Toward Sustainable Communities

American and Comparative Environmental Policy
Sheldon Kamieniecki and Michael E. Kraft, series editors

A complete list of books published in the American and Comparative Environmental Policy series appears at the back of the book.

Toward Sustainable Communities

Transition and Transformations in
Environmental Policy

Second Edition

Edited by Daniel A. Mazmanian and Michael E. Kraft

The MIT Press
Cambridge, Massachusetts
London, England

For information about special quantity discounts, please email special_sales@ mitpress.mit.edu

This book was set in Sabon by SNP Best-set Typesetter Ltd., Hong Kong.

Printed on recycled paper and bound in the United States of America.

Library of Congress Cataloging-in-Publication Data

Toward sustainable communities : transition and transformations in environmental policy/edited by Daniel A. Mazmanian and Michael E. Kraft.
—2nd ed.
    p.   cm.—(American and comparative environmental policy)
Includes bibliographical references and index.
ISBN 978-0-262-13492-7 (hardcover : alk. paper)—ISBN 978-0-262-51229-9 (pbk. : alk. paper)
1. Environmental policy—United States. 2. Sustainable development—United States. I. Mazmanian, Daniel A., 1945–. II. Kraft, Michael E.
GE180.T69   2009
333.720973—dc22
                                                                        2008038557

10 9 8 7 6 5 4 3

Contents

Foreword

The terms "sustainability," "sustainable societies," and "sustainable development" dominate the current debate over present and future environmental policy. Unfortunately, little attention is being paid to the precise definition of these terms, and much confusion surrounds their use. Also complicating our understanding of the meaning of sustainability is whether we are focusing (or should focus) our attention on small, clearly defined jurisdictions at the local level, or whether it is indeed necessary to analyze and achieve sustainability at the national, regional, or global level. The answer to this question has profound implications for the variables we choose to examine, how we structure our analysis and research, and the policy recommendations that are generated.

At the heart of the controversy is the extent to which communities (however defined) can and at what pace move toward the dual goals of vibrant economic development on the one hand and environmental protection and a high quality of life on the other. Moreover, what actions or policies actually constitute successful movement along this path remains open to question. Everyone can agree that both goals are desirable, and many believe that they are attainable, but no one knows exactly how to balance the two and at what societal and governmental level they are most likely to be implemented and effective.

This book edited by Daniel Mazmanian and Michael Kraft is the second edition of a widely cited and highly successful volume that addressed these and similar critical questions concerning sustainability by reviewing and assessing environmental policy successes and failures at the community level (that is, subnational local, regional, and state levels) over an extended period of time, across the United States. Like the first edition, this book deals at length with the various meanings of sustainability and its application in recent years at the community level.

However, much has changed since the publication of the first edition, and the new edition contains an expanded number of case studies of specific places and policy arenas. The chapters are woven together by viewing their specific cases through the lens of the evolution of environmental policy across three overlapping but nonetheless distinct epochs of the environmental movement in the United States. A main theme of the study is the shift of policymaking away from command-and-control approaches and toward policy strategies that are associated with sustainability, particularly at the local and regional level. The book assesses the capacity of the concept of sustainability to serve as a foundation for a new era of environmental policy at all levels of government. As a consequence of evaluating the extent and pace of this overall transition to sustainability-based environmental policy, we come away with a much deeper understanding of the factors that affect the transition within different institutional and political contexts. Both policymakers and students of environmental policy will find this second edition as provocative and stimulating as the first edition (if not more so), especially given the growing importance of the concept of sustainability.

The book illustrates well the purpose of the MIT Press series in American and Comparative Environmental Policy. MIT Press encourages work that examines a broad range of environmental policy issues. The series editors are particularly interested in volumes that incorporate interdisciplinary research and focus on the linkages between public policy and environmental problems and issues both within the United States and in cross-national settings. They welcome contributions that analyze the policy dimensions of relationships between humans and the environment from either a theoretical or empirical perspective. At a time when environmental policies are increasingly seen as controversial and new approaches are being implemented widely, they especially encourage studies that assess policy successes and failures, evaluate new institutional arrangements and policy tools, and clarify new directions for environmental politics and policy. The books in this series are written for a wide audience that includes academics, policymakers, environmental scientists and professionals, business and labor leaders, environmental activists, and students concerned with environmental issues. Hopefully, they contribute to public understanding of environmental problems, issues, and policies of concern today and also suggest promising actions for the future.

Sheldon Kamieniecki, University of California, Santa Cruz
American and Comparative Environmental Policy Series Coeditor

Preface

Anyone attempting to understand the state of environmental policy in the United States today will encounter a wide and bewildering array of laws, programs, and approaches. They range from very stringent and federally directed efforts, such as those in the air pollution and nuclear waste arenas, to an enormous assortment of local, regional, and state water, land-use, urban growth, and resource management policies. There are policies that are quite specific (for example, monitoring the transportation of hazardous waste), and there are some that are exceptionally broad (the congressional mandate to clean up the nation's waters to the point where they are swimmable and fishable). Policies differ in mission and purpose, in who or what is considered the cause of the problem, in who is responsible for remedying the situation, in what strategies are employed to bring about the desired change in behavior by individuals, businesses, and governmental agencies, and in who is expected to enforce the law.

The conventional way of bringing a degree of clarity to this confusing array is to trace the history of a particular type of environmental policy, such as water or air pollution. This was the most common approach in studies of environmental policy in the 1990s when we were writing the first edition of this book, and with few exceptions it remains so today. This "media"-specific approach is valuable and usually sheds light on the many and often unique details that exist within a given policy domain. The drawback to this approach is that it is never clear if the experience in one arena is unique or symptomatic of broader currents within the environmental movement and direction of environmental policy nationwide. An alternative and equally prominent approach is to provide a cross-sectional snapshot, spanning a range of environmental arenas. This is usually informative, but seldom does it lend itself to an understanding of the underlying trends.

We are persuaded that it is most important to understand the broad trends of environmental policy—which we refer to as the underlying environmental movement—and to do so in their boldest relief. Knowing the broad trends helps one fit the particulars from any specific arena into a more understandable overall picture. It is like having a good roadmap that while leaving out most of the details of the terrain, guides one forward in the journey—in this case, to an understanding of how environmental policy has unfolded and continues to unfold. This kind of conceptual clarity is especially necessary in the environmental arena, with its wide range of programs and strategies. Understanding the underlying trends also enables one to make meaningful comparisons, across policy domains—water, air, open space, sustainability—and over time from one era to another. Last, knowing how to distinguish between the kinds of policies and activities that represent past efforts and current conventional thinking, and being able to distinguish these from leading-edge ideas and creative policy proposals, prepares one for active engagement in furthering the environmental agenda and the environmental movement.

The fundamental thesis of this book is that the modern environmental movement can be best understood as the unfolding of three distinctly different but internally coherent epochs: the rise of environmental regulation, the period of flexibility and regulatory reform, and the drive toward sustainable development. This movement begins with the national awakening to the problems of environmental pollution and issues this raised in the late 1960s and early 1970s, and moves through to the merging with the broader movement toward a sustainable future, which extends well beyond the boundaries of environmental policy and the concerns of the first two environmental epochs. Hence, what at first blush might appear to be a chaotic mix of goals, approaches, programs, and activities when viewed in the present can be understood as the cumulative consequence of two past epochs and a third emerging epoch of environmentalism. Furthermore, when viewed separately, each epoch has a fairly coherent internal logic and policy agenda, and understanding environmental policy in the context of each helps distinguish the broad contours of environmentalism. The epochs framework provides a valuable roadmap to the historical evolution, logic, and policy actions of the movement.

The most controversial issue in the environmental movement involves the likelihood of its moving from the goals, strategies, and approaches to protecting and restoring the environment developed in its first two epochs to those needed to achieve a more sustainable society, and by doing so transforming the movement into the third modern epoch. Although the rhetoric of sustainability is being espoused more widely than ever before and has enormous personal and intellectual appeal to environmentalists (and many business and political leaders as well), the reality of the transformation is coming more slowly. Indeed, little scholarly and systematic evidence exists on the extent to which the hopes and aspirations, and the policy promises and public discourse, that have clearly heightened in recent years are being put into practice, or if they can be.

Although theorists and pundits will continue to debate the issues, the world of practice is not standing still. The concerns with air, water, and other pollutants that degrade the health of thousand if not millions of Americans living in communities across the nation, which motivated the initial environmental movement, are overlaid today with global-scale threats to the Earth's upper atmosphere, large-scale endangered habitats, and the planet's natural resource base. The unrelenting onslaught of environmental problems over the past four decades—and as we will argue across three environmental epochs—with some, but far too little, effective response has persuaded many activists and policymakers that sustainability is the only viable path for the future, and to achieve this they must take matters into their own hands. What is needed at this point therefore is a clearer matching up of the theoretical virtues of more sustainable systems with the experiences of sustainability initiatives on the ground.

One of the main purposes of the book is to provide a synthesis of theory and practice by tracing the environmental movement through two critical transformations. These are the transformation from the first epoch, characterized by an array of federal environmental laws and top-down federal regulation, to the second, where emphasis is placed on incentive-based policy approaches and community and regionally based decision making. This is illustrated through initiatives underway within air, water, and land-use policies.

We then move from the traditional environmental concerns to the more comprehensive and complex systems approach that takes into consideration many more factors affecting a community's overall sustainability. Doing so requires moving beyond conventional environmental issues to incorporating a community's physical, psychological, economic, and cultural well-being. The degrees of success of these pilot efforts—applied in air pollution control, land use and growth planning and management, water and watershed management strategies, sustainability strategies—in cities and regions across the nation are extremely valuable, not only for what they suggest about the future direction of the environmental movement, but also for American society as a whole as we look to a more hopeful future.

We want to thank and to recognize our contributing authors for their insights and case studies and their hard work and genial cooperation, without which this collective effort would not have been possible. This is as true for those who revised and rewrote their chapters from the original edition—Lamont Hempel (chapter 2), Daniel Press (chapter 6), and Barry Rabe (chapter 11)—as it is for the new contributors to this second edition—Daniel Fiorino (chapter 3), Nicole Nakagawa (joining Daniel Press), Eliza Barbour and Michael Teitz (chapter 7), Michele Betsill and Barry Rabe (chapter 8), Kent Portney (chapter 9), Mark Lubell, William Leach, and Paul Sabatier (chapter 10), and Marc Gaden (joining Barry Rabe in chapter 11). It has been a pleasure to work with such a talented group of colleagues. We also appreciate the detailed comments on the manuscript by the anonymous reviewers of both the first edition and this new edition; they helped to improve each chapter and develop a more coherent book. We gratefully acknowledge support from the School of Policy, Planning, and Development at the University of Southern California and the Department of Public and Environmental Affairs at the University of Wisconsin-Green Bay. Clay Morgan, Senior Acquisitions Editor for Environmental Studies at MIT Press, inspired this second edition, and to him and his colleagues at the Press who helped turn the idea into a reality, we are deeply appreciative. All who have contributed to the project have superbly done their part. As is only fitting, we take full responsibility for any errors or omissions that remain.

Contributors

Elisa Barbour is a PhD candidate at the Department of City and Regional Planning, University of California, Berkeley.

Michele Betsill is Professor in the Department of Political Science, Colorado State University.

Daniel Fiorino is Director of the Center for Environmental Policy and Distinguished Executive in Residence at American University.

Marc Gaden is the Legislative Liaison and Communications Officer for the Great Lakes Fishery Commission, Ann Arbor, Michigan.

Lamont Hempel is the Director of Environmental Studies at the University of Redlands, and Hedco Professor of Environmental Studies.

Michael Kraft is Professor of Political Science and Public Affairs Emeritus and Herbert Fisk Johnson Professor of Environmental Studies Emeritus at the University of Wisconsin-Green Bay.

William Leach is Assistant Professor in the Department of Public Policy and Administration, and Research Director at the Center for Collaborative Policy at California State University, Sacramento.

Mark Lubell is an Associate Professor in the Department of Environmental Science and Policy at the University of California, Davis.

Daniel Mazmanian is Professor of Public Policy, Sol Price School of Public Policy at the University of Southern California.

Nicole Nakagawa is an Environmental Studies undergraduate at University of California, Santa Cruz.

Kent Portney is Professor of Political Science at Tufts University.

Daniel Press is Professor and Chair of Environmental Studies at the University of California, Santa Cruz.

Barry Rabe is the J. Ira and Nicki Harris Chair of Public Policy at the Gerald R. Ford School of Public Policy at the University of Michigan, where he is Director of the Center for Local, State, and Urban Policy (CLOSUP).

Paul A. Sabatier is a Professor in the Department of Environmental Science and Policy at the University of California, Davis.

Michael Teitz is Professor Emeritus, University of California, Berkeley.

I

Introduction

1

The Three Epochs of the Environmental Movement

Daniel A. Mazmanian and Michael E. Kraft

Since the onset of the modern environmental movement, a great deal has been learned about our ability to direct economic activity, affect human values and behavior, and create a more livable and sustainable world through public policy and government action. The United States has been one of the important crucibles of this learning, with a growing awareness of the interrelationships among social, economic, and environmental systems and the difficulty of changing one without affecting the others in ways both anticipated and not.

A great deal has been accomplished over the past decades through the regulatory enforcement of the range of national environmental laws and policies adopted in the 1970s and 1980s in appreciably reducing air, water, soil, and other environmental pollutants and health risks, on a per capita basis and in total across the nation. Yet it is also true that these gains *are likely to be* short-lived as greater amounts of fossil fuel energy and materials are consumed by an ever growing population and as additional threats to the environment become more prominent—such as the buildup of greenhouse gases, deterioration of the stratospheric ozone layer, rapid decline of species of plants and animals, and depletion of nonrenewable natural resources. Moreover, curbing harmful development and human expansion in one location—a pristine coastline, wetlands, a unique landscape, or an endangered species habitat—does not prevent it from surfacing somewhere else. And that somewhere need not be in North America, but anywhere on the globe, as the world's population grows from 6.7 billion today to 9 billion or more by 2050.

Important politically, the extensive effort by the United States to clean the nation's environment since the 1970s has come at times at the price of economic growth for business and industry, and it has contributed to the migration of some industries from one region to another within the nation and to other countries. Establishing and implementing the nation's environmental laws and regulations also has led to the creation of substantial federal bureaucracies, which can frustrate as much as help remedy environmental problems (Durant, Fiorino, and O'Leary 2004; Eisner 2007; Rosenbaum 2008; Vig and Kraft 2006).

Today, therefore, the decades-long national regulatory policy framework for environmental protection in the United States is undergoing significant reassessment on three fronts. One is its overreliance on command-and-control regulation, which despite notable achievements in the past can no longer be the only or perhaps even the major strategy for achieving environmental sustainability as we look further into the twenty-first century. Among the most important limitations of traditional regulatory policy is its high cost to business and governmental enforcement agencies, its emphasis on remedial rather than preventive actions, and its complex, cumbersome, and adversarial rule-making processes. These weaknesses have proven to be especially significant during times of economic stagnation and diminishing budgetary resources.

Second, national environmental policy often leaves both industry and state and local governments without the flexibility and incentives to achieve environmental quality objectives. Critics argue that the federal Environmental Protection Agency (EPA) often has been unsuccessful at priority setting and program management as it has struggled to balance competing needs and operate within a contentious political environment (Fiorino 2006; Vig and Kraft 2006). Perhaps not surprisingly, management failures and political gridlock at the national level have stimulated considerable policy innovation at the state and local level, an intriguing development that most of the chapters in this volume recount in some detail (Rabe 2006, 2007; Klyza and Sousa 2008).

The third limitation of the regulatory approach is, ironically, its neglect of the broader goal of sustainable development. In the flurry of action by the federal government to develop policies for specific air, water, and other pollutants and to address some of the more visible resource problems, no strategies or policies were developed for working across policy domains, from air and water pollution to energy, agriculture, construction, transportation, land use, and urban planning, in a more comprehensive approach that would simultaneously provide pollution reduction while fostering economic development and quality of life. Even today, while the need to develop a more comprehensive and forward looking strategy is recognized, this task remains beyond the scope of the nation's environmental protection policies, which were largely set down in the 1970s and 1980s, and largely beyond the capacity of the EPA and other federal agencies that are charged with implementing the nation's environmental programs.

As a consequence of being overlooked initially and largely ignored at the national level by Congress and most presidents since the 1970s (with the noted exception of the Clinton administration's effort to foster a dialogue on sustainable practices), the environmental and sustainability movement in the United States has shifted its attention to the subnational level. In doing so, it has recognized that national regulatory strategies that require direct government enforcement, while serving as an important legal and policy framework, need to be complemented with a myriad of public-private and collaborative strategies that bring communities together in pursuit of their common interests in a better future. Many of the most promising sustainability efforts today, albeit unnoticed by the national political establishment in Washington and the nationally oriented media, can be found in the growing application of new approaches at the state, regional, and city levels of government, among the rapidly growing green business and industry entrepreneurs, green industry investors, and nonprofit groups and individuals as they strive to transform themselves and their communities (Coglianese and Nash 2006; Esty and Winston 2006; John 1994, 2004; Morgenstern and Pizer 2006; Portney 2003).

Despite the many obstacles that will need to be addressed in scaling up these experiences to the national level, the lessons being learned at the subnational level demonstrate the potential and promise of sustainable communities as the path of the future. We consider these subnational collaborative, private, and nonprofit sector efforts, especially the adoption of new and more integrated approaches to sustainable growth and development, as beacons for the future and thus make them the primary focus of our attention.

In essence, we believe that American society is reaching a crossroads with respect to environmental protection in several senses of the term and needs to take stock of where it has been and reset its path for the future. Continuation of the environmental regulatory approach initiated in the early 1970s is no longer a sufficient or feasible strategy for realizing the longer-term and more transformative goals of environmental sustainability. Furthermore, the lesson of many years of work in the field leads back to one of the oldest adages of the environmental movement, which is to think and plan globally but act locally. Be it global issues like climate change or local ones of drinkable water, clean air, and nonpolluting industry, acting locally requires mobilizing the capabilities of a broad cross-section of actors across not one but many local communities. Only in this way can the issues of a community's size and scale, together with its human needs and unique culture and ecological features, be adequately molded into an enduring and sustainable future and serve as a model for the nation.

As noted, there has been extensive criticism of centralized command-and-control environmental policy as being too costly, bureaucratic, narrow, and overzealously pursued (e.g., Davies and Mazurek 1998; Eisner 2007; Fiorino 2006). These indictments, though understandable, provide little help in identifying the roots of policy failure and the right direction for the future. It is rather remarkable, actually, that after forty years of the modern environmental movement we have very few systematic assessments of the dozens of policies and hundreds of programs of environmental protection being overseen by the EPA and the fifty states (Harrington, Morgenstern, and Sterner 2004; Knaap and Kim 1998; Press 2007). It has been similar with respect to the principles and policies being adopted on behalf of sustainable development. Although the philosophy of sustainable development has been embraced not only by environmentalists but by a growing segment of business and community leaders, the principles have remained mostly untested. Why this is the case will become more evident in the chapters to follow.

With this as our backdrop, the purpose of this book is to help readers understand the potential of, and thoughtfully engage in the theoretical and practical discussions of, the challenges inherent in moving from a regulatory strategy of environmental protection to one based on principles of sustainability. We believe the best way to do this is to learn from and build on local and regional experiences in sustainability efforts in moving toward a national consensus and policy strategy on sustainable development for the United States.

The chapters that follow in this first section of the book (Part I) focus on the evolution of thinking and understandings of the term sustainability, in chapter 2, and in chapter 3, on the most recent and fully developed practical alternative to command-and-control government regulation, commonly called results-based environmental governance. The change in philosophy in how we govern that is implicit in this new approach and the substantial change in political behavior it will require represent an important step beyond the limitations of the conventional, centrally managed regulatory approach set in place in the early days of the modern environmental era.

Following these discussions, Part II provides intriguing examples of policy experiments in air, land, and water that have begun to move beyond the regulatory approach, into what will be characterized as the second environmental epoch (discussed below). Part III focuses on the more recent generation of policy approaches and community and regional pilot programs and experiments across the public, private, and nonprofit sectors in sustainability that are pointing the way to the future, raising the specter of a second fundamental transformation in the modern environmental movement.

Organizational and Conceptual Overview

Focus on Environmental Epochs

What history tells us is that the response to most environmental problems, whether successful or not, evolves through an organic process of trial, error, and societal learning. It is clear in retrospect that there has been an evolution in the way people think about and frame the issues of environmental protection, and the strategies and policy tools used to address them. To make sense of the present while anticipating the future, it is essential to understand this progression. The progression, which has been incremental when viewed close up and day-by-day, can be more readily and usefully understood when viewed over the course of multiple decades, and, as we believe, as a small number of distinct though overlapping epochs. Each epoch is characterized by a dominant way of defining "the" environmental problem (comprising both a scientific and value component), which in turn leads to a set of policy goals, the use of certain implementation strategies, and other features that must be considered together to capture the essence of the epoch.

Understanding the historical sequence or evolution of these epochs is important also in that policy actors in each learn from the ones that preceded it, ultimately overshadowing (in terms of dominant ideas and focus) and overlaying them (in terms of policies and programs) yet never fully replacing them—along with all the confusion and complexity such progression leads to. Like a good map, the epochs approach attempts to outline the key features of the landscape and show the links between past and present, while indicating how each is distinct in some fairly

Table 1.1
From Environmental Protection to Sustainable Communities

	Regulating for Environmental Protection 1970–1990	Efficiency-Based Regulatory Reform and Flexibility 1980–2000s	Toward Sustainable Communities 1990–present
Problem Identification and Policy Objectives	• pollution caused primarily by callus and unthinking business and industry • establish as national priority the curtailment of air, water, and land pollution caused by industry and other human activity	• managing pollution through market-based and collaborative mechanisms • subject environmental regulations to cost-effectiveness test • internalize pollution costs • pursue economically optimal use of resources and energy • introduce pollution prevention • add policies on toxic waste and chemicals as national priorities	• bringing into harmony human and natural systems on a sustainable basis • balance long-term societal and natural system needs through system design and management • rediscovery of/emphasis on resource conservation • halt diminution of biodiversity • embrace an eco-centric ethic
Implementation Philosophy	• develop the administrative and regulatory legal infrastructure to ensure compliance with federal and state regulations	• shift to state and local level for initiative in compliance and enforcement • create market mechanisms for protection of the environment	• develop new mechanisms and institutions that balance the needs of human and natural systems, both within the U.S. and around the globe • focus on outcomes and performance

Points of Intervention	• end of the production pipeline • end of the waste stream • at the point of local, state, and federal governmental activity	• the market-place, which serves as the arbiter of product viability • provide education and training at several points along the cradle-to-grave path of materials and resource use	• societal level needs assessment and goal prioritization • industry-level attention to product design, materials selection, and environmental strategic planning • individual behavior and life-style choices
Policy Approaches and "Tools"	• policy managed by Washington, D.C. • command-and-control regulation • substantial federal technology R&D • generous federal funding of health and pollution prevention projects	• policy managed more by states and affected communities • federal role shifts to facilitation and oversight • introduction of incentive-based approaches (taxes, fees, emissions trading) for business and industry • creation of emissions-trading markets	• comprehensive future visioning • regional planning based on sustainability guidelines, • Total Quality Environmental Management (TQEM) and life-cycle-design practice in industry • various experiments with new approaches
Information and Data Management Needs	• firm-level emissions • waste stream contents and tracking • human health effects • environmental compliance accounting in industry	• costing out environmental harms and benefits of reduced pollution • provision of readily accessible emissions data (e.g., through Toxics Release Inventory and right-to-know programs)	• sustainability criteria and indicators • eco-human support system thresholds • region/community/global interaction effects (e.g., regarding CO_2 emissions and depletion of ozone layer)

Table 1.1
(continued)

	Regulating for Environmental Protection 1970–1990	Efficiency-Based Regulatory Reform and Flexibility 1980–2000s	Toward Sustainable Communities 1990–present
		• professional protocols for environmental accounting in industry • ecosystem mapping	• utilization of ecological footprint analysis • use of material and energy "flow-through" inventories and accounting • computer modeling of human-natural systems interactions
Predominant Political/ Institutional Context	• rule of law • adversarial relations • zero-sum politics • focus on national regulatory agencies and enforcement mechanisms	• alternative dispute resolution techniques • greater stakeholder and public participation, especially, at the state and local level • reliance on the market place	• public/private partnerships • local/regional collaborations • community capacity building and consensus building • mechanisms created to enforce "collective" decisions
Key Events and Public Actions	• Santa Barbara oil spill • Earth Day • passage of the 1970 CAA and 1972 CWA • passage of National Environmental Policy Act • creation of the Environmental Protection Agency	• Carter administration focus on cost of environmental regulation • election of President Ronald Reagan • Love Canal, Bhopal • RCRA and SARA • growth in state and local environmental policy capacity	• Brundtland report, *Our Common Future* Earth Summit (UNCED) • Montreal Protocol on CFCs, • Kyoto Protocol adoption • Intergovernmental Panel on Climate Change, series of reports • Hurricane Katrina

fundamental ways. The focus on epochs also enables us to stand back from the details and narrow views that come with everyday life and grasp the overall features of the environmental movement at each major juncture in its history.

Finally, there has been dramatic growth in understanding about the environment over the past four decades, with each epoch bringing into clearer focus the interdependence of human and natural systems—and nation-states, continents, and civilizations—and the ultimate limitation of the Earth's ability to sustain infinitely expanding human populations and levels of material consumption. Understanding the "map" of the first two epochs of the modern environmental movement, combined with the growing awareness of the threats to the health of the natural environment at home and around the world, is the basis for our forecast of the epoch to come, viewed from today's vantage point on the cusp of the transformation to a more sustainable civilization. We believe that it is both necessary and likely that the United States will move to a more enduring and sustainable epoch in which concerns for the natural environment and how it relates to all other aspects of our economic and social worlds will play a far more pronounced role in policymaking. We also expect that the transition will occur at widely varying rates and in different forms from one region of the nation to another and across communities.

Table 1.1 presents the three epochs around which the book is organized, beginning largely in the early 1970s with the rise of environmentalism as a social and political movement in the United States and the buildup of the system of federal command-and-control environmental regulation, with its hallmark clean air, clean water, toxics and hazardous waste legislation, creation of the U.S. EPA, and strong federal presence. The third epoch brings into focus the potentiality of sustainable development and sustainable communities as we project further into the twenty-first century. While the movement is global in scope, as are some of the critical issues such as climate change and the overfishing of the world's oceans, our focus will be on how the movement is unfolding in the United States. The second epoch is transitional in several notable respects. It has been marked by the drive for efficiency and flexibility in the regulatory apparatus created in the first epoch. Its rhetoric and politics have been dominated by those with business and property holdings who have seen themselves adversely affected by the generation of environmental laws of the first epoch. Future historians will likely characterize this second epoch as one of bridging. Table 1.1 provides an overview and highlights the critical dimensions of the three epochs and major differences among them in problem identification and policy objectives, implementation philosophies, points of intervention, policy "tools," data and informational needs, political and institutional contexts, and key events and public actions. We believe these features define and differentiate the epochs from one another, and in combination gives each its overall meaning.

We should reiterate that the development of the second and third epochs has not meant the end of the first epoch. Indeed, most environmental policy scholars and practitioners acknowledge that the federally driven command-and-control regulation of epoch one continues to dominate U.S. environmental protection efforts. Many argue as well that the maintenance of some degree of stringent regulation is essential for certain reforms—such as regulatory flexibility or use of market incentives—to work well (Eisner 2007; Fiorino 2006). Yet we believe that the various critiques of the 1970s-era policies, and the reforms based on those critiques, constitute a transitional epoch by themselves, which is ongoing, and that yet another epoch has begun to evolve even as these policy dialogues and experiments continue. In short, the ideas of epoch two and three have been laid on the foundation of epoch one, so far without fundamentally transforming it. Indeed, well into the early twenty-first century, the nation has yet to see the emergence of a new generation of environmental policy, despite many calls for such a transition. Yet one can nonetheless find its seeds in a rich and diverse assortment of activities, particularly at local, state, and regional levels. It is these activities and their implications that we want to explore.

To do so, we seek to present a mapping of each epoch and to explore how useful the mapping framework is in illuminating the critical dimensions of each epoch as they reveal the continuing evolution of the environmental movement. To do this, we have asked several prominent environmental policy scholars and keen observers to contribute, bringing to bear their knowledge of either an important thematic issue—for example, the meaning of sustainability, the need for new governing institutions—or a community or policy arena where a substantive environmental issues is playing out—for example, with respect to air, water, land use, urban design—to assess how well the epochs approach helps illuminate their subject and helps us understand the dynamics in their particular case.

Problem Definition and Policy Objectives

The objective of the first modern environmental epoch was to place center stage the necessity of cleaning up America's polluted waterways, air, and land. Which business and industrial activities were responsible for the pollution was another matter, and was subject to a great deal of debate. For instance, were automobiles, industrial facilities, or climatological conditions the major source of urban air pollution? Whatever the cause, the solutions proposed were almost always costly and therefore contentious. What is clear is that during the first epoch a consensus emerged among scientists, technicians, policymakers, and the public that the issues of pollution and environmental degradation were severe and should be addressed as a top national priority. Despite the criticism that would eventually be heard about the cleanup effort prompted by this consensus, there is little question that the first environmental epoch produced significant improvements in air and water quality in the United States and made important gains in reducing the careless disposal of hazardous wastes and toxic chemicals (Portney 2000; U.S. EPA 2007, 2008; Vig and Kraft 2006).

In addition to policies aimed at specific pollutants, implementation of the National Environmental Policy Act of 1969, with its broad mandate for comprehensive impact assessment and public involvement in environmental policy decisions, spurred significant changes across federal and state bureaucracies. Protection of the nation's natural resources was advanced substantially during this era through new policies and federal mandates for protection of biological diversity and for the stewardship of public lands through what would come to be known as ecosystem management. These include the Endangered Species Act (1973), the Federal Land Policy and Management Act (1976), and the National Forest Management Act (1976), among others (Kraft 2007).

In the second epoch, the focus shifted from strict regulation to balancing environmental objectives with other social and economic priorities, with greater attention to human health effects, and to carrying out more efficiently those environmental policies that were on the books. In a few instances, goals were expanded, such as adding toxic materials and hazardous waste to the environmental policy agenda, the more demanding provisions of the Clean Air Act of 1990, and the greater recognition of the international and global ramifications of pollution. Overall, however, the pace of legislation and coverage of newly identified sources of pollution slowed appreciably in comparison with the first epoch.

What changed most markedly was faith in the philosophy of regulation and strong control by the federal government. It became clear that government alone, especially the federal government, could neither direct nor police all businesses and every community across the nation; nor could it shoulder all the responsibility for stimulating innovative responses to environmental problems (Durant, Fiorino, and O'Leary 2004; Fiorino 2006). This was not simply a reaction to ever-growing government involvement. Underlying the second epoch was the recognition that appreciable progress had been achieved in reducing harmful environmental emissions and enhancing resource protection, in policy if not always in deed. After more than a decade of being front-page news, problems of the environment garnered less and less media attention. These changes occurred within the context of the growing conservative, antiregulation, and anti–federal government political tide that grew throughout the nation in the later part of the 1970s and 1980s, culminating in the Republican Party takeover of Congress in 1994. While this conservative tide was countered to an extent by the Clinton administration's proenvironmental stance, it reached its apex with the victory of President Bush and the conservative wing of the Republican Party in 2000 (Klyza and Sousa 2008; Vig and Kraft 2006).

The lessons of the first two epochs were not lost on those concerned with environmental pollution, the health of the population, and the nation's natural resource base. Although improvements were in fact being made to the nation's waterways, air sheds, and waste sites as a result of the strong, forceful, and aggressively enforced federal and state environmental laws of the first epoch, serious environmental challenges would remain and new ones continue to emerge. These include the loss of biological diversity, the need for habitat management and open space, the possible adverse effects of climate change, and the possibility of a population growth of nearly 50 percent, to some 439 million people in the United States by 2050, and what this implies for pollution and environmental protection.

The close linkage between human population growth, settlement patterns, and industrial activity and the degradation of the environment could not be ignored if permanent solutions were to be found. Problems of the environment were neither simple to address nor isolated from the pace and growth of other human activities, and they could be remedied only with determined, comprehensive, multigenerational efforts.

The realization by a growing number of individuals and opinion leaders from many walks of life that a fundamental transformation in the way Americans relate to the environment and conduct their lives is becoming the hallmark of the third environmental epoch. Pollution reduction, habitat restoration, and determining the most cost-effective methods for achieving these goals pales in comparison to the challenges of sustainability. Focusing on sustainability draws attention to the failure to incorporate into the building blocks of our economic activity in society—including the calculation of the nation's gross national product—measures of environmental health, quality of life, and the full effects of human settlement patterns on the land and the consumption of natural resources.

Significant debate and discussions on how best to incorporate these considerations into policy and action are central to the sustainability movement and to epoch three, as chapter 2 will underscore. For example, the advocates of ecological economics have long argued, in developing their measure of "genuine societal progress," that a more complete national accounting would reveal a downward trend in the genuine per capita level of wealth of Americans, a trend shift reaching back to the mid-1970s. Such assertions have been hotly contested in conventional economic circles. Moreover, the efforts to transform the way we account for the nation's wealth only begs the question of how the intuitively appealing yet vague idea of sustainability is to be defined and measured—and no simple answer has yet been found.

For some advocates, sustainability is understood as a desirable set of pragmatic principles about patterns of consumption, energy use, pollution avoidance, and lifestyle changes to guide everyday action by individuals, business and industry, and communities from the smallest village to the largest of nations. For others, it is an ethical and moral imperative, even a theological creed for humans to live by. The simplest and possibly most encompassing definition of sustainability was provided by the World Commission on Environment and Development (Brundtland Commission 1987, 43): "meeting the needs of the present without compromising the ability of future generations to meet their own needs." What exactly constitutes needs and how to meet them are questions that remain open.

An important intergenerational ethical distinction has been made between "weak" and "strong" definitions of sustainability. In the former, the present generation has an obligation to pass on to future generations an average capital stock—of goods, services, knowledge, raw materials—that is equivalent to today's. In effect, taking all natural and human resources together, the current generation is obliged not to deplete the total stock. Although any given generation may deplete certain resources, as long as those can be replaced through human invention, the process is sustaining. The "strong sustainability" version, in contrast, says that certain natural stocks are essential ecological resources and building blocks for the much broader ecosystem (e.g., the ozone layer and biodiversity), and thus are inappropriate for averaging in with other kinds of assets (e.g., energy-efficient and low-polluting technologies). Not all assets are the same and, for the strong sustainability school, some natural resources and ecological processes are critical; they cannot be depleted below a certain level without dramatic ramifications for sustainability. Thus they cannot be easily averaged into an intergenerational balance sheet.

Ambiguity remains in the concept of sustainability and related concepts such as the "carrying capacity" of the planet. Nevertheless, there is growing recognition that human populations cannot expand indefinitely given the physical limitations of the Earth's land mass and resource base and human dependence on critical ecological processes. It is possible, however, to imagine a trade-off between the absolute size of the planet's population—or that of a town or community—and its energy and resources support systems. A population that consumes less per capita can sustain a larger size over time. For every combination of population size and average resource use there is a limit beyond which the capacity of ecosystems to sustain human beings breaks down. Determining where these thresholds lie is one of the central questions for analysis for the third epoch of environmentalism, as will be made clear in the following chapters.

Implementation Philosophy, Points of Intervention, and Policy Tools

Implementation philosophy goes to the heart of beliefs about how best to achieve agreed upon public policy goals (Mazmanian and Sabatier 1989), and these ideas heavily influence the points of intervention selected and policy tools adopted. Even when different groups and officials can agree on what they want accomplished, determining how best to do so may not be easy. Should people be coaxed or compelled to act a certain way? Should noncompliance be punished, and if so how severely? Should emphasis be placed on educating people and providing them the where-withal to change, or should they be expected to change their behavior, irrespective of costs or their level of awareness of alternatives, as a matter of law? Furthermore, the status, power, and public perception of the groups the legislation is intended to affect often have a great deal to do with the implementation philosophy adopted by political leaders and, in turn, what policy tools are utilized and where.

Seldom explicit, implementation philosophy is usually embedded in the mechanisms that Congress, state legislatures, and communities establish to carry out public policies. Their understanding of the problem and of how best to bring about the desired changes in people's actions are revealed in how they decide to assign various responsibilities. For example, they may assign a task to an existing federal, state, or local agency. Or they may create a new agency for the job, or assign it to an existing regulatory commission, or even assign it to a variety of public-private or even wholly private organizations. They may decide to criminalize certain kinds of behavior—such as disposing of hazardous waste on land—and invoke major penalties for violations, or they may make them minor violations with minimal penalties.

The implementation philosophy of the first environmental epoch was long on process and building new governing institutions, along with oversight of government activities as they affected the environment, but short on actually dictating the behavior of business, industry, and individuals. The signals were clearly mixed, but a combination of both "stick" and "carrot" was utilized.

Probably the most important feature of the first epoch's philosophy was that policy needed to be centralized in the hands of a new comprehensive federal agency: the U.S. Environmental Protection Agency. Given the level of state policy capacity at the time and the failure of most states to aggressively pursue protection of even their own environments, it was widely believed that if the nation's air, water, waste, land use, and related pollution problems were to be addressed successfully, it would have to be done under strong national, uniform guidelines and enforcement by a single agency, along with forceful legislation in critical areas of concern. The most important "seven pillars" of environmental protection legislation from this era are highlighted in box 1.1. For this purpose we exclude the equally important natural resource policies adopted at about the same time, such as the National Environmental Policy Act of 1969. This core of environmental protection or pollution control statutes was

Box 1.1
Seven Pillars of the First Environmental Epoch

(1) The Clean Air Act (CAA). The 1970 act required the EPA to set uniform, national ambient air quality standards to "provide an adequate margin of safety" to protect public health "from any known or anticipated adverse effects" associated with six major pollutants.

(2) The Clean Water Act (CWA). Formally the Federal Water Pollution Control Act Amendments of 1972, the CWA set a national policy for cleaning up the nation's surface water. It established national deadlines for eliminating discharge of pollutants into navigable waters and set as a goal "fishable and swimmable" waters nationwide.

(3) The Safe Drinking Water Act (SDWA). The 1974 act was designed to ensure the quality and safety of drinking water by specifying minimum public health standards for public water supplies. It authorized the EPA to set National Primary Drinking Water Standards for chemical and microbiological contaminants in tap water. The act also required regular monitoring of water supplies to ensure that pollutants stayed below safe levels.

(4) The Resource Conservation and Recovery Act (RCRA). In the 1976 act, Congress required EPA to regulate existing hazardous waste disposal practices as well as to promote the conservation and recovery of resources through comprehensive management of solid waste. RCRA required the EPA to develop criteria for safe disposal of solid waste and the Commerce Department to promote waste recovery technologies and waste conservation. The EPA was to develop a "cradle-to-grave" system of regulation that would monitor and control the production, storage, transportation, and disposal of wastes considered hazardous, and it was to determine the appropriate technology for disposal of wastes. The act was strengthened in 1984.

(5) The Toxic Substances Control Act (TSCA). In this 1976 act, the EPA was given comprehensive authority to identify, evaluate, and regulate risks associated with the full life cycle of commercial chemicals, both those already in commerce as well as new ones in preparation. The EPA was to produce an inventory of chemicals in commercial production, and it was given authority to require testing by industry where data are insufficient and the chemical may present an unacceptable risk.

(6) The Federal Insecticide, Fungicide, and Rodenticide Act (FIFRA). Congress created FIFRA in a 1947 act that established a registration and labeling program housed in the Department of Agriculture that was oriented largely to the efficacy of pesticides. In 1970 Congress established the modern regulatory framework that turned jurisdiction over to the EPA. FIFRA requires that pesticides used commercially within the United States be registered by the EPA. It sets as a criterion for registration that the pesticide not pose "any unreasonable risk to man or the environment,

taking into account the economic, social, and environmental costs and benefits of the use." The act was amended significantly in 1996 with the Food Quality Protection Act.

(7) The Comprehensive Environmental Response, Compensation, and Liability Act (CERCLA or Superfund). Congress enacted CERCLA, better known as Superfund, in 1980 and revised it in 1986 with the Superfund Amendments and Reauthorization Act (SARA). The act is a partner to RCRA. Whereas RCRA deals with current hazardous waste generation and disposal, the Superfund is directed at the thousands of abandoned and uncontrolled hazardous waste sites. The act put responsibility for the cleanup and financial liability on those who disposed of hazardous wastes at the site, a "polluter pays" policy.

developed at a time when it was believed that a "big stick" was necessary to bring about change and that state and local governments either could not or would not be forceful enough. This top-down approach can be contrasted with the decentralized, though still governmental, approach of the second epoch, and the community-based, multisector and more integrative strategy envisioned for the third epoch.

The administrative task this approach presented to the EPA was formidable, particularly for a regulatory bureaucracy struggling to gain legitimacy and sufficient resources to do its job while fending off critics, from both outside and within the federal government. Moreover, what policy and government capacity did exist to deal with air, water, and land pollution was spread among different agencies with little history of coordinated action. In recognizing this history and the inherent difficulty of developing a more integrated approach, Congress and the EPA adopted a pollution or problem-specific organizational structure, which persists to the present, with separate program offices for air and radiation, water, pesticides and toxic substances, and solid wastes and emergency response.

To carry out its expanding mission, the agency's staff grew from about 6,000 in its first full year of operation to approximately 18,000 by the mid-1990s, with two-thirds working in the agency's ten regional offices and in other facilities located outside of Washington, D.C. The agency's operating budget rose from an initial $500 million in 1971, to about $4 billion in the 2000s. However, adjusted for inflation, the operating budget by late in the first decade of 2000 was not appreciably higher than was it was in 1980 (Vig and Kraft 2006). A lack of resources has dampened the agency's ability to keep up with the increased responsibilities that Congress has assigned to it over the years.

Finally, it was initially believed that the demanding new controls over environmental pollution could be put in place without substantially altering the affairs of business, industry, and the consumer. This could be accomplished by placing the emission controls at the "end of the pipe," be it at the tailpipe of the automobile, the tip of a smokestack, or the sewer outflow pipe from a business, industry, or municipal government. Notable exceptions were in the areas of chemicals and toxic materials (see box 1.1, RCRA and TSCA), which require product and materials testing and safety certification, not simply end-of-the-pipe management.

In many respects, the implementation philosophy of the first epoch was effective in developing a strong federal implementing capacity in the form of the U.S. EPA, which in turn carried out the multiple environmental policies nationally. By doing so it helped to foster a similar capacity at the state and local level. In other respects, however, the EPA had become too successful organizationally in the process: big, cumbersome administratively, and ever-present. This contributed to the backlash against the agency and the rise of a counter-philosophy and approach that became the hallmark of second environmental epoch. The backlash emerged first during the 1980s, especially during the Reagan administration, then again, as noted earlier, with the Republican takeover of Congress following the 1994 elections and the election of George Bush in 2000. From the mid-1990s through the 2006 elections, the combination of a conservative Congress and the Bush presidency facilitated a range of legislative, administrative, and judicial assaults that were launched by business and industry, property rights, and antienvironmental groups. Though not successful enough to derail the EPA and undo the environmental movement, this political shift and the actions that resulted did succeed in changing ideas about how best to accomplish environmental objectives (Klyza and Sousa 2008; Kraft 2007; Rosenbaum 2008).

By the mid-1980s, the dominant thinking among members of Congress, business, and the broader public was that a more decentralized and collaborative approach to rule-making and goal setting—within an integrated environmental framework, where costs were accorded greater consideration in pursuing environmental gains—was a better way to accomplish the nation's ambitious environmental agenda. This shift in policy orientation was based on the assumption that the debate was no longer chiefly over the appropriateness of having environmental safeguards. What was most needed was the right opportunity and incentives for business and industry to marshal their creativity and technological know-how to meet the needs of a less-polluting and more energy-efficient society. This new philosophy would balance environmental goals with private-sector costs, be more flexible in application, and be driven by "incentives" rather than governmental prescription and policing (Durant, Fiorino, and O'Leary 2004; Eisner 2007; Fiorino 2006).

Economists had championed this approach for decades. But not until the second epoch did the philosophy take center stage. It was tested in several pilot programs in using market mechanisms, involving stakeholders in setting rules and regulations, and working more to cajole than compel compliance with environmental mandates. This change in philosophy reached a peak in the early 1990s with the EPA's top administrators calling for a move away from pollutant-by-pollutant rules and regulations that had built up over two decades, to integrated ("multimedia"), more decentralized, and collaborative thinking and decision making.

Even as the epoch two changes in thinking was being absorbed into the culture and practices of the EPA, its state counterparts, and business and industry, an even more ambitious philosophy emerged as the environmental movement moved into the third epoch. For these environmentalists, the lesson of the first epoch was not that compromise and cooperation were needed to soften the rigidity of top-down command-and-control, but that a far bolder and comprehensive approach was needed. What was needed was a philosophy and strategy of "sustainability," based on the conviction that more enduring solutions to the problems of environmental pollution, resource degradation, and the looming presence of climate change were required.

The call was for a sustainability approach that envisions a complex web of human and natural systems interactions and linkages, without starting or end point. This goes well beyond the much more constricted and artificial focus characteristic of earlier thinking and policy formulation that treated air, water, and other pollutants separately. Also, linking sustainability concepts to concepts of community has particular advantages, since communities represent the social and physical expression of interdependence.

The implications for policy and action, and for social relations within a community, were profound. It is not yet clear how best to think about the environmental "problem" as one of sustainability, but a number of efforts are underway to scope the necessary boundaries and strategies for action. Furthermore, the absence of precision and clarity has not deterred leaders in the environmental movement, a growing number of those in the business communities, and many subnational public officials, from embracing the movement. As such, while the implementation "philosophy" continues to unfold, it has identified multiple points of action and transformation, as well as micro- and macropolicy tools and guideposts. Which ones will prove the most appropriate will become clear only as the third epoch unfolds.

Information and Data Management Needs

When environmentalism emerged onto the national scene in the early 1970s, there was little questioning the nature of the problem. One did not need to be an expert to appreciate that many of the nation's waterways were polluted to the point of killing off fish and were no longer suitable for drinking and swimming. In extreme cases, their oily surface could even catch fire. Industrial, urban, and agricultural runoff was polluting many underground aquifers, rendering them useless as sources of potable water. Urban smog was an eyesore—literally—in most major urban areas, especially in the hot and dry southwest, where Los Angeles epitomized the problem. Highly radioactive waste was accumulating at the nation's nuclear power plants with nowhere to dispose of it permanently—adding to the public's fear of possible nuclear accidents.

As a response, the passage of new pollution laws was just a first step. The EPA needed to develop, often from scratch, detailed rules and regulations for industry to follow to bring pollution within acceptable levels of public health and safety. Yet the extent of information about pollution and the data-gathering and measurement capabilities of the nation were quite rudimentary. While the intent of Congress to clean up the environment was clear, the practical and technical demands of gauging levels of pollution, their acute and chronic health effects, and tolerable levels of exposure were not.

Congress mandated that the regulations were to be health based, at a time when the science of epidemiology was inconclusive, dose-response rates unknown, and the understanding of the human health effects of differing amounts and duration of exposure to pollutants was modest at best. In short, a great deal of scientific and technical information was needed, and needed fast. It would not be until the mid-1970s, for example, that the EPA, working with lead states such as California, was able to establish reliable monitoring methods for gauging air emissions for a community. It was also unknown which industries were generating what kinds of air and water pollution, and to what extent each could be reduced through new technology and better management, and at what cost.

Who should be responsible for gathering the needed information and how that information should be linked to regional, state, and national strategies for emissions control were debated during the first epoch. In the area of water pollution, where waste was typically dumped into sewers and municipal drainage systems, an entire system of permits and emissions monitoring was developed. Even after more than thirty years, however, there remains only limited monitoring data on the health of the nation's rivers, streams, lakes, ponds, and reservoirs (U.S. EPA 2007).

Air quality measures evolved with greater success, although reliable monitoring and data-collection systems would not be available until late in the 1970s. Still, year-to-year variations reflect not only gains in pollution control but changing economic activity and weather patterns. Also, it is instructive and humbling to realize that even after the federal government spent over $500 million on its massive National Acid Precipitation Assessment Program in the 1980s, uncertainty continues over the effects of acid precipitation on soil chemistry and water quality.

These and similar limitations in monitoring public health and environmental quality persist and constitute one of the major barriers to measuring environmental change and evaluating the impact of public policy efforts (Press 2007). Part of the problem is that the federal government has been unable to consolidate and integrate the diverse array of environmental data programs it does have. Improving the nation's ability to assess interrelationships among different environmental stressors and the impact on health and the environment and to relate this to public policy actions remains a challenge (Gunderson and Holling 2002).

One of the defining characteristics of the second epoch has been the frequency and severity of criticism directed at environmental policy, although fewer questions have been raised about the progress made to date in cleaning up the environment. Rather, critics tend to emphasize the intrusiveness of environmental policies, the substantial costs they have imposed on the private sector and on state and local governments, the inefficiency of command-and-control regulations, and the rapid rise of federal, state, and local bureaucracies associated with the nation's environmental programs (Durant, Fiorino, and O'Leary 2004; Fiorino 2006; Eisner 2007). These critiques resulted in the demand that the administrative and compliance costs of regulations be balanced against pollution reduction and health gains from any given rule or regulation.

The concern of the third epoch goes well beyond prescribing regulations for cleaning up pollution or conventional cost-benefit analysis of their effects. What is being asked for is a method of gauging the multiple ramifications of an action—rule, regulation, activity—within a large and complex array of possible effects, in the near term and well into the future. The level of scientific and technical data, understanding of ecological processes, and analytical capability needed for this kind of assessment is greater than ever before. Only through computer-assisted analysis and simulation will it be possible to conduct the needed analysis in most instances. With only limited data of the sort needed now available, and those with the requisite analytical skills still few in number, a great deal of new kinds of data and analytical capacity is called for, from energy and materials throughput analysis and metropolitan area footprint analysis to green accounting in business and industry.

Predominant Political/Institutional Context
The environmental policy revolution of the 1970s was guided by a set of assumptions about the capacity of state and local governments to identify and act on environmental problems, the willingness of business and industry to minimize costly remedial actions, and the capabilities of a centralized federal government to bring about substantial change in a short period of time. It was assumed, for instance, that business and industry would not voluntarily cooperate in cleanup and, indeed, that they would resist in all manner possible. Policy was designed in this adversarial context. Not surprisingly, both sides lobbied heavily as legislative proposals were formulated and debated in Congress and other venues. They also sought to shape the decisions made by administrative agencies, and they resorted often to the courts to resolve their differences and clarify rights and responsibilities (Kamieniecki 2006; Kraft and Kamieniecki 2007).

The second epoch reflected a desire to find a middle ground through developing new forms of collaboration and participatory policymaking and rule making. With this shift came the emergence of alternative dispute resolution, extensive collaboration, negotiated rule making within the EPA, and similar processes as ways to move beyond gridlock politics and costly legal proceedings. The assumption was that bringing the key stakeholders in a policy arena together would foster greater understanding and cooperation, and allow all parties to focus on areas of shared interest and policy agreement. If nothing else, these changes launched an extraordinary era of searching for common ground and consensual solutions to deeply divisive environmental problems (Kraft 1994; Mazmanian and Morell 1992; Sabatier et al. 2005; Williams and Matheny 1995).

As important as these new decision-making processes are as educational devices and ways of resolving disputes, they have not fully eliminated the suspicions and conflicts among contending parties, nor are they always well suited to resolving fundamental conflicts. Indeed, the confrontational politics used during the Republican-controlled Congress of the late 1990s and early 2000s to weaken environmental policy, and the strong countermovement by a rejuvenated environmental community, attest to the deeper cultural persistence of politics as usual (Klyza and Sousa 2008; Kraft 2007). It would appear that the willingness by the parties to environmental conflicts to use alternative mechanisms for resolving disputes in the second epoch reflects only a partial and strategic commitment on their parts, rather than a fundamental rejection of the older adversarial form of political decision making.

For the third epoch, now in its formative stage, collaboration and cooperation among all affected stakeholders and incentive-based methods of policy implementation are promoted as the preferred approaches for both philosophical and instrumental reasons (Maser 1997; Weber 2003; Wondolleck and Yaffee 2000). What began as experimentation in epoch two is being embraced more deeply in order to reach and assure genuine community-based sustainability. In this vein President Clinton's Council on Sustainable Development of the mid-1990s focused on this approach. With remarkable unanimity, the council's members called for a new generation of flexible, consensual environmental policies that would maximize economic welfare while achieving more effective and efficient environmental protection. The United States, council members said, "must change by moving from conflict to collaboration and adopting stewardship and individual responsibility as tenets by which to live" (PCSD 1996, 1). Such a statement reflected more idealism than realism, but it indicated the kind of political values that were beginning to infuse third-epoch thinking and the effort to seek new forms of governance, starting at the local community level (Hempel 1998).

Analysts examining these trends hail the potential of public education campaigns, collaborative decision making, public-private partnerships, and continued and increasing reliance on market incentives (Durant, Fiorino, and O'Leary 2004; Press and Mazmanian 2006). The transition has only begun, however, and for the present we have an unusual hybrid form of environmental regulation in which new approaches are placed alongside or overlying the old. The potential for significant improvement has been demonstrated when the right conditions present themselves, but the persistence of the formal apparatus of command-and-control regulation in the major environmental protection statutes and their attendant regulations remains and continues to be appropriate in many instances.

What Follows

The chapters that follow provide a combination of illuminating case studies of changes in the thinking and action of the environmental movement, further clarification of the conceptual issues underlying the changes, and concrete evidence of the two major transformations under way: from the first to second as well as second to third epochs. The dates dividing the epochs are never as clear and crisp in practice as described analytically in table 1.1, and the timing and overlapping nature of the transformations fit some cases, such as air and water, better than others, such as sustainable land use planning by cities. Nonetheless, the broad outlines will be revealed and the influence of the growth and learning across the wide array of environmental arenas—trial and error in one epoch, new ideas emerging and becoming dominant in the next, with revised goals and proposed new strategies—is striking. Understanding the environmental movement as it evolves through the three epochs is valuable in understanding the key dimension of societal-level change in general and the transformation of environmental policy in particular. This knowledge should find practical application among those seeking to foster and accelerate the drive toward sustainability.

Meanwhile, as scholars and researchers, we are only beginning our task. To the extent that the epochs framework proves useful in guiding analysis and helping to provide understanding of the changes past and present through our case studies, the framework will beg even more questions of verification and other possible applications. The concluding chapter will address these issues.

The case studies in chapters 4 through 11 provide a cross section of major environmental policy areas in light of the epochs framework. We begin with cases that illuminate the transition from the first to second epoch followed by cases of transitions underway into the third epoch. The cases were chosen because they highlight and illuminate the dimensions of the transition framework combined with their substantive importance as an environmental concern. As one moves from the second to third parts of the book the greater is the shift in emphasis from transitions in environmental protection to sustainability of entire communities and regions, within which environmental concerns become embedded in a far more comprehensive framework.

Before launching into the cases, the complexity and ambiguity surrounding the notion of sustainable communities and environmental governance for the third epoch necessitate further discussion and amplification in order to round out the introductory section of the book. Therefore chapter 2, by Lamont Hempel, provides an historical overview of the origins and implications of the emergent focus on sustainability and why it is having the effect today of repositioning and galvanizing the environmental movement. The chapter serves to underscore the significant departure from the first and second environmental epochs that sustainability represents, but also the difficult transformational challenge it poses not only for the environmental movement but all of society. Chapter 3, by Dan Fiorino, draws our attention to policy and governing approaches that are being introduced to move beyond the dominant regulatory approach characteristic of the first and second epochs—new governing approaches that are better suited to the multisector, collaborative, system-integrating, and multilevel (local through global) approaches to sustainability of the third epoch.

Part II of the book provides a series of case studies of important community- and regionally based efforts at addressing conventional environmental pollution and related land-use problems. Chapter 4, by Daniel Mazmanian, examines clean air regulation, using the case of the transformation from epoch one to two in approach and practice in Southern California, the most heavily polluted urban region in the nation, where some preliminary indications of sustainability thinking infuse the policy process. In chapter 5, Michael Kraft describes extended and committed efforts to use collaborative decision making at the local and regional level in Northeastern Wisconsin to address both point and nonpoint source pollution management under the Clean Water Act. Chapter 6 shifts the focus to land-use policy, which historically has been thought about in terms of parks, recreation, preservation, and aesthetics, but only indirectly thought of as an important component of any lasting sustainability efforts. Here Daniel Press helps us understand the historical context of land-use policy, with emphasis on the important role of local values, interests, and administrative mechanisms and how these have evolved through the epochs, albeit on a very different timescale than suggested in table 1.1.

Part III draws on new and more encompassing efforts, where multimedia, multisector, and multistakeholder strategies are beginning to emerge within communities and regions based on a comprehensive view and the goals of sustainability. The five chapters within this section examine very different contexts within which these programs are being adopted and new practices developed. In chapter 7 Elisa Barbour and Michael Teitz draw our attention to the experiments with regional growth "blueprint" planning in California, exploring and assessing conditions that foster community consensus on growth and development in rapidly expanding communities. In chapter 8, Michele Betsill and Barry Rabe examine a fascinating story in policy leadership at the subnational level regarding one of the most important challenges that will be facing the nation throughout the twenty-first century: climate change. In the vacuum created by eight years of the Bush administration's slow and exceedingly cautious response to the climate change challenge, the subnational response might be viewed as surprising since the issue is being played out mainly on the international stage, among nations, though the case serves as a refreshing reminder of the importance of the bottom up-and entrepreneurial spirit of policy innovation possible in our federal and decentralized system of government in the United States. They examine the nearly half of all the states that stepped into the breach.

In chapter 9, Kent Portney also takes us to the subnational level of government, examining the fascinating range of policy initiatives by the nation's cities to the challenge of sustainability. He probes why some cities are more likely than others to give sustainability policies high priority and why some do better than others in achieving their policy goals. This is followed by the chapter by Mark Lubell, William Leach, and Paul Sabatier that looks at watershed level sustainability planning. Watersheds typically cross long established political boundaries, cut across both public and private lands, and because of this present a host of governance challenges. The authors draw from a number of years of studying watershed partnerships designed to overcome these obstacles, and assess how stakeholders are able to build trust, consensus, and cooperation in the pursuit of sustainability in watershed management. In the concluding illustrative case in this section, chapter 11, Barry Rabe and Marc Gaden explore one of the most ambitious, large-scale, and epoch-spanning regional efforts at environmental restoration: the case of the cleanup and restoration efforts of the Great Lakes Basin bordering the United States and Canada.

Chapter 12, by Kraft and Mazmanian, returns to the central issues of the theory–practice nexus in assessing the extent to which the epochs framework helps us understand the profound changes in the environmental movement past, present, and as we look into the future. Special attention is given to efforts to clarify the concept of sustainability at the community level in its environmental, social, and political dimensions. The chapter addresses the political and participatory dimensions, indeed requisites, of the transformation to sustainability implicit throughout all the illustrative cases.

All of the chapters incorporate an interdisciplinary orientation appropriate to the subject matter. They focus on important illustrations that provide evidence of what works and what does not at the local and regional level, and why. These are not final words on the subjects addressed, nor should they be. We hope our selection of cases conveys a sense of the range of actions begin taken across the nation, and where they do not, we hope others will develop comparable analyses of different cases that can supplement what we are able to offer here. We do think, however, that the cases move the discussion forward and help identify the conditions for successful environmental policy development and implementation. Thus they help to define the basis for policy prescriptions for localities and regions seeking to initiate strategies for building truly enduring sustainable communities.

References

Brundtland Commission (World Commission on Environment and Development). 1987. *Our Common Future.* New York: Oxford University Press.

Coglianese, Cary, and Jennifer Nash, eds. 2006. *Leveraging the Private Sector: Management-Based Strategies for Improving Environmental Performance.* Washington, D.C.: RFF Press.

Davies, J. Clarence, and Jan Mazurek. 1998. *Pollution Control in the United States: Evaluating the System*. Washington, D.C.: Resources for the Future.

Durant, Robert F., Daniel J. Fiorino, and Rosemary O'Leary. 2004. *Environmental Governance Reconsidered: Challenges, Choices, and Opportunities*. Cambridge, MA: MIT Press.

Eisner, Marc Allen. 2007. *Governing the Environment: The Transformation of Environmental Regulation*. Boulder, CO: Lynne Rienner.

Esty, Daniel C., and Andrew S. Winston. 2006. *Green to Gold: How Smart Companies Use Environmental Strategy to Innovate, Create Value, and Build Competitive Advantage*. New Haven, CT: Yale University Press.

Fiorino, Daniel J. 2006. *The New Environmental Regulation*. Cambridge, MA: MIT Press.

Gunderson, Lance H., and C. S. Holling, eds. 2002. *Panarchy: Understanding Transformations in Human and Natural Systems*. Washington, D.C.: Island Press.

Harrington, Winston, Richard Morgenstern, and Thomas Sterner, eds. 2004. *Choosing Environmental Policy: Comparing Instruments and Outcomes in the United States and Europe*. Washington, D.C.: RFF Press.

Hempel, C. Lamont. 1998. "Sustainable Communities: From Vision to Action." Claremont, CA: The Claremont Graduate University.

John, DeWitt. 1994. *Civic Environmentalism: Alternatives to Regulation in States and Communities*. Washington, D.C.: CQ Press.

John, DeWitt. 2004. "Civic Environmentalism." In *Environmental Governance Reconsidered*, ed. Durant, Fiorino, and O'Leary, pp. 219–254.

Kamieniecki, Sheldon. 2006. *Corporate America and Environmental Policy: How Often Does Business Get Its Way?* Cambridge, MA: MIT Press.

Klyza, Christopher McGrory, and David J. Sousa. 2008. *Environmental Policy, 1990–2006: Beyond Gridlock*. Cambridge, MA: MIT Press.

Knaap, Gerrit J., and Tschangho John Kim, eds. 1998. *Environmental Program Evaluation: A Primer*. Champaign, IL: University of Illinois Press.

Kraft, Michael E. 1994. "Searching for Policy Success: Reinventing the Politics of Site Remediation." *Environmental Professional* 16 (September): 245–253.

Kraft, Michael E. 2007. *Environmental Policy and Politics*, 4th ed. New York: Pearson Longman.

Kraft, Michael E., and Sheldon Kamieniecki, eds. 2007. *Business and Environmental Policy: Corporate Interests in the American Political System*. Cambridge, MA: MIT Press.

Maser, Chris. 1997. *Sustainable Community Development: Principles and Concepts*. Delray Beach, FL: St. Lucie Press.

Mazmanian, Daniel, and David Morell. 1992. *Beyond Superfailure: America's Toxics Policy for the 1990s.* Boulder, CO: Westview Press.

Mazmanian, Daniel, and Paul Sabatier. 1989. *Implementation and Public Policy,* with a new postscript. Lanhan, MD: University Press of America.

Morgenstern, Richard D., and William A. Pizer, eds. 2006. *Reality Check: The Nature and Performance of Voluntary Environmental Programs in the United States, Europe, and Japan.* Washington, D.C.: RFF Press.

Portney, Kent E. 2003. *Taking Sustainable Cities Seriously: Economic Development, the Environment, and Quality of Life in American Cities.* Cambridge, MA: MIT Press.

Portney, Paul R., ed. 2000. *Public Policies for Environmental Protection,* 2nd ed. Washington, D.C.: Resources for the Future.

President's Council on Sustainable Development (PCSD). 1996. *Sustainable America: A New Consensus for Prosperity, Opportunity, and a Healthy Environment for the Future.* Washington, D.C.: U.S. Government Printing Office.

Press, Daniel. 2007. "Industry, Environmental Policy, and Environmental Outcomes." *Annual Review of Environment and Resources* 32: 1.1–1.28.

Press, Daniel, and Daniel A. Mazmanian. 2006. "The Greening of Industry: Combining Government Regulation and Voluntary Strategies." In *Environmental Policy,* 6th edition, ed. Vig and Kraft, pp. 264–287.

Rabe, Barry. 2006. "Power to the States: The Promise and Pitfalls of Decentralization." In *Environmental Policy,* 6th edition, ed. Vig and Kraft, pp. 34–56.

Rabe, Barry. 2007. "Environmental Policy and the Bush Era: The Collision between the Administrative Presidency and State Experimentation." *Publius: The Journal of Federalism* 37, 3: 413–431.

Rosenbaum, Walter A. 2008. *Environmental Politics and Policy,* 7th ed. Washington, D.C.: CQ Press.

Sabatier, Paul, Will Focht, Mark Lubell, Zev Trachtenberg, Arnold Vedlitz, and Mary Matlock, eds. 2005. *Swimming Upstream: Collaborative Approaches to Watershed Management.* Cambridge, MA: MIT Press.

U.S. Environmental Protection Agency. 2007. *National Water Quality Inventory Report to Congress (305(b) Report).* Washington, D.C.: Office of Water. Available at www.epa.gov/305b, viewed on August 15, 2007. The report is on the 2002 national assessment database.

U.S. Environmental Protection Agency. 2008. *Latest Findings on National Air Quality: Status and Trends through 2006.* Washington, D.C.: Office of Air and Radiation. Available at: http://www.epa.gov/air/airtrends/2007/, viewed on March 19, 2008.

Vig, Norman J., and Michael E. Kraft, eds. 2006. *Environmental Policy: New Directions for the 21st Century,* 6th ed. Washington, D.C.: CQ Press.

Weber, Edward P. 2003. *Bringing Society Back In: Grassroots Ecosystem Management, Accountability, and Sustainable Communities*. Cambridge, MA: MIT Press.

Williams, Bruce, and Albert Matheny. 1995. *Democracy, Dialogue, and Environmental Disputes: The Contested Languages of Social Regulation*. New Haven, CT: Yale University Press.

Wondolleck, Julia M., and Steven L. Yaffee. 2000. *Making Collaboration Work: Lessons from Innovation in Natural Resource Management*. Washington, D.C.: Island Press.

2

Conceptual and Analytical Challenges in Building Sustainable Communities

Lamont C. Hempel

Whether viewed as a universal truth about intergenerational justice and interspecies harmony or as a half-baked attempt to make a virtue out of mere endurance, the idea of sustainability has successfully invaded the rhetoric, if not the substance, of public debate. It has become a familiar concept in international diplomacy, higher education, corporate public relations, and in almost every other human endeavor that involves the interaction of social and environmental systems.

Sustainability, like democracy, faith, and freedom, is hard to define concisely. As we shall see, the difficulty increases when the concept is expressed in the adjective form, *sustainable*, and paired with words like *development*, *society*, and—the focus of this chapter—*community*. The concept of sustainable community suffers from compound imprecision. Both *sustainability* and *community* are difficult to define in ways that are unambiguous. Putting them together only adds to the operational challenge of cutting the intellectual diamond to fit snugly in the ring of rhetorical authority. Is the chief characteristic of a sustainable community its ability to endure? Or is it the communality of what is sustained? And what is it, exactly, that we want to sustain? Human health and well-being? Ecological wholeness? The so-called *three Es* of sustainability—environmental resilience, economic vitality, and social equity?

Discourses about sustainable communities tend to promote the nostalgic ideal of a simpler, leaner, more virtuous way of life, lived closer to nature and at geographic scales that promote genuine social bonding and prevailing trust. For people interested in simpler times, less traffic congestion, more open space, and an abiding sense of place, the concept of a sustainable community may resonate more for what it recalls from the past than for what it promises about the future. Viewed as a reaction to the dizzying changes wrought by rapid growth and advancing technology, interest in sustainable communities represents, perhaps, a plea for continuity and a return to humanly scaled communities that can withstand Toffler's (1970) "future shock."

But other promoters of the concept of sustainable communities appear quite prepared for—indeed, enthusiastic about—an urban future of rapid change. Their discourses reject the nostalgic urges of history, and focus instead on future settlement patterns, and on the energy, food, and transportation systems they will require in order to succeed. Most of these advocates count on green technologies to solve problems posed by a rapidly urbanizing world. They welcome the challenges inherent in the announcement by the United Nations in 2007 that humanity had moved from a predominantly rural to a predominantly urban existence.

This chapter examines the implications of sustainability concepts and their application in place-based communities. It explores the construction of meaning in beliefs about sustainability, and the conceptual promise and analytical difficulties that those beliefs create for local and regional policymaking. Defining the term *sustainability* with precision is less important for this purpose than understanding the characteristics and goals of the social movement it has fostered. Like other transformative ideas, the concept of sustainability promises to remake the world through reflection and choice, but its potential to engage people's hopes, imagination, and sense of responsibility may depend more on strategic uses of ambiguity than on conceptual precision and clarity. Mobilizing ideas appear to be most effective when they serve as condensational symbols that defy narrow definition, encourage coalition building among diverse interests, and permit just enough comprehension and social absorption to promote convergent political acts. The symbol of sustainability, arguably, is sufficiently ambiguous to be embraced by diverse interests, yet coherent enough to inspire movement in a particular direction.

Conceptual Challenges

No matter what object of sustainability is measured, there is a range of time across which sustainability is not achievable. Communities that may be sustainable over the time frames of modern history—that is, centuries—become faint punctuation marks in the eons of geological history. Even a sustainable Earth eventually succumbs to entropy, asteroid collisions, or other astronomical cataclysms. Nothing is permanent in a physical sense, including our solar system. Accordingly, human communities cannot be sustainable in any strict sense of the term.

Practically speaking, of course, the concept of a sustainable community is temporally acceptable for all human endeavors. In the short run, definitions of sustainability are problematic only insofar as they move from theory to practice. Within the relatively short time frames in which community decision makers operate, the goals of sustainability cease to appear paradoxical. The real difficulty lies not in the relativity of the concept but in its operationalization. Applying sustainability criteria to everyday matters of public policy, business management, and personal consumption is fraught with conceptual and moral hazards. Equally challenging is the problem of envisioning a truly sustainable community in the absence of any concrete examples. And even if persuasive examples could be found and unifying visions embraced, few contemporary institutions or systems of governance appear flexible enough to implement such visions in a timely manner. Building communities in which environmental quality, social justice, and economic vitality cohere in some sustained fashion requires a rare combination of long-range foresight and short-term adaptability.

For hard-bitten realists, the goal of community sustainability is chimerical. We can reduce some of that ambiguity by limiting the use of the term *community* to particular geographic associations of people who share some social, political, historical, and economic interests.[1] But *sustainability* cannot be limited in the same way. It must be understood as less of an object and more of a process. As Folke and Kaberger (1991, 289) observe, "It is not meaningful to measure the absolute sustainability of a society at any point in time." Nor is it reasonable to measure it as a climax or endpoint. Given the second law of thermodynamics, sustainability as permanence is not an option.

Efforts to define and frame concepts of sustainability have typically stressed the principles of support, persistence, balance, and, most important, resilience. A large sample of approaches and definitions is available at www.sustainablemeasures.com. Although some define sustainability in terms of stability, ecologists note that ecosystems with low stability can still exhibit high resilience, thereby suggesting that sustainability has more to do with endurance than with order.[2] Critics, however, respond that if the essence of sustainability is endurance, the concept is neither intellectually interesting nor ethically supportable. Paul Treanor (1996, 6), for example, asserts that "no moral argument can justify the continued existence of existing." Because sustainability assigns value to duration, it provides a basis, in Treanor's view, for radical traditionalism and inflexible forms of political conservatism.

Champions of intergenerational justice, in response, might point out that endurance is a moral imperative when applied to the practices and systems needed to nurture future human societies. At the very least, sustainability implies an obligation to safeguard the existence of future generations.

Development versus Community

By far the most common usage of the word *sustainable* is in combination with the word *development*. Formally introduced in the *World Conservation Strategy* (IUCN 1980), popularized by the Brundtland Commission (World Commission on Environment and Development 1987), and diplomatically embraced at the Earth Summit in 1992, sustainable development has become the "guide star" of international efforts to reconcile economic and ecological imperatives.

Despite its popularity within the U.N. system and across a wide range of opinion leaders, the concept of sustainable development has attracted considerable opposition from environmental groups, most of it centering on the word *development*.[3] William Ophuls (1996, 34) is typical of those who criticize the linkage to development:

Sustainable development is an oxymoron. Modern political economy in any form is unsustainable, precisely because it involves "development"—that is, more and more people consuming more and more goods with the aid of ever more powerful technologies . . . such an economy is based on stolen goods, deferred payments, and hidden costs; it continues to exist or even thrive today only because we do not account for what we steal from nature or for what posterity will have to pay for our pleasures or for what we sweep under the ecological carpet.

Others have emphasized the ways in which debt, trade, and foreign aid have altered the meaning of development and given it a peculiarly Western, industrial focus that fosters accelerated destruction of biological and cultural diversity, particularly in "underdeveloped" countries and regions.[4] This view found frequent expression at the 2002 World Summit on Sustainable Development and helped to convince some observers that sustainable development had become a public relations cloak for corporate globalization (Caplan 2002).

Partly in response to dissatisfaction with the sustainable development concept and partly in response to growing concerns about urban quality of life, a splinter movement of sorts has arisen in an effort to focus sustainability strategies on the social, economic, and ecological well-being of communities. Participants in this movement define community sustainability in ways that highlight relationships between local quality of life and changes in land use, population, consumption, civic participation, and commitment to intertemporal equity. A sustainable community is one in which economic vitality, ecological integrity, civic democracy, and social well-being are linked in complementary fashion, thereby fostering a high quality of life and a strong sense of reciprocal obligation among its members. Ideally, sustainable communities have levels of pollution, consumption, and population size that are in keeping with regional carrying capacity; their members share an ethic of responsibility to one another and to future generations; prices of their goods and services reflect, where practical, the full social costs of their provision; equity mitigation measures protect the poor from the regressive impacts of full-cost pricing; community systems of education, governance, and civic leadership encourage informed democratic deliberation; and the design of markets, transport, land use, and architecture enhances neighborhood livability and preserves ecological integrity (Hempel 1996b, 1998).

The sustainable communities movement tends to be highly decentralized and inclusive, drawing together a growing number of environmentalists, urban public health groups, growth management advocates, civic leaders, municipal planning and redevelopment agencies, environmental justice activists, proponents of local control in government, neighborhood associations, and scholars interested in interdisciplinary approaches to urban problem solving. Although becoming visible in dozens of countries, the movement has not yet achieved any formal coalescence or unification in the organized pursuit of particular policies or institutional reforms. Its most visible face in the United States is probably the "smart growth" movement, which is described below and amplified on in chapter 7 with respect to California's "Blueprint Planning." Internationally, the most visible activities of the sustainable community movement can be seen in the Local Agenda 21 programs of planning and action, the result of an initiative taken in 1992 at the United Nations' Earth Summit. The dispersed nature of the movement is perhaps best illustrated by the thousands of sustainability blogs and Web sites that can now be found on the Internet.[5] Paul Hawken (2007, 223) has identified nearly 9,000 Web sites offering sustainable community ideas. His own community directory and network site, www.wiserearth.org, provides links to more than 1,100 organizations devoted to sustainable community goals, internationally.

Evolving Frameworks

The historical roots of the sustainable communities movement in North America can be traced to many different sources. A partial list of formative developments in the evolution of this movement is provided in box 2.1.

Few individuals have done more to lay the groundwork for today's sustainable community movement than Patrick Geddes and Lewis Mumford. Geddes's *Cities in Evolution* (1915) stressed the integration of environmental protection and social organization in urban design. Noting the corrosive effects of industrialization on geographic community, Geddes observed that "[s]uch swift multiplication of the quantity of life, with corresponding swift exhaustion of the material resources on which life depends has been too much" (1915, 52). His plea for regional planning to combat the "waste and dissipation" of Nature and community strongly influenced the young Lewis Mumford (Luccarelli 1995, 16–28), who went on to become a leader in the 1920s Regional Planning Association of America. Mumford's *Sticks and Stones* (1924) and *The Golden Day* (1926) were among the earliest attempts to address jointly the social and environmental consequences of the loss of community in a "machine civilization." Portraying colonial New England as a promising model for the contemporary design of human settlements, Mumford attempted to reconstruct the communitarian social tradition in a way that would be appropriate for the twentieth century. According to Luccarelli (1995, 49–50), Mumford believed that the attainment of a genuine sense of place, grounded in relation to nature, parallels—and encourages—community. In the early New England that Mumford admired, the techniques of building a livable place—especially town planning—correspond to a culture of community: a commonality based on civic-mindedness and social cohesion. Thus for Mumford, early New England provided both a symbol of commonwealth and an enduring sense of place essential to establishing and maintaining a productive, equitable, and organic relation between built and natural environments. These are the features he praised for creating civic identity and a vibrant regional democracy.

Contemporary Influences

Today's sustainable community movement looks, at first, like an extension of Mumford's vision. It may be more accurate, however, to view it as a reaction to decades of frustration felt by transportation and

Box 2.1
Sustainable Communities: An Issue Evolution Framework

- Garden City movement, led by Ebenezer Howard (1898) at the dawn of the twentieth century.
- Bioregional planning and design insights of Patrick Geddes (1915), Ian McHarg (1969), Kirkpatrick Sale (1985), and the Regional Planning Association of America (Sussman 1976).
- American New Towns movement (e.g., Reston, VA; Radburn, NJ; Columbia, MD) that began in the 1920s.
- Grassroots communitarian movements of the late 1940s (e.g., Fellowship of Intentional Communities, established in 1948).
- Great Society urban programs of Lyndon Johnson in the 1960s.
- The decline of faith in technological progress as a solution to urban problems (e.g., Mumford 1964).
- Spaceship Earth idea (Fuller 1969) and rise of American environmental movement in early 1970s.
- "Limits to growth" arguments of the late 1960s and early 1970s (e.g., Meadows et al. 1972).
- Studies of the resilience of ecological communities (Holling 1973).
- Local self-reliance and appropriate technology movements of the 1970s and early 1980s (e.g., Morris 1982).
- Urban Ecology and Eco-City developments (e.g., Register 1987; Engwicht 1993).
- The strategic coupling of environment and development interests in the sustainable development dialogue of the 1980s (e.g., the Brundtland Commission, 1987) and of the 1990s (e.g., the Earth Summit, 1992, and Habitat II, 1996).
- Architectural visions of neotraditional towns and healthy cities (e.g., Van der Ryn and Calthorpe 1986).
- Social capital debate of the 1990s led by Robert Putnam (1995), Amatai Etzioni (1994), and others.
- Application of industrial ecology concepts, environmental audits, and sustainability indicators in the early 1990s by struggling communities attempting to recover from economic downturns and urban decay (e.g., Sustainable Chattanooga).
- "Smart growth" movement of 1990s and early twenty-first century.
- Rise of sustainable community networks as virtual communities (e.g., Hawken 2007).

land-use planners, municipal officials, neighborhood activists, downtown business leaders, and environmental groups faced with their inability to constrain and effectively manage urban sprawl through the use of planning, zoning, and redevelopment tools. Population and economic growth, market forces, housing preferences, and a culture of consumption have heretofore foiled the best of growth management plans. In a pattern repeated across the country, sprawl has consumed land at a rate far in excess of that needed to keep up with population growth. In the Chicago region, for example, land area developed between 1970 and 1990 grew almost fourteen times faster than population growth. During the same period, the number of people living within Los Angeles city limits increased by 45 percent, while land consumption for development and housing increased by nearly 300 percent (Bernstein 1997, 10). California, with 3.5 million acres already in urban use, is consuming over 60,000 acres of open space each year for urban expansion (Fulton 1991, 2).

Beginning with the cities of Ramapo, New York, in the 1960s and Petaluma, California, in the early 1970s, growth control measures were implemented to reduce and in some cases halt the spread of residential, commercial, and industrial development. But few have succeeded. Despite the adoption of hundreds of local growth management ordinances, the overall pattern has been merely to shift development to nearby communities. Hoping to learn from past mistakes, many concerned citizens and local officials have become advocates of "smart growth"—a movement that stresses regional efficiency, environmental protection, and fiscal responsibility in land use decisions. Its supporters include many sustainability advocates.

One of the most visible sources of sustainable community mobilization has been environmental activists, especially those who have lost confidence in the political capacity of national and international institutions to attack environmental problems in a global or comprehensive manner. Discouraged by the lack of global integration in the management of social and natural systems, these activists have embraced sustainable community ideas as a good way to encourage such integration at the local level. Practicing what Wildavsky (1979, 41) called a "strategic retreat from objectives," many environmentalists have embraced the 1980s slogan "think globally; act locally," thereby framing and attacking an increasing number of regional, national, and global environmental problems at the local level, where they tend to be more comprehensible, accessible, and tractable. Such thinking received a boost at the 1992 Earth Summit, when participating nations agreed to implement Agenda 21 plans for both local and national sustainable development.

The sustainable community concept calls for interdisciplinary and crosscutting approaches to problem framing and policy response. It encourages environmentalists to think carefully about the social and economic needs of a community; developers to understand the rudiments of ecosystem management; civic leaders to recognize the interdependence of communities in both economic and ecological terms; and ordinary citizens to draw connections between civic engagement and quality of life.

Conflicting Goals

Inherent in the process of sustainable community integration are political tensions between the objects of integration. Consider, for example, the aforementioned "three Es" notion of sustainability: environment, economy, and equity. Achieving all three of these goals in a modern community involves tradeoffs and optimization choices that require skill-ful political timing and broad coalition formation. In fact, the three Es can be productively visualized as a triangle of conflicting goals (see figure 2.1), in which movement toward any "E" is met by political resistance from supporters of one or both of the others. Perhaps the most obvious

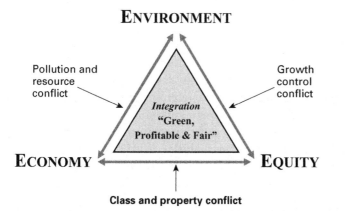

Figure 2.1
Conflicting goals for achieving sustainable communities (adapted from Campbell 1996).

example is the tension between the goals of environmental quality and economic growth, typically viewed as a tradeoff over how much pollution, waste, and natural resource consumption will be tolerated for the sake of economic expansion. Also familiar is the tension between the goals of economic growth and social equity, manifest principally as class and private property conflicts that arise from the concentration and unequal distribution of wealth. Perhaps the least familiar point of tension is found in the urban growth control conflicts that pit environmentalists against champions of equity seeking to secure affordable housing and job creation, often at the cost of open space, habitat loss, and increased congestion. In each case, the ideal of a sustainable community confronts the optimization challenge of becoming green, profitable, and fair, all at the same time.

Adding to this challenge is the growing realization that communities may be less capable of sustaining broad coalitions of diverse citizens than previously thought. Research by Robert Putnam (2007) reveals that homogeneous populations are much more likely to develop sustainable communities than diverse ones. This conclusion runs counter to Putnam's well-known views about social capital and the virtues of diversity, because it suggests that higher homogeneity leads to higher levels of civic engagement and trust, at least in the short run. For many leaders of sustainable community initiatives, this is unwelcome news. It challenges the cherished belief that the goal of sustainability is fully compatible with the goal of strength through diversity.

Competing Orientations

Members of the sustainable community movement differ in the extent to which they incorporate concerns about social justice, the health of ecosystems and other species, and the interests of future generations that do not overlap with their own lives. While some supporters emphasize the technical planning or eco-design features of sustainability (e.g., Aberley 1994; Moughton and Shirley 2005), others stress its political and economic determinants (e.g., Pirages 1996; Roseland 2005). Still others emphasize the moral and ethical dimensions (e.g., Agyemen 2005; Bullard 2007). Recognizing that there is considerable overlap, it is nevertheless possible to characterize these orientations according to the dominant intellectual foundations and frameworks that supporters use in addressing community sustainability. At least five clusters of sustainability approaches can be identified: (1) the natural and social capital approach popular with many economists and political scientists; (2) the urban design–smart growth approach used by many land-use planners, architects, and sustainability-minded local officials; (3) the ecosystem management–urban ecology strategy employed by many ecologists, landscape architects, and natural resource managers; (4) the metropolitan governance orientation that characterizes many civic leaders who seek a regional policy approach to community sustainability; and (5) the neighborhood–ecovillage approach popular with many grassroots activists. None of these are mutually exclusive, nor can they be said to constitute forms of identity that are commonly or self-consciously accepted by participants in the sustainable community movement. Table 2.1 presents a summary of the intellectual foundations, challenges, and relevant indicators associated with each orientation.

Capital Theory

Numerous economists and other social scientists have attempted to define sustainability in terms of shared capital or constant capital. For example, Ismail Serageldin (1995), former vice president of environmental programs at the World Bank, has identified the essential requisites of sustainability as the retention for future generations of four types of capital: natural capital, manmade capital, human capital, and social capital. Building on this idea, Stephen Viederman (1996, 46) adds a fifth type—cultural capital—as necessary to the mission of sustainable communities. Serageldin (1995, 6) defines natural capital as "the stock of environmentally provided assets (such as soil, atmosphere, forests, water, wetlands) that provide a flow of useful goods and services." Using this concept of capital, neoclassical economists have defined sustainability in terms of nondeclining human welfare over time (Pearce, Markandya, and Barbier 1989). Although such definitions rely entirely on anthropocentric utility, they have the virtue of being quantifiable and monetizable. Of course, some things, such as climate "services," remain extremely difficult to measure in dollars.

Critics both within and outside the field of economics have raised basic concerns about this natural capital approach to sustainability (Stern 1997; Common 1995). A typical objection is that the "constant capital" rule assumes unrealistic degrees of substitution of human-made capital for natural capital. Excessive faith in technology leads to assumptions of high elasticity of substitution, though it is apparent to most observers

Table 2.1
Major Approaches to Community Sustainability

Sustainable community orientation	Underlying foundation	Conceptual challenge	Analytical challenge	Key indicators
Capital theory	economics and accounting	nature as capital	elasticity of substitution	natural income accounting
Urban design	land-use planning and architecture	planning vs. markets; "design with nature"	constraints posed by existing environment	density, open space, traffic flows, jobs/housing balance
Ecosystems management	ecology	systems thinking, natural vs. political boundaries	critical loads and stress points; interconnections	urban habitat type; impervious surface area; size of ecological footprint
Metropolitan governance	regionalism	assymetrical interdependence	incentives for intergovernmental cooperation	number of regional councils; joint power agreements; metro tax-base sharing
Eco-villages	neighborhoods	scale effects	technology transfer and replication of local demonstration projects	community gardens; neighborhood associations

that many forms of natural capital, such as the ozone layer, have no known artificial substitutes that can be supplied on a global scale. Some critics dismiss the notion altogether, arguing that nature's intrinsic value precludes natural capital approaches to sustainability (Spash and Hanley 1995).

Natural capital approaches comport with widely accepted accounting schemes that permit measurement across disparate domains of value (Jansson et al. 1994). In the case of social capital, however, even crude attempts at measurement may be futile. According to Coleman (1988, S98), "unlike other forms of capital, social capital inheres in the structure of relations between actors and among actors. It is not lodged either in the actors themselves or in physical implements of production." In other words, social capital is about social relations. In terms of sustainable community objectives, social capital is about personal relations that create trust, norms of acceptance, and a local sense of reciprocal obligation. What those relations are, exactly, and how they are developed and maintained remains very difficult to analyze across time and place.

Urban Design–Smart Growth
The design orientation appears to dominate the literature on sustainable communities. Architects, land use planners, and civil engineers make up the core support group, but a growing number of government and business leaders support community design innovations as the most promising way to revitalize sagging local economies, manage urban growth, and balance demand for transportation, housing, jobs, environmental quality, and social services. Enterprising real estate developers have discovered that projects incorporating sustainability design may add sales appeal and simplify the entitlement process for securing building permits. The rising influence of the U.S. Green Building Council (www.usgbc.org) and its LEED-certified buildings has made sustainable building design a major trend in modern architecture and community design.

As leaders of the design efforts, architects (e.g., McDonough 1992; Van der Ryn and Calthorpe 1986; Kunstler 1996) have attempted to make communities more pedestrian friendly, energy efficient, conducive to public interaction, and aesthetically attractive. Using labels such as the "New Urbanism," "neotraditional communities," and "Green cities," they have mounted campaigns to redesign neighborhoods and communities along lines similar to those championed by Lewis Mumford nearly seventy years ago. Several sets of guiding principles for community design have been prepared as part of these efforts.[6] Among the most important of these design principles is the idea that a community should coexist with nature in a "healthy, supportive, diverse and sustainable condition" (McDonough 1992), and that it should have a well-defined edge, as well as a location, size, and character that permit the close integration of housing, jobs, attractive open space, cultural and recreational amenities, and facilities essential to the daily needs of citizens (Calthorpe 1993).

Although impressed by what these design principles can contribute to the sustainability of new development, many planners and engineers are understandably preoccupied with repairing or restoring the products of past development. The obvious difficulty with most design innovations is that so much of the landscape is already "built out" or settled in ways that appear irreversible and that reflect unsustainable choices. The freedom to select a different course of development or alternative lifestyle is often constrained by the path-dependent outcomes of what has come before (i.e., early design choices of street layout and urban infrastructure have entrained subsequent development and have made it difficult to embark in new directions). Moreover, the political and economic costs of reform render the boldest sustainability designs applicable to only a small number of "boutique" subdivisions, new town demonstrations, or hard-to-replicate experimental communities.

In view of the momentum of past development mistakes, most urban designers point to the importance of infrastructure decisions—especially the allocation of sewer, water, and roads—as fundamental to the success of both new development and redevelopment of existing areas. For many, the design of transportation systems is of paramount importance. David Engwicht (1993), for example, argues that we can sustainably "reclaim" our cities and towns by redesigning transportation on the basis of *exchange* instead of *movement; place* instead of *destination.* The principal challenge becomes one of reducing dependence on private automobiles (Newman and Kenworthy 1989). To that end, design for sustainability usually favors increased density and greater reliance on mixed land uses, both of which encourage walking and greater reliance on public transit. Transit-oriented development (TOD) has become one of the most common strategies for connecting the design approach with the effort by many city planners and officials to promote infill development and higher densification to preserve land and open space.

Ecosystem Management—Urban Ecology

Although this orientation overlaps significantly with environmentally sensitive forms of urban design, the ecosystem approach can be distinguished chiefly by its emphasis on the role of natural systems, such as watersheds, in providing the physical context for planning and management. A major impetus for this approach can be traced to the work of landscape architect, Ian McHarg. His 1969 book, *Design with Nature*, quickly became a classic in the young field of ecological planning. In this approach, the preservation and restoration of ecosystems becomes a fundamental consideration in community design and development (Platt, Rowntree, and Muick 1996). Sociopolitical factors have historically been slighted in ecosystem management, although efforts to integrate the human and ecological dimensions of this approach have been strengthened in recent years (Yaffee et al. 1996).[7]

Because it is essentially a science-based management approach to land and other natural resources, ecosystem management requires careful attention to conservation biology, hydrology, and other aspects of field ecology and natural history analysis. Furthermore, because of its costly scientific monitoring requirements and the multijurisdictional cooperation it needs in order to succeed, the ecosystem approach usually has to be initiated by federal and state agencies, or large nonprofit environmental organizations, such as the Nature Conservancy (Yaffee et al. 1996). This, and the fact that it utilizes natural boundaries for its planning units, means that ecosystem management often operates in some tension with local political jurisdictions. It is by definition a regional approach to sustainability, and thus shares a key feature of the metropolitan approach discussed below.

Bioregionalism, a less science-based ecosystem orientation, has proven very popular with some sustainable community advocates in Europe and North America. Their aim has been to develop a nontechnical understanding of ecological interdependence among ordinary citizens who share a particular bioregion, thus helping the residents recognize their personal stake in the proper management of ecosystems. Relying more on the insights of deep ecology than on scientific research, bioregionalists seek to define human communities as subsystems of ecological communities (Naess 1989). This poses the obvious challenge of reconceptualizing one's place in terms of biophysical features and their interconnections, rather than according to human settlement features, such as roads, towers, reservoirs, and the usual landmarks of the built environment.

Moreover, it changes the human role with regard to nature from that of owner to steward or mere tenant. As one leading advocate of bioregionalism sees it, the challenge is to become "dwellers in the land," interacting in a society whose scale of community, government, and economy is small enough to permit intimate integration with the natural world (Sale 1985).

Metropolitan Governance

A more urban and politically oriented conception of sustainable communities views them as communities interacting within a region that achieve and retain improvements in quality of life without diminishing the quality of life enjoyed by other communities, now and in the future. The zero-sum notion of sustainability implied in this view requires that communities avoid strategies that achieve local sustainability at the expense of other communities. By importing more than their fair share of critical resources and exporting their waste and pollution, a community can improve the quality of life of its citizens by externalizing the costs of improvement, both economically and geographically. Clearly, making air quality improvements in Los Angeles "sustainable" by increasing the city's reliance on coal-fired power plants in Utah is not what community sustainability is about. On the other hand, given differential resources, capabilities, and needs, how can competing communities avoid a certain amount of "beggar-thy-neighbor" behavior? And what constitutes a "fair share" of critical resources among communities?

Given that today's community needs and opportunities can be heavily influenced by international trade arrangements and foreign investment, it is very difficult to devise allocation rules that work to the benefit of both individual communities and regions (or global systems) as a whole. Because of the enormous expansion of economic trade and technology, and in some cases the legacy of colonialism, the locations of a community's economic activity and ecological impact no longer coincide with its geographic location (Wackernagel and Rees 1996). In most countries, communities increasingly appropriate carrying capacity from other communities and regions. The ecological services of one bioregion are used to subsidize the growth of human activities in another. Imported ecological wealth and exported waste permit communities to hide the true costs of unsustainable practices, externalizing them in distant places in the form of huge "ecological footprints."[8]

The point of this "individualistic" account of communities is that sustainability may require something different: a "community-of-communities" approach. Greater regional and global cooperation may be in the offing as communities everywhere face the challenge of reducing greenhouse gas emissions. Sustainability, in climate terms, will require widespread commitment to collaborative solutions. California's new greenhouse gas reduction policy (AB 32) is an excellent example of how local initiatives—for example, air pollution control measures—are being better aligned with state-level initiatives on climate change (see chapter 4).

The practical implication is that sustainable communities may have to be assessed regionally, if not globally. It is the interactions between communities as much as the interactions within that determine each community's potential for sustainability. The political implication of this argument is a renewed emphasis on regionalism and what I have termed *glocal* thinking (Hempel 1996a).[9] Spurred in part by the continuing devolution of power from the federal government to state and local levels, and by the increasing globalization of key economic sectors, the need to develop and connect global and local policymaking is becoming apparent to all but the most reactionary followers of nationalism.

Without a regional vision and the institutional arrangements to facilitate it, the goals of sustainable community end up looking parochial and selfish. Given that over 75 percent of Americans now live in one of 320 metropolitan regions, the "community-of-communities" idea appears to be less far-fetched than our fragmented political system of more than 80,000 local jurisdictions would suggest.[10] As Richard Levine observed (Hiss 1996, 7), metropolitan regions may constitute "the largest unit capable of addressing the many urban, architectural, social, economic, political, natural resource, and environmental imbalances in the modern world, and, at the same time, the smallest scale at which such problems can be meaningfully resolved in an integrated and holistic fashion."

Neighborhood–Ecovillage Development
At the opposite end of the spectrum from would-be planetary managers and globalists are the grassroots activists who want to see sustainability flourish first and foremost at the neighborhood level. They may also promote improvements in overall community design and regional governance, but their overriding interest is in small-scale experiments and

demonstration projects that model the changes they seek for the world as a whole. Like many of the design advocates, they tend to focus on projects that promote pedestrian-friendly villages and public transit–oriented development, backed by mixed-income housing and by mixed-use zoning that permits the integration of commercial and residential space. Most neighborhood activists also have a preference for locally owned businesses, along with attractive public spaces for social interaction. Other desired features include narrow streets, urban infill, plentiful parks and community gardens, access to green power, safe bike trails, organic farmers markets, certified green building designs, and many other features that enhance neighborhood aesthetics, public safety, and the environmental health of all residents.

In essence, supporters of eco-neighborhoods have taken the logic of sustainable communities to the next level (e.g., Barton 2000). They claim, with some justification, that nearly every major sustainable cities program—see, for example, Kent Portney's list of nearly fifty sustainable cities at www.ourgreencities.com—is in reality a loose confederation of neighborhood projects and programs, tied together by a common purpose, coordinated through city and regional offices, and funded in part from grants targeted to or passed through cities and regional authorities. Portney (2003) argues that the wide scope of sustainability actions and political ends in cities such as Portland, Seattle, Chicago, and San Francisco distinguish them from narrower, more scattered, and neighborhood-level activities of many would-be sustainable communities. The fact remains that most cities have been very reluctant to tackle the challenge of sustainability; hence it may make sense to think of the ecovillage movement as a logical first step in a multiphase, multidecade strategy to achieve sustainability at the broader community level. For information about this international strategy, see the Global Ecovillage Network Web site: http://gen.ecovillage.org.

Operationalizing the Concept

With the possible exception of neighborhood demonstration projects, notions of community sustainability frequently trade on lofty sentiments and principles that are difficult, if not impossible, to implement one community at a time. Furthermore, low levels of civic engagement and poor ecological literacy make it difficult to comprehend what is at stake in choices about neighborhood revitalization, regional governance, urban design, ecosystem management, and capital substitution. Most discussion about sustainable communities takes place at the "high-concept" level, rather than in a context of practical problem solving. As a result, efforts to incorporate sustainability goals into public policy may be easy at an abstract level, but once a specific link is made to energy, transportation, land use, population growth, air quality, economic development, and so forth, the utility of the concept begins to erode. Not only is the idea hard to grasp intellectually—because it requires synthetic thinking and integrative minds—but it is also hard to measure in ways that illuminate the concept.

Community Indicators

One of the most promising ways to move from "clouds to concrete" is to construct reliable sustainability indicators that can be tailored to diverse communities and periodically monitored for changes in direction or intensity. These indicators of sustainability measure regional and community-level capacity to meet present and future needs in ways that do not sacrifice important opportunities for future generations. They are essentially integrative measures of economic, social, and ecological health that are designed to gauge a community's systemic balance and resilience over long periods of time. Examples of indicators (see box 2.2 and table 2.2) include the ratio of job growth to population growth, pounds of solid waste landfilled per capita, high school graduation rates, and the green-space–blackspace ratio (open space–paved area). No single indicator is adequate to measure a community's sustainability, but taken in combination a carefully selected battery of indicators can reveal much about a community's movement toward or away from sustainability goals. A growing network of developers and users of sustainability indicators have utilized the Internet to disseminate and test their approaches at the community level.[11]

One of the leading approaches for developing and applying sustainability indicators is ecological footprint analysis, developed by Wackernagel and Rees (1996). They conceive of footprints as accounting tools for calculating human impacts in terms of the land and water areas appropriated for energy and resource consumption and for waste disposal. An ecological footprint is a measure of the load placed on the biosphere by a given population. Footprints are therefore proportional to a community's combined population and per capita consumption of resources (plus associated waste production).

Box 2.2
Examples of Sustainable Community Indicators

- Percent of workforce covered by health insurance
- Greenhouse gas emissions per capita
- Number of domestic violence calls to police
- Number of community gardens
- Landfilled solid waste (tons per year)
- Percent of households that can afford median-priced house
- Water use and wastewater flows (gallons/day/person)
- Net growth in livable wage jobs
- Graduation rate by race and ethnicity
- Energy consumption (BTU per capita)
- Voter turnout in municipal elections
- Pounds of toxics produced and released per year
- Dollar value of repairs or replacement needed in infrastructure investment
- Homeownership rate
- Number of endangered and threatened species
- Community volunteerism by age group (survey data)

More specialized sustainability indicators can be used to measure everything from institutional capacity (e.g., annual tax capacity per household to support community services) to noise exposure (e.g., number of children exposed to air- and ground-traffic noise levels above 50 decibels from 8 p.m. to 8 a.m.). Using advanced information technologies—especially geographic information systems (GIS)—these indicators can be overlaid, mapped, and compared within and across regions to provide sophisticated ways to visualize the complex interactions that influence a community's sustainability index or "scorecard." Geographic information systems provide a practical tool for analyzing how communities are changing over time and why. By integrating layers of information about social, environmental, and economic sustainability, GIS users can produce a color-keyed map of trends and driving forces that interact spatially at the neighborhood, community, and regional levels.

Not surprisingly, while the capability to construct, monitor, and visualize complex sustainability indicators has increased markedly in the past decade, the utilization of such information in policymaking has been rather limited. Political sensitivity about what indicators reveal is not the least of the reasons for this relative lack of progress. Other considerations

Table 2.2
Three Types of Community Indicators

General	Quality of Life	Sustainability
Vehicle miles traveled	Congestion levels	Total vehicular CO_2 emissions/year
Economic growth rate	Income/capita	Ratio of income/capita to municipal debt/capita
Population growth rate	Urban density levels	Ecological footprint (productive land appropriated)
Solid waste (tons/yr)	Solid waste/capita	Percent of solid waste diverted to recycling
Number of parks	Park acreage/1,000 people	Ratio of greenspace-blackspace (paved area)
Size of police force	Violent crimes/10,000 people	Alcohol and drug treatment beds/10,000 people
Housing supply	Median housing price	Percent of adults that can afford median home
Job growth rate	Unemployment rate	Percent of new jobs paying a livable wage
Business permits	Business vacancy rate	Ratio of business startups to business failures
Resource consumption	Water shortages/year	Ratio of renewable water supply to withdrawals
Health facilities	Health insurance coverage (%)	Packs of cigarettes sold per person per year
School facilities	Student-teacher ratios	Number of courses promoting ecological literacy

have also been important: problems of unreliable, invalid, or missing data; problems of data that are not available over time, or not comparable for time series analysis; interjurisdictional conflicts in data collection and interpretation; indicators that are unrepresentative for policymaking, or irrelevant to important community goals; indicators that raise privacy concerns; and indicators that are too complex or esoteric to be understandable by decision makers, let alone the general public. In some instances, the sheer growth of indicators has overwhelmed human capacities to process and interpret the information they contain. The Alberta Round Table on Environment and Economy, for example, initially developed a list of 850 potential sustainability indicators before coming up with a more manageable list of 59 (Maclaren 1996, 197).

Beyond the data analysis and management limitations lies one more critical constraint on the development and use of sustainability indicators: the role of ordinary citizens in their selection and interpretation. Deliberative democracy is, to many people, both a means and an end of the sustainable community movement. If deliberative democracy is conducive to the process of sustainability, and vice versa, it is important that citizens participate in the selection of indicators that will be used to evaluate their community and region. Although such involvement will sometimes lead to the inclusion of indicators that scholars and professional analysts regard as unscientific, irrelevant, or unreliable, to exclude such involvement may reveal, as clearly as any indicator, a basic cause of unsustainability—lack of civic engagement.[12]

Conclusion

Deciding which sustainability approaches and indicators to adopt requires a judicious balancing of technical merit and popular appeal. The capital theory, urban design, ecosystem management, metropolitan governance, and neighborhood approaches all offer important perspectives and insights for use in becoming more sustainable. Each has its limitations as well. Although elements of all five approaches can be included in sustainability strategies, it is apparent that some approaches will have more public appeal than others. For example, urban design is likely to attract more adherents than ecosystem management, and both may have more appeal than capital theory, with its dry academic tone. Moreover, each approach, along with the indicators employed, has to be custom-tailored to suit the needs of diverse communities with unique problems and opportunities.

One perspective in particular—metropolitan governance—deserves special attention as a means for developing the regional policy framework needed to make the other approaches more feasible and effective. For many communities, improved governance appears to be a prerequisite for progress in sustainability. The politics of the metropolitan approach, in combination with the science of the ecosystem approach and the practicality of the neighborhood approach, may offer hope for reducing the parochialism and unplanned growth that threaten the long-term sustainability of many communities. By emphasizing the importance of intercommunity cooperation in achieving sustainability, the metropolitan approach can in theory help to embed the other approaches in the essential workings of local politics and regional policy formation.

In practice, of course, metropolitanism has not fared well in U.S. politics. Like Deborah Stone's (1997) model of society based on the polis rather than the marketplace, the metropolitan vision rests on a little used model of democratic regionalism, rather than on the more familiar models of local control, consumer-driven markets, and design by experts. As such, it promotes the ideal of a community of communities, while at the same time attempting to limit the freedom of individual communities to pursue designs, development strategies, and capital allocations that produce unsustainable outcomes for the region as a whole.

While arguments can be made that such an approach merely shifts the struggle for competitive advantage in growth and consumption from individuals to communities and on to the regional (subnational) level, it appears that most of today's long-term threats to sustainability are more visible and, arguably, more tractable at this level—that is, regional policies may hold greater promise than those arising at the household, neighborhood, local, national, multinational, or global levels. Regionalism, however, is not a panacea. Metropolitan economies could end up competing with one another in ways that are just as debilitating and unsustainable as the competition that now occurs between many central cities and their suburbs. Fortunately, competition among communities and regions need not be (and seldom is) "zero-sum." What makes the metropolitan approach particularly promising for building sustainable communities is its scale of action and exchange: it is big enough to capture key ecological, social, and economic interdependencies, yet small enough to provide a sense of place and social embeddedness. In theory, it affords an optimal scale at which to attempt the integration of governance, social diversity, economic development, and environmental protection.

Eventually it will be necessary to think and act globally in an effort to become more sustainable. The confluence of modernization, globalization, and urbanization in Asia and other regions of the world is being driven by economic and consumer trends that exert strong counterpressure on the goals of sustainability. Metropolitan approaches may become less effective or attractive than state programs, larger regional approaches, federal initiatives, or planetary solutions. For the time being, however, it is at the metropolitan level that sustainability concepts appear most operational and meaningful. This is the level where human communities interact most tellingly with nonhuman nature. It is the primary arena in which conflicting ideals of community, liberty, and ecology will have to be reconciled with the forces of economic globalization.

It remains to be seen if the U.S. political system will adjust to this kind of thinking. The goals of sustainable community may be too Jeffersonian to suit a society shaped predominantly by Hamiltonian precepts. Then again, they may provide an important stimulus for rethinking what quality of life requires in the new millennium.

In *Democracy in America* (1835), de Tocqueville observes that among the key enabling features of American politics are "those township institutions which limit the despotism of the majority and at the same time impart to the people a taste for freedom and the art of being free" (Bradley 1945, vol. 1, 288). A sustainable community is one in which such "taste for freedom" is derived ecologically, as well as politically. Without an ecological reconception of freedom as sustainability, we are left to ponder how and under what conditions, if any, mortal political actors, motivated by short-term incentive structures, will choose to adopt policies that promote genuine sustainability.

Notes

1 The term *sustainable community* has many variations, including green cities, eco-cities, sustainable cities, eco-communities, and livable cities.

2 Common (1995) notes that systems with low stability—for example, temperate forests—can still have high resilience, just as highly stable systems—for

example, tropical ecosystems—can have low resilience compared with temperate ones.

3 Although many writers draw a distinction between development and growth—with growth (interpreted as "bigger") being ecologically unsustainable, unlike development (interpreted as "better")—some critics argue that "development cannot be purified of its historical context" (Sachs 1993, 21) as both a means and end of growth.

4 Of particular relevance here are the arguments made by members of the International Forum on Globalization. Prominent spokespersons include Vandana Shiva, Martin Khor, David Korten, Jerry Mander, Wolfgang Sachs, and Helena Norberg-Hodge.

5 A sample of these sites would include: The International Institute for Sustainable Development (www.iisd.org), the Sustainable Communities Network (www.sustainable.org), the International Council for Local Environmental Initiatives (www.iclei.org), Redefining Progress (www.rprogress.org), and SustainAbility (www.sustainability.com).

6 Perhaps the best known of these guides are the Hannover Principles, developed by William McDonough, dean of the School of Architecture at the University of Virginia, and the Ahwahnee Principles, developed in 1991 by Peter Calthorpe and others at the instigation of the California Local Government Commission.

7 A hybrid of the ecosystem and urban design approaches, applying the characteristics of healthy natural systems to human communities, has been developed by the Chicago-based Urban Sustainability Learning Group (1996). According to their view, a sustainable community is constantly changing through continual interdependent fluctuations in order to maintain itself as the environment changes.

8 Quantifying the total appropriated carrying capacity of a community is extremely difficult, owing in part to conceptual difficulties with carrying capacity itself (Cohen 1995, 237–260). But such quantification is nevertheless important for those who wish to operationalize the concept of sustainability. Ecological footprint analysis is perhaps the best-known technique for this purpose, though it is at best a crude measure of appropriated land and water resources.

9 The rationale for glocalism is derived from the need to connect local policy-making processes that are conducive to deliberative democracy with sustainability strategies that must sometimes be global, or at least regional, in order to be effective. Reestablishing the primacy of community in political life will arguably facilitate the social and environmental sensibilities needed to manage the increasingly global reach of technology and capital.

10 Included in local political jurisdictions in the United States are approximately 3,000 counties, more than 19,000 municipalities, over 16,000 townships, nearly 15,000 school districts, and roughly 30,000 special districts.

11 Examples of popular Web sites include the Global Footprint Network (www.footprintnetwork.org/), Maureen Hart's community indicator network (www

.sustainablemeasures.com), and the International Sustainability Indicators Network (www.sustainabilityindicators.org).

12 For example, the author was once involved in a sustainable community indicator project in which local residents insisted that measures of graffiti removal would provide one of the best sustainability indicators for their neighborhood. Some academic members of the project team regarded the local residents' ideas as shortsighted, crude, or trivial, preferring instead measures that could be derived from the scientific literature.

References

Aberley, Doug. ed. 1994. *Futures by Design: The Practice of Ecological Planning.* Philadelphia, PA: New Society Publishers.

Agyeman, Julian. 2005. *Sustainable Communities and the Challenge of Environmental Justice.* New York: NYU Press.

Barton, Hugh, ed. 2000. *Sustainable Communities: The Potential for Eco-Neighborhoods.* London: Earthscan.

Bernstein, Scott. 1997. "Community-Based Regionalism Key for Sustainable Future." *Neighborhood Works* 20, 6 (November–December): 10.

Bradley, Phillips. ed. 1945. Alexis de Tocqueville's *Democracy in America.* Vol. 1. New York: Vintage.

Brundtland Commission (World Commission on Environment and Development). 1987. *Our Common Future.* New York: Oxford University Press.

Bullard, Robert, ed. 2007. *Growing Smarter: Achieving Livable Communities, Environmental Justice, and Regional Equity.* Cambridge, MA: MIT Press.

Calthorpe, Peter. 1993. *The Next American Metropolis: Ecology, Community, and the American Dream.* Princeton, NJ: Princeton Architectural Press.

Campbell, Scott. 1996. "Green Cities, Growing Cities, Just Cities?—Urban Planning and the Contradictions of Sustainable Development." *Journal of the American Planning Association* 62, 3: 296–311.

Caplan, Ruth. 2002. "Report from Johannesburg: Exposing the Trojan Horse of Corporate Globalization at the World Summit on Sustainable Development." Alliance for Democracy. Available at http://www.thealliancefordemocracy.org/html/eng/1946-AA.shtml.

Cohen, Joel. 1995. *How Many People Can the Earth Support?* New York: W. W. Norton.

Coleman, James S. 1988. "Social Capital in the Creation of Human Capital." *American Journal of Sociology (Supplement)* 94: S95–S120.

Common, Michael. 1995. *Sustainability and Policy: Limits to Economics.* Cambridge: Cambridge University Press.

Dovers, Stephen R. 1997. "Sustainability: Demands on Policy." *Journal of Public Policy* 16, 3: 303–318.

Downs, Anthony. 1994. *New Visions for Metropolitan America*. Washington, D.C.: The Brookings Institution, and Cambridge, MA: Lincoln Institute of Land Policy.

Engwicht, David. 1993. *Reclaiming Our Cities and Towns: Better Living with Less Traffic*. Gabriola Island, BC: New Society Publishers.

Euston, Stanley,.1995. "Gathering Hope: A Citizens' Call to a Sustainability Ethic for Guiding Public Life." Santa Fe, NM: The Sustainability Project.

Folke, Carl, and Tomas Kaberger. 1991. "Recent Trends in Linking the Natural Environment and the Economy." In *Linking the Natural Environment and the Economy: Essays from the Eco-Eco Group,* Folke and Kaberger, eds. Dordrecht: Kluwer.

Fulton, William. 1991. *Guide to California Planning*. Point Arena, CA: Solano Press Books.

Geddes, Patrick. 1915. *Cities in Evolution*. New York: Harper and Row.

Hart, Maureen. 1999. *Guide to Sustainable Community Indicators*, 2nd ed. Available on-line at www.sustainablemeasures.com.

Hart, Stuart L. 1997. "Beyond Greening: Strategies for a Sustainable World." *Harvard Business Review* 75, 1 (January–February): 66–76.

Hawken, Paul. 1993. *The Ecology of Commerce: A Declaration of Sustainability*. New York: HarperCollins.

Hawken, Paul. 2007. *Blessed Unrest*. New York: Viking.

Hempel, Lamont C. 1992. "Earth Summit or Abyss?" Paper presented at the Global Forum, United Nations Conference on Environment and Development, Rio de Janeiro, Brazil (June).

Hempel, Lamont C. 1996a. *Environmental Governance: The Global Challenge*. Washington, D.C.: Island Press.

Hempel, Lamont C. 1996b. "Roots and Wings: Building Sustainable Communities." White Paper, League of Women Voters Population Coalition (January).

Hempel, Lamont C. 1998. *Sustainable Communities: From Vision to Action*. Claremont Graduate University (Hewlett Foundation).

Hiss, Tony, 1996. "Outlining the New Metropolitan Initiative" (Project Report). Chicago: Center for Neighborhood Technology.

Holling, C. S. 1973. "Resilience and Stability of Ecological Systems." *Annual Review of Ecology and Systematics* 4: 1–24.

Howard, Ebenezer. 1898. *Tomorrow: A Peaceful Path to Real Reform*. Later published as *Garden Cities of Tomorrow*. Cambridge, MA: MIT Press, 1965.

International Union for Conservation of Nature (IUCN), United Nations Environment Program and World Wildlife Fund. 1980. *World Conservation Strategy*. Gland, Switzerland: IUCN.

Jansson, Ann-Marie, Monica Hammer, Carl Folke, and Robert Costanza. 1994. *Investing in Natural Capital: The Ecological Economics Approach to Sustainability.* Washington, D.C.: Island Press.

Kunstler, James Howard. 1996. *Home from Nowhere: Remaking Our Everyday World for the Twenty-First Century.* New York: Simon and Schuster.

Luccarelli, Mark. 1995. *Lewis Mumford and the Ecological Region: The Politics of Planning.* New York: The Guilford Press.

Maclaren, Virginia W. 1996. "Urban Sustainability Reporting." *Journal of the American Planning Association* 62, 2: 184–202.

McDonough, William. 1992. "The Hannover Principles: Designing for Sustainability." Report to the City of Hannover, Germany (a guide for international design competitions for EXPO 2000).

McHarg, Ian. 1969. *Design with Nature.* Garden City, NY: Natural History Press.

Meadows, Donella H., Dennis L. Meadows, Jorgen Randers, and William Behrens III. 1972. *The Limits to Growth.* New York: Universe.

Moughton, J. C., and Peter Shirley. 2005. *Urban Design: Green Dimensions,* 2nd ed. Burlington, MA: Architectural Press.

Mumford, Lewis. 1924. Sticks and Stones: A Study of American Architecture and Civilization. New York: Boni and Liveright.

Mumford, Lewis. 1926. The Golden Day: A Study in American Experience and Culture. New York: Boni and Liveright.

Mumford, Lewis. 1964. *The Myth of the Machine.* New York: Harcourt Brace Jovanovich.

Naess, Arne. 1989. *Ecology, Community, and Lifestyle.* Translated and edited by David Rothenberg. New York: Cambridge University Press.

Newman, Peter, and J. R. Kenworthy. 1989. *Cities and Automobile Dependence.* Brookfield, VT: Gower Technical.

Ophuls, William. 1997. *Requiem for Modern Politics: The Tragedy of the Enlightenment and the Challenge of the New Millennium.* Boulder, CO: Westview Press.

Ophuls, William. 1996. "Unsustainable Liberty, Sustainable Freedom." In *Building Sustainable Societies: A Blueprint for a Post-Industrial World*, ed. Dennis Pirages. Armonk, NY: M. E. Sharpe.

Pearce, David W., Anil Markandya, and Edward B. Barbier. 1989. *Blueprint for a Green Economy.* London: Earthscan.

Pirages, Dennis, ed. 1996. *Building Sustainable Societies: A Blueprint for a Post-Industrial World.* Armonk, NY: M. E. Sharpe.

Platt, Rutherford H., Rowan A. Rowntree, Pamela C. Muick, eds. 1996. *The Ecological City: Preserving and Restoring Urban Biodiversity.* Amherst, MA: University of Massachusetts Press.

Portney, Kent E. 2003. *Taking Sustainable Cities Seriously: Economic Development, the Environment, and Quality of Life in American Cities.* Cambridge, MA: The MIT Press.

President's Council on Sustainable Development. 1996. *Sustainable America: A New Consensus for Prosperity, Opportunity, and a Healthy Environment for the Future.* Washington, D.C.: U.S. Government Printing Office.

Putnam, Robert. 2007. "*E Pluribus Unum:* Diversity and Community in the Twenty-first Century." *Scandinavian Political Studies* 30, 2.

Putnam, Robert D. 1995. "Tuning In, Tuning Out: The Strange Disappearance of Social Capital in America." *PS: Political Science and Politics* (December): 664–683.

Register, Richard. 1987. *Eco-City Berkeley: Building Cities for a Healthy Future.* Berkeley, CA: North Atlantic Books.

Roseland, Mark. 2005. *Toward Sustainable Communities: Resources for Citizens and their Governments*, rev. ed. Gabriola Island, BC: New Society Publishers.

Sachs, Wolfgang, ed. 1993. *Global Ecology: A New Arena of Political Conflict.* London: Zed Books.

Sale, Kirkpatrick. 1985. *Dwellers in the Land: The Bioregional Vision.* San Francisco: Sierra Club Books.

Serageldin, Ismail. 1995. "Sustainability and the Wealth of Nations: First Steps in an Ongoing Journey (Draft)." Paper presented at the Third Annual World Bank Conference on Environmentally Sustainable Development. Washington, D.C..

Spash, Clive L., and Nick D. Hanley. 1995. "Preferences, Information, and Biodiversity Preservation." *Ecological Economics* 12: 191–208.

Stern, Andrew. 1997. "Capital Theory Approaches to Sustainability: A Critique." *Journal of Economic Issues* (March) 31, 1: 145–173.

Stone, Deborah. 1997. *Policy Paradox: The Art of Political Decision Making.* New York: W. W. Norton.

Toffler, Alvin. 1970. *Future Shock.* New York: Random House.

Treanor, Paul. 1996. "Why Sustainability Is Wrong." Electronic publication, available at webinter.nl.net/users/Paul.Treanor/sustainability.html.

Urban Sustainability Learning Group. 1996. *Staying in the Game: Exploring Options for Urban Sustainability.* Available from the Center for Neighborhood Technology, Chicago, IL.

Van der Ryn, Sym, and Peter Calthorpe. 1986. *Sustainable Communities: A New Design Synthesis for Cities, Suburbs and Towns.* San Francisco: Sierra Club Books.

Viederman, Stephen. 1996. "Sustainability's Five Capitals and Three Pillars." In *Building Sustainable Societies: A Blueprint for a Post-Industrial World*, ed. Dennis Pirages. Armonk, NY: M. E. Sharpe.

Wackernagel, Mathis, and William Rees. 1996. *Our Ecological Footprint: Reducing Human Impact on the Earth*. Philadelphia: New Society Publishers.

Wildavsky, Aaron. 1979. *Speaking Truth to Power: The Art and Craft of Policy Analysis*. Boston: Little, Brown.

World Commission on Environment and Development. 1987. *Our Common Future*. Oxford: Oxford University Press.

Yaffe, Steven, A. F. Phillips, I. C. Frentz, P. W. Hardy, S. M. Maleki, and B. E. Thorpe. 1996. *Ecosystem Management in the United States: An Assessment of Current Experience*. Washington, D.C.: Island Press.

3

Regulating for the Future: A New Approach for Environmental Governance

Daniel J. Fiorino

The transition from the first to the second and third epochs in environmental protection inevitably will involve changes in our system of environmental regulation. Regulation is the core strategy that the United States and most other industrial nations have used to achieve their environmental goals. Designed originally as a system for pollution control, that regulatory strategy increasingly is unsuited to the demands of a new era of environmental problem solving. The thesis of this chapter is that a regulatory system based solidly on the first era of environmental protection must be adapted to the demands of the second and third eras. The challenge thus becomes one of regulating for the future, not for the past. The response to this challenge is to create a new regulation.

There is little doubt that this country is better off now than it would have been had it not adopted a system of increasingly stringent environmental controls since 1970 (Davies and Mazurek 1998; Kraft and Vig 2006). Surely, if the United States and other nations had carried on with a policy of business as usual since the 1960s, the world would be a far different place. Despite more than a doubling of economic activity and vehicle miles traveled and significant population growth since 1970, emissions of major air pollutants have declined or at least not increased. Discharges of conventional, point-source water contaminants have fallen, although nonpoint sources remain a problem in much of the country. Practices for managing and disposing of hazardous waste are much better than they would have been, and such toxics as DDT, polychlorinated biphenyls (PCBs), mercury, and lead have been greatly reduced or eliminated. It is reasonable to conclude, as has Gregg Easterbrook (1993, 471–472), that environmental protection was a leading success story of postwar liberalism.

Why even think about changing a strategy and policy system that apparently has produced results? The reason is that the existing model—what here is termed the old environmental regulation—increasingly is poorly suited to a rapidly changing world. As the other chapters in this volume suggest, strategies other than regulation will be necessary in moving toward sustainability. Still, regulation as a policy strategy will be an integral part of the transition to the third epoch. The argument here is that regulation will have to change if it is to make that transition possible. Regulation will have to be more collaborative, flexible, and performance-based than it has been until now.

Four changes in particular make it necessary to think about a new environmental regulation. The first is that the problems policymakers face now are different from those that fueled the environmental movement in the 1960s (U.S. EPA 1990; NAPA 1995). The old regulation was designed specifically to deal with pollution from large manufacturing and sewage treatment plants. Those sources are relatively less important today. Water and air pollution increasingly are caused by smaller, scattered, and more diffuse sources that are less amenable just to technology solutions. New problems—climate change, indoor air pollution, persistent pollutants, and loss of habitat—are now on the agenda. Again, technology mandates on their own will not solve these problems. Furthermore, definitions of the environmental "problem" itself have changed, from a narrow focus on pollution control to a broader concern with pollution prevention and, by the 1990s, with cleaner production and sustainability. A regulatory system designed for one set of environmental problems forty years ago must be adapted for different ones today.

A second factor is changes in economic relationships and conditions. By the mid-1990s, these were far more global and dynamic than they had been in 1970, and the trends were accelerating. The concept of globalization had entered the lexicon. Firms now operate in many countries, well beyond the regulatory reach of any one government. At the same time, competitive pressures and the pace of change within the manufacturing sector have increased. In the semiconductor and specialty tape industries, for example, new products must be designed and produced on a six- to nine-month cycle. Firms find it difficult to compete within that cycle when agencies may take a year to approve a new air permit. Moreover, economic activity in the United States has shifted from manufacturing to services, for which conventional regulation is poorly suited.

This combination of global interdependence and rapid rates of change has stretched the capacities of the old regulation, which was designed for different economic conditions.

A third factor is changes in the institutional landscape. The principal change is that the world has become information-rich. Information about environmental performance and conditions exists today that could not have been imagined in the 1970s. This trend began with the Toxics Release Inventory (TRI) and state community right-to-know programs in the 1980s, which compelled firms to report publicly on potentially harmful chemicals released by or stored at their sites. A variety of activist groups, such as the Rainforest Action Network and Greenpeace, use TRI and other information sources, disseminated through the Internet, to provide negative information on corporate practices. These tactics may be effective in changing behavior. A study of pulp and paper mills found that "a painful, well-publicized encounter with a major environmental group produced a sea change in the corporate approach to the environment" (Gunningham, Kagan, and Thornton 2003, 93). Studies have documented the effects that both positive and negative information have on firms (Stephan 2002). These changes in the social landscape present risks for business, but they also offer leverage for activists and regulators to influence behavior in the third epoch of environmental protection.

A fourth source of change is the trend known as the "greening" of industry. In 1975, almost no companies produced environmental reports of any value, environmental management systems (EMS) as we know them today were unheard of, and companies focused their energies on opposition to and eventually reluctant compliance with a range of new environmental laws. In contrast, by 2005, more than half of the global 250 largest firms were producing self-standing corporate sustainability reports (KPMG 2005); some 5,000 U.S. facilities had been certified to ISO 14001 EMS (Environmental Management System) standards; and top firms were using environmental innovation and leadership as a source of business advantage (Gunningham, Kagan, and Thornton 2003, 20–40). A well-documented greening of industry was underway, but regulation was designed, and regulators behaved, as if it were still 1975. To be sure, this trend is limited largely to a subset of large, visible firms, but it offers lessons for how government may influence corporate behavior more generally (Press and Mazmanian 2006).

The Old Environmental Regulation

The concept of the "old environmental regulation" refers to a policy strategy that has dominated environmental protection in the United States since the national regulatory programs were created in the early 1970s. Before 1970, environmental regulation had been left largely to the states. The passage of the Clean Air Act of 1970, however, and of the Federal Water Pollution Control Act (the Clean Water Act) two years later, began a transformation that shifted legal authority to the federal government and greatly increased regulatory controls over industry, especially for manufacturing operations in chemicals, electrical generating, pulp and paper, and other pollution-intensive industries.

The regulatory laws and institutions that were created in the 1970s followed a clear pattern, one that was consistent with the American administrative and legal cultures. They concentrated power in a national regulatory agency (the Environmental Protection Agency, or EPA), which shared authority with states, by authorizing it to issue and enforce technology standards applied to different categories of industry. The EPA and the states also were given authority to oversee compliance with these standards and take legal action to enforce them. At the time, this authority was focused largely on controlling pollution from large, visible sources of pollution at the point of discharge. The relationships between government regulators and industry were designed to be formal and, if necessary, adversarial, as a way to keep agencies independent of industry influence. Although industry would have a say in the standards as they were developed, once they were issued firms would have to comply with them or face legal sanctions and negative publicity. It was assumed that agencies would have the technical knowledge to determine what the best available technologies were and keep the standards up-to-date.

Several characteristics define the old regulation. One is the idea that economic and environmental goals are nearly always at odds. Especially in the early days of the new national programs, in the 1970s, it was assumed that any steps toward environmental protection inevitably would reduce economic growth and competitiveness. Similarly, it was assumed that firms would act in an environmentally responsible manner only if compelled to directly by government rules. Business firms were cast as "amoral calculators" who would subvert regulations at all opportunities to reduce regulatory costs and maximize profits (Kagan and

Scholz 1984). Given this mindset, regulation took on a highly legalistic and adversarial tone, with high levels of distrust between agencies and industry (Kagan 1995).

Still, this model served the nation reasonably well for a few decades. It was a blunt but generally effective tool for changing behavior. In a path that also was taken in other industrial democracies, the United States created a system of laws and rules; a national pollution control agency; a corps of scientific, technical, legal, and policy experts in government and business; and an infrastructure to oversee compliance. Many of the worst pollution problems from the 1960s were at least being tackled, often with success.

By the 1980s, however, flaws in this regulatory model were becoming apparent. New problems were appearing on the agenda, and it was difficult to adapt to them. The technology-based pollution controls were costing more than necessary, and their benefits often were less than the costs (Freeman 2002). With their workloads growing steadily and industry's production processes changing rapidly, agencies were having trouble keeping technology standards current. Mistrust and conflict were interfering with the ability to understand and solve increasingly complex problems. High regulatory transaction costs—reporting, documentation, and cumbersome permitting processes—consumed time and resources, often adding little in the way of environmental results. Even to many strong advocates of environmental protection, it was apparent that a "business as usual" strategy of simply continuing to implement the old regulation on its own terms would be insufficient. In one influential report, the National Academy of Public Administration (NAPA) concluded that the "current environmental protection system cannot deliver the healthy and sustaining world that Americans want" (NAPA 2000, 11). It further determined that environmental laws and "the system they support are not keeping up with changing technology, changing public attitudes, or changing global relationships" (ibid., 18).

Among the criticisms of the old regulation, five are considered here. One is that it impedes innovation. This maybe a surprising claim, because the old regulation was effective in forcing the near-term adoption of technologies like catalytic converters and advanced sewage treatment. However, it has been less successful in creating conditions under which long-term, continuous innovation occurs (Wallace 1995; ELI 1998). By emphasizing end-of-pipe technology controls on pollution sources, for example, regulations close off what often are better options of changing materials, production processes, and product designs (Frondel, Horbach, and Rennings 2007). Agency technology standards may lag behind what is available, so rules often freeze in outdated technologies when better ones could be used. Short and often unpredictable time periods of compliance make it difficult for firms to plan for longer-term innovation. In addition, there is no incentive for firms to perform beyond what is needed to maintain compliance. For these reasons, the Environmental Law Institute concluded in a 1998 study, most firms "fail to develop a culture of continuous environmental improvement necessary to sustain research development, and investment in innovation" (ELI 1998, 5–6). The adversarial and distrustful relationships that characterize regulation in the United States created barriers to the dialogue that is necessary for effective long-term innovation (Delmas and Terlak 2002).

Another criticism is that the existing regulatory system is legalistic, inflexible, and fragmented (Fiorino 2004; NAPA 1995). After nearly forty years, regulatory provisions and processes have become detailed and complex, and compliance checkpoints have proliferated. Seeking to avoid any risk of noncompliance, regulatory agencies have sought to control behavior at minute levels of detail and require near-constant documentation of compliance, even for firms with strong compliance records. In effect, the system is designed around the worst performers. This aspect of the old regulation imposes high regulatory transaction costs on everyone (including the government) and reinforces the distrust that characterizes the system. A consequence of this legalism is that "companies spend considerable sums on lawyers and lobbyists, but comparatively little on creating new and better means of controlling pollution at their plants (a task for which they are uniquely suited)" (Hirsch 1998, 138–139). Further, regulation is a strategy in which uniform rules are applied to diverse circumstances (Bardach and Kagan 2005). This makes it difficult to adapt to new information or opportunities that arise, both for regulated firms and environmental agencies. In the face of rapidly changing problems and dynamic economic social relationships, this lack of adaptability is a major weakness.

The fragmentation of the U.S. pollution control system has been a recurring issue. Congress responded to problems as they emerged on the national policy agenda and support for their passage could be gained. Rather than having an integrated legal framework, the United States created a series of specific authorities enabling the EPA and states to take action against polluters. Between 1970 and 1980, separate laws were passed for air and water pollution, waste management and disposal, drinking water safety, toxic chemicals, and cleanup of hazardous waste sites. Congressional oversight reflected this separation, as did the organization of the EPA and state agencies and the development of expertise within them. This fragmentation by environmental medium was a logical way to respond to a new and complex set of problems at the time, but it has had consequences. Often, problems are shifted from one medium to another, as when sludge created by air pollution controls must be disposed of as a waste, or when air pollution from vehicles becomes a source of water pollution, as it has in Chesapeake Bay. Some environmental problems, such as lead and mercury, require integrated solutions to be effective, and this is difficult in a fragmented system. Other countries, such as Great Britain, have made progress in developing integrated approaches (Gray, James, and Dickson 2006).

A third criticism is that the old regulation costs more than is necessary. The main reason is that it prescribes technologies relatively uniformly across sources and fails to account for differences in pollution control costs among them. In reviewing research on air pollution control, Paul Portney found a purely technology-based approach to be two to fourteen times more costly in reducing emissions than a least-cost approach that allowed for emissions trading (Portney 2000). Emissions trading sets a standard but allows sources with high control costs to obtain credits from sources with low costs. The air quality results are the same or better than under conventional regulation, but the flexibility of the trading mechanisms lowers the overall costs of achieving those results. This principle was incorporated into the 1990 Clean Air Act Amendments. This is an area where there has been progress toward a new regulation. Trading and other market mechanisms are consistent with the design principles presented below and should be further integrated into the regulatory system.

A fourth criticism is that the old regulation is irrelevant to many problems and thus ineffective. We worry not just about controlling pollution from major industrial sources but preventing it, reducing risk, promoting eco-efficiency, and achieving a sustainable economy and society over the long term. We want to use energy, water, and materials efficiently; design environmentally friendly products; assess the impacts of products over their life cycle; preserve habitats and species; and think generally about the effects of today's actions on future generations (Durant, Fiorino, and O'Leary 2004). Many of these issues may not be amenable to a regulatory strategy, but we may be able to address more of them through a modified and enhanced regulatory approach.

A fifth criticism is that regulation faces an "implementation deficit" by making so many demands on government that it cannot be implemented (Dryzek 2005). Regulators simply cannot do everything that the law and their own rules require. The EPA and states regulate an estimated 40,000 stationary air sources; 90,000 facilities with water permits (which actually cover about half a million sources); over 400,000 hazardous waste facilities; and 173,000 drinking water systems (U.S. EPA 1999). Permitting these sources alone is a major undertaking. There also are inspections and enforcement requirements for all of these programs. Add to all of this the steady decline in federal and state environmental agency resources that has been occurring and is likely to continue, and the implementation deficit comes into even sharper focus.

Advocates of the old regulation may argue that we close this deficit by adding implementation capacity. There are two responses to this. First, American society will not support any significant expansion in the regulatory state. There is not enough money, given the financial demands on government, and imposition of more bureaucratic controls is controversial. Second, even if it were possible to expand governmental capacities to close the implementation deficit, say by doubling or tripling the available resources, this expansion would only reinforce the weaknesses that have been discussed. More regulators—rule-writers, permitting staff, inspectors, and so on—would almost inevitably increase the inflexibility and legalism that exist now. We would see efforts to exercise more control, close loopholes, catch paperwork violations, throw barriers in the path of innovation, and elaborate the old regulation in fine detail. Such a strategy would only increase the environmental and social costs of using an old, outdated policy model.

In sum, what is termed here the old regulation was a strategy for the first epoch in environmental protection and very much a product of the times. It has been improved to some degree in the second epoch, but it still is not suited to the changes in problems, economics, society, and the business community that were discussed above. Although the third epoch will require that we use strategies to augment it, regulation still will be an integral part of our environmental policies. If we are to move successfully to a third epoch based on sustainability, we will need to build a new environmental regulation.

The New Environmental Regulation

The new regulation is built on the foundation of the old but will modify it in many ways. It is not meant to dismantle the existing system, which has been vital to our success. Nor does it imply that government will not play a critical role in environmental protection in the future. It does describe a new role for government and a strategy that is more collaborative, flexible, and performance-based than regulation has been until now.

A discussion of the new regulation may begin with the conceptual differences between it and the old version. One conceptual underpinning of the old regulation is that deterrence should be the primary approach to influencing behavior in industry. Rules backed by sanctions are seen as the best, and perhaps the only, way to influence behavior. Under this behavioral theory, the way to make further progress is to issue more rules, exercise closer oversight, and increase penalties to maximize the deterrent effects of the rules. In contrast, the new regulation is based on the premise that many factors influence industry behavior and government should build these into its policy strategies. Under this revised assumption, regulatory and other strategies would change. Positive incentives, such as recognition, more flexible permitting, and alternative compliance strategies could be used to reward and encourage facilities that exhibit strong compliance and environmental performance.

A second assumption of the old regulation is that adversarial relationships almost always produce better outcomes. This has led to the expectation that, to be effective, relationships between government and industry must be legalistic and adversarial. Under a new regulation, this is replaced by the assumption that, except for proven or likely bad actors, collaborative relationships backed by regulatory and other pressures for results offer the best environmental outcomes for society. This is not to suggest that pressure on industry from government and activists is not essential for progress, or that adversarial relationships between government and firms at times are not appropriate. It does mean that the prevailing model of discourse should shift from finding fault and assigning blame to searching for solutions. The changes that have been discussed in problems, institutions, economic relationships, and other aspects of a new epoch make the traditional adversarial approach outdated for all but the unwilling and recalcitrant firms.

A third assumption of the old regulation is that environmental results are best achieved through top-down bureaucratic control. The old regulation relies heavily on a "Weberian" model of problem solving (reflecting the writing of sociologist Max Weber in the early twentieth century), one characterized by hierarchy, extensive elaboration of formal rules, and emphasis on conformance. The new regulation differs by recognizing that goals are best achieved through a more diverse and decentralized strategy that is based on the notions of learning, pressure for results, and horizontal influence, such as through networks. This does not mean that government should not specify rules that define behavior. It does mean that agencies should diversify their policy toolbox and appreciate the varied roles government can play.

The new regulation will reject the notion that all firms are the same in their intentions and capacities, or that the firm itself should be seen as a monolithic black box. It will be designed to account for the differences among firms. Many of the complaints about the old regulation derive from the practice of assuming the worst, because it was built to control the behavior of the most likely noncompliers. Most of the time, the best and most trustworthy facilities must meet the same reporting and permitting requirements as the worst. In contrast, the premise of the new regulation is that some may be trusted more than others. Recognition of these differences should be built into our regulatory designs and incorporated into the relationships between governments and others.

Finally, the new regulation will reject the narrow focus on compliance in favor of a broader emphasis on environmental performance. Having government and industry dedicate their best efforts to ensure full compliance with a detailed set of results has been effective, but it also has had unfortunate consequences. Many compliance issues turn on matters of process or documentation that relate more to maintaining regulatory controls than to environmental effects. Compliance becomes an end in itself. Regulated firms have little or no incentive to do better than comply because government has been concerned not with their success but their failures. The new regulation would recognize that compliance with a core set of standards is essential, but that public policy should be designed as much as possible to define, measure, and encourage continuous improvement. In practical terms, this means government should focus more on making progress on a core set of environmental indicators and less on catching people who deviate from the array of administrative checkpoints that characterize the old regulation.

In sum, rather than assuming industry will act responsibly only under the threat of legal sanctions, the new regulation will recognize the multiple factors that exert pressure on firms—such as communities, investors, insurers, and employees. The idea that adversarial relationships among government and industry are desirable will give way to a preference for collaboration that promotes dialogue, trust, and mutual learning. Instead of assuming that all regulated entities are the same and should be treated as such, it is accepted that differences in performance should be formally recognized. Finally, although compliance with core standards is essential, the broader task of defining, measuring, and encouraging environmental performance will be more prominent in the new regulation than it has been in the old.

Based on these conceptual differences, we may specify a set of design objectives for a new environmental regulation. Five merit discussion.

Use Legally Enforceable, Stringent Performance Standards

A consistent theme in the regulatory literature is that the environmental gains of the last four decades would not have occurred without a coercive push from government. Regulation has forced behavioral changes in industry, increased the costs of mismanaging waste and pollution, empowered communities and citizens, and instilled an environmental ethic in much of society. Nonregulatory pressures have become increasingly important. Still, regulatory pressure is the glue that holds this system of norms and expectations together. Government should set high expectations in responding to pressing environmental issues.

As a source of pressure on industry, however, the new regulation will differ from the old in several ways. In general, government should focus on setting demanding goals and leave firms more discretion in deciding how to meet them. Although prescriptive technology standards may be necessary at times, there should be a strategic preference for enforceable goals over specification of the means of achieving them. There is evidence that many firms would be able to meet more stringent standards in exchange for certainty in what they must accomplish and in how they may accomplish it. An example is the EPA's efforts to develop flexible air permits for large and complex regulated facilities (U.S. EPA 2004). Firms agreed to reduce their emissions below levels specified in conventional air permits in exchange for increased flexibility in determining how to meet those levels.

Demanding, predictable performance goals combined with flexible means will be a hallmark of the new regulation. Pieces of this strategy already exist. The National Ambient Air Quality Standards have been effective in improving air quality; they specify national goals around which specific emission reduction strategies are fashioned. A useful source of experience is the industry covenants used in the Netherlands and discussed below. In the United States, such market incentives as emissions trading or fees on waste and pollution would have a similar effect.

Differentiate among Firms Based on Past and Likely Future Performance

Firms vary tremendously not only in their compliance with the law but in their environmental performance. For some firms, compliance is shoddy and uneven; for others, it is a starting point from which they achieve impressive environmental results. Although regulators are aware in most cases of these differences in performance, they have not been incorporated formally into public policy. Officially, at least, all regulated facilities are treated in largely the same way. They face the same permitting requirements, the same reporting and documentation, and the same inspection levels as anyone else. A principle of the new regulation is that by differentiating among facilities, regulators can overcome some of the limitations in the old regulation as well as deliver more environmental benefits to society.

Regulating through tracks or tiers based on performance offers many advantages. Performance tracks enable government to identify proven high performers, for whom the reporting, inspection, permitting, and other oversight costs of regulation may be reduced. They define a community well suited for collaborative efforts to promote measurement, technological innovation, and information-sharing. Performance tracks allow agencies to give recognition, access, and flexibility that translate into business value. The EPA's Performance Track, discussed below, and other "green clubs" (Prakash and Potoski 2006, 34–80) at the state level offer prototypes for this element of a new regulation.

Promote Continuous Improvements in Environmental Performance

Core normative standards such as those in the old regulation are a necessary but not sufficient condition for promoting cleaner production. Agencies are missing opportunities to achieve better results by not creating mechanisms and incentives for firms to exceed compliance in a process of continuous improvement. If firms are discovering multiple reasons for doing more than complying, as pointed out above, then why should government not determine what is pulling them in this direction, reinforce these efforts, and find ways to induce others to act similarly?

In the new regulation, a system of core performance standards will be used in combination with inducements for continually improving environmental performance. Examples are emissions and effluent trading, which would be expanded, as well as information disclosure, voluntary programs (such as the green clubs discussed below), and other innovative approaches. Think of these as elements in a "pull" strategy that is used together with the "push" strategy of conventional regulation. Positive incentives (carrots) may pull people to improve continuously while negative incentives (the stick of traditional compliance) bring everyone up to legal compliance.

Trading and other tools based on market mechanisms may encourage continuous improvement and innovation by providing economic benefits for firms that exceed standards. Although there still is a long way to go, market incentives have been integrated into the regulatory system more fully than have voluntary programs, which so far have been little more than creative additions at the margins of the old regulation (Fiorino 2006, 133–139). If such programs could be linked with regulatory pressures, they could provide a "sticks and carrots" strategy for inducing firms not only to meet core standards but also to achieve more. In a strategy for cutting greenhouse gases, for example, firms that achieve strict goals for emissions reductions or energy efficiency could be exempted later from the sticks of mandatory actions, such as technology standards or a carbon tax. Conversely, public recognition and expedited permitting provide valuable carrots that can induce firms to go beyond compliance.

Measure Environmental Performance
The EPA and its state counterparts collect large amounts of data from regulated facilities, largely as a way to document compliance. A frequent complaint about the old regulation, however, is that it often fails to provide data on actual environmental performance and conditions (Davies and Mazurek 1998). An exception is the Toxics Release Inventory, created to inform the public about potentially harmful chemicals that are stored at or released by manufacturing facilities, but it provides

only a narrow view of overall environmental impacts and has many limitations. Anyone wanting to compare the relative pollution-intensity or materials-intensity of specific chemical processors or steel makers, or to assess progress over time, would find little in the way of usable data. A centerpiece of a new regulation will be the capacity to track, compare, and evaluate credible and reliable performance indicators at the facility, firm, and industry sector levels (Metzenbaum 2002).

Despite the current limitations in data, there have been steps in the right direction. About a decade ago, a coalition of socially responsible investment firms launched an effort to create formats and protocols for corporate-level environmental and sustainability reporting. Known as the Global Reporting Initiative (GRI), its purpose is to develop voluntary standards comparable to those used for financial reporting. At a facility level, the EPA Performance Track (discussed below) and similar state programs are collecting information from participants on several environmental indicators. The EPA's Sector Strategies Program has tested protocols and formats for tracking results within industry sectors (U.S. EPA 2007). Even some trade associations, such as the American Chemistry Council, are requiring reporting on selected environmental indicators as a condition of membership.

Create Mechanisms and Relationships That Build Trust

Nearly every commentary on U.S. environmental policy laments the high levels of distrust, especially compared to other nations. A former state commissioner and later an EPA regional administrator once observed that the environment "is a public policy field which is almost built on an absence of trust" (Kettl 2002, 184). This distrust has consequences. It is a barrier to dialogue, communication, and innovation. It encourages a low-risk response to technology standards, because firms seek the safety of legal conformity, and it shifts attention from performance to narrow issues of compliance.

Trust may be defined as the view that other parties in a relationship will not act against one's interests, at least not without warning and for good reason. Several factors are associated with building trust in recurring relationships, such as between regulators and firms. Three such factors stand out when thinking of a new regulation. One is credibility in meeting commitments. If firms commit to achieving a result or designing a new technology, or government agrees to not to change requirements for a given period of time, both sides should be able to deliver on those commitments. A second factor is agreement on goals that define mutual commitments and expectations. They provide objective indicators that the desired results are being achieved. A third factor is transparency that assures government, industry, and the public that each party is meeting commitments or making a good faith effort to do so.

The new regulation should be designed to build trust through repeated interactions in which parties are able to set and meet commitments and reach agreement on goals in an atmosphere of transparency. This is why the voluntary programs that the EPA and state agencies have been developing, such as the green clubs discussed below, are important. In addition to encouraging environmental results beyond what the law demands, such programs build trust by engaging government, firms, and others in collaborative relationships where all sides may demonstrate credibility in meeting their commitments.

Sources of Experience in Building a New Regulation
The design of a new environmental regulation need not begin with a blank slate. At various levels of government, many groups are making efforts to augment and modify the old regulation. These provide sources of experience for creating a new approach.

One such source is innovative partnerships that have been emerging at national and state levels. Some of the more interesting are government-sponsored green clubs. These augment conventional regulation by allowing organizations to gain recognition and other benefits for strong records of environmental compliance, management, and results. As of September 2007, the EPA had created nine such clubs, including Climate Leaders, WasteWise, the Green Power Partnership, and the SmartWay Transportation Partnership.

The most comprehensive and rigorous of the EPA's green clubs is the National Environmental Performance Track (Performance Track). Created in 2000 in the waning days of the Clinton administration, it had grown to some 500 members by late 2007. It was the EPA's response to a number of advisory bodies in the 1990s, including the President's Council for Sustainable Development, Aspen Institute, and National Academy of Public Administration. Its purpose was to complement a conventional regulatory strategy with a more positive one that encourages facilities to do better than compliance and use more effective management practices. To qualify, applicants commit to measurable environmental results that go beyond what is required by law, implement an environmental management system, reach out to the community, and demonstrate a record of compliance with environmental regulations at all levels of government. In return, they are recognized in several ways by the EPA; become eligible for regulatory flexibility (such as flexible or expedited permits); and are given opportunities for more constructive interaction with the EPA and state regulators (Fiorino 2006, 144–149).

State environmental agencies also have seen the value of green clubs. By late 2007, some twenty states had created green clubs that are similar in design and objectives to the EPA's Performance Track, and five more were developing one. Although some are more active and successful than others, all share the goal of using positive recognition and other incentives to encourage behavior that goes beyond legal compliance. Among the more prominent examples are the Virginia Environmental Excellence Program, Indiana Environmental Stewardship Program, and Colorado Environmental Leadership Program. In addition to augmenting the traditional stick of regulation with carrots that offer recognition, permit streamlining, and other business value, these programs aim to increase collaboration among government, business, and others as well as to demonstrate the value of environmental leadership.

Some critics have pointed out that green clubs could be used not just to provide recognition or reduce regulatory transaction costs to members, but to relieve them of some of their environmental obligations. This is a legitimate concern that should be reflected in the design of the programs. Members should be shown to be meeting their compliance obligations, reporting systematically on their environmental results, setting an example for others in how they work with communities and government, and upholding the quality of their environmental management activities. Matthew Potoski and Aseem Prakash (2005) have developed a typology of green clubs based on whether or not there are public reports on results, third-party audits of members, and sanctions applied to members (such as removal) that fail to meet program requirements. They classify green clubs that have all three features as "strong sword" programs that will be more credible with the public than clubs having two, one, or none of these features.

Another source of experience in building a new regulation comes from civic environmentalism, which DeWitt John describes as "the process of custom-designing answers to local environmental problems" (John 2004, 219). Many complaints about the old regulation relate to the difficulty of adapting a centralized, uniform, strategy to locally diverse situations.

Civic environmentalism emerged in the 1980s and 1990s as a loose collection of tools, practices, and relationships for responding to these complaints. Most of its applications involve such issues as local and regional ecosystem protection, preservation of forests and other resources, and community-level resource and pollution problems.

Civic environmentalism differs from conventional regulation in several respects. It is adaptive, in that it involves a series of adjustments in strategies and tactics in response to experience and new information. It is eclectic, because different policy tools may be used, including subsidies, regulation, education, effluent trading, and information disclosure, among others. It is collaborative, because many actors work together to develop and implement solutions. Civic environmentalism also is contingent on the characteristics of the problem and the context in which it is being addressed. It is more of a tailored solution to a problem than a fixed response coming from the top down.

As a typical example, consider the problem of protecting a local watershed from overdevelopment and the associated pollution and loss of habitat. Conventional regulation may offer part of the solution by setting technology standards. However, technology controls on industrial sources may already have been effective in lowering point source pollution to nearly zero. The remaining pollution may be due to nonpoint sources, such as agricultural runoff and air deposition from vehicles. Nor does the existing regulatory system help in dealing with land use, wetland preservation, or the legacy of past pollution in the watershed.

An approach based on civic environmentalism starts with the problem and then works backward to solutions. It requires a local "sparkplug" to provide energy and leadership, recognition that existing solutions are insufficient, and the support of key organizations, such as government agencies, local business, and community groups. It also promotes use of creative policy tools. Regulation may be augmented with voluntary action by industry, effluent trading, zoning changes, government funding, incentives for farmers, and other actions. It includes the collaboration, adaptation, trust-building, and emphasis on results that should be characteristic of a new environmental regulation.

Yet a third source of experience comes from other countries. The Netherlands are an example. Into the 1980s, like most other industrial democracies, the Dutch had relied on a top-down, hierarchical approach based on bureaucratic rationality. After years of experience with this conventional regulation, however, there was a growing recognition that this approach would not be sufficient to address the most pressing environmental problems over the long term (de Bruijn and Lulofs 2005). The Netherlands was an economically successful nation, and policymakers were determined to maintain that success. The challenge was to "decouple" continued economic growth and prosperity from environmental degradation by breaking the historical link between growth and environmental harm. In moving beyond conventional regulation, the Dutch adopted a strategy of ecological modernization, in which environmental goals are built into the structure of the economy.

The arguments for change made in the Netherlands in the 1980s resemble those that have been made for change in the United States. It was argued that conventional regulation provided no incentive for continuous improvement, led to cost-ineffective results, failed to keep pace with technological change, and focused too much on end-of-pipe controls. Moreover, it failed to draw sufficiently on industry and other sources of knowledge in devising solutions to pressing issues. A government report issued in 1988 concluded, much as had many reports in the United States, that the old model was "not only inadequate to the challenges of sustainability but also to some extent ineffective" (de Bruijn and Lulofs 2005, 219).

The new approach did not replace what already was in place; it grew alongside of and interacted with the existing system. The foundation of the new approach was a series of National Environmental Policy Plans (NEPP), the first of which was adopted in 1989. The government set quantitative goals for "theme" issues, including such problems as climate, acidification, dispersion of pollutants, water depletion, and resource management (Gunningham and Sinclair 2002; Bressers and Plethenburg 1996). Responsibility for meeting the goals was allocated to groups, such as industry, transport, consumers, and agriculture. Within industry, which is the focus here, targets were then developed for specific sectors, starting with chemicals, base metals, and printing. These sector targets were negotiated with industry associations, which then negotiated specific targets for each firm that were codified in company environmental plans. These plans committed each firm to specific targets and timetables for environmental improvement. Although the sector and company targets are negotiated, the national goals, once set, are not. Officially, participation in the process is voluntary; however, firms that do not take part are subject to conventional technology standards. They have less flexibility and may not be included in the government's commitment not to change the requirements over the life of the agreement. Given the advantages of greater flexibility and certainty offered in these agreements, known as "covenants," most firms have chosen to participate in them.

This brief overview of the Dutch approach highlights its innovative aspects and compatibility with the five design objectives outlined above. The Dutch model combines stringent national goals with flexibility and certainty in deciding how to achieve them. It relies heavily on collaboration to set meaningful sector and company targets. It measures sector and company performance and their effects on achieving national environmental goals. By stressing results over legal conformance, the NEPP approach provides an incentive for firms to continuously improve. Of course, to succeed, the Dutch model requires a high degree of trust among the parties. Government must have confidence that firms will take the steps needed to meet their goals; firms must trust that government will stand by its commitments and not change the rules in the middle of the planning period.

Similarly, government-sponsored green clubs and civic environmentalism reflect several of the design objectives for a new regulation. Both are implemented within the context of existing regulatory standards. They are aimed at creating incentives for continuous improvement and, if designed properly, improving our ability to measure results. Green clubs are designed to differentiate among facilities based on their past and expected future performance. By establishing conditions in which parties demonstrate their credibility in meeting commitments in relationships that may be sustained over time, such initiatives promote trust. Although they do not demonstrate the design objectives for a new regulation as fully as the Dutch planning model, they are useful sources of experience in building a new regulation.

Conclusion: Regulation for the Third Environmental Epoch

This discussion of the old and the new regulations presents them as ideal types that determine how policy objectives actually are achieved on the ground. The ideal type of the old regulation was designed for a first era of environmental problem-solving and increasingly is unsuited to the new epoch, with its long-term focus on sustainability. The old model relies heavily on bureaucratic control, hierarchy, problem fragmentation, conformance with rules, and deterrence through negative sanctions. In contrast, the new regulation offers a more flexible, adaptable, collaborative strategy that is better suited to the challenges and demands of the second and third epochs of environmental protection.

As the examples presented in this chapter and elsewhere in the book demonstrate, an incremental transition toward the concepts and objectives of a new regulation already is underway. It has been and will continue to be a slow transition, given the multiple political barriers that impede change. The old regulation is firmly entrenched, and those who benefit from it politically or economically are skeptical of change. The complex and fragmented legal/regulatory framework that evolved over the last forty years will not be easily modified. Although environmental issues rarely take a top spot on the national policy agenda, concerns about war and national security have pushed most environmental issues aside for now (Bosso and Gruber 2006). Polarization in U.S. national politics makes consensus difficult, especially on such subtle issues as regulatory structures, styles, and relationships. Finally, there is the high level of distrust. Until this is overcome, it will be difficult for people to accept the risks and uncertainties of change.

What may at some point break the gridlock are the demands of pressing issues. The prospect of global climate change and its consequences has generated controversy, but it also has stimulated creative dialogue about policy options and approaches. We are seeing efforts to draw varied interests into a search for solutions; to integrate energy, transportation, and other policy sectors with environmental strategies; to use emissions trading, a carbon tax, and other policy tools in fashioning solutions; to improve the capacity for measuring and benchmarking performance; and to combine voluntary with what almost surely will be regulatory solutions at some point. The need to respond to climate change may stimulate relationships among government, industry, and others that build trust and thus create more opportunities for dialogue that promotes innovation. Within the states and in other countries, a variety of policy innovations are underway that may help modernize the national regulatory system when the political conditions are ripe.

Similarly, the less visible but potentially significant effects of nanotechnologies could stimulate approaches that incorporate the concepts of a new regulation. The growing use of nanoparticles in a variety of products offers major benefits but also potential risks. A recent assessment of the EPA's and the nation's options for responding to these risks (Davies 2007) calls for a diverse and multifaceted response involving dialogue among government, the nano industry, and other interests; a mix of different policy tools; use of positive as well as negative incentives by government, or what is termed "regulation with reward"; an explicitly collaborative approach to developing standards; a reliance on industry codes of conduct verified by the EPA or a third party, based on the principle of "trust but verify"; and the use of insurance and disclosure policies that augment the effects of regulatory standards. Regarding the old regulation, the report asserts that "Nano is still very much an evolving technology, and a cumbersome or overly intrusive regulatory system could prevent it from reaching its full potential" (Davies 2007, 15).

The old regulation has brought us reasonably well through the first and into the second environmental epochs. It will not serve us nearly so well in moving through the second epoch and into the third. Pressure from government applied through regulatory standards still is essential for making progress. From here on out, however, that pressure should be applied in different ways. What is needed now is a more dynamic, adaptive regulatory strategy that creates capacities for learning, allows for collaboration and sharing of responsibility, and promotes continuous improvement and innovation. If we are to move toward a goal of sustainability, and to the third epoch of environmental protection, we should build a new environmental regulation on the foundations of the old.

References

Bardach, Eugene, and Robert Kagan. 2005. *Going by the Book: The Problem of Regulatory Unreasonableness*. Piscataway, NJ: Transaction Publishers.

Bosso Christopher J., and Deborah Lynn Gruber. 2006. "Maintaining Presence: Environmental Advocacy and the Permanent Campaign." In *Environmental Policy: New Directions for the Twentieth First Century*, 6th ed., ed. Norman J. Vig and Michael E. Kraft, 78–99. Washington, D.C.: CQ Press.

Bressers, Hans, and Loret A. Plethenburg. 1996. "The Netherlands." In *National Environmental Policy: A Comparative Study of Capacity-Building*, ed. Martin Janicke and Helmut Weidner. Berlin: Springer.

Davies, J. Clarence. 2007. *EPA and Nanotechnology: Oversight for the 21st Century*. Washington, D.C.: Woodrow Wilson International Center for Scholars.

Davies, J. Clarence, and Jan Mazurek. 1998. *Pollution Control in the United States: Evaluating the System*. Washington, D.C.: Resources for the Future.

de Bruijn, Theo, and Vicki Norberg-Bohm, eds. 2005. *Industrial Transformation: Environmental Policy Innovation in the United States and Europe.* Cambridge, MA: MIT Press.

de Bruijn, Theo, and Kris Lulofs. 2005. "The Dutch Policy Program on Environmental Management: Policy Implementation in Networks." In *Industrial Transformation: Environmental Policy Innovation in the United States and Europe,* ed. Theo deBruijn and Vicki Norberg-Bohm, 203–228. Cambridge, MA: MIT Press.

Delmas, Magali, and Ann Terlak. 2002. "Regulatory Commitment to Voluntary Agreements: Evidence from the United States, Germany, the Netherlands, and France." *Journal of Comparative Policy Analysis: Research and Practice* 4: 5–29.

Dryzek, John. 2005. *The Politics of the Earth: Environmental Discourse,* 2nd ed. Oxford: Oxford University Press.

Durant, Robert F., Daniel J. Fiorino, and Rosemary O'Leary, eds. 2004. *Environmental Governance Reconsidered: Challenges, Choices, and Opportunities.* Cambridge, MA: MIT Press.

Easterbrook, Gregg. 1993. *A Moment on the Earth: The Coming Age of Environmental Optimism.* New York: Viking.

Environmental Law Institute (ELI). 1998. *Barriers to Environmental Technology and Use.* Washington, D.C.: Environmental Law Institute.

Fiorino, Daniel J. 2004. "Flexibility." In *Environmental Governance Reconsidered: Challenges, Choices, and Opportunities,* ed. Robert F. Durant, Daniel J. Fiorino, and Rosemary O'Leary, 393–425. Cambridge, MA: MIT Press.

Fiorino, Daniel J. 2006. *The New Environmental Regulation.* Cambridge, MA: MIT Press.

Freeman, A. Myrick. 2002. "Environmental Policy Since Earth Day: What Have We Gained?" *Journal of Economic Perspectives* 16: 125–146.

Frondel, Manuel, Hans Horbach, and Klaus Rennings. 2007. "End-of-Pipe or Cleaner Production? An Empirical Examination of Environmental Innovation Decisions Across OECD Countries." In *Environmental Policy and Corporate Behavior,* ed. Nick Johnstone, 174–212. Cheltenham: Edward Elgar.

Gray, J., T. James, and J. Dickson. 2006. "Integrated Regulation—Experiences of IPPC in England and Wales." *Water and Environment Journal* 48: 1–5.

Gunningham, Neil, Robert A. Kagan, and Dorothy Thornton. 2003. *Shades of Green: Business, Regulation, and the Environment.* Stanford, CA: Stanford University Press.

Gunningham, Neil, and Darren Sinclair. 2002. *Leaders and Laggards: Next-Generation Environmental Regulation.* Sheffield: Greenleaf.

Hirsch, Dennis D. 1998. "Bill and Al's Excellent Adventure: An Analysis of the EPA's Legal Authority to Implement the Clinton Administration's Project XL." *University of Illinois Law Review*: 129–172.

John, DeWitt. 2004. "Civic Environmentalism." In *Environmental Governance Reconsidered: Challenges, Choices, and Opportunities*, ed. Robert F. Durant, Daniel J. Fiorino, and Rosemary O'Leary, 219–254. Cambridge, MA: MIT Press.

Kagan, Robert A. 1995. "Adversarial Legalism in American Government." In Marc K. Landy and Martin Levin, eds., *The New Politics of Public Policy*, 23–46. Baltimore: Johns Hopkins University Press.

Kagan, Robert A. 2000. "Introduction: Comparing National Styles of Regulation in Japan and the United States." *Law and Policy* 22: 225–244.

Kagan, Robert A., and John T. Scholz. 1984. "The Criminology of the Corporation and Regulatory Enforcement Strategies." In *Enforcing Regulation*, ed. Keith Hawkins and John M. Thomas, 67–95. Baltimore, MD: Johns Hopkins University Press.

Kettl, Donald F, ed. 2002. *Environmental Governance: A Report on the Next Generation of Environmental Policy.* Washington, D.C.: Brookings Institution.

KPMG. 2005. *KPMG International Survey of Corporate Responsibility Reporting 2005.* Available at www.kpmg.com/Rut2000_prod/Document/9/Survey.

Kraft, Michael E., and Norman J. Vig. 2006. "Environmental Politics from the 1970s to the Twenty-First Century." In *Environmental Policy: New Directions for the Twenty-First Century*, 6th ed., ed. Norman J Vig and Michael E. Kraft, 1–33. Washington, D.C.: CQ Press.

Metzenbaum, Shelley H. 2002. "Measurement That Matters: Cleaning Up the Charles River." In *Environmental Governance: A Report on the Next Generation of Environmental Policy*, ed. Donald F. Kettl, 58–117. Washington, D.C.: Brookings Institution.

National Academy of Public Administration (NAPA). 1995. *Setting Priorities, Getting Results: A New Direction for the Environmental Protection Agency.* Washington, D.C.: NAPA.

National Academy of Public Administration (NAPA). 2000. *environment.gov.* Washington, D.C.: NAPA.

Portney, Paul R. 2000. "Air Pollution Policy." In *Public Policies for Environmental Protection*, 2nd ed., ed. Paul R. Portney and Robert N. Stavins, 77–123. Washington, D.C.: Resources for the Future.

Potoski, Matthew, and Aseem Prakash. 2005. "Covenants with Weak Swords: ISO 14001 and Firms' Environmental Performance." *Journal of Policy Analysis and Management* 49: 745–769.

Prakash, Aseem, and Matthew Potoski. 2006. *The Voluntary Environmentalists: Green Clubs, ISO 14001, and Voluntary Environmental Regulations.* Cambridge: Cambridge University Press.

Press, Daniel, and Daniel Mazmanian. 2006. "The Greening of Industry: Combining Government Regulation and Voluntary Strategies." In *Environmental*

Policy: New Directions for the Twenty-First Century, 6th ed., ed. Norman J. Vig and Michael E. Kraft, 264–287. Washington, D.C.: CQ Press.

Stephan, Mark. 2002. "Environmental Disclosure Programs: They Work, But Why?" *Social Science Quarterly* 83: 190–205.

U.S. Environmental Protection Agency. 1990 (EPA). *Reducing Risk: Setting Priorities and Strategies for Environmental Protection*. Washington, D.C.: EPA, Science Advisory Board.

U.S. Environmental Protection Agency. 1999 (EPA). *Enforcement and Compliance Assurance FY98 Accomplishments Report*. Office of Enforcement and Compliance Assurance. Washington, DC: U.S. EPA, June.

U.S. Environmental Protection Agency. 2004 (EPA). *Evaluation of Implementation Experiences with Innovative Air Permits*. Washington, D.C.: EPA Office of Air Quality Planning and Standards and Office of Policy, Economics, and Innovation.

U.S. Environmental Protection Agency (EPA). 2007. *Energy Trends in Selected Manufacturing Sectors: Opportunities and Challenges for Environmentally Preferable Energy Outcomes*. Washington, D.C.: Sector Strategies Division.

Wallace, David. 1995. *Environmental Policy and Industrial Innovation: Strategies in Europe, the US, and Japan*. London: Earthscan.

II

Transitional Approaches in Conventional Media-Based Environmental Policies

4

Los Angeles' Clean Air Saga—Spanning the Three Epochs

Daniel A. Mazmanian

Cleaning the nation's air has been at the top of the public agenda throughout the modern environmental movement. The most important legislation to this effort has been the Clean Air Act of 1970, in which Congress directed the newly established United States Environmental Protection Agency (U.S. EPA) to set national air quality standards to protect public health. These "National Ambient Air Quality Standards" were initially set for five criteria pollutants—carbon monoxide, particulate matter, nitrogen oxide, ozone, nitrogen dioxide, and sulfur dioxide. Lead was later added to the list as was small particulate matter in 1987 and then even smaller "fine" particulates in 1997.

The standards were to be achieved by imposing air pollution controls on all of the nation's industry, businesses, and motorized vehicles. Accomplishing this was going to be an enormous undertaking by the EPA, but so too was the enormity of the air pollution problem. This fact, combined with the vociferous complaints that arose from state and local governments, business, and industry once the EPA began issuing numerous and inflexible regulations, led Congress in 1977 to amend the Clean Air Act to shift to the states and in some instances local and regional air pollution control agencies much of the responsibility for the act's implementation. The hope and expectation was that being nearer to the problem and working more closely with the affected parties, state and local agencies would develop more conciliatory, nonregulatory, and innovative and, thus, less politically volatile approaches to accomplishing the stringent clear air objectives.

Setting aside for a moment issues of cost-effectiveness and political opposition to the EPA, the top-down, federal-state-local government regulatory approach has been relatively successful in reducing air pollution since its inception upon passage of the Clean Air Act. For the nation as a whole, lead emissions have shrunk by 98 percent, largely owing to the federal government's mandating of lead-free gasoline. From 1970 to 2005 the total emissions of the six principal air pollutants regulated under the Act fell by 53 percent (U.S. EPA 2006). Despite this, as recently as 2000, 120 million Americans were still living in "nonattainment areas"—jurisdictions where one or more of the emission reduction criteria were not met.

As for the costs versus benefits, the most comprehensive assessment to date revealed that the benefits to health and the environment have significantly outweighed the dollar cost by a ratio of 42 to 1, according to the EPA study, "Benefits and Costs of the Clean Air Act" (U.S. EPA 2005). Moreover, the emissions reductions were achieved during a period of sustained economic expansion and population growth in the United States. Between 1970 and 2004, as emissions fell by over half, the nation's Gross Domestic Product increased by 187 percent, vehicle miles traveled by Americans increased by 171 percent, energy consumption increased by 47 percent, and the nation's population grew by 40 percent.

The variation in air emission reduction in communities around the nation has been substantial depending largely on differences in weather patterns and topography, economic activity, size and scale of communities, lifestyle, and enforcement commitment and efforts by state and local officials. Thus, although the first epoch of the modern environmental movement saw impressive improvement in air quality overall, further reduction was required, especially in those communities that for whatever reason remained furthest away from meeting the standards of the Clean Air Act.

From the very start, Los Angeles has had the unenviable distinction of being the most heavily air-polluted community in the nation and continues as an "extreme" nonattainment region today. Less well known is that the region has experienced a nearly unbroken pattern of declining health alerts and emissions violations, more dramatic than other western regions such as the San Francisco Bay Area, Sacramento, Phoenix, and Las Vegas (U.S. EPA 2007, 3), and more so than any other major metropolitan region in the nation. The significant (albeit still insufficient) decrease in air pollution in Los Angeles is impressive in view of the fact that it has been achieved despite its unprecedented economic expansion, population growth, and urban sprawl. Possibly least recognized of all, during the first environmental epoch of the 1970s and 1980s, Los Angeles established the nation's largest, most encompassing regulatory command-and-control air-pollution control program in the nation.

Equally important, and in response to that program, at the onset of the second environmental epoch the region's air quality management agency was sharply challenged to reinvent itself to bring it more into alignment with shifting political winds and policy approaches of the second epoch. The agency would need to adjust in order to survive in the new political climate while at the same time maintain the downward trend in pollution reduction the people in the region had been experiencing and had come to expect.

Tracing the rise of the regulatory regime in Los Angeles—which encompasses not just the city and county of Los Angeles, but the adjacent counties of Orange, Riverside, and western San Bernardino—in the first environmental epoch and its subsequent adaptation to the requisites of second epoch will be the major focus of this chapter. In the context of the general focus of the book, the Los Angeles experience highlights the kinds of internal and external factors that led to the undermining of several key tenets of the first epoch and the evolution into the second. In many ways Los Angeles represents an "extreme case study" in view of the depth of the air pollution problem it faces, the extraordinary regulatory regime it developed in epoch one, and the shift it underwent in epoch two. As an extreme case, it also serves to illuminate the outer limits of air pollution as a societal problem, and the lengths to which at least one community has gone to remedy it.

The Los Angeles experience underscores an important point in our effort to understand transitions between environmental epochs. It suggests that a concerted and relatively successful effort to move from the first to second epoch, though a logical and presumably necessary precursor, does not guarantee the transition from the second to the third epoch, that is, to a more sustainable community. Although there are emerging signs that epoch three thinking is taking hold in Los Angeles, the significant changes in policy and action required for this to occur are substantial. The impetus for this will be taken up in the final section of the chapter.

Clean Air Regulation Comes to Los Angeles: Epoch One

Prior to the 1960s it was the responsibility of local governments in California to control air emissions in their communities. Neither the state nor the federal government was involved. County officials in Los Angeles, in 1945, took the lead in addressing air pollution by prohibiting factories from emitting "dark smoke." This was followed in the early 1950s by prohibiting the burning of municipal garbage, first in municipal dumps throughout the county and then in people's backyard incinerators, which had been a common practice. Yet, as scientists began to discover, the problem was more than smoke from dumps, homes, and factories. It was the meteorological conditions of a balmy climate and of atmospheric inversions that traps in the air tons of tiny particles, lead, sulfur dioxide, carbon monoxide, nitrogen oxides, and ozone being emitted by cars, trucks, buses, ships, planes, industrial smokestacks, and the normal operations of business, which is then "cooked" by the sun into photochemical smog.

In the early years, "smog cops" were employed to track down smoke-belching cars on the freeways of Los Angeles (a high-tech version of which today is the use of "remote sensing" devices planted along the freeway to detect gross emitting vehicles). Extensive permitting and facility inspections were eventually instituted by the county and violations were met with fines and civil penalties. Public education campaigns were conducted and some modest emission reduction incentives were provided. As it became evident that local initiatives were insufficient in combating the region's growing air pollution problem, in the 1960s the State of California stepped in and, despite strong opposition from the automotive industry (of importance, an industry centered in Detroit, Michigan, not in California), began to place air pollution restrictions on new automobiles sold in California (Dewey 1997). The state also demanded more aggressive anti–air pollution steps be taken by local governments within the Los Angeles basin. As the issue of air pollution grew in prominence throughout the nation and its roots in automotive emissions became widely known, Congress increased the role of the federal government, most forcefully in the form of the 1970 amendments to the federal Clean Air Act. The cumulative effect on Los Angeles of the expansion in local, state, and federal air regulation over the coming decades was an air pollution control regime greater in capacity, with more funding, and further reach into business, communities, and the lives of individual citizens than could be found anywhere in the nation—or, for that matter, the world.

At the center of the pollution control program in Los Angeles is the South Coast Air Quality Management District (AQMD). The AQMD was established in 1977 by the California legislature to manage, within a single public agency, with greater coordination and comprehensiveness than ever before, the quality of air in the 12,000 square miles of the four-county Los Angeles air basin; which includes the counties of Los Angeles, Ventura, Riverside, and San Bernardino. (The AQMD succeeded the single-county Los Angeles County Air Pollution Control District, which dated back to 1947.) The AQMD is governed by a part-time, appointed board of twelve. Members are appointed one each from the four counties, from cities in the basin, and one each by the Governor of California, Speaker of the California State Assembly, and State Senate Rules Committee.

The mission of the AQMD is to protect public health from air pollution under the guidance of all relevant federal, state, and regional air pollution laws and standards. The AQMD has a strong professional staff with a great deal of autonomy and influence. The staff peaked in the early 1990s at 1,100 persons, and following a series of cuts has leveled off at 800 today. Its operating budget has grown to over 100 million dollars annually, which is raised mainly from within the region, from five major and several minor revenue streams: operating fees assessed against business and industry, permit processing fees, emissions fees, vehicle registration fees, grants/subventions from the EPA and the California Air Resources Board (CARB), and several smaller categories. For several decades, the AQMD has served as one if not the single most powerful region-wide governing agency, affecting economic development, settlement patterns, and lifestyle of residents in the multicounty sprawling megalopolis that is Los Angeles.

Hundreds of air emission controls have been placed on business, industry, and local communities and government agencies, large and small, to reduce the level of the six principal pollutants identified in the Clean Air Act. In the mid-1990s coverage was extended to the emissions of benzene, chromium, arsenic, and more than 100 other toxic chemicals, from approximately 250 of the largest emitters in the region. The AQMD focuses not only on stationary sources of the pollutants, but its activities have had a bearing on land-use and transportation decisions throughout the basin even though it does not have direct regulatory authority in these areas.

The AQMD's strategy for reducing air emissions has stretched from the outright banning of highly toxic and polluting products to supporting research into less pollutive technologies for use in business and industry, and very low emitting cars, trucks, and buses. It has pioneered in efforts to directly affect the behavior of individuals in their driving habits through developing programs of ride-sharing, telecommuting, and shifting driving to nonpeak hours. The AQMD's Commuter Program covers six thousand companies employing two million people, where employers are required to encourage their workers to carpool, use public transit, or bicycle to work rather than drive alone in a car.

The AQMD has led the way in the state and nation in setting standards for emissions from gasoline, solvents, oil-based paints, barbecue lighter fluid, and other commercial products, with the result that most have been reformulated or redesigned by their manufacturers to be less pollutive. A permitting system specifying emission caps on industrial machinery and equipment was instituted, as well as a permit system for an entire facility. Today, there are over 31,000 businesses covered by the AQMD permit program, with emission limits enforced through periodic facility inspections and violators susceptible to fines and civil penalties. Educational campaigns have been conducted to raise the public's awareness of the need for the strong steps taken to reduce air pollution. Research and development has been funded to devise less pollutive technologies for industry, business, transportation, and the home.

Approximately 30 percent of the air pollution in the Los Angeles basin originates from the manufacturing facilities and products that the AQMD regulates directly. However, the remaining 70 percent originates from mobile sources—cars, buses, trucks, trains, airplanes, and ships—which are under the regulatory supervision of the EPA and the State of California's Air Resources Board (CARB), not the AQMD. Although the reach of the AQMD to these mobile sources must perforce be indirect, it is ever-present. For example, with the strong backing of the AQMD, new cars made for sale in California are required to be equipped with pollution controls that make them the cleanest internal combustion engine vehicles in the world, burning the cleanest fuels.

When viewed in terms of the scale of the reach and scope of the challenge, the accomplishments of the AQMD efforts have been notable. The region has seen a significant decline in the most severe health alerts, and stages one, two, and three alerts are almost nonexistent today. The summer smog season of 2004, for example, ended as the cleanest since monitoring began in 1955. In 2004, there were 4 days with health advisory alerts, in comparison with 96 in 1994, with 146 in 1984, and the highest of all, 184, occurring in 1977. Peak concentrations of ozone, one of the toughest emissions to eradicate, have declined from a high of over 200 days in 1980 to under 70 in 2005 (AQMD 2007). This has not come easily.

When Doing Good Is Not Good Enough

Undeterred by the air pollution control strategies that had become synonymous with the AQMD in epoch one, new residents continued to stream into the Los Angeles in large numbers as they had in all but a few years since air emission controls were initiated. They have been attracted by jobs and opportunities, the region's extensive cultural and natural amenities, and its reputation as the immigrant gateway to the United States, most notably from Mexico, Central America, South Korea, and Southeast Asian countries. Since the end of World War II, the population of the four-county Los Angeles air basin has more than tripled in size from 4.8 to over 16.5 million people, at a time when the total U.S. population has doubled in size. Even more dramatic as an impact on air quality, the number of cars in the region has quadrupled from 2.3 to more than 9.5 million, logging over 330 million miles. Similarly, there has been a comparable growth in the number of trucks, trains, ships, and planes entering and leaving the region, and as a consequence, an increase in both air emissions and ever-worsening traffic congestion.

Never has the AQMD had the authority, the political will, or the administrative capacity to curb the region's population growth, despite its obvious link to the air pollution problem of the basin. Consequently, much of the gains in *per person* emission reduction has been and continues to be off-set to a significant degree by the region's continuing growth. By the end of the first epoch, the conundrum seemed almost insurmountable. After more than a decade straining to meet the emissions goals of the Clean Air Act, this led in the early 1980s to resignation among Los Angeles' government and business leaders that the Act's goals would never be met. The issue reached crisis proportion over the AQMD's 1982 Implementation Plan—a plan required by the EPA to be in compliance with the Clean Air Act—to reduce ozone. Rather than spelling out how the region would come into compliance with the ozone standard, the plan did not foresee bringing the region into compliance for at least twenty more years.

The EPA accepted the region's assessment, despite its responsibility to ensure that all state and regional plans take no more than five years to meet the requirements of the Act. In response to the AQMD's position, in 1984, environmentalists from the Coalition for Clean Air, a locally based environmental group, supported by the Sierra Club, turned to the federal court. They filed a suit with the United States Federal District Court in Los Angeles, against the EPA and the AQMD for promulgating a plan that knowingly failed to provide a persuasive and realistic strategy for complying with the Clean Air Act. The suit dragged on for four years until the judge ruled in favor of the environmentalists. It ordered the EPA to develop its own implementation plan for the region in the face of the district's inability to do so. The ruling became the legal backdrop of the renewed efforts and cleanup initiative in the region of the decade to come.

It was at this point in the history of the AQMD that, in 1986, Jim Lents was recruited as executive director of the agency. He had been successful in helping the city of Denver to address its air pollution problem and he was determined to do the same for Los Angeles. Reflecting back on this transition period, Lent would later muse that

The unstated position of the agency between 1977 and 1986 was "we will try to improve the air quality, but Los Angeles is never going to have clean air." ... In 1987, however, we decided that would no longer be the case, that it is our mandate to have air in this basin that is healthy to breathe. (Waldman 1991, 170)

Under Lent's leadership, air pollution policy became a driving force in Los Angeles, affecting everything from energy and transportation decisions—including development of a light rail, low-emitting diesel-powered locomotives, improved internal combustion engines, and the zero-emitting and low-emitting vehicles mandated for the region—to urban planning, waste management, and home and community landscaping. By the end of the 1980s, the AQMD board had emerged as a de facto regional government for the multicounty megalopolis of Los Angeles. The district had developed substantial administrative capacity, employing over a thousand staff, with over a hundred-million-dollar annual operating budget, in a new headquarters building. With authority over the stringent new-source review rules for air pollution being applied to businesses and industries seeking to enter the basin, combined with the provisions in federal, state, and regional law that prohibit any significant deterioration in air quality, the AQMD became a key arbiter of which industries would be allowed in and which ones could realistically afford to stay in the region, and where they would be located.

The AQMD 1991 Plan: The High Point of Command-and-Control Regulation

The release by the AQMD of its 1989 and the slightly modified 1991 Air Quality Management Plan was the toughest, most intrusive set of air emission regulations ever in Los Angeles, or anywhere. They came in three tiers. Tier I comprised 130 measures that were to be adopted in the near term, such as ridesharing and alternative work hours, waste recycling, and using less pollution-emitting building materials. Tier II controls were extensions but also some more stringent applications of the Tier I controls. They included "on the horizon" technologies and policies that could be expected to be developed by the year 2000, such as telecommunication technologies and less pollutive alternative fuels. Tier III regulations were controls that would involve major technological breakthroughs of the type that were expected to emerge over the next two decades, including commercial applications of fuel cells, super-conductors, and widespread adoption of solar power in homes and industry.

Several cost-benefit analyses were conducted on the plan, by the agency, business interests, and environmentalists, though without satisfactory result. Their differences were in part technical, but also economic and political, turning mainly on assumptions about the likelihood of the development and use of new technologies, and who was to bear the cost of the proposed control measures. While it was possible to gauge most of the near-term costs of imposing stricter controls, gauging their long-term costs was more difficult. There was also significant uncertainty and disagreement about the dollar value of human health, the quality of life, and the environment of the basin that would result from the plan. According to the plan, the AQMD would be responsible for caring out many of these provisions, but others would need to be implemented by CARB, the EPA, local governments, transportation agencies, and other special districts and governing entities within the region. The list of control measures was extensive and would require coordination across a myriad of local, state, and federal agencies.

The plan was extremely ambitious. It called for tough new policies and enforcement, and sacrifices by business and industry, the driving public, and all the residents of the basin. It required the full cooperation of all affected local, state, and federal agencies. It proved so sweeping in its potential impact on business and governmental agencies that it prompted the Los Angeles Chamber of Commerce along with a few local political officials to consider establishing a general purpose regional government that would counterbalance the authority over the region being amassed by the AQMD.

The Federal Implementation Plan

If this were not enough, in early 1993 the U.S. Supreme Count denied the EPA's appeal to overturn the decision reached in the U.S. District Court's in 1988, the decision in favor of the environmentalists and against the EPA and the AQMD requiring a plan for reducing ozone in the region. As a result, the EPA was directed by the court to devise a convincing comprehensive plan for the Los Angeles region, a "Federal Implementation Plan" (FIP). The outline of the EPA plan was released in early the next year and reached sectors only barely touched on up to that time by the AQMD, including trains, ships, port authorities, and commercial airlines. The draft plan went so far as to threaten the rationing of gasoline in the basin in order to curtail automotive emissions. Realistically, the EPA knew that even using the full regulatory powers at its disposal it was not likely to win over the local political and economic leaders, who were the main sources of resistance. Therefore, it publicly challenged the region—the AQMD, business, industry, and other community interests—to devise its own new and comprehensive implementation strategy, and thus avoid having the EPA impose one. This was to no avail.

According to the Supreme Count, the FIP was to be in place by February 1995. It was, but it arrived stillborn. The combination of strong political resistance from truckers, shipping and airline industries, local business, the utilities, automotive manufactures, oil companies, local governments, and others was overwhelming. The timing of the release of the FIP, in the midst of the longest recession in the region since the Great Depression of the 1930s, added significantly to the opposition. If there was any remaining doubt about the strength of the opposition to the FIP and what it required, and the shift in the public's concern with the recession in the months prior to the elections of November 1994, it was removed by the election of an antienvironmental Republican Congress in Washington and a Republican majority in the California legislature.

A political resolution to the impasse over the air quality plan for Los Angeles quickly followed the election, negotiated behind the scenes in

Washington. It was agreed that the State of California's air quality plan (the State Implementation Plan or SIP), which already had been approved by the EPA, would be interpreted by the agency to cover the South Coast Air Quality Management District for the purpose of compliance with the Clean Air Act planning requirement. The environmentalists were told that if they did not abide by this resolution and contested it in court, the newly empowered Republican Congress would rewrite the Clean Air Act with a high probability of weakening its goals and strict timelines. The concerns about timing and the adequacy of the region's clean air strategies would again resurface in the coming years, but for the moment the tide had turned. This episode marked a shift in the political influence of the environmental and health care advocates for clean air in Los Angeles and the aggressiveness that had developed in the AQMD. The champions of clean air would have to develop a new approach.

Looking back, two conclusions seem warranted. The command-and-control strategy, the hallmark of epoch one, did bring the region substantially along the path toward attaining federal and state air emission standards. However, under the assumption that the region's population would increase up to 40 percent by the year 2040, with the added economic growth, vehicles miles traveled, and congestion this implied, it was highly likely that emissions, particularly of ozone precursors (NOx and ROGs), would reverse their declining trajectory. Thus, for the region to achieve state and federal emission levels in the face of continuing growth, it would need to reduce hydrocarbons emissions by upward of an additional 80 percent, nitrogen oxides by 70 percent, sulfur oxides by 60 percent, and particulates by 20 percent. If the regulatory strategies for emission reductions had peaked, how then were further significant reductions going to be achieved?

The Pendulum Swings to Efficiency-Based Regulatory Reform and Implementation Flexibility: Epoch Two

From the outset of the struggle to clean the air, the challenge to policymakers had been to achieve a balance between the reduction in the emissions required by law and continuing growth. To the extent that end-of-the-pipe emission controls (such as the catalytic converter on cars and scrubbers on smokestacks), production-line modifications, and less pollutive products could be introduced without undermining the region's economy, increasing regulation did not cause an inordinate amount of economic and social disruption. Despite the complaints from the business community throughout the first two decades under the AQMD and the Clean Air Act, the regulatory strategy worked. In the early 1990s, however, circumstances changed. Los Angeles was engulfed by a deep recession starting in 1990 caused by the end of the cold war and, in turn, the effects on its critically important aerospace and defense industries that had been a major sector of the economy since World War II. This forced all parties to pay attention to the costs of doing business and the costs of government services. It came at a time of a dramatic shift underway in the political climate of the state, one that was conservative in tone and Republican in composition. These two developments joined to make state and local elected officials extremely wary of adding new regulatory burdens and, in several instances, they sought to roll back some already in place. Furthermore, by this point most of the major stationary sources of air pollution in Los Angeles—businesses, industries, the utilities—and the major mobile source—the automobile—had been captured within the command-and-control regulatory net. Even if one wished to substantially reduce emissions further using the conventional regulatory approach, the net would need to be expanded to the thousands of small emitters and minute sources of emission. This was not politically attractive or administratively feasible.

The political shift in the broader society also affected the AQMD's appointed board of governors, which began to mirror the broader political transformation in the state and nation. The new board members moved quickly to change the image and strategy of the agency. A new implementation strategy was declared as their approach became evident when they released the 1993, revised AQMD plan. Market incentives were made the mantra of the new plan. Nearly one hundred market-based measures were identified and a new implementation philosophy was declared, aiming at 75 percent of all smog-causing activities, with proposals for:

• fees on car miles driven and on fuel consumption;
• credits and rebates for cleaner technologies;
• financial incentives to switch to electric vehicles or low-emitting vehicles and fuel cell vehicles;
• planting of carbon absorbing and shade trees;

• credits and rebates for energy efficient houses and businesses;
• expansion of the market-based "cap-and-trade" program for nitrogen oxides (NOx) and sulfur oxides (SOx) introduced the previous year to volatile organic compounds (VOCs).

Removed from the plan were the previous controls on many "indirect sources," special events centers, shopping centers, airport ground access, trip reduction requirements for schools, and other controls on commerce and business.

The new plan was an attempt to reconcile the need for further reduction in emissions—required by the 1990 Clean Air Act, EPA regulations, and the State of California—in the face of enormous political opposition to the stringent control measures previously under discussion and in earlier plans. The only strategy that was likely to work in view of the changed realities was one that avoided forcing a zero-sum trade-off between cleaner air and the growth in people, cars, and business. The region would have to find less top-down, regulatory methods of meeting air quality standards.

The transformation was less of a single strategy than many strategies guided by the principles of regulatory relief (for example, in 1996 alone, permit requirements were eliminated for 10,000 pieces of equipment), efficiency, markets, and an emphasis on new, less pollutive technologies. It included streamlining the permitting process for business and industry to eliminate delays, redundancy, and the different requirements of the local, state, and federal air quality and other regulatory requirements. An extension of streamlining, often proposed but yet to be implemented, is to incorporate within one administrative entity regulatory responsibility for air, water, and other health and environmental pollutants, in a "multimedia" approach to environmental regulation.

The most prominent strategies of the second epoch involved ample use of market incentives, cost-effectiveness and cost-benefit analysis, and risk analysis (Freeman 2006). Although these approaches have their critics, they appear to have the most promise for long-term change.

The Regional Clean Air Incentives Market Program (RECLAIM)

In 1992, and foreshadowing its 1993 Plan, the AQMD adopted the Regional Clean Air Incentives Market program or RECLAIM, as a unique policy for the region though with national implications whereby operators of large industrial facilities would be required to buy and sell emission permits into an open market, in sulfur oxides (SOx) and nitrogen oxides (NOx), as part of the facility's strategy to achieve its required air emissions reduction. The concept was a straightforward application of microeconomic theory (Tietenberg 2006). If top-down, command-and-control regulations could be replaced with a market-based system, the result would be lower total costs to industry, greater flexibility in how industry accomplished emission reduction, and less government bureaucracy.

At the start of RECLAIM, each facility that participated was allocated permits, in pounds, for one year, allowing the emission of NOx and SOx. The allocations were based on a benchmark year. The amount permitted was to be reduced each year thereafter by 5 to 8 percent in order to achieve a region-wide reduction of 83 percent in NOx and 65 percent in SOx by 2003. It was assumed that after 2003 additional targets would be established, depending on the needs of the region. This has occurred.

A permit holder can exercise the permit by emitting up to the allocated amount or reduce emissions and sell the remaining permits back into the market. As an additional incentive, participating companies were granted fast-track, "one-stop shopping" by the AQMD for all their major permit needs. RECLAIM replaced about sixty command-and-control regulations. The overall cost savings to industry was estimated at upward of half of compliance costs of traditional regulation.

Since its inception, RECLAIM has grown into the largest urban region emission trading program in the United States. Within the first two years it had been extended to 329 of 31,000 industrial facilities—including the 300 largest—and covered more than 50 percent of the NOx and 90 percent of SOx emissions from all facilities regulated by the AQMD. Within four years, the number of transactions among facilities had grown to over 400, with nearly 30,000 tons of NOx credits and 30,000 tons of SOx credits chancing hands (AQMD Advisor 1998). Although the program has had its critics (Drury et al. 1999), it continues to be the primary strategy for reducing emissions from the regions largest facilities, with the permissible overall emissions of SOx and NOx covered under the program progressively reduced by the AQMD in each year of the program's existence (AQMD Advisor 2005).

While many environmentalists supported the idea of RECLAIM, others opposed the program because the short-term environmental relief would to be small. This resulted from the political compromise that led to the initial allocation of credits, based on a firm's historic average maximum emissions when the economy was in recession and industrial production was at a low point. Others argued that the program's size (limited to 300 plus large firms) would keep demand and supply of permits limited, and thereby inhibit the development of a large and efficient market. In spite these concerns, the benefits in both the decrease of command-and-control rules and the growing market in trading argues persuasively that RECLAIM is working, and continues as the largest metropolitan experiment to date in emissions trading under the Clean Air Act.

However, and significant in considering future developments, though successful in application to SOx and NOx, RECLAIM failed when the AQMD attempted to apply the program to volatile organic compounds (VOCs), in the mid-1990s. The absence of prior command-and-control regulations over the affected firms and the broad sweep of VOC-emitting businesses appear to have been at the root of the failure to adopt the approach (Dale 2000).

Additional incentive-based approaches to emission reduction were considered in the early to mid-1990s as the new market-based philosophy was being embraced by AQMD. Several of the ideas were prompted by federal transportation law that required transportation planners to design policies that simultaneously reduced highway congestion and air pollution. The simultaneous achievement of both goals can, in theory, be realized through the introduction of market-based schemes, such as congestion pricing, smog fees, gasoline taxes, and incentives for the purchase of smaller and low-emitting vehicles. However, no single "best" approach has been struck upon that simultaneously satisfies all the necessary and sufficient concerns to be adopted—from extent of emissions reduction achieved, simplicity of concept and administration, cost-effectiveness, and equity, to economic impact on the region, intrusiveness, political support, and proportion of the problem addressed. Each approach involves trade-offs between the directness of the economic "signal" to the level of reduced emissions, political acceptability, and so forth.

The approach that came closest to adoption in Los Angeles and statewide was the "vehicle-miles-traveled" fee, or VMT. In the early 1990s the VMT was endorsed by a coalition of business leaders, environmentalists, the regional association of governments, and academics. The VMT is based on the number of miles a vehicle is driven. It has the virtue of

Table 4.1
A Comparison of the First and Second Environmental Epochs in Los Angeles Air Pollution Control Policy

	Regulating for Environmental Protection 1970–1990	Efficiency-Based Regulatory Reform and Flexibility 1980–2000
Problem/Objectives	To reduce air emissions from existing industry and transportation through establishing national health-based standards, imposing end-of-tailpipe emissions restrictions, and using air pollution policy to compel changes in work and lifestyle	To devise a regional growth strategy that utilizes market incentives to encourage development and application of minimally polluting technologies; to foster green business networks and public-private collaboration
Philosophy (Orientation) of Business	Considers pollution a public (not private) sector issue. Rejects the basic premise and methods of the environmental movement; pollution viewed as an externalities problem; adversarial in tone	Recognizes the need to reduce pollution as a matter of law and good business; looks to public policy to provide incentives to reduce pollution and help overcome problems of collective action in industry
Philosophy (Orientation) of Government	To establish environmental standards and oversee business and citizen compliance through top down command-and-control regulation	To be a partner with business in the greening process; to devise win-win policy incentives for economic growth and environmental protection
Philosophy (Orientation) of Environmentalists/Health Interests	To reverse environmental harms caused by modern industrial society and an expanding global population: zero emissions, polluter pays principle, refusal to acknowledge costs, reliance on Federal command-and-control policy and courts, grass-roots social movement politics	Same basic ends though deeply divided on means along lines of cooperation/ cooptation vs. adversarial/deep ecology orientations and strategies

Predominant Political/Institutional Context		
National:	USCAA, CaCAA, NEPA, CEQA, EIRs	ISTEA, EPACT, Clean Cities, DOD's ARPA programs, some sections of the USCAA
LA Regional:	AQMPs, regional rail initiatives and MTAs, utility DSM programs, alternative energy programs	Project CA, LA's New Economy Project, CALSTART, SCE Team Cities, SC Economic Partnership, Aerospace & Defense conversion
Political Style	Adversarial, winners and losers, seen in as zero-sum; insiders and business dominate	Collaborative and inclusive of all interests (corporatist); a search for common ground
Institutional Venue	The legislature and executives offices in Sacramento and Washington, CARB and the air districts; the conventional public policy making arenas; partisan politics	New public-private partnerships and private collaborative forums; more fluid political coalitions; vertical and horizontal linkages across groups and federal, state, and local venues
Power Relationships and Key Players	Elected officials, the recognized representatives of environmental and business groups, industry lobbyists from the leading petro-chemical, energy, and manufacturing sectors	Traditional business and industry leaders plus those from the new high technology industries, a wider array of social and community leaders, universities, technical community
Duration	1970–1995—From Earth Day, passage of NEPA and the 1970 CAA to the issuance of the draft regional Federal Implementation Plan for the Los Angeles region by the EPA in 1994	1990–2000 (and beyond)—From the rise of the new public philosophy and region's economic restructuring, to RECLAIM, and to the market and technology-based strategies of the twenty-first century

being a direct and equitable fee, in that all automobiles are charged the same amount, per mile, for use of the roadways. Several technologies exist for reading a car's mileage electronically; thus the system can be designed to be unobtrusive.

The fee was viewed, also, as a replacement for the state's gasoline tax base that was declining as cars became more efficient. Using the VMT for operating revenue for the state's highway and road system would allow shifting from the tax on gallons of gasoline consumed to miles traveled. To the extent that the VMT became an incentive to move people to public transportation, ride-sharing, and trip reductions, the roadways would be less congested. Air quality would benefit doubly under this scheme, both from the fewer total miles of driving in the basin and the reduction in congestion, which itself is a major cause of auto emissions.

Setting the actual fee level for the VMT was a major point of contention. Representatives of the Los Angeles business community proposed a revenue-neutral one cent per mile, or $100 for every 10,000 miles of travel. Small and Kazimi (1994), using a health-cost criterion, estimated that cost of the health effects of auto emissions could be captured with a three cents per mile fee on cars (equal to approximately thirty cents per gallon of gasoline) and a fifty cents per mile fee on large diesel trucks (to offset their disproportionate contribution to the adverse health effects of the region's air pollution). Environmental Defense Fund, an environmental NGO, argued that a five cent per mile fee would be needed to achieve the optimal amount of reduced congestion and pollution.

The VMT failed to attract sufficient public and legislative support, however, and has not received serious consideration in policy circles since. Nevertheless, it remains as one of the more attractive incentives-based approaches for simultaneously reducing automotive congestion and air emissions in the region.

Table 4.1 captures this transition in sketching out the dimensional features for two of the three epochs of environmentalism presented in chapter 1; the early 1970s–1980s epoch of green regulation and the 1980s–2000 one of regulatory reform, market- and incentive-based approaches, and technology strategies. Here, given their relative importance, somewhat greater elaboration is provided for implementation philosophies of the contending stakeholders, the composition of the stakeholders, their style, and the venues in which they chose to act. Consistent with the general thesis in chapter 1, the broad policy goal of cleaner air remained constant, but the manner in which it is to be achieved, at what cost, and through which methods and mechanisms differed substantially.

Toward Sustainable Communities Los Angeles Style: Epoch Three

The adoption of market-based philosophy and the success of RECLAIM and regulatory flexibility in meeting the region's emission targets, like the command-and-control strategy that preceded it, was judged to be insufficient for achieving the remaining air emissions reduction needed in the region to meet federal and state clean air standards. Standards were becoming ever more demanding, for example, in the stricter regulations promulgated by EPA in 2006 based on new research on the health effects of small particulate matter and the effects to ozone. More dramatic steps would be required and this meant further motivating the public, who would be asked to make additional sacrifices, and inspiring the political and business leaders, who would need to coalesce around a more comprehensive regional strategy.

This leads to consideration of the prospect of Los Angeles moving in the direction of greater sustainability and building the foundation of a third environmental epoch—a move that requires reaching beyond command-and-control and market-based incentives for emissions reduction, to understanding how the region's economy is organized and operated, developing new ways of providing transportation and other infrastructure needs, and embracing significant changes in the way in which the region is governed. In essence, the move would be a fundamental transformation in what Los Angelinos value in their personal and professional lives, their community, and their willingness to make the necessary near-term sacrifices and changes today for a more sustainable future.

The path to sustainability as laid out conceptually in chapters 1 through 3, to be effective as a blueprint for Los Angeles, suggests several necessary though by no means fully sufficient steps in the transition from epochs one and two to three of the environmental movement:

• The entire Los Angeles basin will need to be treated as a single air shed—that is, we need to apply a bubble concept to the region as a whole—covering all sources of air, stationary, and especially mobile sources of emissions.

• A region-wide system of governance and operating institutions will be needed that can integrate the critical components of a more sustainable strategy for the region—not just the regulation of sources of air emissions, but cover transportation, land-use planning, energy, economic development, and quality of life considerations—and regional financing mechanisms to ensure the implementation of regional strategies.

• A combination of incentives and sanctions will be needed to accelerate the redesign of many if not most of today's products and technologies manufactured within and imported into the region to minimize the extreme the use of toxic materials, generate fewer wastes, and consume less energy and natural materials.

• Public agencies overseeing pollution abatement (air, water, toxics, and others) will need to be reengineered from their traditional regulatory approach and culture to one of being collaborators and facilitators in the emerging high-tech, market-based economy of the region.

Most important of all, for the transition to occur the economy of the Los Angeles region will need to be moved to the forefront of the green technology curve. Potentially leading in this transition could be the redesign and remanufacture of the personal automobile. This could outweigh the importance of many of the additional emission reduction changes being imagined for the region. The quantum leap forward in technology has been anticipated since early in epoch one (Lovins, Barnett, and Lovins 1993) and in practice has led to many prototype electric and hybrid cars, and the commercial success of especially Toyota's hybrid car in the California auto market today. Tired of waiting for the technology breakthrough, California venture capitalists recently launched their own new age auto company, Tesla Motors (Shnayerson 2007).

This is only a start, however. The prognosis for the long-term—ten, fifteen, twenty years out—will require additional fundamental change designed to move beyond *minimizing* to *eliminating* harmful auto emissions. A sustainable environment will require accelerating the introduction an entirely new post–fossil fuels economy (possibly based on hydrogen).

For both technical and economic reasons, the transformation will propel business and manufacturing firms forward on the ladder of complexity and cost. Progress will require a host of new cradle-to-grave "total cost assessment" and "life-cycle analysis" management, accounting, and decision-making systems, and "life-cycle design" for products, all of which incorporate direct and indirect environmental costs.

Managers will need to be able to select the overall and multimedia (air, water, noise) least harmful and least costly mix of products and production processes (Freeman et al. 1992; Keoleian and Menerey 1994).

In recognition of these challenges and obstacles, is there any indication that pressure is rising for the changes needed? The answer, albeit guarded and limited, is yes, and it is coming from two major directions.

Two Issues Prompting Epoch Three Air Pollution Policy Approaches in Los Angeles

The air pollution agenda of Los Angeles in recent years has been dominated by a set of interrelated issues brought about by the emergence of goods movement as the fastest growing component of the region's economy. With the globalization of manufacturing and changing patterns of production and distribution over the past two decades, extending today from Asian manufacturers to North American consumers, Los Angles has become the nation's largest containerized shipping port of entry—third largest worldwide—through which pass 40 percent of all containerized goods entering the United States. The jobs and economic benefits of goods movement to the region are substantial. So too the challenges—challenges of distributing goods across the basin and the nation, work force needs and job training, transportation infrastructure planning and development, and coping with the concentration of diesel emissions from the cargo ships, trains, and trucks moving into and out of the port, which has reached a critical threshold. Goods movement has become the growth driver, on the one hand, and on the other hand the most severe air pollution, health, and environmental justice challenge facing Los Angeles.

The California Air Resources Board has forecasted that the currently unregulated NOx from the cargo ships alone is likely to grow to 250 million tons daily over the next fifteen years unless major steps are taken to curb the emissions; this compares to 130 tons from trucks and 77 tons from locomotive trains operating in the state today (Schoch 2005). Moreover, these are emissions that disproportionately affect the health of the children of the mostly poor, working class, and minority populations in the neighborhoods surrounding the ports and along the major trucking corridors leading from the port to the nation's interstate highway system (AQMD 2007; Pastor, Morello-Frosch, and Sadd 2006).

As noted, the AQMD is responsible for addressing the health and equity implications of air emissions in the region under both the EPA policy and its own health and environmental justice policies. Yet, it is the state and federal governments that regulate the trains and trucks involved in the goods movement, under the interstate commerce clause of the federal government. In the case of shipping, oversight is by a mix of federal and international maritime regulations. Nonetheless, this has not deterred the AQMD from insinuating itself through promulgating a set of guiding policy principles and action measures in a "Clean Port Initiative," adopted by its board in November of 2005, imploring the ports of Los Angeles and Long Beach to move aggressively on reducing air emissions, to require shipping companies to bear their share of the costs, and to coordinate with the AQMD and the other critical stakeholders in their planning and implementation. That which AQMD can implement under its own authority it is doing and, where it lacks formal authority, it is working with CARB, EPA, the state legislature, Congress, the two ports and their counterpart ports in Asia, and the transport industries directly, to clean the air.

To accomplish the ambitious goals of the Clean Port Initiative, new technologies, systems management, and logistics measures will be needed, and most if not all the measures being called for will need to be implemented. The dollar costs will be substantial and are being contested, from converting the trucking fleet and trains to low-emitting and nonemitting fuel sources, adding new lanes to relieve truck congestion on the region's highways, construction of a trucks-only highway through the region, construction of a new rail route through the region, and working in tandem with the ports, both in Los Angeles and in Asia. At the same time, Californians voted in 2006 for a $1.2 billion bond measure for air quality improvements at the ports; the two ports have adopted a Clean Ports Action Plan and an Alternative Maritime Power agreement for dock-side ship air emissions; CARB has promulgated new low sulfur emission standards for diesel truck engines; and; through a business-government sponsored program low-emission locomotives are being introduced at the ports. While much of this is being done in the "shadow" of regulation—that is, the fear of federal, state, and regional air quality regulations—it is actually being carried out in a far more multisector public-private framework of negotiation and cooperation. It is being embraced by the chambers of commerce in the region, the respective cities of Long Beach and Los Angeles, and in consultation and negotiation with environmental and health advocacy groups. Providing an even broader multiregional perspective and framework for addressing the goods movement challenges, not only of air pollution but transportation, land-use, and economic development, a "Green Freight Initiative" was launched in 2005–2006 by a coalition of the leading business interests throughout all of Southern California, committed to the proposition that solutions to the environment and health challenges of goods movement will be found by government and industry working together. This is the promise of the business leaders who launched the new initiative and has been affirmed by the governor of the state and his cabinet officers.

In effect, the governance process is a new combination of collaboration and policymaking among all the key stakeholders, with AQMD playing an important but no longer singular or even dominant role, if for no other reason than that it does not have the statutory authority to regulate across all the sectors and issues needed for a successful goods movement strategy.

California's Green House Gases Emissions Policy Will Require a Sustainability-Based Approach for Air Emissions Reduction

The challenge of addressing the ambient air quality of the Los Angles region under the Clean Air Act has been at the center of clean air policy and under the authority of the AQMD for over three decades. The balancing act required of the AQMD (together with CARB and the EPA)— to compel compliance under the law while not undermining the region's economy or generating so great a political backlash as to weaken the Clean Air Act—itself has proven to be a fascinating example of how in order to maintain forward progress the air control "regime" has moved through the command-and-control epoch to market-based strategies and regulatory flexibility. The most recent episode of trying to cope with the nexus of goods movements and ports, and thus ships, trains, and trucks, combined with congestion and transportation, health-related emissions problems, and issues of environmental justice, while enabling Los Angeles to participate in today's global economy, is bringing all the relevant parties together in a more comprehensive and sustainable regional approach to the challenges faced.

While this alone is only a first step into the transformation to a third epoch of the environmental movement in Los Angeles, the process is receiving a monumental push forward by the entry of California into the worldwide attack on elevated greenhouse gas (GHG) emissions, especially CO_2, which have not historically been covered by the Clean Air

Act. Filling this policy void, California has established itself as a first-mover and leading state in the nation and worldwide in addressing climate change through a series of executive orders by the governor, passage of implementing legislation, and setting ambitious goals for GHG emission reductions for the state by 2020 and 2050. At this writing, the processes of rule making, guidelines, public-private coordination, initiatives, and public-private costs and funding agreements are only now unfolding.

It is evident already, however, that the monumental nature of the GHG challenge and expectation that all sectors of the economy and all Californian's will need to be a party to the solution will require embracing as never before the philosophy of sustainability and epoch three approaches, tools, and governing mechanisms. In view of this, it is reasonable to anticipate that in addressing its continuing challenges of ambient air quality Los Angles will be merging this with its looming challenge of reducing upper atmospheric GHG emissions.

It remains to be seen how far Los Angeles, in so many ways America's preeminent trend-setting city of the twentieth century, will be able to remake itself into a sustainable city of the twenty-first century. It will need to address not only the issues of ambient air pollution and greenhouse gases, but also water, transportation, and growth in business and industry, along with urban sprawl, rapid population growth, education, and overall quality of life needs of its people. Even before the transition from the first to the second environmental epoch is complete, the third beckons. But as is evident in this discussion and in subsequent chapters, much more will be needed than a media-specific—in this case, air-pollution-focused—transformational effort.

References

AQMD Advisor. 1998. "First Comprehensive Audit Finds RECLAIM Program Working." July.

AQMD Advisor. 2005. "AQMD Orders Further Emissions Reductions From Region's Pollution Credit Trading Program." March.

AQMD (South Coast Air Quality Management District). 2007. Final Air Quality Management Plan. June 1. Http://www.AQMD.gov/AQMPintro.html.

Dale, Thompson B. 2000. "Political Obstacles to the Implementation of Emissions Markets: Lessons from RECLAIM." *Natural Resources Journal* 40, 3 (summer).

Dewey, Scott. 1997. "Don't Breathe the Air." Doctoral dissertation in History, Rice University. April.

Drury, Richard, Michael Belliveau, J. Scott Kuhn, and Shirpra Bansal. 1999. "Pollution Trading and Environmental Justice." *Duke Environmental Law and Policy Forum* 9: 231–289.

Freeman, Harry, Trees Harden, Johnny Springier, Paul Random, Mary Ann Currant, and Kenneth Stone. 1992. "Industrial Pollution Prevention: A Critical Review." *Journal of Air and Waste Management* 42: 618–656.

Freeman, A. Myrick III. 2006. "Economics, Incentives, and Environmental Policy." Chapter 9 in *Environmental Policy: New Directions for the Twenty-First Century*, 6th ed., ed. Norman J. Vig and Michael E. Kraft, 193–214. Washington, D.C.: CQ Press.

Keoleian, Gregory, and Dan Menerey. 1994. "Sustainable Development by Design: Review of Life Cycle Design and Related Approaches." *Journal of Air and Waste Management* 44: 645–668.

Lovins, Amory B., John W. Barnett, and L. Hunter Lovins. 1993. "Supercars: The Coming Light-Vehicle Revolution." Rocky Mountain Institute. March.

Pastor, Manuel Jr., Rachel Morello-Frosch, and James L. Sadd. 2006. "Breathless: Schools, Air Toxics, and Environmental Justice in California." *Policy Studies Journal* 34, 3: 337–362.

Schoch, Deborah. 2005. "Study Links Diesel Fumes to Illness." *Los Angeles Times*. December 3, B-1.

Shnayerson, Michael. 2007. "Quiet Thunder." *Vanity Fair* (May). Http://www.vanityfair.com/politics/features/2007/05/tesla2005.

Small, Kenneth, and Camilla Kazimi. 1994. "On the Cost of Air Pollution from Motor Vehicles." University of California Transportation Center, Irvine. September.

Tietenberg, Tom H. 2006. *Emissions Trading: Principles and Practice*, 2nd ed. Washington, D.C.: Resources for the Future.

U.S. Environmental Protection Agency (EPA). 2005. "Benefits and Costs of the Clean Air Act." Final Report to Congress on the Benefits and Costs of the Clean Air Act, 1970–1990. EPA 410-R-99-001.

U.S. Environmental Protection Agency. 2006. "Air Emissions Trends—Continued Progress through 2005." Http://www.epa.gov/airtrends/2006/emissions_summary_2005.html.

U.S. Environmental Protection Agency. 2007. "EPA Progress Report 2007: Pacific Southwest Region." EPA-909-R-07-003.

Waldman, Tom. 1991. "LA Air Board Starts a Fresh Wind Blowing." *California Journal* (April).

5

Cleaning Wisconsin's Waters: From Command and Control to Collaborative Decision Making

Michael E. Kraft

The enactment of the Federal Water Pollution Control Act Amendments of 1972, known as the Clean Water Act (CWA), was a key signpost of the new era of environmental policy launched in the 1970s. Passage of the act signaled the nation's determination to clean up its heavily polluted streams, rivers, and lakes through a federally driven regulatory process based on national water quality standards and joint federal-state implementation. The new law provided a comprehensive framework of pollution control standards, tools, and financial assistance. It also established deadlines for eliminating the discharge of pollutants, and it sought ambitiously to "restore and maintain the chemical, physical, and biological integrity" of the nation's waters.

In most important respects, the CWA's reliance on a command-and-control approach that is applied to a single environmental medium (water) places it squarely within what the introductory chapter describes as epoch one. This strategy concentrated on regulating for environmental protection with a focus on business, industry, and municipal waste dischargers, and attempted to control their all too obvious end-of-the-pipe pollution.

The 1972 act was a dramatic break with previous policies that were widely faulted as ineffective and excessively dependent on highly variable state economic resources, bureaucratic capacity, and commitment to water quality goals (Ringquist 1993; Kraft 2007). The new policy also was successful by most measures. It resulted in significant improvements in overall national water quality. Yet the CWA was costly, too, with a cumulative national expenditure of public and private funds estimated at $500 billion over its first twenty years alone (Knopman and Smith 1993).

Not surprisingly, as is the case with other national environmental policies of the 1970s, both formal and informal assessments of the CWA over the past three decades have questioned its efficiency and effectiveness. Such critical evaluations have called for the use of new approaches that promise to reduce costs of compliance, promote greater flexibility and efficiency in implementation, and emphasize pollution prevention and ecosystem-based management, especially within river basins (Davies and Mazurek 1998; Eisner 2007; Fiorino 2006; Freeman 2000; Layzer 2008; and Weber 2003). Most of these strategies are hallmarks of epoch two, as discussed in chapter 1, and some are reflective of epoch three thinking. A key component of the new approaches, which is thought to be essential to long-term success, is the substitution of a more cooperative and collaborative process of decision making for the often adversarial relations between government and polluters that have been characteristic of conventional environmental regulation. This claim is persuasive in theory, but confidence in the efficacy of such collaboration would be enhanced if its use in specific cases were evaluated.

To provide such information, this chapter examines experience with water quality policy in one region of the United States that shares many qualities with other industrialized areas of the nation. It reviews the recent history of the struggle to clean up the Fox-Wolf River Basin in Northeastern Wisconsin, which surrounds metropolitan Green Bay. It highlights the strategies used nationwide as well as within this region during the first two epochs, and discusses the emergence of the third epoch of sustainability. The chapter also focuses on major achievements to date in cleaning up area waters and the remaining tasks, especially the substantial challenge of removing highly contaminated sediments laden with polychlorinated biphenyls (PCBs) deposited years ago through discharges by area pulp and paper mills.[1]

Over time, the Wisconsin Department of Natural Resources (WDNR) and other governmental bodies and industry have made use of all of the techniques available under the CWA and commonly used throughout the nation. A great deal of progress has been achieved in improving water quality through the regulatory mechanisms established by the CWA and through use of pollution prevention and other components of the second epoch of the 1980s and 1990s. Yet the area continues to struggle, as does the rest of the country, with controlling nonpoint sources of water pollution (where the origins are multiple, varied, and diffuse) and with removing highly dangerous toxic chemicals from its streams, rivers, lakes, and bays. Doing so is essential to promote community sustainability in a region where the culture and economic vitality are tied firmly to maintenance of quality surface water. Recent efforts in the region to protect water quality have depended on the use of collaborative decision making and public-private partnerships. The successes and limitations of these approaches hold some lessons for the rest of the nation.

Water Quality Problems and Progress

Water resources and their quality are essential to life and of obvious importance to the nation's economy. Water resources meet the public's need for clean drinking water, and they also support agriculture, industry, electric power generation, recreation and tourism, transportation, and fisheries. In the Fox-Wolf Basin, clean surface waters are the primary source of drinking water for about 100,000 people. Industries throughout the region use water for papermaking and food processing, among many other industrial activities. High-quality surface water also helps to satisfy the public's diverse recreational interests—fishing, swimming, canoeing, sailing, boating, and the simple enjoyment of the beauty of a large body of water flowing through a wooded countryside or the middle of an urban area. The river basin and bay of Green Bay are also vital to the integrity of the Great Lakes; they are a key component of that ecosystem.

Degradation of Water Quality
The quality of the nation's water is affected by a multiplicity of human uses, including point discharges of waste from industry and municipalities and nonpoint source pollution from agriculture and urban runoff. A century and more of industrial development, burgeoning human population, and land-use changes throughout the nation had taken its toll by the time the Clean Water Act was adopted in 1972. The waters of the Fox-Wolf Basin were no exception.

The lower Fox River stretches 39 miles from its source near the cities of Neenah and Menasha in the northwest corner of Lake Winnebago north through the Fox Cities to its mouth at the head of the bay of Green Bay. The lower Fox River Basin encompasses approximately 400 square miles of drainage area in Northeastern Wisconsin, and about 6,400 square miles downstream, including parts of East Central Wisconsin (see figure 5.1). The Fox-Wolf River Basin supports a population of about 750,000 people, and it constitutes the largest tributary to the Lake Michigan Basin and the third largest to the Great Lakes. It also empties

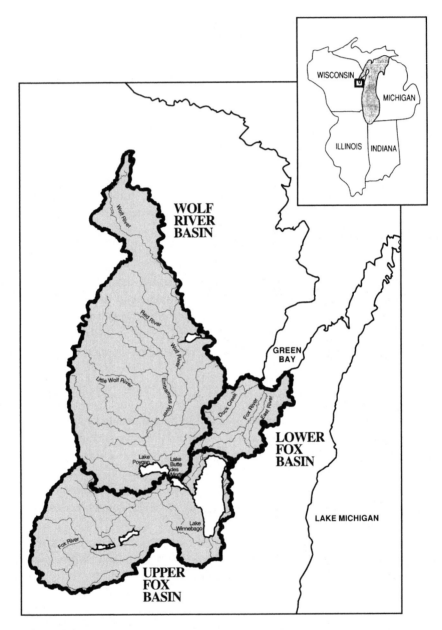

Figure 5.1
The Fox-Wolf River Basin.

into the head of the world's largest freshwater estuary in the bay of Green Bay. The basin is a complex ecosystem that has been transformed substantially over the past century. By the 1920s, 34 pulp and paper mills had been established along the lower Fox, and by the 1990s, the lower Fox received the discharge of thirteen mills, the largest concentration of the paper industry in the world.

Water quality in the region has been adversely affected by the operations of many other businesses and by agriculture, which has increased the runoff of soils, nutrients from fertilizers and untreated animal wastes, and chemicals from pesticide applications. In addition, more than 90 percent of coastal wetlands in the lower Fox River and Green Bay have been lost to land filling, industrial and residential development, and other changes in land use, with substantial damage to ecosystem functions (WDNR 1993).

Among the most serious water quality problems in the area is the presence of persistent toxic chemicals. Varying levels of more than one hundred potentially toxic substances have been identified in the water, fish, and sediment of the Fox River, including polychlorinated organic compounds such as PCBs, dioxins, and furans; mercury, lead, and other heavy metals; pesticides; polycyclic aromatic hydrocarbons; and volatile hydrocarbons (WDNR 1993, 1999; Sullivan and Delfino 1982).

The river and bay have been the object of intensive scientific investigation, particularly for the movement of toxic chemicals through the land, air, and water. Indeed, a Green Bay mass balance study was the first in the world to measure the presence, transport, and fate of bioaccumulating toxic chemicals in a river and bay environment (Mercurio 1995). These and other studies of ecosystem stressors in the region have identified nutrient and sediment loading as perhaps the most important concern related to the loss of many beneficial uses of water resources (WDNR 1988; Harris et al. 1994).

In the 1990s, an estimated 1.5 million pounds of phosphorus flowed into the Fox River and into the bay each year, along with 150,000 tons of suspended solids, the vast majority of which have come from nonpoint sources—algae and soil erosion (WDNR 1993). Not surprisingly, water quality experts argue that to restore area waters, the loading of nutrients and solids must be significantly reduced, wetland habitat protected and restored, and persistent organic chemicals such as PCBs eliminated or reduced to a level where no adverse effects on the ecosystem can be detected (WDNR 1988; Harris 1994).

These toxic chemicals, including mercury and ammonia, remain the toxic substances of greatest concern in the lower Fox River and Green Bay. All pose a risk to ecosystem functions in area waters, and the persistent and bioaccumulative toxics, particularly PCBs, also present a serious risk to human health (Harris et al. 1994; WDNR 1993). Between 1954 and 1997, seven area paper mills discharged an estimated 700,000 pounds of PCBs into the river. Over 64,000 pounds remain today in the river's sediments, with the remainder having washed into the bay, making their removal nearly impossible. Nearly all of the PCBs that continue to enter the bay now come from sediment resuspension and settling rather than from point sources (WDNR 1993, 1999).[2]

Although the PCB risks are not widely recognized by area residents, the federal government considers the lower Fox River and Green Bay to be among the most severely PCB-contaminated sites in the nation. Indeed, the area is comparable to the Hudson River in New York, which the EPA placed on the Superfund National Priorities List in 2002. When dredging operations began in earnest in 2005, projections indicated that the Fox River location will likely be the nation's largest cleanup of contaminated sediments by volume ever attempted.

Progress in Improving Water Quality Nationally and in Wisconsin

In its twenty-fifth anniversary issue, the federal Council on Environmental Quality (1997, 12) noted that across the nation "most of the conspicuous water pollution from point sources has been eliminated. More than 57,000 industrial facilities now operate under a pollution control permit." Other observers have offered a less sanguine view of water quality, in part because of the paucity of reliable data about the thousands of streams, rivers, ponds, and lakes across the nation (Knopman and Smith 1993; Davies and Mazurek 1998). Recent EPA reports of progress under the Clean Water Act reach many of the same conclusions (U.S. EPA 2007).

Some trends are reasonably clear, however. Almost everywhere there has been a major reduction in the raw pollution of surface waters. The proportion of the U.S. population served by wastewater treatment systems rose from 42 percent in 1970 to about 74 percent by 1985, with a resulting estimated decline in annual releases of organic wastes of about 46 percent (Adler 1993). Most of the huge financial investment in clean water since 1972 has been expended on conventional point sources of water pollutants, and as a result, most industries and municipalities have greatly reduced their discharges, consistent with the intent of the Clean Water Act.

Beyond those controls on dischargers, we have other ways to measure progress. The most widely used assessment of surface water quality is the National Water Quality Inventory, a biennial report from the EPA that is based on inventory by the fifty states of their own water resources. Section 305(b) of the CWA requires states to report every two years to the EPA on the extent to which state waters support designated beneficial uses. The review for 2002 (U.S. EPA 2007) was based on surveys within the states that relied on varying methods of assessment. However, caution is usually urged in interpreting the numbers. For example, the states collectively surveyed only 19 percent of the nation's total miles of all streams and rivers, and 37 percent of its lakes.

Based on these limited inventories, for the nation as a whole, about 51 percent of rivers and streams and 48 percent of lakes, reservoirs, and ponds "fully support" such "designated uses" as swimming, fishing, drinking water supply, and supporting aquatic life. About 45 percent of rivers and streams were found to be impaired to some degree, as were 47 percent of lakes, ponds, and reservoirs. In Wisconsin, the numbers were comparable. For example, the state found that about 57 percent of assessed rivers and streams were impaired, as were 57 percent of lakes, ponds, and reservoirs.

Only 520 of 5,521 Great Lakes shoreline miles were assessed by the states, including Wisconsin, and they found only 9 percent of them to fully support designated uses. About 91 percent of the assessed shoreline areas were rated by the states as impaired, largely because of fish consumption advisories and unfavorable conditions for supporting aquatic life—chiefly because of persistent toxic chemicals that enter the food web, habitat degradation, and competition by nonnative species (U.S. EPA 2007). However, a major federal report released in early 2008 seemed to confirm what many in the region have long suspected, that toxic chemical pollution in the Great Lakes also may have serious public health consequences (Harris 2008).

The water quality reports show some improvement over the years, although the most recent data released by the EPA in 2007 paint a generally *less* positive picture than similar reports in the late 1990s. Both in the 1990s and today, these kinds of surveys indicate that many problems remain with the nation's surface water quality. Their causes are also fairly evident. EPA reports have consistently indicated that the leading sources of water quality impairment affecting rivers and streams today are agricultural activities, hydrologic modifications such as water diversions, habitat alterations, urban runoff and storm water, and municipal permitted discharges such as from sewage treatment plants.

In effect, the remaining problems across the nation, and in Wisconsin, are largely nonpoint sources of pollution. Section 208 of the Clean Water Act required all states to assess the contribution of nonpoint sources to water quality and to establish programs to control them. Early efforts under that section to develop areawide water quality management plans were promising. Yet the reality is that since then neither Congress nor the EPA has done much to address such sources, nor have most states. The Water Quality Act of 1987 emphasized again the need to control nonpoint sources, and the EPA has had a modest program to aid the states in addressing them. But as critics note, the budgets have been small compared to what the agency has spent on other water quality programs (Davies and Mazurek 1998, 272).

Cleaning up the Fox River

Improvements in water quality are as apparent in the Fox River and Northeastern Wisconsin as they are nationwide, and these achievements reflect the stringent regulatory framework created by the Clean Water Act in a manner that was typical of environmental protection policy in epoch one. Until passage of the act in 1972, the lower Fox River Basin remained heavily polluted despite many state and local attempts to clean it up. After passage, efforts were far more successful. By the middle to late 1970s, fish and other organisms began to return to the river as wastewater treatment facilities were built or modernized—in part through funds made available by the CWA. By the early 1980s, a world-class walleye fishery had been restored in the seven-mile stretch from De Pere to the mouth of the Fox River in the bay of Green Bay.

Those gains in water quality were achieved mainly through the state-administered permitting system that sought to meet water quality standards set by the CWA. The permits limited overall pollutant discharge in the entire 39-mile stretch of the lower Fox by allowing specified discharges only to the extent that the river was capable of assimilating them. Under Section 402 of the CWA, states implement the National Pollutant Discharge Elimination System (NPDES), contingent upon approval by the EPA. Under Section 307 of the act, the NPDES also has been used to control discharge of PCBs and other toxic chemicals.

The results of this regulatory action were striking. According to one assessment, from 1971 to 1990, total suspended solids discharged by point sources to the Fox River declined by 91 percent. Between 1962 and 1990, biological oxygen demand loadings (a key determinant of river health) fell by 94 percent. The author concluded that "up and down the river, the story is much the same. The cleanup of industrial and municipal discharges over the past three decades has been nothing short of astonishing" (Alesch 1997, 8).

A local journalist captured the same sentiment, with a sober warning of work yet to be done:

Through the diligence of environmentalists, the force of regulators and the cooperation—sometimes reluctant—of paper mills, great strides have been made in cleaning the water in the past twenty-five years. In the summer, fishermen line its banks and boats ply its shimmering waters. Many fish and fowl, once driven out by poison and pollution, are coming home. But it's still a sick river. The Fox remains unfit for swimming and offers up more than a dozen fish species that are unsafe for human consumption. Visitors come to look but not touch. (Campbell 1997)

As is the case nationally, the remaining problems in the Fox-Wolf River Basin are largely nonpoint sources of pollution, especially nutrients and sediments, and toxic chemicals. Many of those chemicals, notably PCBs, are buried in the river's sediments and "leak" into the river through resuspension and biological uptake. They will be a major object of concern for decades to come.

A Shift in Emphasis: Cost-Effectiveness and Collaboration as Guiding Principles

As this brief assessment of progress under the Clean Water Act illustrates, the regulatory apparatus established under the act, representative of the first epoch in environmental policy, could go only so far. The laws and regulations could yield impressive gains in many areas with a high level of political commitment and strong state capacity for administration of the programs (Ringquist 1993). Yet the CWA also faced major barriers because of the high cost associated with meeting stringent water quality standards, opposition from industry and municipalities, and continued contribution to water quality problems of largely uncontrolled nonpoint sources of pollutants. Hence the appeal of the efficiency-based regulatory reforms and collaborative approaches to decision making associated with epoch two. The latter is especially promising as a new policy strategy even if not fully tested.

Both nationally and locally, proponents of collaborative decision making argue that it can replace the often highly adversarial relations between government and industry and between the federal and state governments. Collaboration involves greater participation by a diversity of stakeholders, building of trust, and a freer exchange of information. Together, these characteristics are expected to lead to a more open decision-making process, a greater commitment to achieving environmental quality goals, and consensus on how to achieve those goals. That is, the hope is that such processes can lead to agreement on the most viable solutions and the criteria that should govern choices among them, such as economic cost, technical feasibility, and social acceptability (Layzer 2008; NAPA 1995; Sabatier et al. 2005; Weber 2003). Its advocates believe such collaboration will likely yield more successful policies and programs over time, as measured by achievement of improved environmental conditions.

As is true of most new approaches to environmental policy, however, such expectations are sometimes grounded more in dissatisfaction with past policies and faith in the new efforts than they are in a documented and successful track record. Historically there have been few systematic evaluations of the EPA's environmental programs, and there is even less evidence of how well the new approaches of epoch two have been working, even as the subject remains of great interest to scholars and practitioners (Eisner 2007; Fiorino 2006; Klyza and Sousa 2008; and Morgenstern and Pizer 2007). What remains uncertain is the ease with which such a collaborative style of decision making can be established and maintained over time, and the extent to which it will help to achieve both the desired environmental quality goals and community sustainability. Chapter 10 in this volume offers an extensive review of recent work on these questions.

As will be made evident in the present case study, collaboration may work best in the early stages of the policy process—in the identification of problems, the consideration of alternative policy approaches, and the selection of the tools to be used. Such cooperative approaches may be less suitable, however, for implementation of the chosen policies—when specific action steps must be taken. Implementation success may depend on the existence of sufficient authority at the state or federal level to maintain timely progress in reaching environmental goals. Assessment of experience to date in the Fox-Wolf Basin helps to illuminate these relationships.

Emphasizing Cost-Effectiveness in the Fox-Wolf Basin

The new emphasis on cost-effectiveness as a policy strategy can be seen in the efforts of local organizations in the Fox-Wolf River Basin during the 1990s. Industries and municipalities along the lower Fox River had invested a great deal of money in technological pollution controls under the Clean Water Act, spending an estimated $300 million by 1987. The Green Bay Metropolitan Sewerage District (GBMSD) spent a considerable portion of that amount, and it was as eager as industry to find ways to minimize future costs. Both industries and municipal dischargers pressed increasingly for a different approach, and cost-effectiveness became their watchword. They were convinced that additional investments simply could not be justified on the basis of the expected benefits in water quality, which they believed could be improved only marginally if at all (Alesch 1997). They worried about how to comply with the additional controls they expected the state to impose within a decade as it continued on course to implement the CWA. They also were concerned about the likely impact on an area economy that is heavily dependent on paper making, paper recycling, meat packing, and vegetable processing, all water intensive.

In 1992 government and industry leaders established a not-for-profit corporation, Northeastern Wisconsin Waters of Tomorrow (NEWWT), to assist in developing a new strategy. NEWWT was funded in large part by the municipal sewerage district, which had assumed a major role in actions on local water pollution. The GBMSD was determined to find alternatives to expensive treatment of water problems by the district itself, the cost of which it would have to pass on to area residents. Its new relationship with NEWWT provided a possible avenue for developing such solutions. NEWWT's purpose was to search for cost-effective alternatives to conventional regulation in the watershed. It did so with the blessings of the Wisconsin Department of Natural Resources and its director, George Meyer, an appointee of the longtime Republican governor, Tommy Thompson.

NEWWT recruited a small staff, hired consultants, and developed a computer simulation of the Fox-Wolf River Basin. Of particular concern for dealing with the problem of phosphorus and suspended solids in the river basin was how interdisciplinary analysis of the watershed could improve understanding of the flow of water, nutrients, solids, and other material that affect the quality of the river and bay. Such knowledge also could help in setting pollution control targets to maximize water quality improvements. In short, such analysis was intended to answer the critical question of how citizens, industry, and the state should invest money and energy to have the greatest impact on cleaning up the river and bay.

The research team concluded that about 75 percent of the phosphorus and 90 percent of the suspended solids that reach lower Green Bay came from rural upstream sources. Economic analysis also indicated that the cost of controlling these sources would be significantly less than the alternatives (White, Baumgart, and Johnson 1995). The message could not be clearer. The biggest payoff for the least cost would come through reducing phosphorus and solids from agricultural lands entering the waters. These objectives could be met through planting of vegetation along riverbanks ("vegetative buffers") to minimize erosion, encouraging more efficient use of fertilizers and pesticides, adoption of zoning and livestock exclusion ordinances to minimize animal access to area streams, and improved management of animal wastes, among other actions.

Such efforts to address nonpoint sources of water pollution underscore the long-term and difficult challenge of improving water quality in the basin and in similar settings around the nation. Applying technology to "fix" the point discharges, the key focus of epoch one in environmental policy, can never be sufficient, and it cannot be economically efficient to continue to ratchet up the regulatory requirements on those sources. Yet dealing with the nonpoint sources will take longer and involves working with a greater diversity of people, economic enterprises, and landscapes. One report on the state of the bay tried to respond to the understandable public frustration with the painfully slow process of restoring area water quality based on this new watershed approach:

[T]here are no "fix-it" manuals for large scale ecosystems, and the economic and social matrix of our society resists change. It is not a matter of applying the right technological fix, but rather a matter of changing the whole way we count environmental costs and measure the effectiveness of expenditures. We are in that process and the learning curve is steep. It will take time to mobilize resources appropriate to the scale that is needed. The results, however, should be sustainable because we will come to see ourselves as part of a larger system, the "health" of which is necessary for our own health and economic well-being. (Harris 1994, 24)

NEWWT and GBMSD Favor Collaboration as a Strategy

The search for cost-effective solutions to local water quality problems (a key feature of epoch two in environmental policy) pushed NEWWT as well as the GBMSD to adopt a waterbasin or ecosystem perspective. In doing so, both built on previous efforts by other local groups and the WDNR itself to use an ecosystem approach in dealing with water quality problems in the area (H. Harris et al. 1982; V. Harris 1992). To better reflect this orientation, in 1994 NEWWT changed its name to Fox-Wolf Basin 2000 (FWB 2000), added members to its board of directors from across the watershed, and became the most active proponent in the region of an ecosystem-based approach to improving water quality. Although in some respects FWB 2000 was a grassroots environmental organization, it was also self-consciously dedicated to a collaborative philosophy of working closely with business and government agencies, which distinguished it from many other area environmental advocacy groups. Some of the latter were vocal opponents of FWB 2000, which they considered to be too closely aligned with area polluters. Eventually FWB 2000 evolved into the Fox-Wolf Watershed Alliance, a nonprofit organization with a broader mission of identifying issues and advocating "policies and actions to protect, restore and sustain the water resources of the Fox-Wolf River Basin."[3]

At about the same time it helped to initiate FWB 2000, the GBMSD entered into partnerships with area businesses to promote its new philosophy of pollution prevention and cost-effective approaches to water quality improvement. For example, the GBMSD cooperated with the county's solid waste department to create the state's first full-time center for collection of household hazardous waste that might otherwise have found its way into area waters. The GBMSD generally found a supportive business community that was seeking new ways to enhance its competitiveness in a global economy. Hence it was attracted to cost-effective ways to control area pollution, or to prevent it through changes in production processes (Alesch 1997).

In addition to its many other actions, the GBMSD (with help from Fox-Wolf Basin 2000) prodded the Wisconsin DNR to move more aggressively on its long-standing commitment to using a watershed approach to environmental protection, and to use the case of Northeastern Wisconsin as a pilot program for reorganization of the WDNR itself along ecosystem lines.

These changes represent the beginning of a transition from what we have called epoch two to a focus on sustainability in epoch three. Indeed, DNR Secretary Meyer himself referred to the organizational shift as a "new paradigm," and he linked it directly to other efforts within the state at that time to "cut red tape and costs" and to find alternatives to "the cumbersome, burdensome, and expensive regulatory process" (quoted in Alesch 1997, 18). Meyer suggested that the department, which is the designated agency in Wisconsin for both pollution regulation and management of natural resources, had few choices in a period in which flat budgets left it unable to get its work done without entering into such partnerships. These partnerships were attractive in part because the new partners were expected to add to the total funds available for water quality initiatives.

One of the most intriguing questions raised about these developments is whether a regulatory agency can successfully negotiate such organizational and policy changes without sacrificing the very qualities that have led to improvements in water quality since the early 1970s. That is one of the risks of deemphasizing regulatory approaches in search of more cooperative (and more politically appealing) relations in environmental policy. There is much less question that adoption of a watershed approach and a strategy of flexible, adaptive, and ecosystem-based management represents a major advancement over previous water quality regulation within the state.

The Remedial Action Plan Process as Collaborative Decision Making

One of the earliest efforts at collaborative decision making was well underway by the time the WDNR was considering reinventing itself. It concerns the work of the Lower Green Bay Remedial Action Plan (RAP) during the mid-1980s and early 1990s. The plan grew out of the Great Lakes Water Quality Agreement signed by the United States and Canada in 1972, which highlighted the need to clean up persistently polluted trouble spots or areas of concern—AOCs (Botts and Muldoon 1997; Colborn et al. 1990). One of these was the lower Green Bay and the lower Fox River.

Consistent with the agreement, an informal working group of individuals from local governments, federal agencies, businesses, and other backgrounds (including environmental scientists, citizens, and agricultural interests) met under the auspices of the WDNR to analyze area water quality problems and to set out short-term and long-term corrective measures to restore area waters (WDNR 1993). The Green Bay RAP was one of the first within the Great Lakes Basin to be completed and it has been cited widely in the region as a model for RAP development and implementation. It also has been praised for using citizen involvement and an ecosystem approach to planning and management for water quality improvement (Harris 1992).[4]

Two distinctive characteristics of the RAP merit mention. One is that it adopted a vision of the future of the river and bay rooted in a broad ecosystem view of environmental issues that is evident in both its general goals and objectives and in its specific recommendations to restore ecosystem functions. Achieving those goals would help to realize a "desired future state," in which the full beneficial uses of area waters long impaired by human activities would be restored. Thus, the RAP explicitly, and at an early date, adopted a comprehensive and integrated perspective on water quality founded on beliefs in the importance of sustainability and the tools of ecosystem-based management, consistent with environmental protection in epoch three. This view was broadly endorsed by the working group as the most sensible way to proceed. Indeed, the 1993 update of the plan incorporated specific sustainability goals "to ensure the sustainability of a restored and healthy environment through pollution prevention and the development of sustainable economies, resources, and facilities which support beneficial uses into the future" (WDNR 1993, xxii).

The second characteristic was that the RAP process illustrated well that at local and regional levels, it was indeed possible for diverse stakeholders to come together to define environmental problems and solutions, to help set priorities among competing problems, and to serve as a catalyst for action. The RAP also facilitated the integration of scientific findings and actions by both public and private sector parties, fostered and supported public education on the issues, and facilitated public participation in environmental decision making (Harris 1992). In many ways, the RAP was a successful example of collaborative decision making.

The limitations of the RAP process, however, were equally evident. Between 1988 and 1993, some 38 of the 120 recommended remedial actions were implemented. Another 57 were initiated. But most of the actions taken were relatively short-term and imposed few costs on local business and government. Achieving the more challenging goals would take much more commitment by government and business that was simply not forthcoming in the 1990s. One of the most notable omissions was an ability to deal with nonpoint sources, including toxic chemicals. As the 1993 RAP update made clear, "loads of toxic contaminants from point sources appear to be largely controlled, but nonpoint sources, including contaminated sediments [were] not reduced significantly from 1985 and are substantial, continuing pollutant sources to the AOC" (WDNR 1993, xxi). Hence it was likely that restoration of area waters would take decades of sustained commitment to pollution prevention, cleanup of contaminants, habitat enhancement, and better land-use management, among other actions.

The Problem of Contaminated Sediments: How Well Did Collaboration Work?

Among the most challenging of the tasks identified by the RAP is cleanup of contaminated sediments in the lower Fox River, which is expected to reduce the flow of persistent toxic chemicals into the bay and into Lake Michigan. The chief concern is large deposits of PCBs in the river sediments.

According to the Green Bay Mass Balance Study and other investigations, more than fifty contaminated sediment deposits exist along the lower Fox River. Most of these are just downstream of industrial outfalls. Each deposit is unique and its effect depends on hydrologic conditions, the number and types of contaminants, the extent of contamination, the composition of the sediment, and the deposit's depth, breadth, and location. The high degree of variability means that different forms of treatment or remediation may be necessary at different sites, with sharply varying costs (Harris 1994; WDNR 1993). Most of the PCBs will remain buried in the river, but depending on aquatic conditions, some portion enters the water column or is volatilized into the air and transported downstream or downwind. Because some of the deposits are at significant risk of movement, the timing of their remediation is an important issue. Once the contaminants reach the bay of Green Bay or Lake Michigan, there is no feasible way to remove or remediate them.[5]

Debate over the extent of cleanup necessary and who was to pay the high cost became so fierce that conventional regulatory processes alone had little chance of success. As was the case with achieving cost-effective cleanup of the river through targeting of nonpoint sources of pollution, removal of contaminated sediments seemed a good candidate for the use of collaborative decision making.

Many different approaches to collaboration were tried over a period of several years. For example, in 1992, the WDNR and the paper industry created a Fox River Coalition (FRC) out of concern that dealing with the sediments could easily lead to a legal morass in which local businesses would face costly action under the federal Comprehensive Environmental Response, Compensation, and Liability Act (CERCLA), better known as Superfund (Mercurio 1995). The paper mills (and local public officials) hoped that such collaboration could steer remediation toward cost-effective strategies and a combination of public and private funding. The mills also pressed for further scientific studies to help ensure, in their view, that solutions would be technically justifiable and cleanups not more stringent than necessary.

The coalition brought together some thirty "partners" to explore the technical, financial, and institutional needs for remediation of the sediments. However, the FRC decided early on against inviting environmental and conservation organizations to participate, even though they had been well represented in the earlier RAP process. Minutes of the coalition's meetings indicate that it sought to limit participation to achieve "fruitful discussion and decision making" (Johnson 1996). Ultimately, that decision undermined the credibility of the FRC, as the excluded environmental interests became vocal critics of the process. The FRC had limited success as well because members adopted a consensus style of decision making that in effect meant that any member could "veto" a proposal through a strongly voiced objection. The result was what some observers characterized as a seemingly endless discussion of issues that produced no definitive decisions to take action (ibid.).

The WDNR's summary of the coalition's actions described it as a "national model for successful environmental restoration" and "Wisconsin's greatest hope for achieving successful river restoration in the shortest time possible" (Mercurio 1995, ii). Even the coalition's most fervent supporters conceded that progress was slow, yet they also endorsed this kind of collaboration as a new mold for "a cooperative, nonadversarial approach to the problem" (Alesch 1997, 20). At a minimum, the FRC seemed to help build trust and a good working relationship among the paper mills, the municipal sewage treatment plants, the Oneida Indian Tribe (whose lands lie within the river basin), and state and local government officials—if not local environmental groups. These relationships continued in the late 1990s and early 2000s despite the end of the formal FRC process, and they helped to facilitate later negotiations over cleanup actions.

If the FRC illustrates the potential for local collaboration, other actions in the mid-1990s served as a reminder that federal and state agencies retained considerable regulatory authority. Both the U.S. Fish and Wildlife Service (FWS) and the EPA injected new expectations into the process that spurred more definitive action. The FWS decided to pursue a Natural Resource Damage Assessment (NRDA) as allowed under the Superfund program. An NRDA investigates, evaluates, and quantifies injuries to natural resources, and calculates the amount of monetary damages that can be assessed on responsible parties and used to restore the resources.

The NRDA was favored by local environmental groups as a more dependable way than use of collaborative decision making to resolve the issues and force cleanup of the river. Yet it was by no means clear that the NRDA could achieve those goals. Nonetheless, the threat of an FWS lawsuit based on the damage assessment prodded the FRC to move more deliberately on the technical tasks of assessing the sediment removal problem and available options.

The EPA's intervention in 1997 was perhaps the most decisive action in moving the key policy actors toward a solution. In June of that year, the agency announced that the slow pace of cleanup forced it to seek the state's support for placement of the river on the Superfund National Priorities List (NPL). Agency officials believed that Superfund proceedings could speed up the cleanup process, a concern that they indicated was heightened because lower Fox received a high score on a preliminary assessment of risk to public health and the environment. That measure put it on a par with PCB-related Superfund sites on the Hudson River in New York, the Kalamazoo River in Michigan, and the Sheboygan River in Wisconsin.

State and local government officials and representative of the paper mills were unimpressed. They denounced the EPA action and continued to praise a "public-private partnership" as the model to follow. In contrast, area environmentalists applauded the EPA decision, saying that listing the site would hasten cleanup of the river and force the polluters to pay.

In July 1998, the EPA formally proposed listing the lower Fox River on the Superfund's NPL, arguing that "the site poses very serious human health and ecological risks which are not being adequately addressed"

(Campbell 1998). The agency accepted public comments on its proposal, amid much local concern that a Superfund designation would be a severe stigma on the community and region and would harm economic prospects. The EPA continued to insist, however, that even with a Superfund listing, negotiations over a voluntary cleanup plan between the state and the paper mills would continue. Such an agreement could be reached at any time, officials argued. Moreover, the state, rather than the EPA, would play the lead role.

The relatively high cost of cleanup was a major stumbling block in these negotiations, with estimates ranging from about $600 million to over $2 billion, depending on the technology used and the extent of the cleanup. By 1999, the WDNR released a new study that lowered the estimated costs for "feasible" cleanup alternatives for the river alone (excluding the bay) to between $150 million and $728 million (WDNR 1999). With so much riding on the decisions, the paper mills wanted to defer large-scale cleanup; they also argued repeatedly that the PCBs posed no significant risk to public health and that dredging of the sediments was neither a proven technology nor cost effective. They believed that many of the sediments could be capped and left in place. The consensus of area scientists and agency technical staff, however, was that removal of nearly all of the PCBs from the lower Fox was essential for both human and ecological health.

The EPA never proceeded with the formal Superfund designation, but chose to implement the cleanup plan under Superfund law on an informal basis. Essentially, the EPA used its political clout to push the various parties to come to agreement on a cleanup plan. The EPA and the WDNR worked cooperatively and published a proposed Remedial Action Plan in October 2001, listing various cleanup options. It followed evaluation of several demonstration cleanup projects and a number of public meetings. Finally, the agencies issued two Records of Decision (RODs) in June 2003 that spelled out the necessary actions to remove PCB-contaminated sediment from the riverbed in all areas with concentrations above one part per million. Local environmental groups consistently argued that the cleanup standard was too weak, but other stakeholders considered the final RODs to require fairly demanding cleanup actions that would substantially reduce the environmental and health risks posed by PCBs in the sediments.[6]

Some hydrologic dredging began in 2005, and at one point it involved the removal of about 1,000 cubic yards of sediment each day, with crews working around the clock. The cleanup plan also calls for "monitored natural recovery" in some areas where no dredging would take place, and some areas may be capped rather than dredged if cost and risk estimates justify such actions, such as for deposits close to shorelines or near utilities where dredging could cause damage. Capping involves the use of gravel and sand covers designed to hold the sediments in place.

In June 2007, the WDNR approved a modification to the ROD that would allow greater emphasis on capping of sediments in place and somewhat less reliance on their removal through dredging. The action was strongly favored by the paper companies as more cost effective and opposed by environmentalists and area scientists as providing no lasting solutions given the possibility that the caps might not hold the sediments adequately, particularly under conditions of high water flow.

Even with this significant change, throughout 2007 the WDNR continued to negotiate with the companies over an appropriate financial settlement for the river cleanup, without much success. Moreover, the agency had no firm agreement on a local landfill site to accept the sediments. Those being removed from cleanup actions in 2007 were being sent by truck to a Detroit, Michigan, site that was approved for toxic waste disposal. By November, the EPA and the U.S. Department of Justice, with agreement from the WDNR, finally ordered the paper companies to find a landfill, prepare the area to receive dewatered sediment, and start dredging the most contaminated sections of the river by 2009. Bruce Baker, deputy administrator for the WDNR's Division of Water, characterized the outcome as a disappointment in light of the years of effort to encourage collaborative decision making. On the day the order was announced, Baker said: "The project is no longer a cooperative operation" (Walter 2007). Disputes also continued between the paper mills and their insurance companies over financial responsibility, with one trial in 2008 finding the insurance companies liable for a good portion of the cleanup costs for one of the seven mills involved. Other trials are expected to begin in 2009.

Even when the cleanup is completed, it is likely to be decades before current health advisories for eating fish from the river will be removed. If negotiations with the paper companies over cleanup design, construction, and financial responsibilities are unsuccessful at any time, the companies may still use the courts to resolve remaining conflicts. Doing so might well add to what is already expected to be a long-term series of actions to clean up and eventually restore the river to its former quality.

Conclusions

The Fox-Wolf Basin case illustrates the challenges that most communities and regions face as they attempt to move toward the long-term goal of sustainability. The 1970s-era environmental protection policies have accomplished much, as control of point sources and improved water quality in the Fox River Basin clearly attest. Yet further progress requires adjustment in those policy strategies to enhance society's capacity to deal with the more intractable problems of nonpoint sources, such as runoff from agricultural lands and the river sediments contaminated with PCBs. The high cost and economic impacts on communities of cleanup actions propel the search for cost-effective means and for ways to encourage cooperation between the public and private sectors. Such cooperation can also help to build the mutual trust and consensus that are essential for creating sustainable communities.

The case reported on in this chapter traces the evolution of water quality issues across two of the epochs introduced in chapter 1, and the beginning of the third. It highlights the important efforts at collaborative decision making about water quality issues in Northeastern Wisconsin, a state long considered to be among the most environmentally progressive in the nation. The work of the Remedial Action Plan and the Fox River Coalition is a story of both success and failure. Public-private partnerships were formed, and they helped to establish effective working relations among business officials, state and local policymakers, scientists, environmentalists, and community leaders. Regional water quality problems were thoroughly investigated by the Green Bay RAP and the Mass Balance Study, and, using collaborative and consensual approaches, action agendas were developed to restore damaged ecosystems and protect public health.

Yet cooperation and voluntary cleanup programs, especially those directed at contaminated sediments, could go only so far in light of the high costs of remediation, ill-defined goals, and limited public understanding of the issues. Scientific knowledge by itself could not drive the cleanup process. Support by policymakers, the public, and industry was crucial for success. Without it, neither the RAP process nor the FRC could achieve its goals. After five years of extensive discussion and negotiation, the FRC's public-private partnership resulted in only a modest tangible commitment to cleaning up the river—primarily the agreement to provide $10 million to initiate remediation at two demonstration sites. The major constraints that so limited this process seemed to be a reluctance to pay the high price of cleanup and continuing doubts that the anticipated ecological and health benefits could justify doing so. Under these conditions, the threat of intervention by the EPA and FWS acting under the authority of Superfund helped to spur negotiations over a final cleanup agreement that may lead to some degree of restoration of the area's once pristine waters, but only slowly.

The inability of collaborative and consensual decision making to fully replace conventional command-and-control approaches does not imply, of course, that it has little value. The years of cooperation between business and government and other stakeholders in the region helped to build mutual understanding and trust that will be vital to achieving community and regional sustainability in the future. Equally important is the contribution that such collaboration can make to building public trust and confidence in regional water quality decision making. Of course, if the extended negotiations between the paper companies and the WDNR and EPA fail to lead to firm cleanup commitments, the public may well become disenchanted with the process. The initial broad-based collaboration in this case eventually narrowed considerably by the 2000s to behind-the-scenes meetings between paper companies and the agencies that inspired little confidence among other stakeholders.

Despite this outcome in the long-delayed cleanup of the river, by 2008, a number of interrelated actions in the region hinted at the emergence of epoch three thinking. Local policymakers, citizen groups, and business leaders increasingly began using the language of sustainability. Most of the communities in the region adopted twenty-year land-use plans as a result of a state smart growth policy that required such planning—and they did so through an open and highly participatory process. In the late 1990s the region hosted several conferences on the theme of a sustainable community, and by 2007, the mayor of Green Bay established a Sustainable Green Bay Initiative that touted "collaboration of business leaders, government officials, non-profit organizations and citizens" who were "committed to making Green Bay a more vibrant, resource-efficient and sustainable community."

With respect to the water quality issues themselves, the outcomes in this case suggest that collaboration among community stakeholders works best when diverse parties are seeking agreement on general cleanup goals—particularly as they deal with the inherent uncertainty of environmental and health risks and the anticipated costs of cleanup. This approach to decision making may be less suitable when consensus cannot be easily achieved on specific cleanup schedules, the means to be used, and the allocation of costs—and where participants believe they will benefit from deferring decisions. Under these conditions, the continuing presence of stringent federal environmental laws and standards, such as those embodied in the Clean Water Act and Superfund, complements and reinforces a collaborative decision-making process. In the case of the Fox-Wolf Basin, federal intervention promised to end what had become protracted discussion and delay, and it created a new opportunity for negotiation and agreement on the cleanup of the river.

This experience suggests that hybrid policies and planning processes may be needed to spur community sustainability in epoch three of the modern environmental era. For example, the best aspects of a regulatory framework could be combined with market-based approaches, public-private collaboration, and public education on the issues. Communities could be given sufficient time to resolve local problems on their own through cooperative processes before more formal regulatory requirements, from the federal or state government, take effect. The challenge for each community, region, and state is to design and implement its own distinctive blend of policies and plans that best promises to inspire, support, and nourish a transition toward sustainability. Such a transition also requires a financial strategy to match the policy strategy, and a genuine commitment by the business community to moving forward.

Notes

1. Some portions of the Fox River case study in the first edition of this book drew from Bruce N. Johnson's master's thesis at Northern Illinois University (Johnson 1996), and he was good enough to read over and contribute to portions of the larger chapter as a coauthor. The current version of the chapter relies much less on that case history. It also draws in part from an abbreviated version of the study published in *Public Works Management and Policy* in 2006.

2. A fuller account of these estimates can be found on the WDNR Web site for the Fox River cleanup project: http://dnr.wi.gov/org/water/wm/foxriver/.

3. The quotation comes from the Fox-Wolf Watershed Alliance Web page: http://www.fwwa.org/index.htm, accessed November 7, 2007.

4. As one sign of the breadth of representation, the Citizen Advisory Committee of the initial RAP comprised representatives of business, industry, environmental groups, sports and boating organizations, agriculture, shoreline residents, and local government agencies. Many other groups were involved with the technical advisory committees as well.

5. The Wisconsin DNR Web site for the Fox River cleanup effort, cited in note 2, provides exhaustive detail on the scientific studies, risk assessments, and the various actions recommended and taken over the years.

6. In addition to the formal public comment process that applied to the cleanup plan, natural and social scientists and federal, state, and local agency personnel from the region commented on it through an informal Science and Technical Advisory Committee (STAC) that was a holdover from the Green Bay RAP committees. Whereas the RAP operated under the auspices of the DNR, by the early 2000s the STAC had no formal authority. Nevertheless, it continued to meet to offer technical advice through the kind of collaborative process described in the chapter. I have served as a member of the STAC since 1991.

References

Adler, Robert W. 1993. "Water Resources: Revitalizing the Clean Water Act." *Environment* 35 (November): 4–5, 40.

Alesch, Daniel J. 1997. "New Strategies for Environmental Problems in Wisconsin: Breaking Out of the Box." *Wisconsin Policy Institute Report* 10, 2 (February): 1–26.

Botts, Lee, and Paul Muldoon. 1997. *The Great Lakes Water Quality Agreement: Its Past Successes and Uncertain Future*. Hanover, NH: Institute on International Environmental Governance, March.

Campbell, Susan. 1997. "Future of Fox River at Stake." *Green Bay Press-Gazette*, September 14, 1.

Campbell, Susan. 1998. "Fox Proposed for Superfund: Potential Remains for Voluntary Cleanup." *Green Bay Press-Gazette*, July 10, A1–2.

Colborn, Theodora E., Alex Davidson, Sharon N. Green, R. A. (Tom) Hodge, C. Ian Jackson, and Richard A. Liroff. 1990. *Great Lakes, Great Legacy?* Washington, D.C.: Conservation Foundation.

Council on Environmental Quality (CEQ). 1997. *Environmental Quality: Twenty-fifth Anniversary Report*. Washington, D.C.: CEQ.

Davies, J. Clarence, and Jan Mazurek. 1998. *Pollution Control in the United States: Evaluating the System*. Washington, D.C.: Resources for the Future.

Eisner, Marc Allen. 2007. *Governing the Environment: The Transformation of Environmental Regulation*. Boulder, CO: Lynne Rienner.

Fiorino, Daniel J. 2006. *The New Environmental Regulation*. Cambridge, MA: MIT Press.

Freeman, A. Myrick III. 2000. "Water Pollution Policy." In *Public Policies for Environmental Protection*, ed. Paul R. Portney and Robert N. Stavins, 169–213. Washington, D.C.: Resources for the Future.

Harris, Gardiner. 2008. "Health Report Raises Dispute Over Great Lakes Pollution." *New York Times*, March 3, A15.

Harris, Hallett J. 1994. *The State of the Bay, 1993: A Watershed Perspective.* Green Bay, WI: University of Wisconsin-Green Bay Institute for Land and Water Studies, August.

Harris, Hallett J., Daniel R. Talhelm, John J. Magnuson, and Anne M. Forbes. 1982. "Green Bay in the Future—A Rehabilitative Prospectus." Ann Arbor, MI: Great Lakes Fishery Commission, September.

Harris, Hallett J., Robert B. Wenger, Victoria A. Harris, and David S. Devault. 1994. "A Method for Assessing Environmental Risk: A Case Study of Green Bay, Lake Michigan." *Environmental Management* 18, 2: 295–306.

Harris, Victoria A. 1992. "From Plan to Action: The Green Bay Experience." In *Under Raps: Toward Grassroots Ecological Democracy in the Great Lakes Basin*, ed. John H. Hartig and Michael A. Zarull, 37–58. Ann Arbor: University of Michigan Press.

Johnson, Bruce N. 1996. "A Case Study of the Fox River Coalition: An 'Innovative' Approach to Contaminated Sediment Remediation in the Lower Fox River." De Kalb, IL: Department of Political Science, Northern Illinois University, unpublished paper.

Knopman, Debra S, and Richard A. Smith. 1993. "Twenty Years of the Clean Water Act." *Environment* 35 (January–February): 17–20, 34–41.

Klyza, Christopher McGrory, and David J. Sousa. 2008. *American Environmental Policy, 1990–2006: Beyond Gridlock*. Cambridge, MA: MIT Press.

Kraft, Michael E. 2007. *Environmental Policy and Politics*, 4th ed. New York: Pearson Longman.

Layzer, Judith. 2008. *Natural Experiments: Ecosystem Management and the Environment*. Cambridge, MA: MIT Press.

Mercurio, Jo. 1995. "The Fox River Coalition: A Regional Partnership Dedicated to Cleaning up Contaminated Sediment and Improving Water Quality in the Fox Valley." Madison: Department of Natural Resources, WR-382-95.

Morgenstern, Richard D., and William A. Pizer, eds. 2007. *Reality Check: The Nature and Performance of Voluntary Environmental Programs in the United States, Europe, and Japan*. Washington, D.C.: RFF Press.

National Academy of Public Administration (NAPA). 1995. *Setting Priorities, Getting Results: A New Direction for EPA*. Washington, D.C.: NAPA.

Ringquist, Evan J. 1993. *Environmental Protection at the State Level: Politics and Progress in Controlling Pollution*. Armonk, NY: M. E. Sharpe.

Sabatier, Paul A., Will Focht, Mark Lubell, Zev Trachtenberg, Arnold Vedlitz, and Marty Matlock, eds. 2005. *Swimming Upstream: Collaborative Approaches to Watershed Management*. Cambridge, MA: MIT Press.

Sullivan, John R., and Joseph J. Delfino. 1982. "A Select Inventory of Chemicals Used in Wisconsin's Lower Fox River Basin." Madison, WI: University of Wisconsin, Sea Grant Institute.

U.S. Environmental Protection Agency. 2007. *National Water Quality Inventory: Report to Congress, 2002 Reporting Cycle.* Washington, D.C.: EPA, Office of Water.

Walter, Tony. 2007. "EPA Orders Start to Fox River Cleanup." *Green Bay Press-Gazette,* November 14, A-1, A-7.

Weber, Edward P. 2003. *Bringing Society Back In: Grassroots Ecosystem Management, Accountability, and Sustainable Communities.* Cambridge, MA: MIT Press.

White, David, Baumgart, Paul, and Bruce Johnson, eds. 1995. "Toward a Cost-Effective Approach to Water Resource Management in the Fox-Wolf River Basin: A First Cut Analysis." Green Bay: Northeast Wisconsin Waters of Tomorrow.

Wisconsin Department of Natural Resources (WDNR). 1988. *Lower Green Bay Remedial Action Plan for the Lower Fox River and Lower Green Bay Area of Concern.* Madison, WI: WDNR, PUBL-WR-175-87 Rev 88, February.

Wisconsin Department of Natural Resources (WDNR). 1993. *Lower Green Bay Remedial Action Plan 1993 Update for the Lower Green Bay and Fox Area of Concern.* Madison, WI: WDNR, September.

Wisconsin Department of Natural Resources (WDNR). 1999. *Draft Remedial Investigation, Risk Assessment, and Feasibility Study for the Lower Fox River.* Madison, WI: WDNR, March.

6

Local Open Space Preservation in the United States

Daniel Press and Nicole Nakagawa

A central premise of sustainability is that good land, in sufficient amount and of suitable quality, needs to be passed down from generation to generation. Good land is used for many purposes—agriculture, industry, housing, transportation, recreation, watershed protection, and habitat—and more destructive and irreversible uses clearly prevent future generations from putting land to its optimal, long-run use.

Communities at the municipal and county level exercise tremendous influence on land use within their jurisdictions, and thus one important dimension of any community's sustainability is its ability to preserve land in agriculture, open space, and wildlife habitat, which, in effect, helps preserve long-run options and uses. Also, green spaces, parks, forests, and farms provide an immediate connection to the places where people live. Open space also has an aesthetic appeal. Thus, land preservation is one of the most enduring and rewarding commitments a community can make to future generations.

Looking back on how and why some communities succeed in preserving open space provides valuable insight into the opportunities and constraints faced in the movement toward sustainability. Scholars, social critics, and activists interested in the sustainability of communities can benefit from systematically identifying those communities that are in some way implementing sustainable land-use practices. In this chapter, we examine national trends in local open space preservation, focusing especially on how—or whether—these evolved during the environmental policy epochs described at the outset of this volume.

Although local preservation can refer to the whole suite of land-use tools available to communities (land acquisition, conservation easements, growth limits, zoning, tax incentives), we focus this chapter on land or easement acquisitions, leaving the discussion of "smart growth" and regional planning to chapters 7 and 9. By "local," we refer to substate activities, occurring in cities, counties, and regions, and involving both public and private entities. It's also increasingly apparent that communities differ enormously with respect to their willingness and ability—or "policy capacity" (Press 2002)—to protect local lands, so we also synthesize lessons learned about local preservation successes and failures in the sustainable communities movement.

Community Land Preservation: Recent Trends

Most Americans, especially in the West, think of the federal government as the primary protector and provider of open space held in trust for the public. While the states have always enjoyed substantial holdings (also highest in the West), their parks agencies began making significant acquisitions at the end of the nineteenth century. Many urban residents benefit from substantial local open-space preservation, but don't realize that, in some states, these holdings rival state park systems in their acreage and quality. Ironically, local preservation may "fly below the radar" but can also constitute some of the most valuable and expensive properties protected (publicly or privately), because they are so close to growing urban areas.

Extensive local open-space preservation is a relatively recent phenomenon. The first half of the twentieth century saw slow, steady local land acquisitions, primarily for recreation purposes, often with the state government providing major funding. As the first epoch of the environmental movement swept through the country in the 1960s, local, state, and federal funds for local open-space preservation grew tremendously. Local governments exercised a newfound boldness to regulate on behalf of environmental interests, but this period was to be a short-lived—from about the early 1960s to the early 1980s—ending with the passage of antitax measures in several states (e.g., California's Proposition 13 in 1978 and Massachusetts's Proposition 2 1/2 in 1980). Epoch two strategies emerged out of necessity, beginning in the mid-1980s, when communities were compelled to greatly increase their reliance on public-private partnerships for conservation. This was a time when the federal government dramatically decreased its support for land acquisition, leaving a gap to be filled by local or state governments and private land trusts (Fairfax et al. 2005). Meanwhile, public and private actors alike have become more innovative at cultivating public support for open-space preservation.

Open-space activity over the last ten to twenty years represents a new era, mostly in the sheer number of preservation efforts going on around the country. Between 1988 and 2008, 76 percent of land conservation ballot measures were successful resulting in passage of 1,595 ballot measures (meeting the majority or supermajority vote requirements in their communities) and raising over $46 billion for local open-space preservation.[1] As impressive as this sum may be, it almost certainly does not represent the full extent of local conservation expenditures—these data come from the Trust for Public Land's "LandVote" database, which does not track special district votes and budgets (TPL 2008). Adding in special districts would surely increase these figures by several billion dollars (California alone has over 100 special park and recreation districts, some of which have extensive holdings).

Using data from the Land Trust Alliance (Land Trust Alliance 2007), table 6.1 shows that the mid-Atlantic states passed the largest number of measures (595) between 1988 and 2007, but communities in the West (mostly in California and Colorado) raised the largest amount of money (about $14.7 billion), even though they faced the lowest approval rate (51 percent). That approval rate probably reflects the strong dampening

Table 6.1
Conservation Bonds by Region, 1988–2007

Region	Number of Measures on Ballots	Measures Approved	Approval Rate	Funds Raised
West	183	94	51%	$14.7 billion
Southwest	137	122	89%	$3.4 billion
Rocky Mountain	176	134	76%	$3.7 billion
Southeast	197	154	78%	$5.2 billion
Midwest	265	184	69%	$4.4 billion
New England	410	301	73%	$1 billion
Mid-Atlantic	721	595	82%	$13.2 billion
Total	2089	1584	76%	$46 billion

Source: Trust for Public Land, 2007

effect that antitax measures (also known as TABOR—Taxpayer Bill of Rights—measures) in California, Colorado and Oregon have had on ballot finance measures for open space.[2]

California and New Jersey offer further regional patterns that dramatically highlight differences in taxation constraints and acquisition opportunities. Over the last thirty years, voters in these two states together funded close to half of all the successful open-space measures in TPL's LandVote database. But Californians, constrained by formidable supermajority requirements for bonds passed at the local level, raised nearly three quarters of their funding from state bonds, which require only simple majorities. Voters in New Jersey raised less than half their open-space funds from state bonds. Moreover, residents of the Garden State use local ballot measures far more often (and for much smaller acquisition projects) than Californians. In effect, New Jerseyites used relatively easy simple majority voting rules to purchase small properties in and surrounding scores of townships. Californians purchased much larger, more expensive properties, often for use by the extensive state park system.

Federal grants for state or local preservation have not equaled these levels in decades. Although the U.S. Department of Agriculture makes substantial conservation payments to farmers (generally between $2 billion and $5 billion per year), far less is granted annually specifically for nonfarm open space. One of the most important sources of federal funding for parkland acquisition has been the federal Land and Water Conservation Fund (LWCF). This fund, created in 1964, relies mostly on royalties from oil and gas leases on the Outer Continental Shelf. Although the federal government makes grants to states, these often regrant substantial portions of the fund to cities, counties, and special districts, often on a competitive basis.

Allocations to states declined precipitously between the early 1980s and 2000. The LWCF took in about $29 billion between 1964 and 2006, but only $15 billion dollars have been used, nationally, for park and habitat acquisition (Vincent 2006). The all-time high was around 1977–1978, when Congress approved about $800 million per year for parks and national preserves; since the early 1980s, Congress has spent $100 million to $300 million per year for parks and preserves, though the fund actually stopped making state grants altogether for a few years during the 104th and 105th Congresses of the late 1990s. After a spike in state allocations from 2001 to 2005 (when states received between $90 million and $140 million), the fund has provided less than $30 million, overall, for land acquisition. Thus, by way of comparison, from 1988 to 2006, when states and communities raised about $36 billion for land preservation, federal grants to states equaled $762 million, about 2 percent of the state and local totals.

Do these preservation trends mean that urban sprawl and development are slowing, or are we actually adding to the nation's "conservation estate" (lands under some kind of formal protection) while losing open space and farm acreage to development? The answer necessarily varies depending on where in the country we look, but nationally, urban land area quadrupled between 1945 and 2002, with steady increases of about 8 million to 13 million acres per year.[3] Meanwhile, cropland decreased 14 million acres (about 3 percent) between 1977 and 2002 (Lubowski et al. 2006), so, by these measures we are not appreciably decreasing the country's rate of urbanization. According to the National Resources Inventory (NRCS 2007), the greatest increases in "developed land" over the last 25 years occurred in California, the Great Lakes (2.2 million acres more, 1982–2002), New England and the mid-Atlantic states (4.9 million more), and the South, around the Gulf of Mexico.

The Growth Machine Meets the Open Space Network

In 1976, the urban sociologist Harvey Molotch aptly termed local land-use institutions as "growth machines" (Molotch 1976). This intuitive, catchy moniker perfectly conveyed how city councils, county boards, and planning commissions design their land-use policies to attract growth—for tax revenues and local development goals. Cities, towns, and counties find themselves caught in a growth spiral, approving more development to raise funds for the schools, sewers, police, and parks that new housing tracts and strip malls inevitably demand. The growth machine is never sated, especially if local governments cannot raise adequate revenues because of TABOR or other antitax measures. Indeed, careful urban development and redevelopment studies demonstrate that most residential growth costs more (in some cases resulting in 10 percent fiscal deficits) than it brings in (Burchell and Mukherji 2003; Fausold and Lilieholm 1999). So why do cities and counties keep sprawling? First, because the largest contributions to local elections come from developers; second, because local officials get caught in a kind of Ponzi scheme, approving new developments whose tax revenues are adequate to pay for existing infrastructure and service needs, but not those required by the newest projects (Press 2002).

In some cases, local open-space preservation succeeds as a response to rampant development and sprawl. In some parts of the country, local policy entrepreneurs put so much effort into building networks, institutions, and rules to counter the growth machine that they, in effect, create enduring preservation machines or "open space networks," which are excellent examples of epoch three environmental governance.

In their excellent history of U.S. land acquisition, Fairfax et al. (2005) persuasively show that there's not much new under the sun in this policy domain. Americans have always been opportunistic and creative when it came to protecting their landscapes. That said, preservation in the early twenty-first century is not just an updated replicate of the early twentieth century. Today's open space networks build on what preceded them, by (1) increasing preservation activity, (2) using a greater diversity of policy tools, and (3) blurring the formal relationships between governments at all levels, between public and private institutions, and land ownership types (e.g., easements or fee simple).

A Critical Mass

In epoch one, local open-space preservation was pursued in more of a "top-down" fashion than it is today; elites (in and out of government, but generally in leadership positions) and technocrats were mainly responsible for initiating open-space preservation efforts, while implementation was left largely to regional and state managers. Conservation funds of any real importance were appropriated and distributed far from the preservation sites, with minimal input from local interests.

Such a system involved relatively few actors. A few members of the state legislature, a member of Congress, and one or two agency officials could arrange for a federal budgetary earmark to allocate considerable land acquisition funds to a region, county, city, or township. Consider, for example, how California allocated park bond money in 1964 versus 2006. Proposition 1, the "State Beach, Park, Recreational, and Historical Facilities Bond Act of 1964"—a state law one page long—allocated $150 million to various state and local agencies and named only two individuals with any responsibility or authority to spend the funds: the administrator of the Resources Agency and the director of the Department of Parks and Recreation. Looking forward to Proposition 84, a $5.5 billion

Table 6.2
Land Trusts on the Web

Land Trust Alliance	www.lta.org
Directories of local land trusts	www.ltanet.org/findlandtrust/
The Nature Conservancy	www.nature.org
The Trust for Public Land	www.tpl.org

bond act, entitled the "Safe Drinking Water, Water Quality and Supply, Flood Control, River and Coastal Protection Bond Act of 2006," named twenty-one individuals, departments, and conservancies in eight pages of small print. The inclusion of more decision makers directly correlates with the increasing complexity and specificity of these bond acts.

The numbers and roles of nongovernmental organizations have changed as well. For example, in 1982, the Land Trust Exchange (later, the Land Trust Alliance [LTA], a national clearinghouse based in Washington, D.C.) counted 400 land trusts active in the United States with an annual operating budget of just a few million dollars (Land Trust Exchange 1985). By 2006, that figure had risen to about 1,700 land trusts with annual operating budgets of over $400 million and endowments topping $1 billion. Land trusts now employ or involve 6,000 professional staff, over 90,000 volunteers and 15,000 dedicated board members (Land Trust Alliance 2006, 2007). According to the 2006 Annual Report of the LTA, land trusts were responsible for protecting some 37 million acres nationally, an area the Land Trust Alliance likes to compare to the size of New England (Land Trust Alliance 2007).

Like public open-space efforts, land trust activities are not uniformly distributed, as the LTA points out:

The states with the highest total acres conserved are California, Maine, Colorado, Montana, Virginia, New York, Vermont, New Mexico, Pennsylvania and Massachusetts. Notably, Colorado and Virginia are two of the few states offering a state tax incentive for conservation, operating in tandem with the federal incentive—a likely factor in the rankings. (Land Trust Alliance 2006)

A Changing Toolkit

In addition to a dramatic increase in the volume of local open-space activity, the policy tools employed by major players continue to change in fluid, innovative ways. During epoch two, local land trusts, park districts, and conservation organizations sought public-private partner-ships for open-space preservation, often relying on tax incentives and conservation easements instead of outright (and expensive) land acquisi-tion, the method of choice in epoch one.

While acquisition can be the surest way to remove a developable property from future threats, it is an expensive strategy. Currently, parks and open space authorities routinely pay $5,000 to $100,000 per acre for new acquisitions, expensive, desirable parcels that are attrac-tive precisely because they are close to rapidly expanding cities and towns. Moreover, land acquisition and management costs have gone up tremendously, much faster than the growth of local parks and open-space agency budgets (Press 2002). As costs have soared, local governments and nongovernmental organizations have turned to other conservation options, including special area zoning, transferable devel-opment rights (TDRs, in which development options are spatially shifted) and conservation easements (in which development rights are donated or sold by landowners). In 2006, the Land Trust Alliance reported that

Local and state land trusts increased the acres protected by conservation ease-ments by 148 percent. These private, voluntary agreements saved 6,245,969 acres as of 2005, versus 2,514,566 just five years ago. Easements allow land-owners to take advantage of IRS approved tax incentives. The use of such ease-ments has been on the rise for more than a decade. Easements are sometimes the only way family farmers can afford to conserve their working farm, ranch or timber lands. (Land Trust Alliance 2006)

Although these methods of conservation tend to be less expensive than outright purchase, they have their own limitations. Special area zoning, for example, regulates development rights in order to promote a wide range of public interest goals, including sensitive or riparian habitat protection, agricultural land preservation, erosion control, and watershed management, to name only a few. It is the most contro-versial of the alternatives to outright purchase, relying as it does on the private sector to bear the costs of preservation—hearkening back, in fact, to epoch one command-and-control regulation. Furthermore, a change in city councils or boards of supervisors can quickly undo these protections.

TDR negotiations tend to go smoothly only if there are relatively abundant and uncontroversial sites to transfer development—which is not the case with the many TDRs involving sensitive habitats (usually wetlands). Conservation easements can offer attractive "income and estate tax deductions equal to the value of the development rights retired" (Wright 1994), but landowners are often reluctant to give up development rights in perpetuity. Purchasing development rights for conservation easements can be quite expensive, to the point of negating the potential savings of buying the rights separate from the land. In the case of donated and purchased conservation easements, the transaction costs (time, energy, legal counsel) of negotiating agreements among landowners, conservation groups, and local governments can be quite high (Fairfax and Guenzler 2001). Finally, the public's interest in granting tax relief to properties encumbered by easements is not well served unless there is some transparency to the easement terms and their enforcement (Morris, forthcoming).

Nonetheless, the numerous land trusts that sprang up around the country during the last twenty years, as epoch two thinking and strategies took hold, have provided precisely the sorts of resources needed to overcome the transaction costs of negotiating conservation easements and purchased development rights. One of the largest purchased development rights agreements in the nation was negotiated in 1996 by the Monterey County Board of Supervisors, the Big Sur Land Trust, and a landowner with a substantial coastal ranch. The Monterey County Board of Supervisors used $11.5 million of state bond act funds, leftover from Proposition 70 of 1988, to purchase the development rights to 3,550 acres of the El Sur Ranch (Rogers 1996).

Open-Space Governance

Daniel Mazmanian and Michael Kraft suggest that, in epoch three, "collaboration and cooperation among all affected stakeholders and incentive-based methods of policy implementation are promoted as the preferred approaches for both philosophical and instrumental reasons" (this vol., p. 25). These are *networking* and *governance* approaches to policymaking, and they very accurately characterize the relationships forming today between an ever widening set of open-space stakeholders.

As an example, consider a local community wishing to expand its park services or acquisitions, launch a new open-space district, or complete an assessment of its open-space resources and needs. In epoch one, such tasks would have fallen to the local town aldermen, city counselors, or planning commissions. Depending on their local capacities, these institutions would either forgo such tasks, deeming them too complex or expensive, or would take them on as best they could, possibly learning "from scratch" along the way. Beginning in epoch two (during the mid- to late-1980s), NGOs that had specialized narrowly on land deals began to transform themselves into what some are calling "conservation organizations," often with help from national organizations.

The best example is the Trust for Public Land (TPL). Traditionally, TPL brokered land deals, leveraged multiple funding sources, and "flipped" properties, often from private owners to (slower-moving) public agencies. Today, TPL spends much of its time on epoch three approaches, especially at the local level. In addition to providing extensive information about land preservation (including the LandVote database described earlier), TPL develops local policy capacity by providing important services to communities that they might not otherwise have the expertise or resources to secure on their own. Drawing on a city or county's own statistics, TPL conducts detailed, tailored feasibility analyses resulting in reports that include a local (1) fiscal portrait (budget, bonded indebtedness, debt ceilings, bond ratings, and taxable assessed valuations), (2) menu of conservation finance options (constitutional and statutory provisions, property tax, parcel tax, general obligation bonds, districts as financing mechanisms, special districts and identification of current tax limits), and (3) election analysis (voter turnout and election results for recent fiscal questions, such as bond issues or tax increases, all at the relevant jurisdiction). Importantly, TPL provides these feasibility reports free of charge. If a community finds the feasibility report encouraging, TPL then helps local leaders assess voter support through extensive polling followed by mobilization. These mobilization efforts are called "green printing," and involve multiple community meetings and strategy sessions that encourage residents to articulate their own conservation preferences.

TPL is not alone in these sorts of efforts. In California, the Institute for Local Government, the nonprofit research arm of the California League of Cities, provides comprehensive reports, such as the sophisticated "Funding Open Space Acquisition Programs" manual (Institute for Local Government 2007).

Even private philanthropy approaches conservation differently. For example, the David and Lucile Packard Foundation, one of the country's largest, launched an ambitious, $175 million, five-year program, the

Conserving California Landscape Initiative (CCLI) in 1998. While CCLI paid for traditional land acquisitions in California's Central Coast, Central Valley and Sierra Nevada, the program followed a "strategic giving" or "venture philanthropy" philosophy, "(a) targeting specific geographical regions and NGOs, (b) grant leveraging, (c) promoting conservation partnerships, (d) capacity building of NGOs, and (e) employing a multidimensional approach to conserve land" (Delfin and Tang 2006). When the foundation announced the official end of the program in August 2003, it could claim major credit for preserving over 342,000 acres and leveraging its donations with approximately $700 million in matching funds.

Community Sustainability or Playgrounds for the Rich?

Aside from its growing sophistication and wide governance model, has the open space network been able to deliver local preservation benefits widely? Who supports local open-space preservation? Though many factors are at play, socioeconomic status and demographics are strong predictors of the appearance of open-space initiatives on local ballots, as well as voter support. Communities with large populations, low population density, rapid growth in surrounding areas, and highly educated and environmentally concerned residents most frequently asked their voters for ballot-box open-space support (Nelson, Uwasu, and Polasky 2007; Kline 2006). Similar factors also lead to voter approval for open space (Nelson, Uwasu, and Polasky 2007; Kline 2006; Press 2003).

Solecki, Mason, and Martin's (2004) case study analyzing the spatial characteristics of a $1 billion open-space land acquisition ballot measure in New Jersey reports several common findings. First, open-space land acquisition is less of a priority in urban areas, and support for it is more concentrated in New Jersey's more affluent "wealth belt" (north-central New Jersey) where rapid land conversion is occurring. Second, voter participation and support will likely be lower in densely populated, older urban areas.

There is general agreement that wealthier, more educated, and generally more liberal voters provide the most consistent support for local preservation, but the role of development pressure is not at all clear. Are voters reacting to sprawl that they can see or is the effect really too hard to measure? Howell-Moroney (2004), Kline (2006), and Nelson, Uwasu, and Polasky (2007) all argue that population density and development pressure correlate strongly with increased local preservation, but Romero and Liserio (2002, 349) argue that open-space preservation is not a function of sprawled development, "for it is no more likely to occur in communities characterized by low population density than in those that already demonstrate relatively more concentrated development patterns."

Regardless of the role development pressure plays in spurring preservation efforts, local open space unequivocally benefits wealthier communities—who can more easily afford open-space bonds and who do, in fact, vote for them—principally by raising property values (Irwin 2002; Lutzenheiser and Netusil 2001). Land and housing economists refer to the economic benefit of open space on surrounding properties as "enhancement value." Open space in rural areas tends not to create much enhancement value since there's a lot of open space anyway, but in "urban or urbanizing areas where open space is scarce or diminishing . . . enhancement value will be high" (Fausold and Lilieholm 1999, 310). And in their study of the Minneapolis-St. Paul area, Anderson and West (2006) point out that "the value of proximity to open space is higher in neighborhoods that are dense, near the central business district, high-income, high-crime, or home to many children."

A Few Cases from Around the Country

National figures tell an impressive story, but of course, local open-space preservation happens in particular places with their own unique, often idiosyncratic, personalities, opportunities, and obstacles. The following three illustrative examples, drawn from the Highlands Greenbelt (involving Connecticut, New Jersey, New York, and Pennsylvania), the Chelsea Creek project in Boston, and the Turquoise Trail/Gutierrez Canyon of New Mexico, each in their own way depict local actors well versed in epoch two strategies, but also well on their way to epoch three approaches to sustainability. Thus, these cases show communities strategically stitching together funding from both the public and private sectors, and local, state, or federal governments. Gone is the exclusive reliance on top-down, elite decision making; moreover, regulatory tools are often leveraged by market incentives. Perhaps just as important, local policy entrepreneurs justify preservation efforts on societal grounds at least as much as they do on ecological principles.

The Highlands Greenbelt
The entire Highlands Greenbelt includes the states of Connecticut, New Jersey, New York, and Pennsylvania. It totals almost 3.5 million acres and supplies drinking water to some fifteen million people (Highlands Water Protection and Planning Council 2006). This region is divided into two zones: the Planning Area, which only permits development authorized by the community, and the Preservation Area, which "severely curtails development" (Barry 2007). However, of all the Highlands states, it is New Jersey that has made the most substantial efforts to conserve the natural beauty of this region. New Jersey "exhibits the most regulatory willingness [and] is the only state of the four to have passed state-level Highlands Protections" (Alloway 2007). The New Jersey Highlands Region alone consists of 860,000 acres, 7 counties, and 88 municipalities (Somers 2007).

Nearly one-third of the New Jersey Highlands (NJH) is dedicated to open space (New Jersey Highlands Coalition 2006), presenting a tremendous number of recreational opportunities for local residents and those trying to escape the congestion of urban life. It not only provides critical habitat for some 250 endangered, threatened, and rare species, but also protects valuable drinking water supplies. The region's "forests, wetlands, wells, streams and reservoirs" (ibid.) provide half the state—five million people—with 770 million gallons of water a day. Thirteen percent of the NJH is dedicated to agriculture and half of the region is forested land (ibid.). Despite these efforts to conserve open space, almost 3,000 acres of land are lost to development each year (ibid.).

Since the 1900s, New Jersey has conducted extensive studies of the region, and conservation efforts have emerged at both the state and local levels. Nonprofit organizations such as the New Jersey Highlands Coalition, New Jersey Conservation Foundation, Trust for Public Land, and the Nature Conservancy have acted as "deal makers and landowners" (Somers 2007), acquiring land, providing grants, and initiating conservation easements. Many of the towns, recognizing the value of the land as well as development threats, have willingly approved local taxes to protect the region, often with the active involvement of the state as principal land buyer and broker. Julia Somers, director of the New Jersey Highlands Coalition, stated that the largest landowner is the State: "For over twenty years the State of New Jersey has actively owned public land, making funds available to local conservancies." Legislation such as the Pinelands Protection Act, the Hackensack

Meadowlands Recreation and Development Act of 1979, the New Jersey Highlands Act, and the Highlands Water Protection and Planning Act have provided much-needed funds and regulation to protect the region (Kahn 2007).

Federal involvement has been limited. Two key pieces of legislation have been the Food, Agriculture, Conservation, and Trade Act of 1990, and the Highlands Conservation Act of 2004. The Food, Agriculture, Conservation, and Trade Act of 1990 provided funds for the USDA's Forest Legacy Program, which paved the way for studies in the region and also helped states "buy conservation easements and forest land threatened with development" (Alloway 2007). The Highlands Conservation Act of 2004 earmarked "$10,000,000 per year for each of fiscal years 2005 through 2014" (U.S.D.A. 2006) to all the Highlands states. Somers (2007) notes that the region has only received about two million of the ten million allocated and emphasizes that the "counties and municipalities and the nonprofits absolutely dwarf what the federal government has put into land conservation."

Perhaps the biggest obstacle the NJH region has faced is the hesitation of other Highlands states to take action. The State of New Jersey and its residents are leading the way with environmental regulation and protection that, according to Somers, is a decade ahead of the federal government. New Jersey's efforts to protect open space and limit development have also resulted in lawsuits by both developers and private landowners. A recent case, which could reach the Supreme Court, is being filed by Castle Rock Estates, LLC. The plaintiffs claim that New Jersey's preservation act "gives the state Department of Environmental Protection unlimited power to take property without just compensation" (Kahn 2007, 2).

A major project in the works right now is the Highlands Regional Master Plan. It includes all the Highlands states, and a draft was released just last year. The stated purpose of the plan is to "protect, restore and enhance water quality and water quantity in the Region" and includes important goals relating to the protection of agriculture viability, ecosystems, species and communities, as well as scenic and history resources (Highlands Water Protection and Planning Council 2006, 1).

Boston's Chelsea Creek

Bordering the banks of Boston's Chelsea Creek are the communities of Chelsea, East Boston, and Revere. These communities, composed of primarily low-income households, suffer from both a lack of open space and a lack of access to open space (in this case, Chelsea Creek itself). In fact, East Boston only has two access points to Chelsea Creek, while Chelsea and Revere have none (Chacker 2006). The Urban Ecology Institute (2007) reports that "Chelsea and East Boston suffer some of the lowest rates of green space per capita in the Boston area." Furthermore, residents suffer the ill effects of local industry and pollution. Storing jet fuel for Logan airport, heating fuel for a majority of New England communities, and 130,000 tons of road salt, Chelsea Creek is considered by the EPA to be "the second most polluted waterway in Massachusetts" (Chacker 2006). A 2005 Northeastern University study placed Chelsea third on a list of the most environmentally overburdened cities. Thus, the Chelsea Creek case invokes open space issues as much as environmental justice issues. Chelsea Creek has long been regarded as an industrial area by agencies such as the state Department of Environmental Protection, but it is also a place many people call home.

Efforts to clean up, restore, and preserve Chelsea Creek have been ongoing since the 1960s (TPL 2006) and have been spearheaded by local grassroots organizations. In 1998, the Chelsea Creek Restoration Partnership (CCRP) was formed. It integrates both conservation and environmental justice into its agenda and is composed of five different organizations: the Chelsea Green Space and Recreation Committee, the Neighborhood of Affordable Housing, the Urban Ecology Institute, Green Space (Chelsea Human Services Collaborative), and the Chelsea Creek Action Group. Their stated mission is to:

Reclaim land along Chelsea Creek and to transform the creek into an environmentally sound natural resource, a public health benefit rather than a public health threat; a vital economic engine for jobs in Chelsea and East Boston; a publicly accessible recreational asset; and an educational resource for youth and adults from both sides of the river. (Urban Ecology Institute 2007)

Project funding has been provided by local businesses, individuals, foundations, the Trust for Public Land, and the local groups listed above (Chacker 2006). However, it does not appear that either the State of Massachusetts or the federal government has been actively involved in this effort since 2003.

Working with local residents, businesses, other nonprofit organizations, and some government agencies, CCRP has completed a number of projects along Chelsea Creek. In almost all cases, the active involvement and input of the community has been a key factor in the success of these projects. In 2003, Chelsea Creek's first park was established. Once a contaminated, abandoned site, the 4.5-acre Condor Street Urban Wild allows public access to Chelsea Creek. CCRP, in collaboration with the EPA and Boston Parks Department, obtained $1.2 million for this project. Revitalization of the Hess Site (an oil tank farm owned by Hess Corporation) in East Boston and Mill Creek/Parkway Plaza (a vital salt marsh located just north of Chelsea and Revere) can be credited to local involvement in the "visioning process" (Urban Ecology Institute 2007) of the future of these sites.

The Eastern Minerals Salt Pile presents a major hazard to both public health and the environment. One hundred and thirty thousand tons of road salt produce ferrocyanide-containing pollution and are located directly on the banks of Chelsea Creek (Chacker 2006). The company owning the pile has remained in business despite the fact that it is in violation of state law. It was only after the involvement of the Chelsea Creek Action Group (CCAG) that the Department of Environmental Protection issued notices of noncompliance and fines. CCAG's involvement also led to the implementation of "measures to reduce pollution and improve the air and water quality for nearby residents" (Urban Ecology Institute 2007).

Since 1994, TPL has been working with local groups to create greenways within East Boston and Chelsea. The first project began with 3.5 acres, and, today, TPL continues to add acreage to the greenways. More projects are being created that seek to establish a physical connection between these two communities and open space. TPL hopes to one day construct and plan for "the long-term stewardship of the greenway" (Trust for Public Land 2006). In the meantime, today's "greenway features include paths for pedestrians and for bicyclists/skaters, an interpretive center housed in a renovated Conrail caboose, signage, and decorative lighting" (ibid.). The Greenway Connections Feasibility Study, released in July of 2004, evaluates the need for more public access to open space and proposes new projects for the area.

The Turquoise Trail and Gutierrez Canyon of New Mexico

The East Mountain Area of Bernalillo County encompasses a total of 3,696 acres, 300 acres of which are designated as the Gutierrez Canyon Open Space (City of Albuquerque 2007b). The Gutierrez Canyon Open Space, managed and owned by the City of Albuquerque, was purchased in 1963 and was "one of the first pieces of land the City set aside for the preservation of nature" (City of Albuquerque 2007a). It provides recreational opportunities such as biking, hiking, and horseback riding, but, more important, the area contains groundwater resources and "also serves as a refuge for species displaced by encroachment of development into wildlife habitat (Larroque 2007, 4). Initially, the only access points to this open space were through residential neighborhoods and private property. Thus, an expansion program was proposed to provide a trailhead and adequate parking facilities. The Gutierrez Canyon Open Space Expansion Project, approved on September 3, 2007, will add 420 acres to the preexisting Gutierrez Canyon Open Space and provide access to the Turquoise Trail. This undeveloped and relatively roadless land is "located roughly between Gutierrez Canyon on the east and N.M. 14 to the west. The residential areas of Piñon Ridge and Sierra Vista in Cedar Crest lie north and south" (Larroque 2007, 4).

For many years, residents using recreational opportunities in the area believed that the 420 acres belonged to the local school district. However, it was actually owned by Tijeras/Milne LLC. Earlier in the year, when it was discovered that the 420 acres would be up for sale, local resident John Peterson helped form the Turquoise Trail/Gutierrez Canyon Preservation Coalition. Working with the Trust for Public Land (TPL), the Coalition's goal was to ultimately purchase the land. This portion of the East Mountains already experiences development pressures from communities on both sides and residents were concerned that the area might be sold to developers: "Residents of the East Mountains area have long pointed to the region's 'rural character' as one of its most prized assets, as well as one of its most threatened resources" (*Albuquerque Journal* 2007, A4). A community survey conducted in 2005 showed that 80 percent of the area residents believed that the preservation of rural character was important.

The success of this land acquisition can be attributed to the multifaceted collaboration effort. This effort has resulted in the creation of local organizations (e.g., the Turquoise Trail/Gutierrez Canyon Preservation Coalition and the Turquoise Trail Preservation Trust) and also garnered support from TPL, state officials, city council members, and Lieutenant Governor Diane Denish. Representative Kathy McCoy sponsored *HB 782*, which "calls for $1 million from the general fund to help Albuquerque purchase the 480 acres" (Gomez 2007, B2). Senator Sue Wilson

Beffort has also introduced a similar bill. Key legislation, led by City Councilors Isaac Benton and Martin Heinrich, resulted in the approval of the purchase of the 420 acres. Five hundred thousand dollars resulting from this legislation was combined with $1.25 million from the New Mexico State Legislature and $250,000 from the State Energy, Minerals, and Natural Resources Department (City of Albuquerque 2007b). An additional $300,000 was allocated via funding by Governor Bill Richardson in July of 2007.

Another important aspect of this conservation effort was the role of the 2006 *East Mountain Area Plan* (an update of the 1992 *East Mountain Area Plan*). The plan outlined five major goals for open space within Bernalillo County, all of which could be characterized as epoch three values and strategies:

1) Work with private and non-profit entities to establish and maintain a network of educational and recreational facilities, parks, trails and open spaces that promotes recreation, tourism, cultural activities, trail corridors, protection from natural and manmade hazards, and conservation of natural and visual resources
2) Secure long-term funding (20+ years) sources for Bernalillo County Open Space (BCOS)
3) Develop resource management plans for BCOS properties that conserve and enhance natural resources while providing opportunities for public education and recreation
4) Preserve and enhance water resources on BCOS properties
5) Form partnerships with agencies and community organizations to build BCOS capacity for land management by BCOS and other conservation partners (Bernalillo County 2007, 18)

The main mode of open-space conservation that this document noted was outright land acquisition. This plan also included data on surveys conducted within the community as well as a history of the area, existing conditions of land use, the natural environment and development, and an "action plan" for the county.

In July 2007, TPL ranked Albuquerque "first place nationally for its percentage of land devoted to open space—one quarter of its total area, not including recent purchases" (City of Albuquerque 2007b). With the continued support of its residents, the City of Albuquerque will no doubt be able to hold this title for many years to come.

Each of these cases mirrors the trends identified earlier in the chapter: (1) in a true bottom-up fashion, communities (and sometime regional actors acting on behalf of several communities) make concerted efforts to articulate both preservation goals and strategies for getting there; (2) local entrepreneurs make sophisticated use of outside policy capacity, that is, state and federal expertise and dollars or private aid; (3) communities identify new goals and justifications for local open-space preservation (e.g., environmental justice); and (4) local actors frequently use innovative policy tools (e.g., making water pollution violations pay for riparian or watershed land conservation).

Conclusion: Challenges for Local Open-Space Preservation in the Near Future

In what sense is the evolution and maturation of the open-space governance system—what we have termed in this volume epoch three thinking and action—helping communities become more sustainable? While local preservation enjoys a long, rich history dating back two hundred years, epoch three approaches broaden local efforts far beyond their traditional scope. In addition to justifying preservation for habitat and watershed protection, local preservationists today more often accept some new development as a necessary precondition for preservation, in effect, extracting land or funds from developers in exchange for permit approvals—what Jeffery Milder calls "development for conservation" (Milder 2007).

Epoch three strategies also surely increase policy capacity and probably help cultivate place attachment; over time, communities are developing stronger cultures of preservation. Thus, the lands themselves help keep options open to future generations and that includes choices for dealing with the kinds of habitat drift induced by climate change. But it's entirely possible that climate change and sprawl will go too fast for even this mature network to keep up with—that's almost certainly going to be the case in some parts of the country. Moreover, increasing land and stewardship costs, along with climate change, could exacerbate the already inequitable distribution of local open space.

Stewardship
As climate change strains species and ecosystems, communities will need to be ever more creative and bold with their open-space management.

But open-space management (or, more broadly, stewardship) is one of the great question marks characterizing recent local preservation efforts. In essence, communities know too little about what they have protected and devote appallingly small budgets to infrastructure, maintenance activities, and management personnel (Holloran and Press 2007; Petersen, Press, and Vasey 2007).

How can it be that Americans willingly pay billions of dollars to acquire valuable open space, but turn miserly and short-sighted when it comes to stewardship? Stewardship suffers partly because a wicked combination of short political attention spans along with extremely tight annual budgets conspire to favor acquisition over stewardship. The drama in preservation is in the acquisition deal, not in the day-to-day management. Donors far prefer to have their name on a high-profile project (a building, a new open-space preserve) than to pay for seemingly prosaic maintenance. For their part, community leaders and politicians need to demonstrate their achievements within short time spans (usually measured by electoral cycles); a long-term restoration project or invasive species eradication won't fit the bill as well as a well-publicized acquisition.

It's also a lot easier to raise money for one-time, unique expenditures than committing an institution to making payments for many years, as anyone managing an overstretched annual budget can attest. An alternative to general fund expenditures might be to set up stewardship endowments. Indeed, some land trusts won't even accept land gifts unless donors also endow management funds (Press 2002). Similarly, local and state bond measures commit taxpayers to land and easement purchases, not management. State constitutions typically disallow legislatures and agencies alike to set up endowments using borrowed money; this would, in effect, consist of arbitrage (taking advantage of a low interest rate on borrowed money to make higher interest on invested funds).

These essentially structural impediments to stewardship also mean that we know very little about the country's growing local "conservation estate." Ideally, new acquisitions would receive careful baseline assessments (e.g., species, soils, roads, structures), which would then be updated on a regular basis. Infrastructure (roads, fences, culverts) should be maintained and repaired, especially if preserved lands attract a lot of active use. Such efforts require steady, meaningful monitoring, which, in turn, requires "feet on the ground."

None of this great stewardship will come cheaply, of course, and costs vary enormously. A group of British researchers estimated that conservation costs ranged from 10 cents per square kilometer per year in the Russian Arctic to over $1 million per square kilometer per year in some western European areas that had high restoration costs (Balmford et al. 2003), while reserves in Florida cost about $40 to $165 per acre per year to manage (Main, Roka, and Noss 1999).

In 2004, the Center for Natural Lands Management (CNLM) conducted a thorough assessment of stewardship costs for the U.S. Environmental Protection Agency, and developed software for estimating stewardship expenses for any particular parcel. Using their software, CNLM conducted 28 case studies of preserves in three states, ranging in size from 13 acres to over 100,000 acres. Not surprisingly, the group found that stewardship costs—as well as the kinds of activities—vary tremendously, but were always expensive, as the report points out:

Annual management costs averaged $51 per acre per year for all 28 projects (the median was $122 for the sample). The range in cost per acre per year is $6 to more than $2,100. Therefore, for a 100-acre preserve, the annual cost could range from as little as $600 to as much as $210,000 per year. Although the cost of stewardship cannot be predicted with any acceptable level of confidence from the size of the preserve, the economies of scale are dramatic. Costs ranged from around $1,000 an acre per year for many smaller projects to well under $100 an acre per year for the larger projects. (CNLM 2004, v)

Given these structural and political impediments to stewardship financing, a major challenge of epoch three open-space preservation lies in matching gains in local policy capacity with real, measurable, and accountable—in short, sustainable—land management.

Environmental Justice

We usually think of environmental inequities involving undesirable land uses and toxins disproportionately affecting poor and minority communities. In recent years, scholars and activists have used spatial data to show that poor communities of color not only suffer more from environmental bads, but enjoy much less access to environmental goods, like open space, as well. These "park-poor and nature-starved" (Wolch 2007) communities tend to be composed of primarily low-income, minority groups of color. Wolch, Wilson, and Fehrenbach (2005) go as far as calling this a form of environmental racism.

A recent report analyzing access and use of the San Francisco Bay Area's East Bay Regional Parks District (EBRPD)—the most envied jewels of urban open space in California—found that:

• Low-income minority communities are predominantly located in the East Bay "flatlands," whereas affluent communities are primarily located at higher elevations and on hillsides, where most of the East Bay parks' acreage is located.

• Parks tend to be visited by people who live close to them; since the hillsides tend to have the most expensive housing, the East Bay's parks tend to get few visits from low-income minority visitors.

• Part of this inequity problem relates to inadequate transit options. Many low-income minority residents do not own cars; parks tend to be poorly served by buses or light rail. (Kibel 2007)

If we ever hope to "move from urban landscapes of fear to geographies of hope" (Wolch 2007) whereby access to open space is no longer a privilege but a right, then "ecological citizenship must go beyond its historic adherents (the hikey-bikeys and tree hugging set) and move into the mainstream" (ibid.), adopting many of the principles of epoch three environmentalism:

As a new sort of urban regime takes shape, focused on regulating socioenvironmental relations, lines of authority are blurred, partnership is the order of the day, and almost anything goes in the scramble for funds. (Ibid., 380)

The Chelsea Creek case in Boston and the Cornfields Park in Los Angeles (another inner-city project spearheaded by an ethnically diverse coalition) provide rare exceptions that must become the norm if community sustainability will be enjoyed equitably in the future. Including urban parks in old "rustbelt" (Ferris, Norman, and Sempik 2001) communities would not only provide access to open space but would also influence health, prosperity, and social cohesion, simultaneously building social capital and environmental policy capacity (Wolch, Wilson, and Fehrenbach 2005).

Future success will depend on innovative partnerships pursued at all levels of government, and with active participation by NGOs and civil society. But many economic and political obstacles will remain. One valuable lesson from past efforts is that open space must become understood as a vital community asset, equal to a thriving downtown, a modern stadium, or safe, vibrant schools. Local actors working for sustainable communities would do well to track and publicize compelling indicators—the acres of parks and open space per 1,000 residents is a tried and true measure; the ratio of green space to "black space" (pavement) and access to all residents are also valuable data. However, advocates of community sustainability will find their best asset in their region's land itself. The more a community's residents can experience the immediate and varied experience of open space, the more they will come to know and protect it, and seek to extend its reaches. For those willing to listen, a community's hills, woodlands, and streams tell us that sustainability, an idea so elusive in the abstract, is as certain as the open land at the edge of town.

Notes

1. Open-space measures fared very well in the November 2007 off-year elections, sometimes with odd results. New Jersey voters overwhelmingly supported $200 million of open-space bonds, but rejected bonds for stem cell research and a proposal to dedicate some of the current sales tax to property tax relief (Ian Urbina, "Voters Split on Spending Initiatives on States' Ballots," *New York Times*, November 8, 2007).

2. Interestingly, only about half of the states allow for initiatives and referenda, but many more communities at the local level make use of these ballot measures for conservation financing.

3. The year 2002 shows a decrease in urban area over 1997 but only because of reclassification by the census.

References

Albuquerque Journal. 2007. "Locals Can Help Save Open Space." *Albuquerque Journal* (22 Feb.): A4.

Alloway, Kristen. 2007. "Open-Space Group Lands Slice of Highlands. Seller of 12-acre Parcel in Butler Gives Up Plans for Condo Project." *Star Ledger* (18 May): 29.

Anderson, Soren T., and Sarah W. West. 2006. "Open Space, Residential Property Values, and Spatial Context." *Regional Science and Urban Economics* 36, 6: 773–789.

Ando, Amy, Jeffrey Camm, Stephen Polasky, and Andrew Solow. 1998. "Species Distributions, Land Values, and Efficient Conservation." *Science* 279: 2126–2128.

Balmford, Andrew, Kevin J. Gaston, Simon Blyth, Alex James, and Val Kapos. 2003. "Global Variation in Terrestrial Conservation Costs, Conservation Benefits, and Unmet Conservation Needs." *Proceedings of the National Academy of Sciences of the United States of America* 100, 3: 1046–1050.

Barry, Jan. 2007. "Feds' $1.98M 'A Good Beginning'; Money Allocated to Preserve Highlands." *The Record* (26 Mar.): L01.

Bernalillo County. 2007. *East Mountain Area Plan 2006*. Http://www.bernco.gov/live/departments.asp?dept=7346&submenuid=19645. Accessed 14 September 2007.

Burchell, Robert W., and Sahan Mukherji. 2003. "Conventional development versus managed growth: The costs of sprawl." *American Journal of Public Health* 93, 9 (September): 1534–1540.

Center for Natural Lands Management. 2004. "Natural Lands Management. Cost Analysis. 28 Case Studies." Prepared by the Center for Natural Lands Management for the Environmental Protection Agency. Grant x83061601. Fallbrook, CA, October. Accessed at http://www.cnlm.org/cms/images/stories/cnlm_docs/management_issues/epa_case_studies.pdf.

Chacker, Stacey. 2006. "Chelsea Creek Restoration Partnership." Http://www.cwp.org/ urbanrivers/StaceyChacker2.pdf. Accessed 6 August 2007.

City of Albuquerque. 2007a. East Mountain. Http://www.cabq.gov/openspace/eastmountain.html. Accessed 13 September 2007.

City of Albuquerque. 2007b. Unanimous Approval of Gutierrez Canyon Open Space Purchase and Preservation. Http://www.cabq.gov/blogs/councilhighlights/2007/09/unanimous_approval_of_guttiere.html. Accessed 13 September 2007.

Delfin, Francisco, Jr., an Shui-Yan Tang. 2006. "Philanthropic-Strategies in Place-Based, Collaborative Conservation: The Case of the Packard Foundation's Conserving California Landscape Initiative." *Nonprofit and Voluntary Sector Quarterly* 35, 3 (September): 405–429.

Eagles, Paul F. J. 2002. "Trends in Park Tourism: Economics, Finance, and Management." *Journal of Sustainable Tourism* 10, 2:132–153.

Fairfax, Sally K., and Darla Guenzler. 2001. *Conservation Trusts*. Lawrence: University Press of Kansas.

Fairfax, Sally K., Lauren Gwin, Mary Ann King, Leigh Raymond, and Laura A. Watt. 2005. *Buying Nature: The Limits of Land Acquisition as a Conservation Strategy, 1780–2004*. Cambridge, MA: MIT Press.

Fausold, Charles J., and Robert J. Lilieholm. 1999. "The Economic Value of Open Space: A Review and Synthesis." *Environmental Management* 23, 3: 307–320.

Ferris, John, Carol Norman, and Joe Sempik. 2001. "People, Land, and Sustainability: Community Gardens and the Social Dimension of Sustainable Development." *Social Policy and Administration* 35, 5: 559–568.

Gomez, Matt. 2007. "Bills May Help Add Open Space; Some East Mountain Residents Want to Expand Gutierrez Canyon Site." *Albuquerque Journal* (23 February): B2.

Highlands Water Protection and Planning Council. 2006. "Highlands Draft Regional Master Plan: Release for Public Comment." Http://www.highlands .state.nj/us/njhighlands/master/draft.rmp.html. Accessed 6 August 2007.

Holloran, Pete, and Daniel Press. 2007. "Obstacles to Land Stewardship in California." Oakland, CA: California Policy Research Center (CPRC) report.

Howell-Moroney, Michael. 2004. "What Are the Determinants of Open-Space Ballot Measures? An Extension of the Research." *Social Science Quarterly* 85, 1 (March): 169–179.

Institute for Local Government. 2007. "Funding Open Space Acquisition Programs." Http://www.ilsg.org/openspace.

Irwin, Elena G. 2002. "The Effects of Open Space on Residential Property Values." *Land Economics* 78, 4 (November): 465–480.

Kahn, Debra. 2007. "CONSERVATION: Highlands States Willing to Step Up for Watershed Protections." *Land Letter* 10, 9 (12 April).

Kibel, Paul Stanton. 2007. "Access to Parkland: Environmental Justice at East Bay Parks." San Francisco, CA: Golden Gate University of Law. Accessed at www.ggu.edu/law.

Kline, Jeffrey D. 2006. "Public Demand for Preserving Local Open Space." *Society and Natural Resources* 19: 645–659.

Land Trust Alliance. 2007. Land Trust Alliance 2006 Annual Report. Washington, D.C.: Land Trust Alliance. Accessed at http://www.lta.org.

Land Trust Alliance. 2006. 2005 National Land Trust Census Report. Washington, D.C.: Land Trust Alliance. Accessed at http://www.lta.org.

Land Trust Exchange. 1985. 1985–86 National Directory of Local and Regional Land Conservation Organizations. Bar Harbor, ME: Land Trust Exchange.

Larroque, Andre. 2007. "Group Seeks Public Purchase of 480 Acres." *Independent* 9, 4 (24 Jan.): 4.

Lubowski, Ruben N., Marlow Vesterby, Shawn Bucholtz, Alba Baez, and Michael J. Roberts. 2006. "Major Uses of Land in The United States, 2002." Washington, D.C.: United States Department of Agriculture, Economic Research Service, Economic Information Bulletin Number 14.

Lutzenheiser, Margot, and Noelwah R. Netusil. 2001. "The Effect of Open Spaces on a Home's Sale Price." *Contemporary Economic Policy* 19, 3: 291–298.

Main, Martin B., Fritz M. Roka, and Reed F. Noss. 1999. "Evaluating Costs of Conservation." *Conservation Biology* 13, 6: 1262–1272.

Milder, Jeffery C. 2007. "A Framework for Understanding Conservation Development and Its Ecological Implications." *BioScience* 57, 9: 757–768.

Molotch, Harvey. 1976. "The City as a Growth Machine: Toward a Political Economy of Place." *American Journal of Sociology* 82, 2 (September): 309–332.

Morris, Amy Wilson. 2008. "Easing Conservation? Conservation Easements, Public Accountability, and Neoliberalism." *Geoforum* 39, 3: 1215–1227.

Natural Resources Conservation Service. 2007. "National Resources Inventory 2003, Annual NRI." Http://www.nrcs.usda.gov/TECHNICAL/land/nri03/nri03landuse-mrb.html. Accessed 11 October 2007.

Nelson, Erik, Michinori Uwasu, and Stephen Polasky. 2007 "Voting on Open Space: What Explains the Appearance and Support of Municipal-Level Open Space Conservation Referenda in the United States?" *Ecological Economics* 62: 580–593.

New Jersey Highlands Coalition. 2006. Http://njhighlandscoalition.org/index .htm. Accessed 20 August 2007.

Petersen, Brian, Daniel Press, and Michael Vasey. 2007. "Reforming Land Use and Conservation Policies in the Face of Climate Change." Paper presented at the Ecological Society of America annual meeting, San Jose, California, August 8–10.

Press, Daniel. 2002. *Saving Open Space: The Politics of Local Preservation in California.* Berkeley, California: University of California Press.

Press, Daniel. 2003. "Who Votes for Natural Resources in California?" *Society and Natural Resources* 16: 835–846.

Rogers, Paul. 1996. "Big Chunk of Big Sur Preserved." *San Jose Mercury News,* December 4, A1, A18.

Romero, Francine Sanders, and Adrian Liserio. 2002. "Saving Open Space: Determinants of 1998 and 1999 'Antisprawl' Ballot Measures." *Social Science Quarterly* 83, 1 (March): 341–352.

Solecki, William D., Robert J. Mason, and Shannon Martin. 2004. "The Geography of Support for Open-Space Initiatives: A Case Study of New Jersey's 1998 Ballot Measure." *Social Science Quarterly* 85, 3 (September): 624–639.

Somers, Julia. 2007. Personal interview. 24 August.

Tarrant, Michael A., and H. Ken Cordell. 1999. "Environmental Justice and the Spatial Distribution of Outdoor Recreation Sites: An Application of Geographic Information Systems." *Journal of Leisure Research* 31, 1: 18–34.

Trust for Public Land (TPL). 2006. Completed Projects—Parks for People—New England. Http://www.tpl.org/tier3_cd.cfm?content_item_id=19825&folder_id =905. Accessed 26 July 2007.

Trust for Public Land (TPL). 2008. LandVote Database. Accessed at http://www .tpl.org/tier2_kad.cfm?folder_id=2386.

Urban Ecology Institute (UEI). 2007. Chelsea Creek Restoration Partnership (CCRP). Http://www.urbaneco.org/Chelsea_partnership.asp. Accessed 6 August 2007.

U.S.D.A. (Forest Service). 2006. Http://www.na.fs.fed.us/highlands/conservation/ index.shtm. Accessed 24 August 2007.

Vincent, Carol Hardy. 2006. "Land and Water Conservation Fund: Overview, Funding History, and Current Issues." Congressional Research Service Report to Congress. Http://www.nationalaglawcenter.org/assets/crs/RL33531.pdf. Accessed 11 October 2007.

Wolch, Jennifer. 2007. "Green Urban Worlds." *Annals of the Association of American Geographers* 97, 2: 373–384.

Wolch, Jennifer, John P. Wilson, and Jed Fehrenbach. 2005. "Parks and Park Funding in Los Angeles: An Equity-Mapping Analysis." *Urban Geography* 26, 1: 4–35.

Wright, J. B. 1994. "Designing and Applying Conservation Easements." *Journal of the American Planning Association* 60, 3: 380–388.

III

Toward Community, Regional, and State Strategies for Sustainability: Leading Examples of the Transformation Process

7

Blueprint Planning in California: An Experiment in Regional Planning for Sustainable Development

Elisa Barbour and Michael Teitz

California is a laboratory for growth planning, facing difficult choices about how to accommodate growth and development while also meeting environmental goals such as the state's new greenhouse gas emissions policy. Regional planning agencies in the state have become innovators in strategic planning for growth. By the early 2000s, regional agencies in the four largest metropolitan areas (the Los Angeles, San Francisco Bay, San Diego, and Sacramento areas) had begun a process called "blueprint" planning to coordinate long-range plans for transportation investment, air quality, and land use with local governments. The approach is now expanding across the state, as the state government launched a program in 2005 to encourage its adoption in other metropolitan areas.

Blueprint planning forms a good test case of strengths and weaknesses of voluntary, multiissue and multijurisdictional growth planning—the sort of collaborative governance model many advocate for addressing sustainability concerns, as Mazmanian and Kraft describe in this volume. The blueprint process responds to state and federal mandates for transportation and air quality planning, but it is also "bottom up" in that it depends on achieving consensus among the multiple local governments in each region on a "preferred growth scenario." As blueprints have begun to incorporate multiple policy objectives in areas such as energy and habitat conservation, some are coming to resemble comprehensive metropolitan plans. They explicitly seek to address the "three Es" of sustainable development simultaneously—economic health, environmental quality, and social equity (Mazmanian and Kraft, this vol.; Hempel, this vol.). This chapter considers the origins of blueprint planning and whether and how the blueprint model works to achieve sustainable development.[1]

The Logic of Blueprint Planning

Blueprint planning in California is only beginning to take on in a self-conscious way the task of regional sustainability planning. The process started during the 1990s as a narrower imperative on the part of regional transportation planning agencies to devise new methods to cope with fiscal and environmental constraint. Federal and state reforms during that decade had provided regional agencies new authority over transportation investment, even as many roadways were growing congested and funds for new roadway capacity remained low compared to previous decades (Hanak and Baldassare 2005). At the same time, federal reforms required that the agencies help advance air quality goals.

In that context, regional agencies became innovators in strategic growth planning because they had little choice. To carry out their responsibilities, these agencies had to work to improve coordination of transportation, air quality, and land-use planning at a metropolitan scale. Since then, blueprint planning has gained increasing political momentum at the state level because of its potential for reconciling "progrowth" and "antigrowth" conflicts and state and local needs and priorities through a politically palatable approach. "Antigrowth" pressures have included environmental concerns about loss of natural habitat and global warming from greenhouse gas emissions from transportation. In addition, community activists and local governments express concerns about accommodating new housing, even as homebuilders and many state officials seek to increase housing supply. Blueprint planning has provided an interface and forum for managing and reconciling such statewide and local concerns, and in the process, it has transformed traditional regional transportation planning—once an arcane and technocratic realm—into something more participatory and broad-based.

Blueprint Planning in Context: Antecedents and Influences

Blueprint planning emerged in response to specific mandates and conditions in California during the past decade. But its antecedents and influences are older and wider. As a variant of regional planning, blueprint planning traces its roots to a long historical tradition. As a form of state-supported comprehensive growth planning, it connects to state policies adopted elsewhere during recent decades and provides a California variant. Practically speaking, it draws much from the toolbox of smart growth planning techniques described by Hempel in this volume. Additionally, as blueprint planning takes on greater environmental responsibilities, it also connects to ecosystem-based sustainability planning. We explore these connections in this section and the next.

The ideas of regionalism and regional planning have a long history, antedating sustainability and sustainable development as explicit policy issues in the United States, but having much in common with them. As Hempel notes in this volume, we might see a version of today's sustainability theories in the ideas of geographers such as Patrick Geddes and planners such as Lewis Mumford. These authors advocated a form of regional planning and settlement that would recover for the modern, technologically driven world both a more human scale and a balance with nature (Geddes 1950; Mumford 1961).

The twentieth century, with its unparalleled growth in population, economic output, and wealth, effectively marginalized these ideas as against capitalist, market-driven economic development. Nonetheless, there remains an important legacy of regionalism and regional planning useful for the emerging effort to achieve sustainable development. The idea of region serves as a reminder that political boundaries are inadequate to address the issues underlying the drive for sustainability, and yet we still need to define both the issues and the policy responses to them in spatial terms appropriate to effective policy.

Where we should draw boundaries for purposes of managing growth is not self-evident. Social and economic activity is increasingly linked across space through new technologies and the rise of globalized production processes. The climate change issue underscores how human activity in local places produces wider impacts, and the effect of the global sum of such activities in turn affects localities. Policy solutions also span multiple scales, requiring action by national governments and international bodies, as well as major corporations, but also individual actions at a local scale. Somewhere between these two scales stands the potential action of state and local governments. The past decade has seen, in particular, a proliferation of efforts within local communities, through an increase in theory and practice on "sustainable cities" planning.

Such local action runs into serious problems when attempting to define sustainability policies that need to be executed within a larger spatial frame. In the urban-metropolitan context, these problems are especially visible with regard to policies that address environmental concerns, such as air pollution, carbon emissions, and conservation of natural habitat, through efforts to change or coordinate transportation and land-use patterns. In order for sustainability policies to act effectively on transportation or land use, it is necessary for them to operate at a scale that captures interactive social processes that manifest substantially within regional frameworks, including labor and housing markets and associated transportation flows. These functional processes generally do not coincide with any political jurisdiction.

The growth of urban areas has been accelerating, defying political boundaries, in some cases even international ones. It requires very large infrastructure and housing investment, and its form may have profound consequences for environmental sustainability. However, planning for urban growth is difficult where political power and responsibility are fragmented, as is generally the case in metropolitan regions in the United States. As suburban development proliferated in the decades after World War II, the major elements of growth management—land use, infrastructure, and environmental planning and policy—were fragmented across levels of government and jurisdictions. The state and federal governments took over the job of providing large-scale infrastructure systems—highways, water supply, universities—through single-function, top-down planning and facilities-building agencies, but they left land-use authority to local governments. During the 1970s, the state and federal governments also took on the role of regulating environmental quality in response to public concerns about negative consequences of growth. The environmental regulatory bureaucracies paralleled the state and federal approach to managing large-scale infrastructure investment through single-function, top-down agencies, as Mazmanian and Kraft discuss in this volume. Thus, institutionalization of environmental values tended to reinforce the state's "stovepipe" planning system, which remained largely disconnected from local land-use practice. In the process, growth management became fractured, not just among levels of government, but also even for the policy areas under state or federal control, because single-function agencies rarely coordinated plans carefully.

Thus, complex policy issues that manifest themselves at the metropolitan scale generally have no political and organizational counterparts. Where regional agencies exist, they rarely have independent authority. Instead, they have been formed either as single-purpose technical agencies responsible to higher levels of government, or as voluntary forums for local governments and others to coordinate mutual concerns.

The dilemma, then, is how to address sustainability issues in a metropolitan regional context, while overcoming the problem of fragmentation, providing appropriate technical expertise for complex issues, and generating broad community consensus. In some states—New Jersey, Oregon, Washington, and Florida among them—the problem has been addressed through passage during recent decades of comprehensive state-level growth planning laws and processes that incorporate regional and local planning components. However, in California, such a "top-down" approach has been stymied by the diversity and sheer number of metropolitan regions, and the history of strong support for local government "home rule."

For these reasons, "new regionalist" initiatives such as blueprint processes are considered more promising for attempting the challenge of coordinated growth planning in California. Reformers promote "collaborative regional governance" as more flexible and politically palatable than establishing a new layer of regional government or a new set of state growth mandates. Regional planning is advocated as a framework to connect and align local, state, and federal processes across multiple issue areas.

These precepts for sustainable regional development planning have a parallel in the "ecosystem" concept prevalent in environmental sciences (Jepson 2001). Environmental policy increasingly emphasizes the importance of ecosystems as a basis for sustainability planning. The ecosystem concept encompasses dynamic, complex, and interactive processes among humans and other species with and within their natural environment, across multiple scales in time and space (Folke et al. 2002; Berkes 2004; Mitchell and Lankao 2004). As Mazmanian and Kraft note in this volume, environmental programs increasingly aim to address the social and economic needs of local stakeholders. We describe California variants of such programs later in this chapter. Policymaking and implementation in this context must grapple with inherent uncertainty in social-natural processes, and "adaptive management" is advocated to include deliberate experimentation and feedback processes for "learning by doing" (Clark, Crutzen, and Schellnhuber 2004; Gallopin 2004).

An important parallel between the ecosystem approach and the collaborative regional governance approach is that in both cases, the scale of policy initiatives is meant to capture key social and natural functional processes in coherently defined "places" in which processes nevertheless transcend boundaries (such as air pollution flows within and across regional air basins, and flows of goods and people within and across regional labor markets). Collaborative metropolitan planning gained impetus from arguments that regions form the key economic "units" within an increasingly globally connected economy (Hamilton, Miller, and Paytas 2004). In a similar fashion, ecosystem planning, such as for natural habitat, works to preserve and restore coherent bioregional habitats even as it recognizes interpermeability across a wider natural environment. Thus, both the ecosystem and metropolitan regional concepts popular today aim to set coherent frames for comprehensive planning processes viewed as very complex, inherently unpredictable, and transcending boundaries from the local to the global scale.

A parallel can also be drawn on the temporal scale between the "adaptive management" approach advocated in environmental sciences and metropolitan planning processes such as for California blueprints. The blueprint process is fundamentally connected to long-range regional transportation planning, which, since passage of the Federal-Aid Highway Act of 1962, has been required to be conducted by regional agencies as a "comprehensive, continuing, and cooperative" process to define plans, programs, and operations consistent with regional objectives. Blueprint planners are transforming the traditional approach into one more participatory and comprehensive in its policy goals, and in doing so they are implementing the adaptive management model of learning by doing.

Because of the conceptual links between ecosystem planning through adaptive management, and comprehensive, collaborative metropolitan growth planning, the blueprints form a good case study of sustainability planning. But do they (or how do they) define, measure, and work to achieve sustainability? In evaluating the blueprints, we make use of the Ecological Society of America's guideposts for ecosystem management, namely to define clear, operational goals and objectives for sustainability, to reconcile spatial and temporal scales through collaboration among stakeholders and long-term commitment, and to ensure that institutions are accountable and adaptable (Christensen et al. 1996).

Why Did Blueprint Planning Emerge?

In California by the late 1990s, a constellation of issues created pressure for more coordinated growth policy. The state's system of growth management had served well in supporting post–World War II suburban development, but it had started to run up against internal contradictions.

Problems such as rising traffic congestion and overcrowded schools alerted state residents that infrastructure facilities were strained. Meanwhile, housing affordability problems had become acute, with 15 of the 25 most unaffordable metropolitan housing markets in the nation located in California (Fulton 2000). This issue added to state policymakers' concern about the need to promote new development to accommodate a growing population.

Policymakers began connecting worries about housing affordability with concern about housing location and type, noting that most new housing built during the 1990s had been single-family homes at the fringe of the state's urban areas (California Department of Housing and Community Development 2000). Seeking affordable housing, many Californians had moved inland away from more expensive coastal zones, and inland areas experienced more rapid population growth. Commuting pressure to coastal job centers worsened on many key routes.

Even if voters could be convinced to provide new funds for roadways, planners had grown wary of highway expansion as a means of reducing congestion, as any new capacity might be quickly used up by travelers shifting from other routes or modes or times of day. Transit had been expanded in the state's major metro areas during the 1980s and 1990s, but this alternative had provoked its own backlash because of cost overruns and disappointing ridership levels (Hanak and Barbour 2005). In the highways-versus-transit debate, neither side seemed to be winning.

Longer commutes also raised concerns about air quality, with most of the state's metropolitan regions out of compliance with federal standards, and mobile sources forming the largest source of polluting emissions (California Air Resources Board 2007). Concern about global warming heightened the imperative to reduce the persistent rise in vehicle travel occurring in the state. Meanwhile, as new development in inland areas butted up against remaining natural habitat for threatened and endangered species, legal conflicts erupted especially in Southern California, a global "hotspot" for at-risk biodiversity.

Thus, accommodating new growth and development through outward expansion into agricultural and other "greenfield" areas faced significant long-term environmental and fiscal limitations. In California as elsewhere in the nation, "smart growth" options gained support as an alternative. For transportation, planners increasingly sought methods to use existing facilities more efficiently, through solutions tailored to needs of specific regions and corridors. Rather than rely mainly on expanding the supply of facilities (transit and roads), the new strategies often called for managing demand instead, such as through introducing high occupancy vehicle lanes to accommodate carpools, and more flexible forms of transit. Research had demonstrated that higher job and residential density near transit stations increases ridership, and so more compact "infill" development near transit was advocated (California Department of Transportation 2002).When such development became more attractive to homebuilders because of price spikes for new housing during the dot-com boom of the late 1990s, infill development near transit looked like a potential solution to multiple problems. It might simultaneously increase affordable housing options (multiunit development) while also lessening pressure on the environment (air quality and open space) and public service needs (transportation, water, and power).

But the infill "solution" faced its own set of constraints. Policies with potential regional benefits—such as permitting more infill housing—may entail local costs in the form of higher service demands as well as community opposition. Proposition 13—the landmark voter initiative passed in 1978—and subsequent voter measures had limited local government revenue-raising ability, especially from property taxes. Local governments increasingly "fiscalized" land-use choices with an eye to consequences for their budgets. Local governments often viewed housing, especially multiunit housing, as a "fiscal loser," unable to pay its way in terms of associated service and infrastructure costs. Other than heavy industrial, multiunit housing was considered the least favorable land use among city managers in the state (Lewis and Barbour 1999).

Not only local governments but also community residents sometimes resisted infill development. Ironically, one tool at their disposal has been the California Environmental Quality Act (CEQA), a law that came under intense scrutiny by the middle of the first decade of the 2000s at the state level. CEQA forms an exception to top-down, bureaucratic environmental policy, and it is closely connected to local land-use planning. A strong state version of the National Environmental Policy Act, CEQA requires that all government regulatory actions affecting development be subject to environmental review, and where possible, mitigation. Proposed development projects are evaluated in terms of their potential direct and cumulative effects on a range of environmental and quality of life criteria (including such factors as noise, traffic, and aesthetics).

Developers have long argued that CEQA is used as a "NIMBY" tool to resist development. Some research has shown that the most common challenges raised under CEQA, and the most common mitigation measures adopted, are for traffic, noise, and service shortages—concerns related more to infrastructure and service deficiencies than environmental protection (Johnston and McCartney 1991; Barbour and Teitz 2006). This research suggests that CEQA is used less by environmentalists to address environmental concerns than by neighborhood residents worried about quality of life concerns that might better be addressed through local or regional growth planning processes than through project environmental review.

The basic problem is that CEQA works poorly as an environmental policy tool when clear state or regional environmental standards are missing, or if they cannot easily be translated into project-level criteria (Landis et al. 1995). This situation prevails in relation to many environmental concerns, and as a result, piecemeal application of CEQA can even result in mitigation actions detrimental to environmental quality (ibid.). For example, lowering a residential project's density can help mitigate traffic congestion or open space problems at the local scale, but when viewed regionally it might only compound the problems if development is pushed to outlying areas. If, instead of being displaced, the development fails to occur, then the so-called mitigation may compound housing shortages. Considering such effects, some critics charged that CEQA's project-level focus is "the antithesis of sustainability on the scale of the metropolitan region and the State" (Sargent et al. 2004, 3).

To address such concerns, many have advocated strengthening CEQA review at the plan, rather than project, level (see Barbour and Teitz 2005). Such a reorientation could enable CEQA to more effectively accommodate regional or local strategies that trade off increases in negative effects in one geographic area in exchange for corresponding reductions in another (Landis et al. 1995). Examples include trade-offs between local congestion increases and regional congestion improvements obtained from transit-oriented infill projects, or trade-offs between preserving natural habitat in large blocks in certain areas, in exchange for allowing development in others.

By the 2000s, CEQA reform had become a hotly debated topic linked to discussions about strengthening planning for growth and improvement. Governor Arnold Schwarzenegger's administration targeted

CEQA reform as one way to address housing production problems, advocating an easing of CEQA review. But although some environmentalists acknowledged the benefit of easing CEQA restrictions on infill development, they considered this appropriate only as part of a larger package of reforms that would also identify and protect natural resource areas (Metro Investment Report 2004). If local project review could be "tiered" off stronger regional environmental plans, a new frame could be set for reconciling interests in a more coordinated way. In this context, the future of metropolitan growth planning may well be tied to CEQA reform in the years ahead—a topic explored more fully later in this chapter.

Thus, by the late 1990s and early 2000s, regional and statewide consequences of local land use and development were coming under scrutiny. However, no consensus had emerged about how to reconcile "progrowth" and "antigrowth" forces and attitudes, such as concerns about the need for housing production and regional economic development, on the one hand, and resistance to community change and environmental disruption, on the other. Even as demographic and market forces made infill development more attractive to the homebuilding industry, many older, developed areas lacked adequate infrastructure to support such development. Local governments, frustrated by fiscal limitations, were in no mood to surrender land use control, one of their few remaining areas of substantial discretionary authority. Environmental lobbyists supported policies to contain sprawl, but like community activists they did not want CEQA's basic principles to be weakened. Regional planning frameworks might help align some of these interests, but in California, regional planning mandates would be difficult to impose from the top down in a one-size-fits-all manner, because of the complexity, power, and distinctiveness of the state's regional economies.

Federal and State Reforms Set the Stage

Regional agencies in California took on these growth planning challenges by the late 1990s because they had little choice. They became innovators in strategic growth planning by the early 2000s because the state government was doing little to advance such planning, and regional agencies—especially for transportation—faced responsibilities making such an approach necessary.

Federal and state reforms during the 1990s had devolved authority and responsibility for transportation planning to the regional level, while also requiring conformity with air quality mandates. It is important to recognize the key role these reforms played in producing blueprint planning, because the process is sometimes mischaracterized, even by participants, as purely "bottom-up" and voluntary. Instead, the federal and state reforms established a new institutional frame of responsibility and authority, vested in the collaborative structure of the regional agencies.

The federal Intermodal Surface Transportation Efficiency Act (ISTEA), passed in 1991, required metropolitan planning organizations (MPOs) to take the lead in developing long-range (minimum twenty years) regional transportation plans (RTPs). MPOs, designated under federal law for regional transportation planning, generally coincide with Councils of Government (COGs), established in most urban areas in the state as voluntary forums for local governments to consider common concerns. Governance of the larger COG/MPOs generally operates on a combination of population and one-government, one-vote bases.

ISTEA directed about one-fifth of federal funds for California to the MPOs. Their investment plans were required to be "fiscally constrained," or in other words, to be based on realistic funding prospects. This measure gave the plans new weight with local governments (Goldman and Deakin 2000). Plans were required to address multiple policy objectives including energy conservation and efficient use and maintenance of facilities. Flexibility for programming funds across modal categories was increased to promote more direct comparisons of costs and benefits of options such as transit or highway expansion. In 1997 the state completed its own form of devolution through passage of Senate Bill 45, which gives regional agencies authority to program *all* long-range state and federal capital investment funds allocated for metropolitan regions in the state—75 percent of all such funds statewide.

These reforms provided the COG/MPOs with a huge new carrot—programming billions of dollars in transportation investments. This alone did not produce blueprint planning, however. COG/MPOs also faced a big stick as ISTEA, coupled with amendments to the Clean Air Act passed in 1990 required that transportation plans conform to regional air quality plans. This effectively established a "pollution budget" in nonattainment areas. The nexus thereby created between transportation and air quality planning has been a key driver of blueprint efforts. These reforms have the characteristics that Fiorino characterizes in this volume as the "new" form of environmental regulation; they combine outcome-oriented standards across policy areas with flexible implementation techniques and incentives for participation among multiple stakeholders.

Thus by the late 1990s, COG/MPOs were poised for change, facing tough challenges with greater authority to address them. Their technical modeling indicated that traffic congestion and vehicle travel would increase substantially in years to come, even as meeting air quality requirements posed an immediate challenge. In this context, transportation planners turned to land use as one lever for improving outcomes, in particular through promoting infill development near transit.

A serious reorientation of local land-use policy within a regional context would take some doing, however, because transportation agencies have no direct control over local land use. California has a long tradition of respecting the "home rule" authority of local governments—cities and counties (the latter in unincorporated areas)—over general land use matters. Reorienting land-use policy to promote regional transportation and environmental objectives inverts the traditional planning relationship and requires much closer coordination between regional transportation agencies and local officials and planners. In traditional regional transportation planning models, land use and development plans of local governments were taken *as given*. By contrast, the smart growth approach considers development and land use *alternatives* in light of their local and regional impacts. This new approach is a key defining characteristic of blueprint planning.

A consensus-building process was required, given how contentious growth conflicts had become and how jealously local land-use power is guarded in California. COG/MPOs were institutionally well suited for the job. In the state's planning framework, COG/MPOs act as an interface between local governments and state and federal programs, and have no independent authority as such. Governed by representatives of local governments and other entities such as transit districts, COG/MPOs are not directly accountable to voters. Rather, maintaining membership is the key to their success, and COG/MPOs must devise policies that can gain broad support from member local governments.

The COG/MPOs' structure provides unique advantages and disadvantages in coordinating growth policy. To the degree they are effective in integrating local and regional policies and objectives, COG/MPOs can reintegrate the basic elements of growth management. That is because they bring together regional systems-level planning functions (for transportation and air quality, in response to state and federal mandates) with the community-level land-use authority of local governments (cities and counties). They bring infrastructure, land use, and environmental policy closer together at a regional scale than any other institutions. Furthermore, the COG/MPO decision-making structure may help ensure policy compliance if policies reflect consensus across multiple agencies and jurisdictions.

However, the voluntary, collaborative nature of COG/MPOs has long made it difficult to develop plans and programs with a strong regional systems focus. Their structure tends to foster a "lowest common denominator" approach to policymaking, based on horse-trading or aggregating individual government objectives, that steers away from controversial policies that could create winners and losers among local government members. COG/MPOs face a strong structural incentive to use a "peanut butter" approach to allocating benefits or mandates—that is, to spread them equally and thinly across jurisdictions. And in relation to land use, COG/MPOs cannot actually mandate, they can only advise.

Environmental Models for Blueprint Planning

By the late 1990s, institutional innovations in environmental planning also provided new guidance for integrating economic and environmental goals—and reconciling long-standing conflicts—through collaborative land-use planning. A particularly important model was the state's Natural Communities Conservation Planning Program (NCCP), established in 1991 to help overcome legal conflicts over endangered species. Rapid land development in Southern California had resulted in conversion of much habitat and precipitous drops in the populations of many species (Pollak 2001a,b). Environmentalists were frustrated that the Endangered Species Act (ESA), among the stiffest of environmental mandates, was failing to prevent extinctions because of the inadequacy of preserving small, unconnected parcels of land for one species at a time, and only after species were in trouble. Landowners were frustrated by the cost and inconvenience of permitting under the ESA (ibid.).

The NCCP takes a preventive, long-term, ecosystem approach to reconciling species preservation with increased demand for urban development. The program develops bioregional, multispecies habitat preserves through cooperative agreements among federal and state agencies, local governments, environmentalists, landowners, and others. The initial focus of the program has been Southern California but it has moved northward, with twelve plans approved and permitted and about twenty more under development across the state.

The NCCP program exemplifies the same recipe as the transportation-air quality programs described earlier—combining outcome-oriented performance objectives with incentives for cooperation and flexibility in implementation. Through coordinated mitigation and regulatory relief, NCCP plans can provide more certainty both for landowners and for the status of the environment than can a more piecemeal regulatory approach. In exchange for agreeing to provide mitigation as required in the program, landowners receive valuable assurances that they will avoid economic consequences from future changes in species status (sanctioned through a federal policy called "no surprises"). Meanwhile, environmentalists favor the program's landscape-scale approach and the resources the program can produce for assembling large-scale reserves. The program demonstrates that the state government can overcome piecemeal regulation and link local mitigation with more comprehensive planning, without establishing new mandates or administrative bodies. This was possible because the tough substantive standards of the Endangered Species Act provided focus and because the state aligned incentives to facilitate voluntary coordination.

The benefits of the NCCP form a mirror image of CEQA's piecemeal approach, but so do its weaknesses. In contrast to CEQA's narrow framework (considering and mitigating environmental impacts at only one location at one point in time), the NCCP aims to coordinate multiple interests over time and across large geographic areas. Experience shows this is not easy to negotiate in practice. Although originally envisioned as a program to be organized at a bioregional scale, in practice the NCCP has been devolved to politically defined subregions—in particular to the county level. The plans have been protracted in development and have not always secured adequate funding. Continuing legal challenges have addressed the program's ability to meet adaptive management goals (Krist 2007). The "no surprises" assurances, needed to guarantee landowner participation, transfer the assumption of risk of future uncertainty in species preservation costs to the federal and state governments or, possibly, even to the species themselves. Thus, the program has not provided as much certainty for the status of the environment as it has for development. For this reason, the NCCP program has divided the environmental community.

The Basics of Blueprint Planning

Blueprint planning evolved independently in the four largest metro areas in the state (the Los Angeles, San Francisco Bay, San Diego, and Sacramento areas). By 2004, each had adopted a blueprint (Barbour and Teitz 2006). Starting in 2005, the state department of transportation systematized and extended the work through an annual appropriation of $5 million for competitive grants for MPOs across the state and, through the process, provided the moniker "blueprint planning." MPOs in sixteen metro areas have launched blueprint processes.

Blueprint planning seeks mainly to coordinate long-range regional and local plans for transportation investment, air quality, and housing, although other policy areas such as energy and habitat planning are also starting to be incorporated. The original, concrete objective has been to develop long-range land-use and housing projections that encourage more compact development than do current local policies. MPOs have long developed (and regularly updated) long-range projections as a basis for regional transportation and air quality plans. However, in the traditional approach, local development policies were taken as a given.

Blueprints substitute a coordinated outreach process—a so-called visioning process—for what traditionally was mainly a technical exercise undertaken by a few planners. Essentially, visioning processes are consensus-building exercises to define a preferred course of future development and create the momentum necessary to support policy changes to carry it out. The projections provide a relatively unconstrained venue for considering future development preferences because they are not actual land-use plans and they need not specify detailed implementation procedures. Still, when member local governments of COG/MPOs adopt a blueprint land-use scenario, they are effectively pledging to implement—at least eventually—whatever policies are needed to support the projected land uses. Blueprint processes culminate with the development of incentives to encourage local governments to implement the preferred scenario.

The Visioning Process

COG/MPOs partnered with interest group stakeholders in coordinating multiyear visioning processes. The effort was more effective in the two smaller regions—the San Diego and Sacramento areas—than in the two larger ones. In the smaller regions, working committees were established including local officials, planners, and outside stakeholders such as representatives of business, environmental, and social equity organizations. With a much smaller number of local jurisdictions in these regions, the COG/MPOs were able to develop more fully integrated decision structures and convene something resembling a single regional conversation about growth among the key stakeholders.[2]

The task of convening a regional planning discussion was substantially harder in the two larger regions. In the Los Angeles area, the visioning process was organized mainly by the COG/MPO itself, with less involvement from other organizations than occurred in the other cases. In the San Francisco Bay Area the process was launched entirely by an extragovernmental coalition of stakeholder groups called the Bay Area Alliance for Sustainable Development. This distinctive strategy reflected a history of contentious regional politics, and ongoing stakeholder efforts to prod the regional agencies into more concerted action. This fractured governance approach would prove to be a problem later on when trade-offs had to be faced.

In preparing for the visioning stage, blueprint organizers first identified smart growth goals or principles to provide focus. In each case, "sustainability," "healthy ecosystems," or "preserving natural resources" was included among project goals, but in no case did any of these concepts form the overarching goal (except perhaps in the name of the San Francisco coalition). Performance indicators and data were developed to permit testing of land-use alternatives. The performance indicators were related to project goals and objectives, such as transportation mobility, air quality, open space preservation, and jobs-housing balance. However, clear performance targets were not established. In other words, although the indicators could help identify land-use scenarios that were "better" or "worse" in relation to project goals, they would not be used to gauge whether specific outcomes could be attained, nor were the indicators weighted in relation to one another.

In this regard, the original blueprints were not true sustainability planning processes of the sort characterized by Mazmanian and Kraft in this volume as "third epoch" efforts. Without identifying measurable sustainability objectives, the blueprints processes cannot determine whether and how sustainability goals can be reconciled and implemented. However, the "visioning" efforts were couched as an exploratory process to engage local communities in a wider regional conversation about growth, and so they left some questions open.

The visioning stage consisted of public workshops organized over a year or more for targeted stakeholders and the public. Participants evaluated development options and distilled preferred scenarios. The workshops occurred between 2001 and 2004, with total attendance ranging from about 1,000 at 13 workshops in the Los Angeles area to about 5,000 at 38 workshops in the Sacramento area.

Three of the regions—Los Angeles, the Bay Area, and Sacramento—used a map-based visioning process. At the workshops, participants distilled development options using interactive mapping exercises. For example, the Los Angeles project employed a "chip game" in which participants accommodated projected growth through stacking chips representing development at different densities. In the Sacramento and San Francisco Bay Area cases, a staff person at each table ran an interactive computer program called PLACE³S to estimate projected outcomes of interest for different land-use scenarios. The technique allows participants to visualize future land uses and gain immediate feedback on key indicators measured both regionally and locally.

Blueprint organizers compiled and synthesized results from the workshops and developed alternative scenarios for final consideration. They included a projected future "base case" scenario that represented no change from current policies. The organizers then used computer models to evaluate the scenarios in relation to multiple performance measures. At a culminating regional workshop, participants selected a final "preferred scenario." In every region, the preferred scenario incorporated more compact development than the "current trends" base case.

Scenario Modeling

Comparing the performance measurement of development scenarios among the regions is difficult because they employed neither the same performance measures nor the same timeframe.[3] However, in all cases, the smart growth preferred scenario promised regional benefits, in comparison to the "current trends" base case, from reduced auto use and travel time, air quality improvements, and preservation of open space.

The Sacramento process projected the most substantial benefits from its preferred scenario compared to the projected future base case, but in part this reflected a much longer (fifty-year) timeframe for that exercise.

All the preferred scenarios projected a shift away from auto use, but this was only slight in the San Francisco Bay and Los Angeles areas. Transit access was projected to improve substantially under the smart growth scenarios (in the Sacramento region, 38 percent of new housing growth over the fifty-year plan period, and in the San Francisco Bay Area, half of new housing built during the twenty-year plan period, would be near transit, compared to little or none under the projected base cases). However, given the small share of all trips made on transit, the overall modal shift was marginal.

The smart growth alternatives also promised savings in travel time and daily vehicle miles traveled (VMT)—a 26 percent reduction in VMT in the Sacramento area compared to the projected base case, for example. Projected VMT savings were much smaller in the Los Angeles area; nevertheless, the reduction helped in achieving air quality conformity requirements. The Sacramento blueprint projected a 15 percent reduction in per capita carbon dioxide and small particulates vehicle emissions from the preferred scenario compared to the base case; air quality improvements were smaller in the other two regions. Projected gains in preservation of open space were substantial—112,000 fewer greenfield acres would be converted to greenfield development in the Bay Area and surrounding commuter counties over the duration of the plan, and 357 fewer square miles would be urbanized in the Sacramento area (a savings of more than half).

Some of the visioning processes evaluated housing-related outcomes. For example, the Sacramento process modeled proximity of housing and jobs within communities, and the share of residents living in neighborhoods with good pedestrian features. In both cases, the share doubled under the smart growth scenario compared to the base case. The Bay Area process went furthest in modeling equity-related measures. For example, 41 percent of new units projected to be built would be affordable to very low or low income residents under the smart growth scenario, compared to 16 percent in the base case. The smart growth scenario included a 46 percent increase in housing in the region's most impoverished communities—more than three times that of the base case.

The Sacramento area COG/MPO extended scenario modeling to address infrastructure-related issues including infrastructure costs, water demand, and flood danger. The results are instructive in relation to potential benefits of smart growth. The agency's infrastructure cost model suggested that overall savings from the blueprint scenario would be $14 billion. However, the modeling also indicated that for many reinvestment sites, the preferred alternative would be more expensive than the base case because of infrastructure deficiencies for accommodating envisioned levels of reinvestment. This analysis confirms the common complaint that infrastructure costs of infill development can be prohibitive, especially in older areas, presenting complex local/regional trade-off in costs and benefits. Modeling of flood danger indicated similar trade-offs, because some of the areas slated for more compact development lack adequate flood protection. However, funneling new development to areas with adequate protection would produce more sprawl and other environmental impacts. Facing these difficult trade-offs, the agency began developing a flood control strategy with other agencies.

These projected trade-offs among development alternatives underscore the value of blueprint scenario modeling. Smart growth is not always a win-win scenario, although often it is depicted that way. Modeling should help inform decisions—the tough ones, not just the easy ones. Research suggests that important trade-offs may be at stake in considering smart growth. For example, more compact development may exacerbate local congestion rather than alleviate it (Wachs 2002). Indeed, increasing congestion is the mechanism by which higher density may encourage more walking and transit use and less car use.

Adopting the Preferred Scenario

The next step in the blueprint process was for the COG/MPOs to consider adopting the preferred development scenario, produced through the visioning process, as its official housing and land-use projections. The COG/MPOs in the Los Angeles and Sacramento regions adopted the preferred scenario. In each case, a "wedge" of projected compact development diverged from current local policies.

In the San Francisco Bay Area, however, the process broke down as conflict erupted about the proposed wedge. Business leaders had considered it a priority to provide enough housing within the region for the projected increase in the workforce, rather than let new housing for regional workers "spill over" to surrounding agricultural counties. However, environmentalists prioritized protecting open space within the region. These interests were reconciled in the preferred scenario by funneling more development into central urban areas. However, the affected cities would not all accept the densities prescribed. The COG adopted projections containing a smaller smart growth "wedge" than in the preferred scenario. It allowed about half of new development to spill out of the region. This spillover growth functioned as an escape valve allowing the COG to avoid reconciling the growth conflicts.

The San Diego process followed a different path than the other three. Rather than a map-based scenario-building process, the San Diego COG/MPO developed a comprehensive regional plan in 2004 with policies for housing, transportation, energy, infrastructure, and environmental protection. Then, priority growth areas were targeted for more compact development—just as in the other cases. But in the San Diego area, the official projections reflect current local plans, a distinction relating to a lesson learned earlier in the region. In the early 1990s, the San Diego area COG/MPO had adopted a smart growth land use strategy, but abandoned it by the late 1990s because of noncompliance from participating jurisdictions. In the new approach, areas are targeted for more compact development and resources identified to support it—just as in the other regions—but projections are not set "ahead" of current policies. The San Diego experience provides a valuable lesson for all the COG/MPOs. If projections are unrealistic—if they are not translated into real policies and practices in the medium term, not just the distant future—the credibility of the blueprint process could be undermined. Furthermore, the COG/MPO could risk losing federal approval of the scenarios as the basis for transportation and air quality plans.

The San Diego and San Francisco Bay processes raise interesting questions about political pragmatism in blueprint planning. On the one hand, the blueprints will not become "third epoch" sustainability processes until they identify clear sustainability objectives and implement policies to achieve them. On the other hand, it is perhaps less useful to focus on the size of the wedge of more compact development in a *given* blueprint—whether it is "enough" to accomplish desired outcomes—than to consider how to strengthen the process in an ongoing fashion. The term "blueprint" has an end-state finality to it, but, in fact, COG/MPOs update their official land-use projections for each new regional transportation plan every four years. Thus, modifications can be incorporated over time, if visioning is transformed into an ongoing, iterative process focused clearly on goals and performance targets.

Implementation and Monitoring

After the preferred scenarios were adopted, the next stages in the blue-print process were implementation and monitoring. Implementation is critical to blueprint effectiveness because the preferred scenarios are only advisory. COG/MPOs can only influence local policy by providing incentives or through peer pressure. The basic blueprint implementation task is to realize the region's preferred growth vision by supporting local communities in undertaking and approving development projects, zoning and general plan changes, and other measures to close the gap between the preferred scenario and current practice.

Implementation strategies have fallen into three basic categories. The first has been to target resources to identified priority development areas, such as technical assistance and competitive grants for development projects that support blueprint goals. Currently, three of the regions provide about $10 million in regional transportation funds annually for such competitive grants. However, the total level of funding is very low compared to all regional development activity and transportation investment. Furthermore, the grant programs face a difficult trade-off between concentrating resources on fewer projects with greater overall impact and spreading resources more widely to maintain political buy-in.

A more assertive approach adopted by two of the COG/MPOs (in San Diego and the Bay Area) is to condition allocation of discretionary funding for new transit expansion on supportive local land-use plans and policies. In a related move, the Bay Area MPO adopted measurable objectives for supportive land uses that apply to transportation corridors, encouraging cooperation among jurisdictions that share each corridor as a resource. This strategy embodies the same recipe for success noted earlier—combining clear performance objectives with flexible implementation by local actors.

Organizational strategies are a third main implementation technique. These include promoting corridor-scale planning and aligning various regional planning processes. In multicounty regions an important strategy is to engage county-level transportation agencies, which control substantial transportation funding, but rarely pursue integrated transportation–land use planning. Until their leverage is brought to bear, blueprint planning will not achieve its full potential.

The final step in blueprint planning is monitoring of results. In an adaptive management loop, results from such performance monitoring should then feed back through an iterative decision process into a new round of blueprinting. The regions do monitor progress on sustainability indicators. However, they have not yet adopted clear performance targets as the basis for determining investments.

How Effective Is Blueprint Planning?

Thus far, the blueprint experiment shows great promise but also certain weaknesses. Its promise relates especially to the innovative process being developed for considering alternative development futures. Its weaknesses relate especially to the lack of adequate incentives to ensure implementation of preferred scenarios on the ground.

The power of the blueprint process derives, in particular, from its combination of technical modeling with outreach and engagement. Undertaking a modeling process in a participatory framework allows communities to consider and address cumulative consequences of development choices made locally and regionally. Thus, blueprint planning is already helping achieve a key sustainability goal—connecting and integrating planning for the three Es in relation to state, regional, and local needs and priorities.

However, the key to blueprints is implementation, and in this regard, blueprint processes still face an uphill battle. Financial resources that have been provided to support blueprint outcomes are small compared to the overall level of development activity.

Other challenges for blueprint planning relate to scale. The blueprint process has gained considerable momentum for influencing outcomes in the two smaller regions studied. More than three-quarters of cities in these regions are engaged with the COG/MPO in blueprint implementation.[4] In the Sacramento region blueprint planners report that developers now often advocate for their project proposals as being "blueprint-ready." However, blueprint involvement has been markedly less widespread in the two larger regions, not just due to their larger territories and populations, but also to their jurisdictional complexity. More effective subregional planning may be necessary in these regions to achieve the engagement among neighboring jurisdictions that has helped advance the process in the smaller regions.

Governance problems also arise at a wider scale than the metro area. Even as some COG/MPO regions may be "too big" in certain ways, they may also be too small in others. This problem has been evident when metropolitan development has "spilled over" the jurisdictional boundaries of existing COG/MPOs. In two of the blueprint processes—San Diego and the San Francisco Bay Area—a substantial share of new housing needed to accommodate projected employment growth was allowed to spill over beyond the metro region's boundaries. In such cases state action may be required to reconfigure COG/MPO jurisdictional boundaries, strengthen planning requirements for adjacent COG/MPOs, or otherwise address the problems.

Another challenge has been how to integrate social equity and environmental land use and water planning effectively into blueprints. Only one blueprint evaluated equity outcomes in much detail (the Bay Area's). And although each of the four COG/MPOs aims to incorporate regional environmental plans such as for habitat preservation and water quality into their efforts, few have advanced very far. A fully comprehensive regional plan requires more than designating priority areas for *more* concentrated development; the counterpart is designating natural resource and working landscape lands that are *off-limits* to development. Only through adding in this piece of the puzzle can political consensus be fully achieved between regional environmental and economic development goals. With most development in the state still occurring at the suburban and rural fringe of metropolitan areas, blueprints that focus mainly on infill and disregard development in "greenfield" areas might prove ineffective.

The State Government Role

Support from the state government is needed for blueprint planning to be effective. Until 2005, direct state support was minimal. However, as state policymakers began to pay close attention to the issue of global warming in recent years, they have also paid closer attention to blueprint planning as a consequence.

Blueprint planning depends on state government support in spite of its voluntary nature. The process emerged in response to state and federal programs, without which the regional experiments would not have been launched. Blueprints are fundamentally about redistributing resources to promote different outcomes, and unless mutual benefits are obvious to participants, policy consensus may be prone to collapse. State or federal government action is generally required to implement redistributive policies, because such policies are often perceived as creating "winners and losers." Furthermore, the state government establishes the overall framework of regulatory mandates and fiscal incentives that local governments face when they make land-use choices, and to the degree that this framework does not support smart growth principles, blueprints may be working against the tide.

The state government provided little direct support for blueprints until 2005, when the state began providing incentive grants to encourage blueprint planning in metro areas. State support was then boosted substantially in 2006 through passage of a housing bond that included funds that, for the first time, aimed to shape the overall pattern of local development activity. The bond included $1.15 billion to support transit-oriented development and local infrastructure for infill projects. The programs mirror the incentive grant approach being implemented by the regional agencies. Criteria for allocating infill grants include consistency with a regional blueprint as one factor for ranking project proposals.

More than any other state government action so far, passage of global warming legislation in 2006 has served to draw attention to blueprints. The legislation, Assembly Bill 32 (AB 32), calls for reducing greenhouse gas emissions statewide to 1990 levels by 2020. The governor signed an executive order (S-3-05) that calls for further reductions to 80 percent below 1990 levels by 2050. With about 40 percent of the state's greenhouse gas emissions coming from transportation, reducing VMT is viewed as one means to avoid global warming (California EPA 2007). In turn, state policymakers consider blueprint planning to be an important tool for helping reduce VMT (California Department of Transportation 2006).

A legislative bill (Senate Bill 375) introduced in 2007 and passed in 2008 advances blueprints as a vehicle for achieving climate change reductions from land use. SB 375 quickly became the most hotly debated land-use bill at the state capitol, because it brought to the fore the policy conflicts described in this chapter. The bill helps align many policy elements we have discussed, including regional transportation funding, air quality mandates, local land use planning, and CEQA reform.

SB 375 establishes a new state framework for metropolitan growth planning in California that largely follows the blueprint model. SB 375 seeks to align state and local plans and priorities, but it relies on incentives rather than mandates to encourage local compliance. The legislation calls on the state Air Resources Board to set greenhouse gas emissions targets for blueprints to achieve. It also makes state funding for transportation projects in metropolitan areas contingent on their consistency with blueprints, and it coordinates planning schedules for local and regional transportation and housing plans. SB 375 retains the largely voluntary framework of blueprints, by using CEQA relief to encourage local governments to enact supportive land uses, rather than mandating it. Compliance with blueprints forms a basis for obtaining CEQA regulatory relief for infill projects, which should help shift environment-development conflicts from the project-by-project level to a more proactive, regional frame. However, some measures that would have substantially constrained local land used powers, such as measures to protect natural resource areas, were watered down in SB 375. As a result, SB 375's approach—like the regionally defined blueprint processes that preceded it—is likely to be more effective in promoting infill development than in preventing conversion of greenfields at the fringe of developed areas.

Blueprints and Sustainability Planning

Blueprint planning is a viable experiment in planning for sustainable development. It moves regional development in a more sustainable direction. Its collaborative governance approach helps integrate state, regional, and local priorities and needs in a context of much conflict between "no-growth" and "pro-growth" forces and attitudes. Its frame links local choices to wider—even global—consequences. And it focuses attention on tough choices involved in achieving the three Es simultaneously.

Blueprint planning has worked even when consensus has fallen apart, such as in the case of the San Francisco process. Sustainability planning is as much about bringing trade-offs to light—trade-offs between local and regional costs and benefits of development, or among broad policy goals—and working to resolve them, as it is about defining a given set of prescriptive goals (Campbell 1996; Godschalk 2004).

But although blueprint planning is a true experiment in sustainability planning, it still falls short of the mark. The processes have not yet adopted clear performance targets as the basis for determining investments, although they are all working to better clarify objectives. Nor have blueprint processes fully integrated planning across policy domains and jurisdictions. It might be considered daunting to expect regional agreement on measurable sustainability objectives. However, confronting that challenge also helps drive blueprint planning forward.

The state's new climate policy sets a tough performance target for sustainable development that blueprints are being called upon to help address. Blueprints' value as a climate policy tool reflects their value for sustainability planning more broadly. However, ongoing tension regarding attempts to constrain local land-use powers also suggests that achieving tough sustainability objectives will severely test the blueprint's voluntary, collaborative decision-making structure. Blueprint planning has been viewed as politically palatable because it is seen as compatible with local home-rule authority. A more centralized approach may be needed to achieve the state's climate policy goals, especially the steep emissions reductions called for after 2020.

The best approach moving forward may already be apparent in the regional planning innovations this chapter has described—namely, the NCCP program and the blueprints themselves. So far, these voluntary models have achieved only halting and incremental progress toward sustainability goals. However, these programs have taken root because the state and federal governments set clear, outcome-oriented mandates for environmental quality and then the state and regional agencies provided incentives to encourage implementation among local actors. The standards provide focus, while the incentives bring participants to the table for arduous planning processes. The SB 375 framework may prove to be too weak to be effective in achieving the state's environmental goals. If so, then incentives for local compliance with blueprints may need to be strengthened, or more stringent measures may be required. However, even if that occurs, elements of the blueprint model are likely to remain essential in achieving planning coordination in a state as diverse as California—in particular, the model's emphasis on encouraging local flexibility in implementing state policy goals and encouraging broad-based regional processes that align state and local needs and priorities.

In many ways, achieving sustainable development is fundamentally a governance challenge, given the magnitude of the task as well as the institutional impediments. For that reason, the controversy generated by SB 375 could be viewed as a hopeful sign. As policymakers debate how to make regional sustainability planning work in California, the process is still advancing.

Notes

1. The authors wish to thank the Public Policy Institute of California for supporting this project.

2. The Los Angeles Area has 187 cities, the San Francisco Bay Area has 101, the Sacramento area has 23, and the San Diego area has 18.

3. See Smart Growth Strategy/Regional Livability Footprint Project 2002; Southern California Association of Governments 2004; Sacramento Area Council of Governments 2005a,b,c,d, 2006. The performance measures described here are a sample of all measures modeled for the blueprints.

4. We conducted a survey of city planning directors in the four regions in February 2006, with a 52 percent response rate. Planning directors from the two smaller regions were more familiar with blueprint processes; over two-thirds of survey respondents were "very familiar" with the blueprint process compared to about one-quarter in the larger regions. Respondents from smaller areas were also more likely to consider the blueprint processes effective and influential on local planning and development choices. A higher share of cities in the smaller regions (over three-quarters) was targeted for land-use changes in the blueprints, according to the survey respondents (the share was closer to half in the larger regions). Over three-quarters of cities in the smaller regions, but less than a third in the larger regions, were engaged in blueprint implementation. However, the perceived influence of the blueprints was fairly low overall.

References

Barbour, Elisa, and Michael B. Teitz. 2005. *CEQA Reform: Issues and Options.* San Francisco, CA: Public Policy Institute of California.

Barbour, Elisa, and Michael Teitz. 2006. *Blueprint Planning in California: Forging Consensus on Metropolitan Growth and Development.* San Francisco, CA: Public Policy Institute of California.

Berkes, Fikret. 2004. "Rethinking Community-Based Conservation." *Conservation Biology* 18, 3 (June): 621–630.

California Air Resources Board. 2007. *Proposed State Strategy for California's 2007 State Implementation Plan.* January. Sacramento, CA.

California Department of Housing and Community Development. 2000. *Raising the Roof—California Housing Development Projections and Constraints 1997–2020.* Sacramento, CA.

California Department of Transportation. 2002. *Statewide Transit-Oriented Development Study.* September. Sacramento, CA.

California Department of Transportation. 2006. *Climate Action Program at CalTrans.* December. Sacramento, CA.

California Environmental Protection Agency. 2007. *Proposed Early Actions to Mitigate Climate Change in California: Draft for Public Review*. April. Sacramento, CA.

Campbell, Scott. 1996. "Green Cities, Growing Cities? Urban Planning and the Contradictions of Sustainable Development." *Journal of the American Planning Association* 62, 3 (summer): 296–312.

Christensen, Norman L., Ann M. Bartuska, James H. Brown, Stephen Carpenter, Carla D'Antonio, Robert Francis, Jerry F. Franklin, James A. MacMahon, Reed F. Noss, David J. Parsons, Charles H. Peterson, Monica G. Turner, and Robert G. Woodmansee. 1996. "The Report of the Ecological Society of America Committee on the Scientific Basis for Ecosystem Management." *Ecological Applications* 6, 3 (August): 665–691.

Clark, William C., Paul J. Crutzen, and Hans J. Schellnhuber. 2004. "Science for Global Sustainability: Toward a New Paradigm." In *Earth Systems Analysis for Sustainability*, ed. Hans J. Schellnhuber, Paul J. Crutzen, William C. Clark, Martin Claussen, and Hermann Held, 1–28. Cambridge, MA: MIT Press.

Folke, Carl, Steve Carpenter, Thomas Elmqvist, Lance Gunderson, C. S. Holling, and Brian Walker. 2002. "Resilience and Sustainable Development: Building Adaptive Capacity in a World of Transformations." *Ambio* 31, (August): 437–440.

Fulton, William. 2000. "Housing Rises on Sacramento's List of Priorities." *California Planning and Development Report* 15, 1 (January).

Gallopin, Gilberto C. 2004. "What Kind of System of Science (and Technology) Is Needed to Support the Quest for Sustainable Development?" In *Earth Systems Analysis for Sustainability*, ed. Hans J. Schellnhuber, Paul J. Crutzen, William C. Clark, Martin Claussen, and Hermann Held, 367–386. Cambridge, MA: MIT Press.

Geddes, Patrick. 1950. *Cities in Evolution*. Oxford: Oxford University Press.

Godschalk, David. 2004. "Land Use Planning Challenges." *Journal of the American Planning Association* 70, 1 (winter): 5–13.

Goldman, Todd, and Elizabeth Deakin. 2000. "Regionalism through Partnerships? Metropolitan Planning Since ISTEA." *Berkeley Planning Journal* 14: 46–75.

Hamilton, David K., David Y. Miller, and Jerry Paytas. 2004. "Exploring the Horizontal and Vertical Dimensions of the Governing of Metropolitan Regions." *Urban Affairs Review* 40, 2: 147–182.

Hanak, Ellen, and Elisa Barbour. 2005. "Sizing Up the Challenge: California's Infrastructure Needs and Tradeoffs." In *California 2025: Taking on the Future*, ed. Ellen Hanak and Mark Baldassare, 113–156. San Francisco, CA: Public Policy Institute of California.

Hanak, Ellen, and Mark Baldassare, eds. 2005. *California 2025: Taking on the Future*. San Francisco, CA: Public Policy Institute of California.

Jepson, Edward J. 2001. "Sustainability and Planning: Diverse Concepts and Close Associations." *Journal of Planning Literature* 15, 4: 499–510.

Johnston, Robert A., and Wade S. McCartney. 1991. "Local Government Implementation of Mitigation Requirements under the California Environmental Quality Act." *Environmental Impact Assessment Review* 11: 53–67.

Krist, John. 2007. "Court Ruling Offers Warning to Habitat Plan Negotiators." *California Planning and Development Report* 22, 2 (February).

Landis, John D., Rolf Pendall, Robert Olshansky, and William Huang. 1995. *Fixing CEQA: Options and Opportunities for Reforming the California Environmental Quality Act.* Berkeley, CA: California Policy Seminar, University of California, Berkeley.

Lewis, Paul G., and Elisa Barbour. 1999. *California Cities and the Local Sales Tax.* San Francisco, CA: Public Policy Institute of California.

Metro Investment Report. 2004. "The Need to Reform California's EIR Process Affirmed by PCL's Fred Keeley." Los Angeles, CA (July).

Mitchell, Ronald B., and P. Romero Lankao. 2004. "Institutions, Science, and Technology in the Transition to Sustainability." In *Earth Systems Analysis for Sustainability*, ed. Hans J. Schellnhuber, Paul J. Crutzen, William C. Clark, Martin Claussen, and Hermann Held, 387–408. Cambridge, MA: MIT Press.

Mumford, Lewis. 1961. *The City in History: Its Origins, Its Transformations, and Its Prospects.* New York: Harcourt, Brace and World.

Pollak, Daniel. 2001a. *Natural Communities Conservation Planning (NCCP): The Origins of an Ambitious Experiment to Protect Ecosystems.* Sacramento, CA: California Research Bureau.

Pollak, Daniel. 2001b. *The Future of Habitat Conservation? The NCCP Experience in Southern California.* Sacramento, CA: California Research Bureau.

Sacramento Area Council of Governments. 2005a. *Special Report: Preferred Blueprint Alternative.* January. Sacramento, CA.

Sacramento Area Council of Governments. 2005b. *Housing and Land Use Committee Meeting Agenda: Infrastructure Cost Analysis, Draft Results.* May 2. Sacramento, CA.

Sacramento Area Council of Governments. 2005c. "The Cost of Growth: Initial Blueprint Infrastructure Cost Analysis." Sacramento, California: *Regional Report* (October).

Sacramento Area Council of Governments. 2005d. *Regional Planning Partnership Meeting Minute: Blueprint 2050 Water Demand Analysis.* October 20. Sacramento, CA.

Sacramento Area Council of Governments. 2006. *Item #06-5-5, Housing and Land Use Committee Meeting Agenda.* May 1. Sacramento, CA.

Sargent, David, Paul Crawford, Chris Clark, and David Early. 2004. *Sustaining California: A White Paper on the Unintended Negative Consequences of the California Environmental Quality Act (CEQA) and a Proposal for Positive Change.* December.

Smart Growth Strategy/Regional Livability Footprint Project. 2002. *Final Report.* October. Sacramento, CA.

Southern California Association of Governments. 2004. *Southern California Compass: Growth Vision Report.* June. Los Angeles, CA.

Wachs, Martin. 2002. "Fighting Traffic Congestion with Information Technology." *Issues in Science and Technology* (fall): 43–50.

8

Climate Change and Multilevel Governance: The Evolving State and Local Roles

Michele M. Betsill and Barry G. Rabe

When the threat of climate change first appeared on the international political agenda in the late 1980s, it was framed as a "global" issue in that its causes and impacts transcend the boundaries of any single country. The standard assumption was that global environmental problems such as climate change, ozone depletion, and biodiversity loss could only be governed through international cooperation in the form of multilateral agreements. Throughout the 1990s, the international community devoted enormous time and energy to negotiating two multilateral climate change treaties: the 1992 United Nations Framework Convention on Climate Change and its 1997 Kyoto Protocol.

A pair of earlier environmental policy experiments was repeatedly invoked during this period as models for creation of a seamless global regime to constrain carbon emissions. The international ozone depletion accords were commonly characterized as establishing a precedent for multinational collaboration that could be modified as necessary over time. In turn, the American experience with emissions trading for sulfur dioxide was widely invoked as a cost-effective policy that could readily be adapted for an international carbon-trading market established through international negotiations. Under such prevailing models, there was no need to consider any subnational governmental roles such as those for states and local governments in a multilevel system such as that of the United States.

A decade later, there is growing awareness that the scale of environmental problems need not dictate the scale or form of governance mechanisms. Scholars and practitioners increasingly recognize that global problems involve multilevel governance, with governance activities occurring at a variety of jurisdictional levels from the international to the local (Hooghe and Marks 2003). In fact, while national governments and the media focused their attention on international treaty negotiations, subnational governments around the world have taken up the challenge of dealing with climate change and consequently have challenged its global framing. In the case of the United States, state and local governments have been central actors in climate change governance, assuming leadership roles amid prolonged inertia by federal government institutions. Between 1975 and 2008, Congress held 323 hearings on various aspects of climate change but proved consistently incapable of passing legislation; the George W. Bush administration further opened the door to subnational leadership through its repudiation of Kyoto and virtually all other federal policy options. As a result, there has been a clear shift from the classic government, top-down approach reflective of epoch one thinking toward a more decentralized, epoch two approach where the state and local levels constitute the primary loci of governance.

This dramatic evolution may be best illustrated by the political figures who can lay claim to national leadership on the climate change issue. Under conventional thinking, it would be assumed that recent presidents, congressional leaders, and heads of federal agencies such as the Department of State and the Environmental Protection Agency would be the dominant forces, engaged in ongoing international negotiations while implementing the American part of any such bargain through federal laws and institutions. Instead, more than a decade after the signing of the Kyoto Protocol,[1] the elected officials in American life who can best lay claim to national leadership operate at the subnational level, including governors such as California's Arnold Schwarzenegger, Massachusetts' Deval Patrick, and Florida's Charles Crist, and mayors such as New York City's Michael Bloomberg, Chicago's Richard Daley, Seattle's Greg Nickels, and Salt Lake City's Rocky Anderson.

Although the focus of this chapter will be on the United States, it should be noted that this transition from epoch one to epoch two thinking on the climate change issue is by no means an exclusively American phenomenon. Similar patterns are evident in Australia, which until December 2007 was also a non-Kyoto country. Even in nations that have ratified the Kyoto Protocol, including member states of the European Union, the opportunities and challenges for engagement across governmental systems and levels are increasingly evident. As London Mayor Ken Livingstone has said, "It is in cities that the battle to tackle climate change will be won or lost." In neighboring Canada, ratification of the

Kyoto Protocol by the federal Parliament in 2002 has not translated into any significant federal action. Instead, major cities are clearly the most active and innovative forces on climate policy in Canada, though they are beginning to be joined by such provinces as British Columbia and Manitoba. Toronto Mayor David Miller, among the leading figures on taking steps to reduce actual greenhouse gases in Canada, has noted, "Where national governments can't or won't lead, cities will."

This chapter is intended to explore the odyssey of climate policy over the past decade, both describing and analyzing the unexpectedly prominent roles for state and local governments. It will offer an overview of various policy initiatives at both levels and consider factors underlying such a range of actions. States began enacting climate-related policies in the late 1980s with cities following in the early 1990s. To date, more than 700 American local governments and nearly all state governments have engaged in some form of climate change policymaking (U.S. Conference of Mayors 2007). This chapter summarizes recent trends in the development of state and local climate change policies from a multilevel governance perspective and considers longer-term ramifications that emerge from such a reframing.

We begin with a discussion of the ways in which state and local governments have taken up the issue of climate change, highlighting key trends and examples of best practice. We note that national and transnational networks have been central in mobilizing local officials on the climate issue, but that such networks have been less significant in the development of state climate policies. At each level, we find considerable variation in the extent to which government officials have engaged the issue of climate change, and argue that subnational climate policy in the United States tends to be characterized by some key elements of both the second and third environmental epochs outlined in chapter 1.

In the next section, we discuss the ways that state and local governments are beginning to interact vertically across jurisdictional boundaries. From a multilevel governance perspective, it becomes clear that interactions between governance activities at different levels shape policy development, implementation, and effectiveness (Berkes 2002; Young 2002). Surprisingly little is known, in climate change or other spheres of domestic policy, about this interactive effect. Many scholars have examined carefully the "horizontal diffusion" of policy within one level of government, such as renewable energy mandates that might spread across multiple states over time or an energy efficiency program for public buildings that might gain popularity in multiple municipalities over a certain period (Berry and Berry 1990; Godwin and Schroedel 2000). But as scholars have begun to explore the interactive effects between state and local actions in recent years, they are finding more activity than generally anticipated. In turn, there appear to be distinct patterns and relationships that may offer some insight into the evolving development of subnational climate policy (Shipan and Volden 2006).

Subnational Climate Change Policy in the United States

The federal government retains substantial authority in many spheres of American public policy, consistent with its extensive constitutional powers and experience of recent decades. In fact, numerous areas of public policy have moved toward greater centralization in the current decade, as evident in such policy areas as homeland security, education, medical care, elections governance, and a number of areas related to environmental protection (Conlan and Dinan 2007). So it is not by any means inevitable that climate change or any other policy area moves toward decentralization. Nonetheless, the formal powers of state and local governments remain extensive, allowing considerable latitude for more decentralized governance.

All fifty states have their own constitutions, nearly half of which have been fully revamped over the past four decades to formally expand many state government powers. They retain dominant oversight of a number of areas directly relevant to greenhouse gas emissions, such as electricity sector regulation, and have received devolved authority from Washington, D.C., for playing the lead role in implementation of many federal environmental and energy programs. In turn, they retain significant powers to generate their own revenues through varied taxation sources and command considerable powers of regulation and unilateral policy development. Local governments are more varied, linked in part to the very nature of the constitution of the state in which they are located. In many instances, municipalities retain considerable authority through "home rule." This often translates into substantial control over local land-use decisions through zoning and varied planning tools, strategies for promoting economic development and diversification, and even direct oversight of core governmental functions such as police and fire protection, as well as public education. Just as state and federal authorities are linked in many ways, local governments are not autonomous but embedded in a larger system of multilevel governance. But both state and local levels retain enormous legal and political room to attempt to reduce their greenhouse gas emissions. If they want to move forward on climate change, they are generally empowered to do so. As we shall see, a surprisingly large set of them have decided to follow this very course of action.

State Climate Policies
The sheer volume and variety of state climate initiatives is staggering, and the proliferation of activity shows no sign of slowing as we approach the end of the current decade. The clear majority of American states have enacted at least one piece of climate legislation or issued at least one executive order that set formal requirements for reducing greenhouse gases. More than half of the states have passed multiple laws designed to achieve such reductions, forty-seven have completed greenhouse gas inventories, and twenty-nine have set forth action plans to guide future policy. In twelve instances, states have formally established statewide reduction commitments for future years and decades, linked to policies designed to attain these reduction pledges.

Renewable energy has been a particularly popular area of engagement, with twenty-eight states having enacted renewable portfolio standards (RPS) that mandate a formal increase in the amount of electricity distributed in a state that must be generated from renewable sources (Rabe and Mundo 2007). Fourteen states have formally agreed to follow California in seeking a federal government waiver to establish the world's first carbon dioxide emissions standard for vehicles; most of these very states banded together to win a U.S. Supreme Court case designed to force the federal government to allow states such discretion and returned immediately to the courts after the Bush administration initially rejected the proposal. Thirty-six states have programs intended to expand development and use of ethanol and other non-carbon-based fuel sources, and twenty-one states are actively involved in establishing regional zones for capping and trading carbon emissions from electrical utilities (Rabe 2008b; Pew Center on Global Climate Change 2007).

Most of these policies can be best characterized as "home grown" initiatives, whereby relatively small networks of advocates coalesced to design and secure support for enactment. So-called policy entrepreneurs embedded in state agencies such as environmental protection and energy development often played pivotal roles in both idea-development and coalition-building, seeking allies from various interest groups and then establishing links to key elected officials (Rabe 2004). Such entrepreneurs proved particularly skilled in advancing the case that any effort to improve environmental quality would also bolster state economic development through development of new energy sources and technologies, thereby adding political appeal.

As these policies have diffused across individual states and expanded, there is increasing evidence of the development of larger intrastate networks as well as growing interstate interaction. In particular, more states are beginning to work collaboratively with other, usually neighboring states, attempting to coordinate their policies and literally regionalize their efforts so as to maximize likely emissions reduction and achieve economies of scale to reduce costs. This often produces greater political conflict, as more diverse constituents are likely to be influenced by emerging policies, but that has not slowed the momentum of state-based policy development.

New York State illustrates this pattern, having launched a number of modest climate strategies in the early and mid-1990s, many of which were focused on increased energy efficiency. Early in the current decade, former Republican Governor George Pataki called for a more ambitious set of policies. This included a state RPS, which was enacted in 2004 and called for all state electricity generators to reach a 25 percent level of renewable energy use by 2013. But New York also decided to explore the possibility of developing a carbon emissions trading program, following earlier experiments in neighboring New Hampshire and Massachusetts. The state concluded that such an enterprise was promising but made more sense if mounted on a regional basis. Consequently, it launched a multiyear process known as the Regional Greenhouse Gas Initiative (RGGI). This has involved intensive negotiations over several years between officials in ten northeastern states. Several other states such as Pennsylvania and Illinois are exploring the possibility of joining RGGI. A series of memoranda of understanding has been drafted between these states, designed to launch a regional carbon-trading program focused on the electricity sector in 2009. RGGI sets short- and longer-term reduction targets and can be modified to add additional states that choose to join. RGGI leaders are also clear that they are amenable to working with either local governments such as the District of Columbia or the federal government, as long as the core principles and ambitious reduction goals of the initiative are not compromised (Rabe 2008a).

On the West Coast, California is laying claim not only to national but rather world leadership on climate change. The state has long-standing commitments to energy alternatives and environmental protection and has one of the lowest rates of per-capita greenhouse gas emissions among the fifty states. Moreover, its rate of emissions growth has been relatively low since 1990, despite considerable population and economic growth during this period. Nonetheless, the state has attempted to build on this record through a near-constant flurry of activity during the past half-decade. After a wave of early efforts to establish a renewable portfolio standard and the legislation to cap carbon emissions from vehicles, the Democratic legislature and Republican Governor Schwarzenegger teamed up in 2006 to enact the California Global Warming Solutions Act. This calls for steady reductions over each of the next several decades, culminating in a level of statewide emissions that are 50 percent below 1990 levels by 2050. These reductions are to be attained through a dizzying array of new policies, including a carbon cap-and-trade program that would include electricity generators but also cut across other sectors. California also has established a program to mandate reduced carbon content in fuel over the next decade, further intensified its efforts in renewable energy and energy efficiency, and is scrutinizing virtually every corner of the state economy for possible emission reductions.

Much like New York, the state has also begun to build multistate networks, most notably attempting to emulate the RGGI experience through its sponsorship of the Western Climate Initiative. This has resulted in signed cooperative agreements designed to produce a common cap-and-trade zone with Arizona, New Mexico, Oregon, and Washington. Moreover, California is looking for ways to partner with jurisdictions outside U.S. boundaries, whether neighbors such as the Mexican state of Baja California and the Canadian province of British Columbia or even noncontiguous players such as the United Kingdom. In fact, the state is participating in conversations with RGGI and the European Union about establishing a cross-continental emissions trading mechanism, despite the absence of support from the U.S. federal government. Six Midwestern states signed a similar agreement in December 2007, although they are not as advanced in working out essential details. Not every climate-oriented state is as active as New York or California, but, collectively, they underscore a broad and expanding state commitment to take a lead role on this issue. Moreover, there is some evidence to suggest that the relative stabilization in U.S. greenhouse gas emissions since 2003 is at least partly attributable to the collective impact of state climate policies as they have moved into the stage of implementation.

Municipal Climate Policies

The flurry of climate change activity at the municipal level in recent years has been equally staggering. One of the unique aspects of municipal climate action is the presence of networks through which local authorities become engaged with the issue of climate change. The first network to become active in the United States was the Cities for Climate Protection (CCP) campaign, which was initiated in 1993 by the International Council for Local Environmental Initiatives (ICLEI).[2] Today, the CCP has more than 650 members around the world, including more than 160 in the United States. The CCP is characterized by a "milestone" approach in which members agree to conduct an emissions inventory and projection; set a target for controlling emissions; create a local action plan for achieving that target; implement policies from the plan; and monitor and report on their progress. The CCP network supports members through the provision of best practice information and software tools for measuring and monitoring emissions (Bulkeley and Betsill 2003). The largest municipal climate network in the United States is organized around the U.S. Mayors Climate Protection Agreement (USMCPA). In 2005, Seattle Mayor Greg Nickels launched an effort to encourage mayors in the United States to commit to reducing local emissions 7 percent below 1990 levels by 2012 (the U.S. Kyoto Protocol target) and lobbying state and federal officials to take stronger action on climate change. To date, more than 880 mayors have signed on to the agreement, and the initiative has been endorsed by the U.S. Conference of Mayors and ICLEI.

Local authorities join climate networks for a variety of reasons, many of them unrelated to the issue of climate change (Betsill 2001; Kousky and Schneider 2003). CCP members often highlight the cobenefits of local climate action, such as cost savings and improvements to local air quality. Such cobenefits can be useful in recruiting new members as well as allowing interested officials to "sell" the CCP initiative at home where some people may be skeptical of climate change and/or view it as a matter for other levels of government. Some local governments see network participation as an opportunity to exercise leadership on the climate issue, both in their own communities and in the absence of serious action at the federal level. Others admit to joining because of "peer pressure" from neighboring communities. A growing number of local officials view the climate change issue as requiring urgent action, citing the vulnerability of their communities and/or a moral imperative to protect future generations (Warden 2007). Regardless of motivation, local governments rarely join municipal climate protection networks or become active in developing climate protection policies in the absence of a policy entrepreneur situated within the city government.

At the municipal level, most climate-related policies are concentrated in the waste, energy, and transportation sectors. In the waste sector, local governments promote recycling programs to divert waste from landfills, and many capture landfill methane.[3] Activities in the energy sector include retrofitting municipal buildings with energy-efficient lighting and window film to reduce energy use, requiring that new municipal buildings meet Leadership in Energy and Environmental Design (LEED) standards, and green power purchases. Many local authorities have adopted light-emitting diode (LED) traffic lights, which require significantly less energy to operate and less frequent repairs, thus generating savings on electricity and labor costs. In the transportation sector, local governments may provide incentives for the use of public transit systems and/or promote carpooling and biking programs. Many also have adopted a "green fleets" program whereby they purchase hybrid or highly fuel-efficient cars for the municipal fleet. Other types of policies include tree planting programs, green purchasing, and in some cases involvement in emissions trading.

Portland, Oregon, is often recognized as a leader in municipal climate protection policy (e.g., Bailey 2007). Portland was one of fourteen municipalities worldwide to participate in ICLEI's Urban CO_2 Reduction Project, the pilot project for the CCP campaign, and in 1993 became the first city in the United States to adopt a climate protection strategy (Betsill 2001; City of Portland and Multnomah County 2005). In 2001, the city began working with the Multnomah County government and revised the plan. Together, the city and county have adopted a number of policies and programs aimed at reducing emissions 10 percent below 1990 levels by 2010. In the transportation sector, the use of public transit is up 75 percent since 1990 thanks to the addition of two light rail lines and a streetcar. The city and county have purchased hybrid vehicles as well as vehicles that run on biodiesel for their fleets. In the energy sector, the city partners with the state-sponsored Climate Trust and local energy providers to provide incentives for businesses and households to improve energy efficiency, and the city has set a goal of purchasing renewable energy for 100 percent of its energy use (Armstrong 2006). Portland has one of the highest numbers of LEED-certified buildings in the country and has converted all of its traffic lights to LED bulbs. The city also has the highest recycling rate (54 percent) in the country. Thanks to these programs and considerable support from local residents and businesses, Portland's 2004 emissions were only slightly higher than 1990 emissions (and well below the projected "business as usual" level) despite rapid population growth. Perhaps most impressively, Portland's per capita emissions were 12.5 percent lower during this period.

The portfolio of climate policies in specific cities varies considerably and reflects local concerns and competencies. This can be seen clearly in the cases of Fort Collins and Boulder, Colorado. Both cities are members of the CCP campaign, but only Boulder has signed the USMCPA. Fort Collins has not joined this initiative because of concerns that it would not be able to achieve the 7 percent reduction goal given that it is already facing difficulty in meeting its own target to reduce community-wide emissions 30 percent below predicted worst-case 2010 levels (City of Fort Collins 1999). In contrast, Boulder had already adopted the Kyoto target for itself in 2002, so there was little cost in joining the USMCPA (City of Boulder 2006).[4]

Boulder's climate protection program is fully integrated into a wider sustainability initiative aimed at securing a "sustainable energy future" and reflects a commitment to "protect the natural environment of the Boulder Valley while fostering a livable, vibrant and sustainable community" (City of Boulder 2006, 5). It is within this political context that Boulder voters in November 2006 approved the first (and thus far only) municipal carbon tax on electricity consumption, which is expected to generate more than $860,000 in 2007 (City of Boulder 2007). Revenues will be used to fund GHG reduction projects, including programs aimed at helping lower-income residents enhance energy efficiency. Fort Collins has pursued climate protection separate from its wider sustainability efforts (although it is exploring the implications of more fully integrating these programs) and tends to focus on those policies that can be justified on economic as well as climate protection grounds.

Fort Collins has the advantage of a municipally owned utility so that it has greater capacity to set policies on electricity generation and efficiency. For example, in 1998, Fort Collins Utilities became one of the first utilities in the country to offer wind energy to its customers, and, in 2003, the city set a goal of achieving 15 percent of its energy from renewable sources by 2017 (City of Fort Collins 2005). The Utilities Department also provides assistance with energy-efficiency projects through assessment, rebates, and low-interest loans. Boulder has been relatively successful in working with its electricity provider, Xcel Energy, to achieve its climate goals, although this requires constant negotiation. The city contested a ruling that would have allowed Xcel to obtain renewable energy credits from power generated by the city's eight hydroelectric plants, and, in a settlement, the city and Xcel agreed to split the renewable energy credits equally.

Unfortunately, we do not have good data on the exact number of cities that are adopting different types of climate protection policies. The USMCPA does not require reporting, and in 2005, only 6 percent of US-CCP members engaged in monitoring and reporting. We do know that the vast majority of U.S. cities engaged in climate protection have done so since 2005, through the USMCPA, and thus are unlikely to have developed a significant portfolio of climate protection policies at this point. This also means that we do not have a good estimate of the impact of local climate policies on GHG emissions. In 2005, CCP members reported 23 million tons of reductions in CO_2 equivalent. On the one hand, this can be assumed to be an underestimate given that the majority of CCP participants did not report such data. On the other hand, research suggests that many local governments confront a number of obstacles in moving from the rhetorical commitment to climate change embodied in network membership to action on the ground (Betsill 2001; Bulkeley and Betsill 2003; Collier 1997; DeAngelo and Harvey 1998; Yarnal, O'Connor, and Shudak 2003). These obstacles include the need for a political champion within the local authority, access to financial resources, jurisdiction over emissions-producing activities, technical expertise and dedicated person hours, the weighing of climate protection against other local priorities, and political will.

Subnational Climate Change Policy and the Three Epochs

There is considerable variation in the extent to which state and local government officials have engaged the issue of climate change, making it difficult to characterize subnational climate policy in terms of a single environmental epoch as outlined in chapter 1. There has clearly been a dramatic shift in attention from the national and international arena of action (epoch one) toward a more decentralized approach focused on the state, local, and community levels (epoch two). At the state level, most governments have adopted methods for reducing greenhouse gas emissions that will also contribute to economic development. For example, many states tend to favor their "home grown" sources of electricity when designing RPS policies and generally tailor all climate policies to maximize anticipated economic advantage to the state. In other words, they have subjected climate policies to the cost-effectiveness test in ways that are consistent with the second epoch. This same trend is also evident in many municipalities where authorities often justify new policies and programs in terms of their potential economic benefits. In a minority of cases at the local level, municipal governments have integrated climate protection into a broader sustainability agenda that emphasizes collaborative, intersectoral, community-based approaches, reflecting the early signs of a shift from the second to the third epoch. As discussed below, growing awareness of the complex vertical and horizontal connections between various levels of governance provides additional evidence that a shift to epoch three thinking may be underway.

Vertical Interaction: A Growing State-and-Local Nexus?

Until recently, state and local climate change policymaking has occurred in parallel policy arenas with little vertical interaction between governmental levels. State officials have tended to look to other states (and more recently, the European Union) for ideas about how to mitigate greenhouse gas emissions. They have paid minimal attention to the role of local officials in achieving that goal and instead focused on interstate linkages, such as how to maximize any economic development boost from promoting renewable energy technologies. Similarly, local officials have looked to other municipalities and transnational municipal networks for guidance. Within the CCP network, local officials often framed climate-related policies in terms of other local concerns such as air quality and energy efficiency so that there was little need to reach out to other levels of governance.

There are preliminary signs that this lack of vertical interaction may be changing. In this section, we note that state and local governments are becoming increasingly aware of interdependencies and areas of policy overlap that require some form of coordination across levels. We find that some forms of intergovernmental interaction may have a synergistic or "snowball" effect, with policy innovation in one state or locality influencing diffusion to other state and local jurisdictions. In short, these involve multilevel relationships that make new policy adoption more likely, whether through formal collaboration, financial incentives, or perhaps some coercive pressures. On the other hand, other forms of intergovernmental interaction may actually reduce the incentives for diffusion, serving as a "pressure valve" of sorts whereby one jurisdiction's efforts might actually deter additional policy development, either by taking a dominant role in a particular area or providing some form of disincentive (Shipan and Volden 2006).

We begin by reviewing a number of instances in which state and local level climate governance activities have begun to intersect. This discussion highlights the complex relationship between state and local climate protection where synergies across levels cannot be assumed. We identify a number of potential areas of conflict before turning to a discussion of several institutional innovations designed to facilitate synergistic interactions between state and local governments. Thus far, our review of the evolving state and local climate relationship suggests far greater proclivity for the snowball effect, with numerous instances of multilevel engagement taking many different forms, consistent with epoch three as outlined in chapter 1.

Formal Interdependencies and Policy Overlap

Although there has been scant formal vertical interaction between state and municipal governments in the past, there is awareness, especially at the local level, that there may be a growing number of situations in which some form of shared authority necessitates formal collaboration between state and local governments if a particular policy initiative is to go forward. A municipality, for example, may need state funding or regulatory approval to move ahead with a policy, just as a state may need to work with a local government in a case where local land-use controls must be modified to secure a state aim. Such interdependencies are not surprising from a multilevel governance perspective. Young (2002, 263) argues that "as the density of institutions operating in a social space increases, the likelihood of interplay between or among distinct institutions rises." The overall system of climate governance is becoming highly complex, particularly at the subnational level in the United States where the number of state and local governments engaging in climate policy making increases daily. These policy arrangements are bound to come into contact with one another, and "the resultant interactions can be expected to loom large as determinants of the performance of individual institutions" (ibid.). In other words, it is important to consider how governance arrangements at one level are shaped by arrangements at other levels. Of course, this could become even more significant in the event that the federal government enters the climate arena with significant legislation in coming years, raising questions of its linkages with existing bodies of state and local policy.

One salient example of state-and-local interdependence involves one of the nation's largest states, New York, and its most prominent municipality, New York City. While New York State has emerged as a national and international leader on climate change, as discussed above, New York City has not shied away from the issue either. The Big Apple already has a very low rate of per capita greenhouse gas emissions, owing both to its population densities and some history of involvement in trying to curb emissions. But Mayor Michael Bloomberg has decided to expand this role dramatically, through a 127-point plan unveiled in 2007 to address long-term sustainability to help New York contend with projected population growth in coming decades and improve the overall quality of life for its citizens. Bloomberg's proposal addresses land use, air and water quality, energy efficiency, alternative energy, mass transportation, massive tree-planting with the intent of improving environmental quality throughout the city, and the specific goal of reducing New York's greenhouse gas emissions by 30 percent over the next quarter-century. Bloomberg has described this as "the most dramatic reduction in greenhouse gases ever achieved by any American city" (Kolbert 2007, 23).

Many of these 127 provisions can be taken unilaterally but others require active support from the state government in Albany. For example, Bloomberg borrowed an idea popularized in London to reduce transportation-based emissions and vehicle gridlock through establishment of an $8 "congestion charge" for any motor vehicles entering the portion of Manhattan south of 86th Street between 6 a.m. and 6 p.m. But it required a series of state government approvals, with specific roles to be played by the governor, the legislature, and state commissions with some degree of oversight of this area of transportation management. If approved, New York City was also asking for state support to provide approximately $200 million to help cover the considerable costs of putting in place the infrastructure and personnel to make sure such a system operated properly, above the revenue expected to be collected from the congestion charge itself (Patrick 2007). Despite strong support for the city plan from Governor David Paterson and many other key stakeholders, the State Assembly killed the proposal in April 2008 by failing to bring it forward for a vote.

There are also areas in which city and state interests could converge—or collide—in electricity use. The state's RPS exempts small and municipally owned electricity generators, so any attempt to maximize renewable generation across the state will require some form of state-city agreement. At the same time, Bloomberg wants to pay for some of his energy efficiency initiatives and create an incentive to reduce electricity through establishment of a $2.50 monthly surcharge on all electric bills in the city and has hinted at emulating the Boulder approach through some form of carbon tax across multiple sources of energy derived from fossil fuels. The surcharge encroaches somewhat on state domain, given strong state authority in controlling electricity regulation and pricing, and will again necessitate some form of intergovernmental collaboration; and a carbon tax would raise additional intergovernmental issues. Each of these instances underscores the kinds of formal interdependencies that may become increasingly common as the scope of state and local climate initiatives expands. Thus far, New York appears to be moving toward the path of collaboration, perhaps facilitating a snowball effect, but much remains to be determined.

The collision between state and local jurisdiction over electricity development and generation is also emerging in cases where state efforts to constrain expanded use of fossil fuels may serve to restrict local preferences. In Florida, for example, 2007 legislation authorized the state's Public Service Commission to prioritize approvals for renewable energy and energy conservation activities, placing construction of any new coal-fired facilities at the bottom of the cost-effectiveness approval hierarchy. This decision had a chilling effect on a plan by four cities, including Tallahassee, to support the development of an 800-megawatt coal plant, leading them to suspend planning in July 2007 owing to the likely outcome of a state review. A similar dynamic is increasingly evident in states across the country, including some such as Kansas and North Carolina that have little previous history of engagement on climate change.

State and local governments are also interacting within the growing market for emissions reductions. A number of state and local governments have joined the Chicago Climate Exchange, a system in which members make voluntary, but legally binding, commitments to reduce GHG emissions 1 percent per year below a baseline. Members that achieve reductions beyond that commitment may sell excess credits to those members that fail to meet their targets. The states of Illinois and New Mexico have joined the Chicago Climate Exchange as have the cities of Aspen, Colorado; Berkeley, California; Boulder, Colorado; Chicago, Illinois; Fargo, North Dakota; Oakland, California; and Portland, Oregon (Chicago Climate Exchange 2008).[5] Conceptually, this means that state governments could purchase emissions reduction units from local governments and vice versa. Under the rules of the Chicago Climate Exchange, state and local governments commit to reducing emissions within their own operations (e.g., government-owned buildings and vehicle fleets), so there is little question about who can claim credit for reductions. This is a fairly efficient allocation of governance tasks where each level of government has an incentive to focus on those emissions over which it has direct control. However, we can imagine potential conflicts as state governments move toward creating regional cap-and-trade systems that cover multiple sectors of the economy. The line between "state" and "municipal" emissions reductions may become blurred in these systems, and there is a great deal of uncertainty about whether and how emissions reductions units might be transferred across trading systems (e.g., between the Chicago Climate Exchange and RGGI). Such developments may inhibit the ability of local governments to participate in the carbon market in the future.

Potential Conflicts

These kinds of interdependencies and policy overlap are only likely to expand in coming years, given the sheer expanse of state and local policies on common policy areas. The examples discussed in the previous section suggest that as the system of subnational climate governance becomes more complex, synergies between state and local policies cannot be assumed (Betsill and Bulkeley 2006, 2007; Fairbrass and Jordan 2001). Municipalities are particularly susceptible to difficulties in instances where they have limited "vertical autonomy" (DeAngelo and Harvey 1998). As in the New York case, local officials may have to appeal to state policymakers to create an enabling environment for local climate protection, through policies giving local authorities greater autonomy and/or providing resources. In New York, Mayor Bloomberg's chances of getting support from Governor Paterson are relatively good, given that New York state is a recognized leader in state-level climate protection. The prospects for such snowball effects are less clear for local governments located in less climate-friendly states. Of course, as more and more states establish targets for achieving GHG reductions, they will need to turn to local authorities for assistance in controlling emissions under municipal jurisdiction, creating additional opportunities for synergy.

We can say with relative certainty that as more and more cities become active in the area of climate change and as states adopt a wider range of policies for climate protection, vertical interactions will become increasingly common. We can anticipate a number of issues that may create difficulties when state and local climate policies interact, particularly as one or both levels attempt to influence the shape of possible federal policy. There appears to be a competition between state and local governments in seeking to shape the development of future federal climate change policy, and a number of officials have sought to link their names to this issue. One of the central objectives of the USMCPA and the related work of the U.S. Conference of Mayors is to create a powerful political force urging the federal government to adopt policies and programs to meet or exceed the Kyoto target and to establish a national emissions trading system. Similarly, the RGGI states collectively, as well as individual states such as California and New York, have all proclaimed a desire to serve as models for future federal policy. Governor Schwarzenegger has gone so far as to submit a letter to Congress offering help with policy design, and the leadership of the National Governors Association (NGA) has begun to bring best-practice cases into congressional hearings. There is significant political capital at stake, which may create difficulties if these various actors find themselves promoting competing alternatives, especially if they give undue advantage (such as early-reduction credits or expanded tax incentives) for policies emphasized at one level (Rabe 2008b).

There could also be resources at stake if the federal government takes action on climate change leading to rent-seeking behavior on the part of state and local governments. The U.S. Conference of Mayors strongly advocated for the creation of the Energy Efficiency and Conservation Block Grant (EECBG) program as part of the Energy Independence and Security Act of 2007 (U.S. Conference of Mayors 2008). The block grant provides resources to local governments (city and county) to develop and implement energy efficiency and conservation strategies. Seventy percent of the block grant funds are for local governments while 28 percent will go to states, although states are required to pass at least 60 percent of these funds through to cities and counties that do not receive direct funding.[6] This allocation process creates competition between cities and states and raises questions about whether and how investments made at one level would contribute to policy goals at the other.

Institutions for Vertical Interaction

Fortunately, conflicts between state and local governments in the area of climate policy are not inevitable. As in any system of multilevel governance, a central challenge is to take steps to facilitate interactions across levels of government and to ensure that such interactions create synergies (Young 2002). In the last couple of years, we have observed the emergence of several institutional mechanisms for state and local collaboration on the climate change issue, suggesting a range of possibilities for expanded engagement in the future. In this section, we present examples of such intergovernmental context. This does not purport to offer a comprehensive list of all possible forms of synergistic vertical interaction but rather constitutes an attempt to prompt additional work on this new, but relatively neglected, form of climate change governance.

Multi-Jurisdictional Policy Networks   The vast majority of networks that link agencies and policy professionals from common policy areas are horizontal. They generally work along parallel but separate tracks, either connecting state officials or local-level counterparts but rarely bringing them together. Organizations such as the National Association of Counties (NACO) or the U.S. Conference of Mayors (USCM) represent subsets of the locally based networks that have been active on the climate change issue, joined by such state organizations as the NGA, the National Conference of State Legislatures (NCSL), the Environmental Council of the States (ECOS), and the National Association of State Energy Officials (NASEO).

There are some signs, at least symbolic ones, that there may be greater recognition of state and local interdependencies among these organizations, at minimum in joining common cause against any possible federal encroachment on the policies they have established to date. In 2007, for example, ECOS, which represents the lead environmental agencies of each state, issued a resolution on reduction of greenhouse gas emissions. It noted that "many states and municipalities have already implemented or plan to implement measures to reduce greenhouse gas emissions" and called upon Congress to respect and work with existing policies in developing any future federal legislation. More than half of the states represented in ECOS began meeting separately in less formal settings in 2007 and 2008, attempting to define a more aggressive stance in any future negotiations with Washington that would include formal latitude to "go beyond" federal standards in any future federal policy. In turn, a 2007 resolution by NACO called for any future federal policy "to protect the ability of states/localities to adopt more stringent legislation" than anything that might emanate from Washington, D.C.

At the same time, there may be at least some indication of organizational collaboration that formally integrates state and local representatives and involves more than passage of resolutions. The National Association of Clean Air Agencies (NACAA) has become increasingly active on many aspects of climate change, and represents air pollution agencies in 54 states and territories and more than 165 major metropolitan areas. The NACAA has a leadership structure with formal divides between state and local officials, with copresidents in 2007 from the State of Nebraska and the City of Tucson. The organization has specialized committees to address global warming, energy, and emissions and modeling, all of which have become active in examining climate change and working to promote common strategies among these various subnational units. The organization's most recent statement of "global warming principles," issued in May 2007, notes that "following the historical model of air pollution control in the United States, states and localities are leading the way in addressing global warming" (NACAA 2007). In turn, given these historic and current roles, the principles strongly oppose any preemption by the federal government that would preclude either states or localities from taking "more stringent actions." They also note that "Federal legislation should reflect the extremely active role state and local governments have played, and will continue to play, in reducing greenhouse gas emissions." Alongside this strong statement, NACAA members anticipate working cooperatively across state and local boundaries in implementing a range of policies, including carbon cap-and-trade activities involving one or more states, given shared jurisdiction over various aspects of this form of regulation.

Litigation   Both states and municipalities have considerable latitude to pursue legal approaches to attain their environmental policy goals, either against private entities causing environmental insult or against other governments deemed negligent in their oversight duties. Of course, litigation can take the form of multilevel governments joining common cause or literally squaring off against one another. Thus far, the climate change issue reveals an increasing number of ways in which litigative strategies might be mounted, and both states and municipalities are clearly looking ever more closely at the "legal option." Consistent with other areas of intergovernmental legal relations, this can lead to either collaboration or conflict.

In the most prominent climate change court case to date, the 2007 U.S. Supreme Court decision in *Massachusetts v. EPA,* the plaintiff received considerable local government support in challenging federal reluctance to declare carbon dioxide as an air pollutant under the Clean Air Act Amendments. The U.S. Conference of Mayors filed a supportive *amicus* brief in the case and the cities of Baltimore, New York, and Washington, D.C., all formally joined Massachusetts and eleven other states in pushing the case through the federal court system. Other mayors also went on record as having supported the legal challenge and welcoming the verdict in favor of the subnational plaintiffs. As Mayor Bloomberg noted, "Global warming threatens New York City and every city, and it is our duty to use this case and every other opportunity we have to prevent this situation from getting even worse" (Sierra Club 2006). Clusters of states and municipalities have begun to team up on possible legal sequels to the 2007 federal case, now that the capacity of subnational governments to bring successful suit on climate change against their federal partners has been established. This includes a return to the courts by many states and localities after the U.S. Environmental Protection Agency rejected California's request for a vehicular carbon emissions waiver following the 2007 Supreme Court decision.

At the same time, increasingly active state attorneys general may also choose to bring suit against local governments if in fact they feel that this provides an opportunity to advance a state climate strategy. In California, for example, Attorney General (and former Governor) Edmund Brown, Jr., has begun to explore a number of possible climate-related legal challenges, including pressure on local governments to expand use of the California Environmental Quality Act (CEQA) to include possible climate change impacts in overseeing a wide range of land-use management decisions. Brown has begun to threaten suits against local governments that he feels are delinquent in adding possible climate impacts when making CEQA decisions, and he filed suit in June 2007 against the County of San Bernardino. In this case, the state contended that the county's Final Environmental Impact Report (FEIR) that was included in its March 2007 General Plan update (as required under the CEQA) lacked provisions to inventory or reduce greenhouse gas emissions. A negotiated settlement was reached in August 2007, but Attorney General Brown has threatened additional legal steps through interpretation of the CEQA or other statutes at the local level and his counterparts in other states have begun to explore similar initiatives.

Advisory Committees   In a variety of states, we find state and local officials sitting side-by-side on committees related to climate policy. As of March 2008, twenty-two states have initiated climate change advisory groups through the legislative and/or executive branch, and local officials are involved in those advisory groups in twelve of the states (Pew Center on Global Climate Change 2008). It should be noted that in all cases, local officials are one of many stakeholders and that the process is primarily focused on providing recommendations for state-level policy. Nevertheless, this offers one vehicle for opening dialogue between state and local officials. In Illinois, for example, state and local officials have reciprocal membership on their respective advisory groups. The commissioner for Chicago's Department of the Environment is a member of the state's Climate Change Advisory Group, and the state has a formal seat on Chicago's climate change task force. While there was informal interaction between state and local authorities before, this more formal mechanism may prove useful in furthering an understanding of how state and local government agencies are approaching the issue and searching for policy options that are mutually beneficial.

The Colorado Climate Project is a slightly different model (Colorado Climate Project 2007). While similar in its intent—to inform state climate policy—it is a private initiative of the Rocky Mountain Climate Organization, and local officials have taken a lead role. Project directors include the mayors of Denver, Lakewood, and Fort Collins, and at least eight other municipalities are represented on the various working groups. The state is formally represented by a single member of the Colorado General Assembly, which reflects the political reality in the state at the time the project was created. Newly elected Democratic governor Bill Ritter appointed a climate change advisor in April 2007 who attends meetings of the Climate Action Panel. In another private initiative, ICLEI has launched a task force to enhance links between state and local actions in California (Pew Center on Climate Change 2007).

Conclusion

State and local climate change policies have proliferated over the past decade and we see no sign of this trend slowing. States will continue to expand the number and range of policies and programs aimed at controlling greenhouse gas emissions. At the local level, we expect that the number of cities engaged in climate change policy will continue to grow, and that local authorities will also increase the number and range of climate-related policies and programs. These developments are consistent with a transition between epochs one and two as outlined in chapter 1. In some jurisdictions, there appears to be some movement, particularly on the local level, toward a more holistic view of climate protection as part of the broader sustainability agenda as suggested in the third epoch.

Although the historical development of state and local policies has been relatively independent, we anticipate an increasingly interactive effect as the sheer number of engaged jurisdictions and policies continues to proliferate and many take a very far-reaching approach that transcends traditional governance boundaries. The looming question is whether the interactions between state and local climate policies will lead to intergovernmental conflict or collaboration. The early evidence gives us some cause for optimism; as state and local officials have become aware of their interdependencies and areas of policy overlap, they have been adept at creating new institutional mechanisms to facilitate policy coordination. This suggests movement toward epoch three thinking. That said, we foresee a number of potential areas of conflict in the future, especially as the federal government begins to develop its own approach to climate governance. In the case of climate change, the transition between epochs is not linear and involves ongoing political struggles and contestation.

Notes

1. The Clinton administration signed the Kyoto Protocol, but it has never been ratified by the U.S. Senate.

2. Today, the organization is known as ICLEI—Local Governments for Sustainability.

3. Methane is a greenhouse gas.

4. Boulder's target is actually more ambitious than the USMCPA in that it applies to community-wide emissions rather than just municipal government emissions.

5. Three county governments are also members: King County, Washington; Miami-Dade County, Florida; and Sacramento County, California.

6. The remaining 2 percent is targeted to tribal programs.

References

Armstrong, Michael. 2006. "Climate Protection in Portland." PowerPoint presentation, November. Available at http://www.portlandonline.com/osd/index.cfm?c=41917.

Bailey, John. 2007. *Lessons from the Pioneers: Tackling Global Warming at the Local Level*. Minneapolis, MN: Institute for Local Self-Reliance. Available at http://www.newrules.org/de/pioneers.pdf.

Berkes, Fikret. 2002. "Cross-scale Institutional Linkages: Perspectives from the Bottom Up." In *The Drama of the Commons*, ed. E. Ostrom, T. Dietz, N. Dolsak, P. C. Stern, S. Stonich, and E. U. Weber. Washington, D.C.: National Academy Press.

Berry, Frances Stokes, and William D. Berry. 1990. "State Lottery Adoptions as Policy Innovations: An Event History Analysis." *American Political Science Review* 84, 2: 395–415.

Betsill, Michele M. 2001. "Mitigating Climate Change in US Cities: Opportunities and Obstacles." *Local Environment* 6, 4: 393–406.

Betsill, Michele M., and Harriet Bulkeley. 2006. "Cities and the Multilevel Governance of Global Climate Change." *Global Governance* 12, 2: 141–159.

Betsill, Michele M., and Harriet Bulkeley. 2007. "Looking Back and Thinking Ahead: A Decade of Cities and Climate Change Research." *Local Environment* 12, 5: 1–10.

Bulkeley, Harriet, and Michele M. Betsill. 2003. *Cities and Climate Change: Urban Sustainability and Global Environmental Governance*. London: Routledge.

Chicago Climate Exchange. 2008. "Current Members of CCX." Available at http://www.chicagoclimatex.com/content.jsf?id=64. Accessed 19 March 2008.

City of Boulder. 2006. *Climate Action Plan*. Available at http://www.ci.boulder.co.us/files/Environmental%20Affairs/climate%20and%20energy/cap_final_25sept06.pdf.

City of Boulder. 2007. "Climate Action Plan Tax: Frequently Asked Questions." Available at http://www.bouldercolorado.gov/files/Environmental%20Affairs/climate%20and%20energy/cap_tax_faq_26mar07_final.pdf.

City of Fort Collins. 1999. *Local Action Plan to Reduce Greenhouse Gas Emissions*. Available at http://www.fcgov.com/airquality/lap.php.

City of Fort Collins. 2005. *City of Fort Collins 2003/2004 Climate Protection Status Report*. Available at http://www.fcgov.com/climateprotection/pdf/2003-04climatestatusreport.pdf.

City of Fort Collins. 2006. *Climate Wise: Annual Report*. Available at http://www.ci.fort-collins.co.us/climatewise/pdf/climate_wise_annual_report_2006_final.pdf.

City of Portland and Multnomah County. 2005. Global Warming Progress Report. Available at http://www.portlandonline.com/shared/cfm/image.cfm?id=112118. Accessed 7 July 2008.

Collier, Ute. 1997. "Local Authorities and Climate Protection in the EU: Putting Subsidiarity into Practice?" *Local Environment* 2, 1: 39–57.

Colorado Climate Project. 2007. "Background-Colorado Climate Project." Available at http://www.coloradoclimate.org/background_Climate_Action_Panel.cfm.

Conlan, Tim, and John Dinan. 2007. "Federalism, the Bush Administration, and the Transformation of American Conservatism." *Publius: The Journal of Federalism* 37, 3 (summer): 279–303.

DeAngelo, Benjamin, and L. D. Danny Harvey. 1998. "The Jurisdictional Framework for Municipal Action to Reduce Greenhouse Gas Emissions: Case Studies from Canada, the USA and Germany." *Local Environment* 3, 2: 111–136.

Fairbrass, Jenny, and Andrew Jordan. 2001. "Protecting Biodiversity in the European Union: National Barriers and European Opportunities?" *Journal of European Public Policy* 8, 4: 499–518.

Godwin, Marcia L., and Jean R. Schroedel. 2000. "Policy Diffusion and Strategies for Promoting Policy Change: Evidence from California Local Gun Control Ordinances." *Policy Studies Journal* 28, 4: 760–776.

Hooghe, Lisbet, and Gary Marks. 2003. "Unraveling the Central State, But How? Types of Multi-level Governance." *American Political Science Review* 97, 2: 233–243.

Kolbert, Elizabeth. 2007. "Don't Drive: He Said." *New Yorker* (7 May): 23.

Kousky, Carolyn, and Stephen H. Schneider. 2003. "Global Climate Policy: Will Cities Lead the Way?" *Climate Policy* 3: 359–372.

NACAA. 2007 (National Association of Clean Air Agencies). Global Warming Principles. Available at http://www.4cleanair.org/Documents/NACAAGlobalWarmingPrinciples050107FINAL.pdf. Accesses 7 July 2008.

Patrick, Aaron O. 2007. "Life in the Faster Lane." *Wall Street Journal* (July 7): W1.

Pew Center on Global Climate Change. 2007. *Climate Change 101: Understanding and Responding to Global Climate Change*. Arlington: Pew Center on Global Climate Change.

Pew Center on Global Climate Change. 2008. "States with Active Climate Legislative Commissions and Executive Branch Advisory Groups." Available at http://www.pewclimate.org/what_s_being_done/in_the_states/climatecomissions .cfm. Accessed 19 March 2008.

Rabe, Barry G. 2004. *Statehouse and Greenhouse: The Emerging Politics of American Climate Change Policy.* Washington, D.C.: Brookings Institution.

Rabe, Barry G. 2008a. "Revisiting Regionalism and the Case of Multi-Level Climate Governance." In *Intergovernmental Management for the 21st Century*, ed. T. Conlan and P. Posner. Washington, D.C.: Brookings Institution.

Rabe, Barry G. 2008b. "States on Steroids: The Intergovernmental Odyssey of American Climate Policy." *Review of Policy Research* 25, 2: 105–128.

Rabe, Barry G., and Philip A. Mundo. 2007. "Business Influence in State-Level Environmental Policy." In *Business and Environmental Policy*, ed. M. E. Kraft and S. Kamieniecki, 265–298. Cambridge, MA: MIT Press.

Shipan, Charles R., and Craig Volden. 2006. "Bottom-Up Federalism: The Diffusion of Antismoking Policies from U.S. Cities to States." *American Journal of Political Science* 50, 4: 825–843.

Sierra Club. 2006. "Powerful Coalition Petitions Supreme Court to Order EPA to Obey the Law." Press Release, 31 August.

U.S. Conference of Mayors. 2007. "Cities That Have Signed On." Available at http://usmayors.org/climateprotection/ClimateChange.asp. Accessed 11 November 2007.

U.S. Conference of Mayors. 2008. "The Energy Efficiency and Conservation Block Grant (EECBG)." Available at http://usmayors.org/climateprotection/ documents/eecbghandout.pdf. Accessed 19 March 2008.

Warden, Toby. 2007. "The Social Ecology of U.S. Cities and Global Warming 2005–2007. Think Globally, Act Locally, Govern Virally: US Mayors Take the First Step." Ph.D. Thesis, University of California, Irvine.

Yarnal, Brent, Robert E. O'Connor, and R. Shudak. 2003. "The Impact of Local versus National Framing on Willingness to Reduce Greenhouse Gas Emissions: A Case Study from Central Pennsylvania." *Local Environment* 8, 4: 457–469.

Young, Oran R. 2002. "Institutional Interplay: The Environmental Consequences of Cross-Scale Interactions." In *The Drama of the Commons*, ed. E. Ostrom, T. Dietz, N. Dolsak, P. C. Stern, S. Stonich, and E. U. Weber. Washington, D.C.: National Academy Press.

9

Sustainability in American Cities: A Comprehensive Look at What Cities Are Doing and Why

Kent E. Portney

A generation ago, the idea that American cities would be taking great initiative toward building what we currently call "sustainability" would have been unthinkable. Sustainability, an evolving concept that involves the protection and improvement of the biophysical environment, seemed like a luxury cities could not afford. Faced with enormous social and economic problems, cities' first priority seemed destined to be the pursuit of virtually any kind of economic development to stem the tide of inner-city deterioration. To the extent that something akin to sustainability was part of the urban policy equation, it was rooted in neoclassical economic views that greater economic development automatically translated into what was good for the city. Environmental deterioration was the inevitable, inexorable, price to be paid for keeping jobs and holding the line against social and economic decline. Today, for a variety of reasons, this has changed in many urban areas all around the country.

Although the common wisdom might suggest that cities either can't or won't do much to become more sustainable and to protect the biophysical environment, this view has not kept up with the realities on the ground. Over the last fifteen years, new ways of thinking about city policies have emerged, with a special focus on healthy cities, livability, and sustainability (Selman 1996). This new way of thinking argues that cities have much more leverage in pursuing economic development than they once thought. It also suggests that the traditionally accepted trade-off between economic development on the one hand and environmental protection on the other is a false one. Particularly in the last two decades, as U.S. cities have lost a high proportion of their manufacturing employment base and undergone a transformation to service-based economies, many local governments have come to realize that they do not have to accept high levels of environmental degradation in order to sustain a healthy economy. They have also come to realize that high rates of economic growth do not necessarily translate into making the city a desirable place to live. Cities like Chattanooga and Pittsburgh, which once struggled with the health effects of severe air pollution largely created by manufacturing industries (especially steel mills), have adopted new economic development strategies that seek to add to the employment base without bearing the environmental costs.

Of course, not all cities have come to this realization. Many cities still pursue economic development strategies without regard for the impact on the local, national, or global biophysical environment. For example, there are probably only about 45 cities with populations of at least 100,000 that now have adopted comprehensive sustainability policies or programs (Portney 2003). Still others have adopted policies and programs that at least address some specific sustainability or environmental issues, such as climate change and global warming. Although many others have made pledges to work toward achieving results that are consistent with sustainability, such as the more than 880 U.S. mayors who have signed on to the U.S. Conference of Mayors Climate Change Agreement, and the more than 190 U.S. cities that have joined the International Council for Local Environmental Initiatives' (ICLEI) Climate Change Programme, most of these cities have not actually changed their local policies and programs in response. Yet collectively, American cities may well have done more to contribute to the sustainability of the Earth over the last decade than has the federal government in Washington. This chapter reviews the depth and breadth of what cities are doing to try to become more sustainable.

Sustainability, City Politics, and City Policies

Environmentalism fits imperfectly within the conventional scholarly literature on urban politics. A predominant school of thought focuses on the challenges cities face in maintaining economic viability. To put it bluntly, the dominant view is that cities need business much more than business needs cities. As the service sector has boomed and manufacturing has declined, central cities find themselves challenged by suburbs and exurbs that can offer corporations more attractive sites, a more enticing quality of life for employees, and lower property taxes. It's difficult to argue with this logic, and examples of cities beset by decline while their adjacent suburbs have prospered come easily to mind.

This view of cities in economic decline is clearly hostile to the notion of cities as vibrant centers of environmentalism. And yet liberal advocates have succeeded in a broad range of cities in convincing local governments to establish serious, substantive programs to fight pollution, global warming, and other environmental ills. If it were just the wealthy, "yuppified" cities like Seattle or Austin, scholars could simply acknowledge such cities as rare exceptions. Instead, cities like Phoenix, Jacksonville, and even Cleveland have begun demonstrating an impressive commitment to environmentalism and sustainability. The exact relationship between economic development and the breadth and depth of sustainability programs is unclear, but successful environmentalism is too widespread to dismiss as anomalous. Why is it that so many cities have adopted programs that appear to increase the regulation of business? If cities are in economic peril—and many still are—why is it that postmaterial concerns frequently triumph in light of the obvious need to produce more jobs and more tax revenue? If the portrait painted here is correct, then it is important to understand the fabric of the changes that have occurred.

What, precisely, is the trade-off between environmentalism and economic development? At this stage in the world economy, are modern American cities really giving up the chance to enhance their economic base by embracing environmentalism? And hasn't recent literature emphasized that cities with the brightest future are global cities, cities that are information hubs and centers of financial commerce? Indeed, recent urban economics research seems to show that the assumed trade-off is not as clear-cut as one might think (Nelson and Peterman 2000; Ihlandfeldt 2007) and may even work in the opposite direction (Jeong and Feiock 2006). Although this is a fair criticism of the cities-in-peril perspective, it is naive to assume that modern cities put little at risk in aggressively attacking climate change, pollution, and other environmental problems. Perhaps most germane, there seems to be a persistent perception among policymakers that there is considerable risk because environmental protection costs money: improving mass transit, remediating brownfields, restricting development, retrofitting old buildings, building new LEED-certified buildings, and other such initiatives have serious cost and revenue implications.[1] Even where systematic analysis shows that investment in such improvements would produce substantial savings in the long term, concern over up-front costs means more immediate spending, and that means higher taxes. Moreover, businesses are sensitive to labor costs, taxes, and regulation.

This classic trade-off may seem moot because more and more of America's economic growth comes from the service sector and not from manufacturing. Yet for all the attractiveness of the low-polluting service economy, cities still find it difficult to attract major new economy businesses. Large computer companies are fond of leafy "campuses" in the exurbs, biomedical complexes are typically found in suburbs close to major universities, and the constant mergers and acquisitions in the telecommunications industry have led to many new headquarters located just about everywhere but in large cities. In short, the new economy and the recent emphasis by cities on sustainability does not appear to be a match made in heaven.

Cities are clearly involved in another trade-off, one involving lifestyles. By developing lifestyle neighborhoods and adopting smart growth strategies, many cities are trying to entice individuals to make decisions to live within their boundaries rather than in suburbs where commuting time and lack of a sense of community are counterweights to the attraction of larger homes and better schools. After decades of decline, the 2000 census demonstrated that urban populations are growing, and this strategy appears to be well timed. What political scientists need to do is to try to get beyond a constrained view of the environment versus economics trade-off to a more complex set of dynamics. In a sense, the next stage in urban research is to think rigorously about these two different trade-offs, and to determine the interplay between environmentalism, lifestyle choices, and economic prosperity. But what does such a strategy look like? The discussion of the sustainability programs in specific cities below provides a glimpse into what this strategy looks like today. Whereas some cities never seem to get beyond the environment versus economic growth trade-off debates, many others have indeed moved forward.

Chapter 1 outlined the basic characteristics of the third epoch of the environmental movement, and the sustainable cities initiatives discussed below could not provide stronger evidence of this epoch. Following the lead of some European cities (Beatley 2000), the U.S. cities that have progressed the farthest—such as Seattle, Portland, Denver, and others—started to develop a new understanding of their cities sometime in the early to mid-1990s. Since that time, this new understanding has blossomed into a more integrated approach to pursuing changes, has yielded many new "tools" and management techniques, and in many cases has produced a new political culture that supports, rather than impedes, the pursuit of local sustainability. The end result is that at least several dozen major cities today have started to chart a new course that takes them deeply into the third epoch of the environmental movement.

It is important to build a clear picture of the kinds of policies and programs that make up cities' sustainability programs. One might certainly wonder whether these programs, taken as a whole and implemented as fully as possible, would actually contribute to making the world more sustainable. But this is a question for another time. Here, the challenge is just to provide some understanding of what cities are doing. Embedded in the discussion are some lessons about how different cities have approached the political challenge—how to make the local political landscape safe for the pursuit of sustainability. The pursuit of local sustainability often clashes with mainstream views about what cities ought to be doing and with entrenched interests, especially real estate and development interests, that have a stake in continuing the unsustainable path. Sometimes advocates of sustainability must navigate political waters that are fraught with dangers and impediments, and although research on the effective ways of overcoming these dangers is in its infancy, there are some preliminary lessons that can be taken from cities' experiences.

What Does a Sustainable City in the United States Look Like?

Is there any such thing as a sustainable city? For many people, the basic concept of sustainability at the local level is impossible to imagine. The idea that any city could ever become fully sustainable is, to some, an oxymoron (Rees 1997). Even so, efforts have been made to try to measure how sustainable U.S. cities actually are by looking at the quality of the biophysical environment and many other factors. Presumably, cities whose air quality is worse are less sustainable than cities whose air quality is better. SustainLane, for example, conducts an annual analysis of how sustainable U.S. cities are, taking into account air and water quality, how long it takes to get to work, how congested the roads are, the amount of solid waste diverted from landfills, and many other factors to estimate which cities are the most sustainable today. Such analysis points to Portland (Oregon), San Francisco, Seattle, and Chicago as the most sustainable cities (SustainLane 2007).

What the SustainLane rankings do not explicitly tell us is how much of the sustainability is due to explicit efforts, especially efforts of city government, and how much of it is due to factors essentially outside of the control of the cities themselves. For example, whereas cities can certainly take responsibility for internalities such as the air emissions emitted within their borders, they typically can do nothing about externalities such as those emissions originating elsewhere that happen to affect the ambient air quality. A particular city could work very hard to reduce local emissions, only to have that effort overwhelmed by pollution traveling from faraway places. Poorer quality drinking water might be the result of explicit activities within the city, but it could also be the result of factors outside of the city's control. Of course, externalities can also be imposed by cities on others. If a city simply deals with its solid waste by sending it out of the city, that creates externalities for someone or someplace else, and this may well contribute to unsustainability. For this reason, it is important to understand what cities are doing to try to become more sustainable. How hard is a city trying to become more sustainable? Is the city taking responsibility for trying to make progress in areas where it does have some ability to affect sustainability?

Sustainability at the local level does not happen by accident. Indeed, if some cities are becoming more sustainable, it is inexorably the result of a concerted and coordinated effort on the part of many people and parties in the city, in the metropolitan area and region, and even perhaps the state. In most places, the coordinated effort is spearheaded by the city government when it decides to pursue sustainability as a matter of local public policy. Without doubt, city governments can have a substantial affect on how sustainable they are, even if they can never become entirely sustainable. Today, there are probably on the order of 45 major U.S. cities and many other smaller municipalities that have decided to adopt sustainability policies, and many others have adopted specific policies that appear consistent with a desire to try to become more sustainable. Although we may not know exactly what a sustainable city is, we can certainly make some judgments about how much effort a city is making to try to become more sustainable.

What kinds of policies and programs tend to be part of a city's coordinated public policy effort to try to become more sustainable? There are probably about 35 different policies and programs cities have adopted in this endeavor. No city has adopted and implemented them all. Yet together they provide a snapshot of what is possible for cities to accomplish. For the sake of brevity, I have organized these 36 policies and programs into seven groupings, although these groupings are largely arbitrary in the sense that some programs could easily fit under more than one category.

Smart Growth

So-called smart growth policies and activities represent the central alternative concept to traditional economic growth. The primary target of smart growth is urban sprawl—the tendency for the development of low-density expansion of cities across a large geographic area, spilling outside of the boundaries of any one local government jurisdiction to the suburbs and exurbs of major central cities.

In terms of specific policies and programs, this includes city efforts to engage in eco-industrial park development, targeted or cluster economic development, eco-village (urban infill and transit-oriented housing) projects or programs, and brownfield redevelopment projects. Eco-industrial parks represent efforts to attract environmentally friendly business to the city. In the best of all worlds, an eco-industrial park would be designed to include a business that uses or processes the waste from other businesses, and ultimately reduces the total amount of solid and hazardous waste produced and "exported" to other places.

Targeted or cluster economic development is based on the same underlying principle that cities need to designate specific types of low or nonpolluting industries to form the basis for their economic development strategies. Urban infill housing represents an effort to develop or redevelop parts of the city so that new housing is in close proximity to amenities, such as shopping areas, employment centers, and public transportation. Such housing projects are designed to reduce reliance on the automobile, and ultimately to require less energy and produce less pollution in the process. Brownfield redevelopment projects focus on trying to remove existing hazardous waste sites, or brownfields, that otherwise prevent productive use of parcels of land. Usually, brownfield redevelopment is combined with other smart growth activities so that the recovered land is used for eco-industrial parks, urban infill housing, open space, or some other environmentally friendly activity.

Land-Use Planning

Land-use planning and zoning policies and programs include the use of zoning to delineate environmentally sensitive growth areas, comprehensive land-use planning that incorporates environmental protection, and especially in cities that do not have zoning authority, the use of tax incentives for environmentally friendly development. Most cities in the United States have the legal authority to zone the land in their jurisdiction and to use that zoning authority to determine how the land will be used.

Traditionally, zoning has been used for a variety of purposes, such as ensuring that housing would be separated from industrial areas, often ensuring that people would have to drive to work. In cities that are trying to become more sustainable, particular attention is paid to how environmentally sensitive a given area is when land-use decisions are made. Instead of allowing a polluting industrial facility to be built along the banks of a river or lake, such cities now use their zoning authority to prevent that kind of facility from being located where the industry could do serious environmental damage. Some cities use various kinds of tax or fee rebates to create incentives to achieve the same results.

Transportation

Transportation planning and policies include mass transit, limits on downtown parking spaces, high-occupancy vehicle lanes on city streets, alternatively fueled city vehicle ("green fleet") programs, and bicycle ridership programs. Sometimes as part of a city's sustainability or climate change initiative, efforts will be made to reduce the need for single-occupant motor vehicles, especially in the commute to work. Since the passenger vehicle is one of the largest contributors to air emissions that contribute to climate change, and may well produce a wide array of health problems, cities trying to become more sustainable must make efforts to reduce reliance on the automobile. This inevitably means developing and maintaining mass transit systems, putting limits on the number of downtown parking spaces (which often drives up the price of parking), addition of high-occupancy vehicle (HOV) lanes on city streets, replacing city vehicles with lower-polluting alternatives (including hybrid vehicles and converting vehicles to use biodiesel fuel), and the development of bicycle lanes, paths, and trails.

Pollution Prevention

Pollution prevention and reduction includes solid and hazardous waste recycling, air emissions reduction programs (volatile organic compound [VOC] reduction or climate change programs), recycled product purchasing by city government, hazardous waste site remediation, asbestos abatement, lead paint abatement, and pesticide reduction programs. Whereas traditionally cities have seen pollution prevention as the responsibility of the federal and state governments and the private sector, more and more cities are now adopting policies that are explicitly designed to reduce the streams of various kinds of pollution in their cities. Often combined with transportation and energy programs, pollution prevention targets the sources of air, water, and ground pollution. As discussed in more detail later, this often means that the government will be working with local businesses to help them understand cost-effective alternatives to pollutive practices.

Energy and Resource Conservation

Energy and resource conservation usually focuses on green building programs, renewable energy use by city government, residential energy conservation programs (independent of green building), alternative energy (biofuels, wind power, solar, hydroelectric) offered to consumers, and water protection and conservation efforts. Especially in cities where there is great concern for climate change, local energy reduction programs form the central battlefront in the war against air emissions.

Cities also are doing more and more to promote green building, especially to promote LEED-certified green building design, sometimes through the local building codes and sometimes through technical assistance to architects, contractors, and builders; these efforts are designed to make sure that new buildings use less energy than older ones. Many cities are now pushing hard to ensure that consumers have green energy alternatives—so that consumers can at least have the option of purchasing electricity that is generated through lower polluting technologies. While nearly all cities make efforts to ensure that water is used responsibly, many cities are making more aggressive efforts that include replacing chlorination as a way of purifying drinking water.

Sustainability Indicators

Sustainability (livability) indicators projects represent explicit statements by city governments or local nonprofit organizations that any progress toward becoming more sustainable must be measured and monitored over time. An indicators project will typically explicate dozens of specific indicators of sustainability, such as the amount of energy consumed in the city, the quality of the air or water, and many others, so that baselines can be established against which future progress is to be measured. Typically, cities with indicators projects issue periodic reports that show the extent of progress and identify areas where greater effort needs to be made. Increasingly, sustainable city indicators are incorporated directly into cities' strategic plans and performance management systems rather than existing as stand-alone programs (Brugmann 1997a,b; Pinfield 1997).

Environmental and Social Justice

Environmental and social justice programs make explicit efforts to ensure that the local operational definition of sustainability takes special notice of the uneven distribution of the environmental and public health challenges and tries to ameliorate these differences. As cities work toward becoming more sustainable, some explicitly try to be sure that the benefits of sustainability are relatively equally shared across all neighborhoods and peoples. Although only a few cities have such policies or programs, for many people this represents the true core of what it means to become more sustainable (Warner 2002; Agyeman, Bullard, and Evans 2003).

Governmental and Organizational Coordination

Administrative, organizational, and managerial coordination of the environmental protection function represents an important component of any local sustainability effort. This includes whether a single government or nonprofit agency is responsible for implementing sustainability programs; whether sustainability is an explicit part of a citywide comprehensive plan; whether the city council, as well as county or metropolitan planning agencies, is involved; whether the mayor or chief executive officer is involved; whether the business community is involved; and whether the general public is involved through public hearings, a visioning process, neighborhood associations, or other public participation programs. Many cities now have departments of sustainability and have a specific person who is in charge of developing and coordinating their sustainability efforts.

No city has adopted all of the policies and programs discussed in the sections above. So how do cities rank? Based on a simple counting of the number of these programs and policies the 45 cities have adopted and implemented as of January 1, 2007, Seattle has done the most of any city in the country, adopting and implementing 31 of the 36 programs. A few cities have adopted such policies since that time, such as Philadelphia, Salt Lake City, and Racine (Wisconsin), to name three, and these cities are not yet included in the rankings. Table 9.1 shows the list of cities that have made the pursuit of sustainability official policy, and how they seem to stack up against each other. Among those on the list, Denver, Albuquerque, Los Angeles, Minneapolis, and Oakland are not far behind Seattle. This, of course, does not mean that these cities have achieved sustainability. It does mean that these cities appear to be working hard to try to become more sustainable through local public policies and programs.

What Are Specific Cities Doing to Try to Become More Sustainable?

The discussion so far has been fairly abstract; it has not discussed what specific cities are doing. Yet to get a realistic picture of what is possible, city-specific efforts hold the key. This chapter focuses on the efforts of the cities of Seattle, Portland, Denver, Austin, and Chicago, with additional discussion of Grand Rapids, Los Angeles, and New York City. At the end of this chapter, there is a list of city-specific Web sites that provide greater detail concerning what these cities are doing to try to become more sustainable.

The pursuit of local sustainability is a truly daunting task. It requires a coordinated effort across many city agencies and departments, and may even involve government agencies outside of the city, such as a regional planning agency. Most cities that engage in trying to become more sustainable do so by developing some sort of comprehensive or strategic plan that outlines all the specific areas, programs, and policies that are relevant to the task. Such comprehensive plans usually include specific goals and timetables, performance indicators (ways of measuring whether the goals are being achieved), assignment of responsibilities for achieving the goals, and where needed, proposals for creating new programs. Many sustainability plans explicitly tie the sustainability goals to state laws and local ordinances, making sure that the city has the

Table 9.1
Sustainable Cities and the Number of Sustainability Programs They Have Adopted and Implemented (as of January 1, 2007)

Rank	City	Number of Programs
1	Seattle	31
2	Portland, OR	30
2	Denver	30
4	Albuquerque	29
5	Los Angeles	28
5	Minneapolis	28
5	Oakland	28
8	Boulder	27
8	San Jose	27
8	Chicago	27
11	Santa Monica	26
11	Scottsdale	26
11	San Diego	26
14	Columbus	25
15	San Francisco	25
16	Kansas City	23
17	New York City	23
17	Sacramento	22
19	Tampa	19
19	Anchorage	19
19	Vancouver	19
22	Austin	18
22	Cambridge	18
22	Chattanooga	18
22	Tucson	18
22	Washington	18
22	Grand Rapids	18
28	Baltimore	17
28	Buffalo	17
30	Phoenix	16
31	Boston	15
31	Jacksonville	15

Table 9.1
(continued)

Rank	City	Number of Programs
31	Pittsburgh	15
34	Brookline, MA	14
34	Cleveland	14
34	Atlanta	14
37	St. Louis	13
38	Orlando	12
39	Indianapolis	11
39	Santa Barbara	11
41	Milwaukee	9
41	New Haven	9
43	Olympia, WA	8
44	Lansing/E. Lansing	7
44	Cincinnati	7

legal authority to conduct the programs. Sometimes the plans also include explicit analysis of budgetary issues—what is the city currently spending and how might that spending have to change? The preparation of such plans is a lengthy, time-consuming process, one that is usually revisited and updated periodically. Some cities start this process small, focusing on areas of greatest need, and build toward a more robust effort. But the cities with the most impressive efforts are those that have successfully incorporated sustainability throughout their comprehensive strategic plans.

Sustainability in Seattle and Portland

Perhaps the city most closely identified with the pursuit of sustainability in the United States, the city that has adopted and implemented more sustainability-friendly policies and programs, is Seattle. Portland, Oregon, is a close second. According to SustainLane's 2006 rankings, no city in the United States is more sustainable than Portland, with Seattle close behind. Together, these two cities stand as icons of how to do sustainability correctly. They not only share location in the Northwest part of the country, they also share the fact that both cities are extraordinarily participatory places. They both have extensive systems of neighborhood associations that provide residents with opportunities to be involved in their own communities as well as decisions made by city government. Although there are many possible alternative explanations for why these two cities have done so much, one cannot escape the obvious conclusion that it might have something to do with how engaged the local population is.

Seattle is a city of a little over half a million people located in the Pacific Northwest on Puget Sound. This city's efforts got under way in earnest well over a decade ago, with the resident-initiated effort that became known as Sustainable Seattle, Inc., a local nonprofit organization that assembled the city's first comprehensive sustainable indicators project (AtKisson 1996). Since that time, the Seattle government has enthusiastically gotten on board, devising and implementing a city comprehensive plan entitled "Toward a Sustainable Seattle." This plan presents in great detail all of the policies and programs pursued by the city in its effort to try to become more sustainable, and it establishes specific goals that the city seeks to achieve in this effort. Perhaps most important, it provides a comprehensive statement of how the city intends to continue to pursue sustainability well into the future. With at least 31 different policies and programs all designed to advance the achievement of greater sustainability, Seattle has just about every kind of program that any city could possible enact. Although the plan is far too complicated to discuss in detail here, one "element" of the plan will help to illustrate its approach.

As noted earlier, land-use planning and zoning represents one of the most central issues in determining how sustainable a city can be. When cities allow human activity on environmentally sensitive land without regard to possible deleterious environmental consequences, environmental degradation often results. Avoiding such consequences is both difficult and an absolute necessity for any city trying to become more sustainable. Seattle's comprehensive plan "Land Use Element" describes the three major goals that guide all other land-use policies and programs, including zoning. These goals state that the city seeks to: (1) provide for a development pattern consistent with the urban village strategy by designating areas within the city where various types of land-use activities, building forms, and intensities of development are appropriate; (2) foster neighborhoods in which current and future residents and business owners will want to live, shop, work, and locate their businesses, and also provide for a range of housing types and commercial and industrial spaces in order to accommodate a broad range of families, individuals, income groups, and business; and (3) encourage, through the city's land-use regulations, development that protects the public's health and maintains environmental quality.

Articulating such land-use goals represents an important part of any sustainability plan, but the goals must also be accompanied by policies and programs that make up an action plan. The real challenge is in how to define such policies and programs that actually achieve the goals. In Seattle, the plan presents the citywide zoning system, showing where growth is to be guided and areas where specific kinds of development would be inappropriate. It specifically tries to ensure that, for example, parking lots are not placed in close proximity to neighborhoods or in areas that would encourage greater use of the automobile. The zoning system contributes to creating "urban villages" that allow for a wide array of mixed uses to ensure that residential areas are not segregated from commercial areas, and makes possible the development of high-density housing that typically reduces the need for energy.

Even with all the programs and policies that make up Seattle's sustainability program, perhaps the single most notable aspect of the city's effort—the signature program—is the groundbreaking sustainability indicators project that was spearheaded by the nonprofit group Sustainable Seattle, Inc. (AtKisson 1996). A sustainable indicators project focuses on trying to clarify and determine the most relevant and important areas that need to be improved, such as air quality, water quality, energy consumption, and the like (Portney 2003: 31–62). For each area, at least one measure is developed, and this measure is then tracked over time to see if it is improving, staying the same, or declining. Through extensive public meetings and discussions, Sustainable Seattle managed to produce an impressive indicators document that served as the foundation of sustainability performance measurement by city government, and the document has stood as a template for many other cities that have decided to create their own indicators projects.

Portland, with a population of a little over half a million people, has a sustainability program that is also quite impressive. Not only is Portland's Comprehensive Plan thoroughly imbued with goals that are related to sustainability, it has a citywide Office of Sustainable Development responsible for implementing programs related to energy efficiency, renewable resources, waste reduction and recycling, global warming, green building, and sustainable food systems, and for coordinating sustainability policies across all other bureaus and agencies of city government. An example of how aggressive Portland has been in its pursuit of sustainability can be found in its efforts to address its energy needs. In 2007, the city established a biofuels investment fund that awarded nearly half a million dollars in grants for the development of various biofuels consistent with its renewable fuels standards. This represents one of many specific programs in Portland designed to conserve energy, to make energy consumption more efficient, and to pursue a wide array of green energy sources, including the installation of a fuel-cell electric generation facility that uses methane from its wastewater treatment facilities.

Perhaps the most important aspect of all of Portland's sustainability activities relates to its efforts to truly engage in regional growth planning (Leo 1998). Partly in order to comply with Oregon's statewide growth management policies, Portland has worked very hard to coordinate its policies with those of surrounding cities and towns mainly in Multnomah County. For example, the city established the Portland/Multnomah County Sustainable Development Commission, one of the city's many citizen advisory panels, in order to promote greater regional cooperation. This commission, composed of six residents from Portland and five from surrounding cities and towns in the county, focuses on sustainability education, greening internal government operations across the region, and a broad range of advice on sustainable economic development. Additionally, the city has made concerted efforts to participate actively in regional growth and its management, operates an extensive system of public transit, and has used annexation to ensure that areas outside of the city end up being developed in ways that assist, rather than under-mine, the city's pursuit of sustainability. Indeed, one of the major ele-ments of the city's comprehensive plan is "metropolitan coordination," outlining specific policies and programs through which city operations are consistent with those of the Metropolitan Service District, the plan-ning agency with responsibility for the metropolitan area.

In Seattle and Portland, there seems to be little doubt that the pursuit of sustainability enjoys fairly widespread popular support, and this support is articulated through the many opportunities that residents have for being engaged in their communities and government. Whether through citizen advisory panels, neighborhood associations, or directed planning-based resident participation processes, residents have rarely stood in strong opposition to the pursuit of sustainability. Occasionally, such opposition does materialize over specific proposals and projects that would seem to be consistent with sustainability. For example, when Seattle attempted to design a program to increase housing densities in established residential neighborhoods, area residents opposed and defeated such efforts.

Sustainability in Denver and Austin

Of course, the common wisdom is that cities like Seattle and Portland represent easy targets for advocates of local sustainability. Cities whose populations are perhaps less attuned to environmental protection and sustainability, so the argument goes, wouldn't be nearly as receptive to the idea. Cities that are much more attuned to the needs of local businesses, and where the business community exercises far more political leverage, would perhaps not be very interested in pursuing sustainability. Yet there are several such cities that have been aggressive about trying to become more sustainable. Two of these cities, Denver and Austin, demonstrate that the common wisdom is wrong.

Denver is a city with a population size almost identical to that in Seattle. Located in the Rocky Mountains, Denver has a long history of experiencing rapid population and economic growth and decline. The boom or bust cycles have now been largely replaced by a more stable approach to sustainability. With at least 30 of the programs and policies that contribute to becoming more sustainable, like the much smaller city of Boulder to the north, Denver is right near the top of the heap. Under the guidance of Mayor John Hickenlooper, who signed the U.S. Conference of Mayors Climate Change Agreement in 2005, Denver's pursuit of sustainability is well represented in the city's comprehensive plan and in its Greenprint Denver program. Perhaps the most impressive aspect of Denver's sustainability effort is how comprehensive it is. With special emphasis on energy and natural resource conservation programs, along with explicit efforts to reduce greenhouse gas emissions, there is almost no area of sustainability that the city has not addressed. This may seem somewhat surprising in a city that has traditionally been dominated by efforts to cultivate the business community, but with a mayor who has been a business owner, Denver's sustainability programs have a great deal of credibility across the city.

As one of the key elements of its sustainability strategy, Denver has placed a great deal of attention on trying to improve and protect air quality. Its Greenhouse Gas Reduction Plan (GGRP) includes near-term goals to reduce per capita greenhouse gas emissions by 10 percent by 2012, to require LEED Silver certification of new city buildings, to construct a solar power plant, to develop a biogas to energy power plant that uses gas captured from a waste disposal site, and to reduce overall energy usage by 1 percent a year. It also includes replacing the city's fleets of vehicles with hybrid and biodiesel vehicles. Longer-term goals are even more ambitious.

Denver's commitment to sustainability has been much more associated with a particular individual than that in most other cities. Mayor Hickenlooper has been a significant influence on the rapid involvement of the city with sustainability. What has made this possible is the fact that Hickenlooper is himself a former business owner. With a background in petroleum geology, and then as the owner of a chain of brew-pubs in the Denver area, Hickenlooper brought with him into office in 2003 a high level of credibility with the business community. As he began advocating a variety of sustainability and environmentally proactive policies, he was able to bring the business community along in support. Much like the experience in Grand Rapids, discussed later, Hickenlooper has been able to bridge the gap between advocates of sustainability and the business community by applying the concept of the "triple bottom line," a way to incorporate environmental costs and benefits into the city's finance and planning.

Austin, Texas, a city of over 700,000 people, faces a statewide political culture that would seem anything but conducive to trying to become more sustainable. Yet, perhaps largely because of its particular array of high-technology industries that form the bulk of its employment base, and the presence of the main campus of the University of Texas, it has pursued an impressive array of policies and programs designed to do just that. One of the areas where Austin has been a real leader is in the development of renewable green energy. Electricity is supplied to the City of Austin and surrounding areas by Austin Energy, Inc., a city-owned utility. As an agency of the city, Austin Energy represents the primary mechanism for the city to achieve its goals of reduced air emissions, and has invested in providing its electricity from renewable sources, primarily from 165 large wind turbines (windmills) located in West Texas. It offers consumers the "GreenChoice" option which is priced a little differently than the conventionally generated electricity, often costing residents less than electricity generated with fossil fuels. Approximately 55,000 homes in Austin now take advantage of this option. Austin Energy has also invested in solar and biogas electric generation and offers residential customers energy efficiency services and technical assistance on green building.

Other Examples: Large and Small Cities
What about the really big cities of the United States? Is the pursuit of sustainability something that is too daunting for very large cities? We certainly have the impression that New York, Chicago, and Los Angeles are cities that have more than their share of social, political, and economic challenges. In spite of this, or perhaps because of it, these cities have taken some extraordinary steps to try to become more sustainable. Indeed, in terms of how hard they are trying, these three cities are all among the most impressive in the country.

Sustainability in New York City   In late 2006, New York Mayor Michael Bloomberg announced the city's comprehensive "PlaNYC for a Greener, Greater New York," an effort to articulate a wide array of goals and programs to work toward becoming more sustainable. With a population of over 8,000,000 people, New York City operates at a scale larger than many U.S. states. The plan focuses on five specific areas: the land, where programs are designed to produce more affordable housing, to create and maintain more open space, and to clean up a considerable number of the city's brownfield sites; water, where efforts are focused on prevention of water pollution, water conservation, and improved techniques of water purification and distribution; transportation, with programs designed to expand the capacity of public transit and better management of traffic congestion, which might include instituting a London-style congestion fee; energy, calling for investment in electric generating infrastructure in order to reduce air emissions that result, working to cultivate the market for green energy, and energy conservation; air and climate change, with extensive efforts to reduce motor vehicle emissions from private cars, taxicabs, buses, and city fleet vehicles. This includes eliminating the city's motor vehicle sales tax on cars with very low emissions. The city's green building program, operated by its Sustainable Design Division of the Department of Design and Construction, applies to all city-owned buildings and construction. Given the number of buildings the city owns and operates, the magnitude of the impact produced by this program is impressive. As of 2007, over 40 major city building projects have incorporated sustainable design strategies, with many more planned.

Sustainability in Los Angeles   Los Angeles, with a population of about 3.8 million people, is a relative newcomer to the pursuit of sustainability as well. Its cross-agency SustainLA program represents an effort to coordinate the activities across many different departments and agencies. Operated mainly by the city's Environmental Affairs department, this program focuses on making improvements in numerous areas. Partly as a result of the city's heavy reliance on the automobile and the poor air quality that results, and partly in response to California's very stringent air quality standards, much of Los Angeles' sustainability efforts have focused on air quality, transportation, and energy. These also include efforts to address water quality, land use, solid waste and recycling, hazardous materials and wastes, natural resource management (parks, waterways, open space), green building, and numerous specific programs to promote green businesses. For example, the city has adopted a LEED standard for all public buildings.

With all the environmental and sustainability challenges faced by Los Angeles, there is probably none greater than that associated with the problem of metropolitan sprawl. For many, Los Angeles represents the poster child for the need to pursue an aggressive set of smart growth policies. And that is what the city has started to try to do. The city's General Plan contains numerous elements that seek to create increasing numbers of urban infill housing and urban village projects, designed as mixed-use areas to support population growth and density within the city itself. As the General Plan's housing element notes, "It is the overall housing goal of the city of Los Angeles to create a city of livable and sustainable neighborhoods with a range of housing types and costs in mutual proximity to jobs, infrastructure and services." Although significant progress toward accomplishing goal of creating urban villages is slow and incremental, projects such as this are evident throughout the city. Perhaps equally important is the attempt to integrate the planning of such villages with other city programs, most notably public transit. It is not by accident that many of the city's urban infill housing projects appear in close proximity, for example, to the relatively new subway system. This is part of the city and metro-regional strategy to build in— not out—on the 2 percent of the city's land adjacent to new rail, bus, and train stations. Presumably, coordinating the creation of desirable downtown housing with ready access to public transit will reduce the city's heavy reliance on the passenger vehicle for commuting.

Sustainability in Chicago   When in 2005 Chicago Mayor Richard Daley committed the city to become the most environmentally friendly city in the world, he set the stage for the city to embark on a very ambitious array of programs and policies in the pursuit of sustainability. Even though Chicago was not the first Midwest city to begin working on sustainability issues, in rapid order, it has established itself as the regional leader on these issues, perhaps much like Seattle and Portland stand as regional leaders in the Pacific Northwest. What makes Chicago's efforts important is how comprehensive they are, how much commitment there is at the top, and how aggressively they have targeted the accomplishment of specific programmatic results.

Focused mainly on Conserve Chicago Together, the comprehensive sustainability initiative in the city, an aggressive effort has been made to define and implement numerous policies and programs designed to move Chicago toward becoming more sustainable. Its "Environmental Action Agenda: Building the Sustainable City" policy statement articulates high-priority goals on energy conservation and green building, a comprehensive "mobility" policy involving public and other forms of transit, sustainable infrastructure and resource management (management of the water, land, air, and solid and hazardous waste), and education and outreach. The annual report provides details on accomplishments from the previous year. Some examples of accomplishments in 2005 found in the 2006 report include the purchase of solar panels to generate 1.27 megawatts of electricity for heating water in city buildings, purchase of 113 hybrid vehicles added to the city's vehicle fleet, installation of 20 green roofs, certification of 22 city buildings as LEED green buildings, creation of a program to provide incentives for city employees to ride bicycles to work, and many others. Clearly, Chicago treats the pursuit of sustainability as a comprehensive challenge involving virtually all departments and programs.

What about smaller cities? Does a city have to have a population of at least half a million people to be able to take sustainability seriously? Perhaps not. Although many of the highly rated cities do have fairly large populations, the City of Grand Rapids, Michigan, represents a city that has made remarkable progress toward trying to become more sustainable.

Sustainability in Grand Rapids   One of the most impressive and rapid transformations in trying to become more sustainable is found in the western Michigan city of Grand Rapids. Traditionally thought of as a fairly conservative area, home to former President Gerald R. Ford, Grand

Rapids has made enormous strides in recent years. Spearheaded by Mayor George Hartwell, this city of about 185,000 people has both used the pursuit of sustainability as a means for promoting economic development and used their need to rebuild their economy as a means for becoming more sustainable. Like much of Michigan, Grand Rapids was once highly dependent on manufacturing industries for their employment base and economic vitality. Over the last fifteen to twenty years, it has experienced significant declines in this manufacturing base, and finding sources of jobs to replace those has been a real challenge. Yet Grand Rapids has not shied away from the challenge.

In terms of sustainability related programs, it has created and implemented about as many as any similarly sized city in the country. It boasts the largest number of "green buildings" per capita in the country, including its relatively new civic center and major new buildings constructed for the city government and for Grand Valley State University. Through the creation of the position of sustainability coordinator, the city has worked with virtually all of its various agencies to ensure that the city is working collaboratively toward trying to become more sustainable. Indeed, what is perhaps most notable about this city's sustainability efforts is how open and collaborative it is. Primarily through the creation and operation of the Community Sustainability Partnership, practically every possible "stakeholder" or interested party has been involved in discussions of the directions in which the city should move, including numerous colleges and universities, the Western Michigan Sustainable Business Roundtable, the Grand Rapids Area Chamber of Commerce and West Michigan Hispanic Chamber of Commerce, numerous specific businesses, and many dozens of neighborhood organizations. The net result has been the pursuit of sustainability with very little political opposition. Consistent with experience in other cities, there is a healthy amount of skepticism, but this skepticism is tempered by a widespread recognition that sustainable development is an idea whose time has come.

As with Denver and a few other cities, the strength and goodwill of the mayor has been instrumental in bridging the gap between hardcore sustainability advocates and doubters, especially those in the business community. The mayor, an ordained minister and a local business owner, used his abilities to communicate with business leaders to build consensus about the value of the pursuit of sustainability. Much of his effort has been grounded in the use of the "triple bottom line" as a focusing concept in the city's Sustainability Vision Statement 2006–2010, its comprehensive plan. The triple bottom line approach represents an effort to bring full cost accounting that includes assessment of the costs of environmental impacts and the benefits of environmental protection into the city's policymaking processes. The effectiveness of this approach is that it adapts the bottom line concept that every business person knows and understands, and it does so in a way that merges the need for financial efficiency with concern for the biophysical environment. This approach seems to make it likely that potential opposers of new sustainability-related programs that may cost money will temper their opposition as long as they understand what these expenditures produce for the triple bottom line.

Why Do Cities Choose to Pursue Sustainability?

Perhaps the most difficult question to answer definitively is why some cities elect to chart a path that they believe will make them more sustainable. It is probably safe to say that cities choose such a path when they are convinced that it is highly consistent with their needs and values. More specifically, some cities look to sustainability policies to create a competitive advantage for their economic development activities. Chattanooga, Tennessee, for example, seems to see the pursuit of sustainability as a way to grow the local economy, and to do so without returning to the days when they had serious air pollution. Other cities focus on sustainability as a way to save money, especially on energy costs, and seem only willing to move down the path toward sustainability when it's fiscally feasible. Still other cities look to sustainability policies as a mechanism through which quality of life issues can be addressed. Indeed, one of the principal drivers for large numbers of cities is the sense that the local population demands that the municipal government address livability and quality of life issues. In short, many cities understand that keeping their population base, and attracting new residents, requires attention to protecting and improving the biophysical environment.

Conclusion

The pursuit of sustainability is alive and well in U.S. cities. The third epoch of the environmental movement, discussed in chapter 1, focuses on sustainable communities defined broadly, with special emphasis on the rise of a local eco-centric ethic. The result is a deeper understanding of the need to balance long-term societal and natural system needs, and a reexamination of the assumed trade-off between the pursuit of economic development and the protection of the environment. This chapter shows that many U.S. cities have taken on this challenge and have moved well into the third epoch. Indeed, they are helping to define this epoch. Instead of deferring responsibility for the biophysical environment, these cities have started to take explicit responsibility for managing, protecting, and repairing it; instead of embracing policies and programs that simply shift environmental impacts elsewhere in place or time, these cities have started to look to their larger metropolitan and regional areas in an effort to achieve greater coordination. New methods of governance have emerged that embrace collaborations between government and the private sector and nonprofit sectors, all working toward a new vision of what makes their cities livable and sustainable.

Thus far, no fewer than 45 major U.S. cities have decided that the pursuit of sustainability is a valuable and important goal to be achieved through municipal policies and programs. This pursuit of sustainability has taken many forms, and has been adopted for a number of different reasons. Today, there are at least 35 different specific policies and programs cities have developed and implement in this pursuit. These policies and programs, ranging from revisions in zoning and land uses, to protection of green space, to commitment to green building, energy efficiency and climate change efforts achieved through greenhouse gas emission reductions, conversion to alternative and green energy sources, and many others, are all designed to try to improve and protect the quality of the environment for the short and long term. Many of these cities have incorporated their full range of policies and programs into a comprehensive strategic plan designed to provide guidance to all city policymakers and administrators.

Interest in the pursuit of sustainability at the local level is motivated by many goals. Sometimes, as in Chattanooga and Milwaukee, sustainability is seen as the way to engage in twenty-first century economic development. Sometimes it is seen as a necessary condition for maintaining and attracting residents by making the city an appealing and desirable place to live. Still others are motivated more purely by a desire to help protect the environment and to do something to combat climate change.

Whatever the specific motivation, cities have made enormous strides in transforming their governmental operations, their local economies, and their pollution profiles.

This chapter has documented some of the many city-based policy and program changes that are characteristic of the third epoch as manifest in specific U.S. cities. These changes have ushered in an era replete with opportunities for extensive research needed to determine which of these policies and programs seems most effective in achieving sustainability goals. What is the long-term environmental effect of the policies pursued in Seattle, Portland, and elsewhere? What kinds of programs seem better able to contribute to balancing long-term societal and natural system needs? How do these policies influence the kinds of economic development in the city, and the patterns of economic development outside of the city? What kinds of urban political and governance structures seem best able to embrace the pursuit of sustainability? These are the kinds of questions that will animate future research as the third epoch of the environmental movement unfolds.

Note

1. LEED is an acronym for Leadership in Energy and Environmental Design, a program sponsored by the U.S. Green Building Council.

References

Agyeman, Julian, Robert Bullard, and Bob Evans. 2003. "Introduction: Joined-up Thinking: Bringing Together Sustainability, Environmental Justice and Equity." In *Just Sustainabilities: Development in an Unequal World*, ed. Julian Agyeman, Robert Bullard, and Bob Evans, 1–16. Cambridge, MA: MIT Press.

Agyeman, Julian, and Bob Evans. 1995. "Sustainability and Democracy: Community Participation in Local Agenda 21." *Local Government Policy Making* 22, 2 (October): 35–40.

AtKisson, Alan. 1996. "Developing Indicators of Sustainable Community: Lessons from Sustainable Seattle." *Environmental Impact Assessment Review* 16: 337–350.

Beatley, Timothy 2000. *Green Urbanism: Learning from European Cities*. Washington, D.C.: Island Press.

Bowman, Ann O'M. 2006. "Environmental Issues in Big City Politics." Paper delivered at the 2006 Meeting of the American Political Science Association, Philadelphia.

Brugmann, Jeb. 1997a. "Is There a Method in Our Measurement? The Use of Indicators in Local Sustainable Development Planning." *Local Environment* 2, 1 (February): 59–72.

Brugmann, Jeb. 1997b. "Sustainability Indicators Revisited: Getting from Political Objectives to Performance Outcomes—A Response to Graham Pinfield." *Local Environment* 2, 3 (October): 299–302.

Bulkeley, Harriet, and Michele M. Betsill. 2003. *Cities and Climate Change: Urban Sustainability and Global Environmental Governance.* London: Routledge.

Costanza, Robert, Herman Daly, and Thomas Prugh. 2000. *The Local Politics of Global Sustainability.* Washington, D.C.: Island Press.

Downs, Anthony. 2000. *Dealing Effectively with Fast Growth.* Washington, D.C.: Brookings Institution Center on Urban and Metropolitan Policy, Policy Brief no. 67, November. Available at http://www.brook.edu/dybdocroot/comm/policybriefs/pb067/pb67.htm.

Ihlandfeldt, Keith R. 2007. "The Effect of Land Use Regulation on Housing and Land Prices." *Journal of Urban Economics* 61, 3 (May): 420–435.

Jeong, Moon-Gi, and Richard Feiock. 2006. "Impact Fees, Growth Management, and Development: A Contractual Approach to Local Policy and Governance." *Urban Affairs Review* 41, 6 (July): 749–768.

Kahn, Matthew. 2006. *Green Cities: Urban Growth and the Environment.* Washington, D.C.: Brookings Institution Press.

Leo, Christopher. 1998. "Regional Growth Management Regime: The Case of Portland, Oregon." *Journal of Urban Affairs* 20: 363–394.

Nelson, Arthur C., and David R. Peterman. 2000. "Does Growth Management Matter? The Effect of Growth Management on Economic Performance." *Journal of Planning Education and Research* 19: 277–285.

Pinfield, Graham. 1997. "The Use of Indicators in Local Sustainable Development Planning: A Response to Jeb Brugmann." *Local Environment* 2, 2 (June): 185–188.

Portney, Kent E. 2003. *Taking Sustainable Cities Seriously: Economic Development, the Environment, and Livability in America Cities.* Cambridge, MA: MIT Press.

Portney, Kent E. 2005. "Civic Engagement and Sustainable Cities in the U.S." *Public Administration Review* 65, 5 (September/October): 577–589.

Portney, Kent E. 2007. "Local Business and Environmental Policies in Cities." In *Business and Environmental Policy: Corporate Interests in the American Political System*, ed. Michael E. Kraft and Sheldon Kamieniecki, 299–326. Cambridge, MA: MIT Press.

Potapchuk, William. 1996. "Building Sustainable Community Politics: Synergizing Participatory, Institutional, and Representative Democracy." *National Civic Review* 85, 3 (fall): 54–59.

Press, Daniel, and Alan Balch. 2002 "Community Environmental Policy Capacity and Effective Environmental Protection." In *New Tools for Environmental Protection: Education, Information, and Voluntary Measures*, ed. Thomas Dietz and Paul Stern, 183–200. Washington, D.C.: National Academies Press.

Rees, William E. 1997. "Is 'Sustainable City' an Oxymoron?" *Local Environment* 2, 3 (October): 303–310.

Selman, Paul. 1996. *Local Sustainability: Managing and Planning Ecologically Sound Places*. New York: St. Martin's Press.

SustainLane. 2007. *The SustainLane 2006 US City Rankings*. Found at: http://www.sustainlane.com/us-city-rankings/. Accessed 10 October 2007.

Warner, Kee. 2002. "Linking Local Sustainability Initiatives with Environmental Justice." *Local Environment* 7, 1 (February): 35–47.

Further Reading: Web Sites about Specific Cities Sustainability Efforts (all Web sites last accessed October 9, 2007)

Albuquerque: http://www.cabq.gov/sustainability

Anchorage: http://home.muni.org/iceimages/Planning/f2020_introduction.pdf

Atlanta: http://www.aia.org/static/state_local_resources/adv_sustainability

Austin: http://www.ci.austin.tx.us/sustainable/

Baltimore: http://www.ci.baltimore.md.us/government/planning/

Boston: http://www.cityofboston.gov/environment/

Boulder: http://www.ci.boulder.co.us/ (under "Departments" and "Environmental Affairs")

Brookline, MA: http://www.townofbrooklinemass.com/Parks/pdf/Sustainability Inventory.pdf.

Buffalo: http://www.ci.buffalo.ny.us/files/1_2_1/Mayor/COB_Comprehensive _Plan/section_2459290796.html

Cambridge: http://cambridge-live-sustcity.runtime-collective.com/ccm/portal/

Chattanooga: http://www.chattanooga.gov/Files/NCCIReportF.pdf

Chicago: http://egov.cityofchicago.org/ (under "City Departments" and "Environment")

Cincinnati: http://www.sustainablecincinnati.org/

Cleveland: http://www.nhlink.net/enviro/scp/description.html and http://www.ecocitycleveland.org/

Columbus: http://getgreencolumbus.com/

Denver: http://www.greenprintdenver.org/

Grand Rapids: http://www.grand-rapids.mi.us/index.pl?page_id=415

Indianapolis: http://www.indygov.org/ ("Indy GreenPrint" under "Newsletters")

Jacksonville: http://www.jaxgreen.org/12/

Kansas City, MO: http://www.kcmo.org/planning.nsf/web/about?opendocument

Lansing/East Lansing: http://www.urbanoptions.org/sustain/slhome.htm and http://www.cityofeastlansing.com/

Los Angeles: http://www.lacity.org/ead/EADWeb-Sustainable/sustainable.htm and http://www.sustainla.org/

Milwaukee: http://www.city.milwaukee.gov/PowerGreen13218.htm

Minneapolis: http://www.ci.minneapolis.mn.us/sustainability/GreenPrint07_home.asp

New Haven: http://www.cityofnewhaven.com/CityPlan/pdfs/PlanningPrograms/ComprehensivePlan/SectionXEnvironment.pdf

New York City: http://www.nyc.gov/html/planyc2030/html/home/home.shtml

Oakland: http://www.sustainableoakland.com/Page774.aspx

Olympia, WA: http://www.ci.olympia.wa.us/community/sustainability/

Orlando: http://greenorlando.com/category/sustainability

Phoenix: http://phoenix.gov/PLANNING/gpsum.pdf

Pittsburgh: http://www.sustainablepittsburgh.org/

Portland, OR: http://www.portlandonline.com/osd/

Sacramento: http://cityofsacramento.org/planning/long-range/citywide-and-regional/sustainability.cfm

San Diego: http://www.sandiego.gov/environmental-services/sustainable/index.shtml

10

Collaborative Watershed Partnerships in the Epoch of Sustainability

Mark Lubell, William D. Leach, and Paul A. Sabatier

Chapter 1 of this volume uses an "epochs" framework to analyze the evolution of environmental policy from the command-and-control heyday of the 1970s through the more decentralized, collaborative epoch of sustainability. This chapter argues that collaborative watershed partnerships are one of the pillars of the sustainability epoch. It is hard to argue with this statement given the massive growth in watershed partnerships in the last twenty years, with concomitant excitement about the approach from scholars, practitioners, and politicians. Kenney (2001, 188) states emphatically that collaborative partnerships are "the most significant and exciting development in natural resources management since the environmental movement of the 1960s and 1970s."

The origins of the watershed movement can be roughly traced to the late 1980s and early 1990s. Although we know of no accurate estimate of the number of partnerships, we believe that partnerships are still growing in number, and there are easily over 1,000 partnerships nationwide. Partnerships are active in every U.S. state, and there are known to be approximately 150 to 300 active in California (California Resources Agency 2002), about 90 in Oregon (Oregon Watershed Enhancement Board 2004), and at least 35 in Washington (Washington Department of Ecology 2003). According to an analysis of data from the National Watershed Network, there were 958 watershed partnerships in 1997, and 75 percent of those were created after 1990 (Lubell et al. 2002). Kenney et al. (2000) identify 346 partnerships in the Western United States and estimate that 91 percent of those were started after 1990. The watershed partnership phenomenon has spread all over the world, especially in Canada and Australia (Margerum 1995; Marshall 1998). Pretty (2003) estimates approximately a half-million watershed groups throughout the world.

Like the other environmental policy epochs, the watershed partnership phenomena can be characterized by how it defines environmental problems, preferred implementation strategies, information/data management needs, and predominant political context. Watershed partnerships focus on "unsolved" environmental problems that have continued to challenge more centralized institutions. Chief among these problems are nonpoint source pollution from urban and agricultural sources, habitat and biodiversity loss, and ecosystem degradation. These problems are linked in terms of coming from diffuse and complex sources, involving the decisions of many individual people and organizations, and spanning administrative and jurisdictional boundaries. Thus solving these problems requires cooperation from many stakeholders with diverse and often conflicting social values.

Given the need for cooperation, the preferred implementation strategy relies heavily on collaborative decision processes, incentives, and voluntary participation. The decision processes usually are structured into various committees, each of which gives some input into a broader executive committee charged with developing a resource management plan. The inclusive decision structure usually includes economic and environmental interest groups, local governments, state/federal agencies, scientists, Native American tribes, and sometimes specific outreach to environmental justice groups. Whereas the resulting management plans typically consider the implications of existing regulations, the actual restoration activities utilize grant money and incentives. The use of regulatory processes or litigation is often a signal that the partnership is failing to achieve cooperation. In many cases, the partnership is only advisory to a government agency, which retains the final approval over a specific plan.

The best (but not all) watershed partnerships explicitly adopt an "adaptive management" information and data strategy. Adaptive management views policymaking as an experiment in the context of uncertain ecological processes. Scientists are purposely involved in the process in order to inject appropriate theory and research design. A good adaptive management program collects extensive environmental data over long time periods, and then changes policies as appropriate to meet policy goals. Such extensive monitoring can be very costly, and adaptive management is also challenged by the short-term incentives of politicians, the difficulty of changing bureaucratic organizations, the desire of businesses to have a stable set of policy rules, and criticisms from citizens who do not understand why government cannot get it right in the first place.

The predominant political context is local, decentralized, and focused on civic engagement. Watershed partnerships are designed to reflect the social, economic, and environmental preferences of local communities. At the same time, they eschew centralized, standardized rules in favor of bureaucratic flexibility and policy rules modified to fit local circumstances. Accordingly, they are quite diverse in both their decision structures and management strategies. The partnerships strive to engage stakeholders in the policy process, and to have them take responsibility for their own backyards. The political context of partnerships usually spans the economic, social, and environmental goals of sustainability.

Do watershed partnerships contribute to the goal of sustainability? Despite a predominantly positive view of watershed partnerships among scholars and practitioners, there is a growing host of criticisms about both their efficacy (e.g., Coglianese 2003; Lubell 2004a) and legitimacy (McCloskey 1996; Kenney 2000). Do watershed partnerships really achieve sustainability goals, or are they merely symbolic policies that provide an illusion of progress but fail to solve underlying problems? Do watershed partnerships inappropriately devolve decision making to local stakeholders, and undermine the public accountability of national governance institutions? Do watershed partnerships divert cooperation away from existing governance institutions in a way that undermines past successes? Are watershed partnerships consistent with the principles of democratic governance (Leach 2006a)? If stakeholders are to make informed decisions about whether to continue supporting and participating in watershed partnerships, we need to better understand how they have worked in the past, and how they might be designed in the future to maximize their benefits for environmental problems and democratic processes.

In this chapter, we summarize the current state of knowledge about the factors influencing the success of watershed partnerships. We begin by discussing a conceptual framework for watershed partnerships that identifies aspects of the collaborative process, participants, and context that may influence effectiveness. We next summarize the findings from the watershed partnerships literature, focusing in depth on the National Estuary Program study (Mark Lubell, John Scholz, Mark Schneider) and the Watershed Partnership Project (Bill Leach, Paul Sabatier, Neil Pelkey, Chris Weible, and others). These studies are notable for their use of large empirical datasets to identify the factors associated with partnership success. The conceptual framework presented in this chapter receives further testing through a new set of parallel analyses of the NEP and WPP data. We originally developed the framework and analysis for a working paper commissioned by the National Research Council (Lubell and Leach 2005).

A Conceptual Framework for Watershed Partnerships

In this section, we discuss the conceptual framework for explaining the effectiveness of watershed partnerships presented in figure 10.1. The solid arrows in the framework represent causal links supported by analyses of the WPP and NEP projects, and by building on the framework presented in *Swimming Upstream: Collaborative Approaches to Watershed Management* (Sabatier et al. 2005; hereafter referred to as *Swim-*

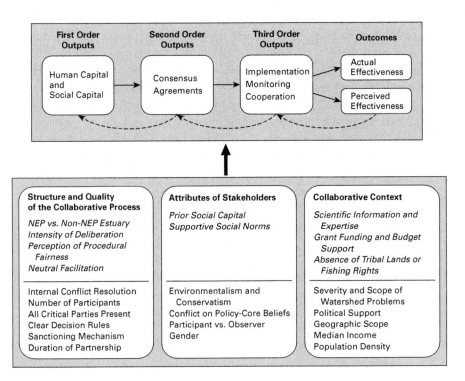

Figure 10.1
Conceptual model of watershed partnerships.

ming Upstream). The framework draws links between partnership outputs and outcomes, our dependent variables, and the structure, participants, and context of the partnership. To foreshadow our conclusions, figure 10.1 lists in italics (above the lines) those factors that we have confirmed to affect partnership success through multiple analyses of the WPP and NEP data, as well as findings from other researchers. Below the lines (in normal print) are variables that are hypothesized to affect success, but do not receive consistent support across analyses.

The framework draws extensively on three theoretical approaches that have been used to analyze partnerships: institutional rational choice (IRC), the Advocacy Coalition Framework (ACF), and social capital. The IRC approach focuses on how institutional structures shape the incentives and behaviors of involved actors and, along with the attributes of the environmental problems and community, ultimately determine the benefits and costs of cooperation. The ACF describes how actors form coalitions on the basis of shared belief systems, where stakeholders' basic social values shape their perceptions of environmental problems and preferred policies. The social capital literature argues that partnerships encourage cooperation by developing norms of reciprocity, trust, and networks of civic engagement. We will refer to each of these theories in the discussion below, and more extensive discussion is available in *Swimming Upstream*.

One limitation of this framework is that we assume that outputs and outcomes at any given time are linked in a one-way sequential chain running from the building of social capital, to the forging of policy agreements, to policy implementation, to outcomes. It is certainly plausible that the relationships are reciprocal over time (as depicted by the dashed arrows); for example, improved environmental outcomes leading to higher levels of consensus and policy agreement. However, we feel that the causal arrows depicted in the framework are most likely stronger than the reciprocal relationships. For example, Leach and Sabatier (2005a) find that trust relationships influence the extent of partnership agreements, but not vice versa. However, we do not have adequate data to test all of the possible more complex causal relationships, so we maintain the sequential chain as a simplifying assumption.

The Sequential Purposes of Watershed Partnerships

As mentioned in the introduction, the purpose of watershed partnerships is to solve the environmental problems and associated social problems that have not been adequately addressed by command-and-control regulations. These types of problems receive top billing in the environmental projects of the National Estuary Program: 42 percent address habitat preservation, 44 percent wildlife protection, and 58 percent nonpoint source pollution (Lubell 2004b), and in West-coast watershed partnerships: 70 percent water quality, 57 percent habitat, and 57 percent salmon or steelhead. The watershed partnerships identified by the Natural Resources Law Center (Kenney et al. 2000) also identify water quality and habitat degradation as the most frequent problems.

That is not to say watershed partnerships do not address traditional issues like point source pollution. The integrated, ecosystem approach advocated by most partnerships tries to consider all the potential causes of environmental problems in the watershed. However, because watershed partnerships tend to emphasize problems that are not adequately managed by existing institutions, they are best thought of as complements to (not substitutes for) existing policies.

Achieving the ultimate goal of watershed protection requires three instrumental goals along the way, which we label first-, second-, and third-order outputs. First-order outputs are building human and social capital among the partnership stakeholders. Social capital is defined as trust, networks, and norms of reciprocity, all of which are known to be an important basis for cooperation (Colman 1988; Putnam 1993, 2000). Many partnerships begin with some type of conflict and high levels of distrust between stakeholders. Repeated interactions among stakeholders who have had few previous opportunities for face-to-face deliberation allows partnerships to break out of the "vicious" circle of noncooperation and move into the "virtuous" circle of reciprocal cooperation (Putnam 1993). In addition, many stakeholders enter the process with low levels of human capital in terms of the technical aspects of the policy options under deliberation. The educational and scientific activities of the partnership help build human capital for making better-informed decisions.

Second-order outputs are the forging of policy agreements, which are embodied in watershed management plans. The consensus decision-making procedures of partnerships are designed to produce agreement on the characteristics of watershed problems, policy goals, required information, the best policy tools, and the economic and environmental consequences of proposed policies. This agreement is then translated into some type of watershed management plan that describes the range of actions different parties should take. The management plan can be conceptualized as a contract between the multiple stakeholders involved, where each stakeholder is given some responsibility to execute the terms of the contract.

Third-order outputs are the specific projects and monitoring that are completed to implement the terms of the plan, including any provisions for adaptive management. These include restoration projects, changes in land-use practices, revised water quality regulations, and the like. Plan implementation is challenging because there are few hierarchical relationships among stakeholders and limited formal mechanisms for enforcing the agreement. Thus, implementation in watershed partnerships requires broad cooperation, both across stakeholders and within each organization or interest group that is party to the agreement. Cooperation among signatories occurs chiefly through peer pressure and appeals to norms of reciprocity, and through the threat of political embarrassment should any party decide to renege on a prior commitment.

The Structure of Watershed Partnerships: Form Follows Function

Collaborative policies have several distinct structural and process features; the extent to which a particular partnership incorporates these structural features may influence effectiveness. The focus on the structural features of the partnerships is the main contribution of the institutional rational choice approach to the study of cooperation and watershed partnerships.

Inclusive and representative participation is particularly important to the success of watershed partnerships. In all forms of policy processes, nonparticipants can potentially cause disruptions by challenging the final decision (as can participants if they dislike the decision). But in watershed partnerships, a nonparticipant can thwart the objectives of the partnership simply by refusing to negotiate or using alternative venues (e.g., courts) to undermine any partnership agreements. The reason many collaborative groups organize themselves around hydrological boundaries is to include all the public and private entities whose land-use activities influence watershed conditions. One possible disadvantage of the inclusive nature of partnerships is that increasing the number and heterogeneity of participants makes collective action more difficult (Olson 1965; Libecap 1989).

Because participation is voluntary, watershed partnerships generally utilize some type of consensus decision-making rules. Cooperation is usually higher when there is agreement on structure of the decision rules, and the rules are clear to participants. Consensus decision-rules are especially useful for decision making in the face of scientific uncertainty because they do not force participants to make commitments until they are comfortable with the relative risk and potential payoff. In some cases, consensus rules are supported by provisions in the management plans that are designed to sanction noncooperators. The most common type of sanctioning mechanism is that of conditional statements that specify the appropriate response of other actors to nonfulfillment of the contract (e.g., if actor X does not complete this project, then actor Y does not have to provide funding).

Partnerships often retain the services of a professional neutral facilitator to actively structure the dialogue at partnership meetings, and/or a watershed coordinator to handle the administrative tasks associated with hosting partnership meetings and applying for grants on behalf of the partnership. However, in probably the majority of partnerships, these tasks are handled by one or more participating stakeholders—typically staff of either a lead convening agency, or of a relatively neutral agency such as a university cooperative extension office or a resource conservation district (Leach and Sabatier 2003).

Structural features like consensus rules and neutral facilitation are used to enhance the capacity for conflict resolution within the context of the partnership, and also the overall perception of procedural fairness. Consensus and cooperation are much less likely when stakeholder conflicts are moved to alternative venues like the courts, legislature, or agency rule-making. Once the conflict moves to more traditional political venues, it is likely to be plagued with all the traditional problems of environmental policy that partnerships are designed to avoid. The process may be viewed as unfair if certain categories of stakeholders are excluded or if their interests are not being heard and reflected in the management plans. A process might also be seen as unfair if one particular group or coalition dominates.

Some other structural characteristics of the partnership may also matter; these may or may not be measured in a particular study. Older partnerships that have survived a hazardous political environment usually engage in a broader range of activities. Sometimes a partnership will be organizationally housed in a particular agency, but even then the partnership staff sometimes is funded from multiple sources. Some partnerships rely on a local agency (e.g., a county or resource conservation district) to serve as the official applicant for grant funds. Other partnerships opt out of agency sponsorship, and instead set up their own nonprofit 501(c)(3) organization as a mechanism for obtaining grants. Others forgo grant funds and operate strictly on the participants' in-kind contributions of time, labor, or materials.

Attributes of Stakeholders in Watershed Partnerships

The effectiveness of watershed partnerships is also influenced by the characteristics of the stakeholders who are participating in the process. One of the most important participant traits is social capital, which we treat as both an instrumental goal of partnerships and a catalyst for other forms of partnership success. But stakeholders also enter partnerships with established levels of social capital, and these preexisting networks, norms of reciprocity, and trust may provide a good foundation for reaching consensus on watershed management plans. Some stakeholders have a formal role in a partnership, and others may only be outside observers. Formal participants are more likely to exhibit a commitment to the process.

Stakeholders also bring different types of social values and belief systems into the partnership process. The Advocacy Coalition Framework argues that when stakeholders have belief systems congruent with the structure and purpose of watershed partnerships, they are more likely to cooperate, and less likely to use alternative venues to question the effectiveness and legitimacy of any outputs. Belief systems are important because social values affect how people process information, form beliefs about policy effectiveness, and make decisions about cooperation. The WPP and NEP projects focus on four key social values that are generally discussed in partnership processes:

Environmentalism   Preference for environmental protection over economic development and a general belief in the value of biodiversity.

Conservatism   Preference for private property rights and a belief that the market is superior to government for determining allocation of natural resources.

Inclusiveness   Preference for maximum public participation in policy decisions.

Consensus norm   Belief in resolving environmental policy issues through consensus-based decisions.

The main prediction is that differences in social values among stakeholders will impede the attainment of consensus-based policy agreements. Another prediction is that norms of inclusiveness and consensus are conducive to partnership success because they are fundamental assumptions of every collaborative process and are congruent with goals of the partnership. Unlike the case of traditional environmental regulation, the effects of environmentalism and conservatism are unclear in the context of watershed partnerships. Environmentalists might be more likely to support collaborative partnerships because they direct attention and resources to environmental problems. However, many prominent environmentalists have opposed collaboration on the grounds that, among other things, it tends to coopt government agencies charged with upholding environmental laws (McCloskey 2000; Wilson and Weltman 2000). The hypothesis for conservatism is equally unclear. Conservatives generally resist any type of coercive environmental regulation, but the emphasis of watershed partnerships on voluntary compliance may lead conservatives to prefer partnerships over command-and-control structures.

The Context of Watershed Partnerships

The context of watershed partnerships is generally defined by the physical–biological attributes of the watershed itself, the state of scientific knowledge about relevant socioecological parameters, the surrounding political and policy environment, and the structure of the communities within that watershed (Ostrom 1990).

The severity of environmental problems in a watershed is a particularly important factor because the benefits of collaboration are greatest when there is some problem to solve. For that reason, watershed partnerships are more likely to evolve in degraded watersheds (Lubell et al. 2002), and individual stakeholders are more motivated to participate if they believe problems are severe. There is some discussion (mostly among practitioners) about preservation of relatively pristine watersheds as another important motivation for forming a partnership, and certainly some of the National Estuary Program partnerships are in less-developed watersheds. However, there has been no clear demonstration in the watershed partnership literature that preservation is considered as important as restoration of degraded watersheds.

One of the most important contextual factors is the availability and quality of scientific information and expertise. If stakeholders believe the science is murky or biased, they are much less likely to forge a policy agreement. Poor science generates uncertainty and allows divergent social values to continue to divide stakeholders. Partnerships will use mechanisms like guest speaker series, public meetings, and research reviews to communicate scientific information to other stakeholders. In addition, partnerships very often commission new research that is designed to inform specific policy questions within the partnership. Therefore, scientific knowledge is not strictly an attribute of the partnership context, but may also be an indicator of the quality of the collaborative process itself.

Partnerships can be supported or undermined by administrative and policy decisions from higher levels of the federal system, such as state/federal legislation, court decisions, rule-making, and budgets. Partnerships, like any other organization, thrive on administrative support in the form of grants, budget allocation, and personnel. These resources can be secured by political entrepreneurs who fight to bring these resources to bear on local projects. Partnerships can also be deprived of these same resources by unfriendly actors. It is very rare for a partnership to survive without at least some political support from higher levels.

The presence of Native American tribes in a watershed often adds an additional layer of complexity to the collaborative process. Native Americans have experienced a long history of abuse and broken treaties at the hands of U.S. government officials, which may make them reluctant to enter new agreements (Cronin and Ostergren 2007). Many Native American tribal representatives in the WPP cases subscribe to a biocentric set of social values that potentially conflicts with the European values of other stakeholders. Tribes govern themselves with a variety of traditional formal and informal institutions and cultural norms, making it difficult for nonnative stakeholders to understand whom to negotiate with, or the proper etiquette (Jostad, McAvoy, and McDonald 1996). These issues suggest the need for extra effort to bridge the cultural gap with Native American tribes, which often rely heavily on natural resources, have been forced to live in more degraded watersheds, and have local knowledge that can be invaluable for policymaking.

Watersheds with broad geographic scope, for example the Columbia River Basin and the San Francisco Bay Delta, possibly face greater challenges for collaboration such as a greater number and complexity of problems, greater number of actors, and longer travel distances to partnership meetings. Also, many partnerships tend to focus on a core conservation area, and in large watersheds this may leave many of the causes of local problems outside the scope of the partnership.

Summary of Existing Watershed Partnership Research

In this section, we summarize findings from existing research from the NEP and WPP that can provide some explanations for partnership success. We provide supporting evidence from other studies of watershed partnerships as well. However, this is not meant to be a review of the entire watershed partnership literature. We refer the reader to Leach and Pelkey 2001 for a more extensive discussion.

We believe that the WPP and NEP projects are the two best existing studies of watershed partnerships in terms of the breadth of quantitative data, number of partnerships considered, and the potential for comparison to watersheds without partnerships (NEP study). However, it is important to be explicit about the strengths and weaknesses of the research designs for these projects. A common weakness of both projects is measuring only attitudes and/or outputs. The NEP project relies mainly on attitudes and beliefs about policy effectiveness, cooperation, and conflict resolution as the dependent measures of success. The WPP also uses attitudes and beliefs, but adds archival data about the number and extent of watershed projects. Neither project—nor any other research that we know of—measures environmental outcomes in a systematic and comparative fashion. Although many researchers are actively searching for ways to fill this void (Meridian Institute 2003; CBCRC 2004), one of the outstanding questions in partnership research is the use of environmental indicators to evaluate effectiveness.

The main advantage of the WPP is the use of over 70 partnerships in California, Oregon, and Washington. This provides enough data for a reliable aggregate-level statistical analysis, at least with statistical techniques that do not rely on asymptotic assumptions (e.g., linear regression), especially for the contextual variables that vary across watersheds. For each partnership, the WPP relies on three to five in-person interviews and a mail-administered survey of all participants (with an average response rate of 65 percent). The WPP does not include measures from watersheds without partnerships. Therefore it is impossible for the WPP to evaluate the effectiveness of partnerships in comparison to traditional governance institutions.

The NEP project uses stakeholder survey data from 20 estuaries with the NEP, and 10 estuaries without the NEP. The NEP study provides the comparative aspect that is lacking in the WPP, and averages 36 respondents per estuary (57 percent response rate across all estuaries) in Wave 1 of the survey, allowing fairly reliable estimates of central tendencies within watersheds. However, with only 30 watersheds, the aggregate-level analyses have limited statistical reliability. There will necessarily be a fairly large error term in any aggregate-level multivariate analysis. Because of this, any of the new analyses reported below use individual respondents as the unit of analysis.

Previous Findings from the National Estuary Program Study

The four most relevant papers from the NEP are Lubell (2003; 2004a,b) and Schneider et al. (2003). Each of these papers uses a different measure of outputs to draw conclusions about what explains the success of partnerships. Lubell (2003) uses perceived effectiveness of estuary policies as the dependent variable. Perceptions of policy effectiveness are higher among stakeholders who believe that science is adequate; conflicts can be resolved within existing institutions; and institutions have fair processes. Perceived effectiveness is also higher for those who trust other stakeholders and have policy-core beliefs congruent with the structure of collaborative institutions. On average, stakeholders from NEP watersheds view policies as more effective than stakeholders from non-NEP watersheds (controlling for nonrandom selection). However, there are interactions between policy-core beliefs and the institutional setting: the positive effects of the NEP are concentrated among environmentalists who believe policy should be inclusive. Lubell (2003) confirms many of the causal relationships hypothesized in figure 10.1.

Schneider et al. (2003) focus the analysis directly on the structure of policy networks within the estuaries. The primary conclusion is that networks within the NEP have higher frequencies of interaction, and are more likely to span multiple interests and levels of government. At the same time, NEP networks are positively associated with several attitudes that form the basis for cooperation: trust, perceived effectiveness, fairness, and conflict resolution. Taken together, Lubell (2003) and Schneider et al. (2003) make a strong case that the NEP increases social capital, and that social capital is linked to important indicators of success.

Lubell (2004a) goes a step further by measuring the number of cooperative activities engaged in by stakeholders and the perceived level of consensus on several watershed issues. The same basic factors explain cooperation and consensus: scientific knowledge, trust, fairness, conflict resolution, and policy-core values. The analysis also finds that cooperation and consensus is higher among stakeholders who believe that agency budgets and commitment to estuary policies had increased. NEP stakeholders also show higher levels of consensus relative to non-NEP, but the NEP appears to be operating indirectly by improving the other intermediate beliefs (e.g., trust, scientific knowledge). However, NEP stakeholders have the same level of cooperation as non-NEP stakeholders (with a small possibility of *less* cooperation), which indicates the potential for symbolic policy.

Lubell (2004b) takes a different approach by measuring the level of conflict resolution for 112 conflicts and the level of cooperation for 102 environmental projects nested within NEP and non-NEP estuaries. The project/conflict analysis confirmed many of the previous conclusions, but also added some new findings about the watershed context. Projects with a broader geographic scope and limited level of stakeholder representation had less cooperation. The ability to resolve conflict was negatively affected by changes in higher-level policies, but positively affected by changes in key personnel. One possible interpretation of this finding is that changing the rules creates uncertainty, whereas changing people may allow for political entrepreneurship.

The NEP informants reported two key lessons for partnership coordinators: act as neutral mediators between conflicting parties, and spend more time building the infrastructure for cooperation rather than trying to implement management actions normally within the scope of particular agencies. Building the infrastructure for cooperation includes scientific research, public awareness campaigns, facilitating communication, and leveraging interagency cooperation. That is not to say that NEP managers completely avoid implementation; over 50 percent were involved in some type of implementation activity. But their time was more heavily weighted toward the infrastructure for cooperation.

Previous Findings from the Watershed Partnerships Project

Findings from the WPP study regarding factors influencing partnership success have been reported in a number of publications and working papers, each focusing on a subset of independent and dependent variables designed to test hypotheses from either the practitioner literature or from the three theoretical frameworks described above. In all, the

WPP study has focused on six measures of success: level of agreement, restoration projects (i.e., project implementation), monitoring projects, perceived effects on human and social capital, perceived effects on watershed conditions, and interpersonal trust. Leach, Pelkey, and Sabatier (2002) describe in detail how the first five of these success measures is measured and how it varies across partnerships.

Leach and Sabatier (2005b) describe and model interpersonal trust. The most important predictors of interpersonal trust include stable interpersonal relationships, small group size, generalized social trust, norms of consensus, perceived procedural fairness, clear decision rules, political stalemate, congruence on policy-related beliefs, and an absence of devil-shift (the belief that one's opponents are more powerful than one's allies). Surprisingly, null or negative correlations exist between trust and social network density, as measured by membership in voluntary associations. Overall, theories derived from the Advocacy Coalition Framework do at least as well as those based on rational choice assumptions.

Leach and Sabatier (2005a) focus on how trust and social capital influence partnership agreements, project implementation, and perceived outcomes in the watershed. The chapter finds that trust is important for promoting agreements, especially among older partnerships. Younger partnerships, however, frequently overcome distrust to reach complex agreements. Agreements are also more likely in partnerships where the watershed is in a state of crisis (flooding is a particularly powerful stimulus), and where the stakeholders share strong norms of reciprocity and wield adequate authority to negotiate on behalf of the organizations they represent. Trust and social capital do not directly affect the implementation of restoration projects, but do indirectly affect implementation by influencing agreements (as in the sequential outputs hypothesized in figure 10.1). Once agreements are reached, project implementation primarily depends on two basic resources: time and money.

Leach and Sabatier (2003) focus on the role that partnership facilitators and coordinators play in influencing these same measures of success. They found that both professional facilitators (trained and hired neutrals) and layperson/stakeholder facilitators can be effective. However, in general, agreements were positively correlated with facilitators who were disinterested (i.e., neutral nonstakeholders), but negatively correlated with those who were hired, trained, and/or *perceived* as being effective. The result holds up even when controlling for the severity or intractability of the problems in the watershed.

Parallel Analysis of WPP and NEP Data

Previous NEP and WPP analyses have not explicitly considered the integrated conceptual framework presented in figure 10.1. Below, we briefly report the results of a new analysis of the NEP and WPP data that attempts to address all the key elements of the conceptual framework in a similar manner. Tables 10.1 and 10.2 summarize how each study measures the key dependent and independent variables. As the tables show, neither study measures all the variables. When a given variable is included in both studies, it is measured differently in each study. Having different methods actually enhances the strength of the combined analysis when the same variable measured in two different ways has a similar effect on dependent variables.

The new analyses are presented as regression models in tables 10.3 and 10.4. The regression models show that the attributes of successful partnerships differ from less successful partnerships. More specifically, the models provide a quantitative means of testing hypotheses about which contextual, structural, and stakeholder attributes are most important for explaining variation in success across partnerships. From a technical standpoint, any variables that have positive coefficients will increase the likelihood of success, while negative coefficients decrease the likelihood of success. Thus, to the extent these results are correct, the potential for any particular partnership to succeed or fail can be partially evaluated by assessing the strength of each variable in that partnership (e.g., how good is the scientific information?). The regression analyses complement figure 10.1 by quantitatively demonstrating those variables that are more important (above the lines in figure 10.1) or less important for explaining success (below the lines in figure 10.1).

The new analyses explicitly take into account the sequential nature of partnership goals by including earlier outputs as independent variables in the equations predicting the later outputs. This setup essentially creates a set of structural equations and requires two simplifying assumptions to make accurate regression estimates. First, there are no reciprocal linkages between the sequential outputs and outcomes. As mentioned previously, though there may be some reciprocal linkages over time, we feel the causal direction is stronger in the order we describe. Second, we assume there is no correlation between the error terms of each regression equation. This is admittedly a strong assumption, and there are techniques for estimating the models in the presence of correlated errors (namely, instrumental variables). However, these techniques have strict

Table 10.1
Measurement of Selected Dependent Variables in NEP and WPP Studies

Dependent Variables	NEP Study Measurement	WPP Study Measurement
Outcomes		
Policy effectiveness	Stakeholder perceptions	Index measuring the perceived effect upon twelve ecological and social parameters in the watershed, weighted by the perceived importance of each parameter. (index)
Third-Order Outputs		
Project Implementation	N/A	Index measuring the number, scope, and completion of partnership projects, weighted by the estimated likelihood that the project would not have happened (at all, as soon, or as well) without the partnership.
Cooperation	Incidence of seven types of cooperation	N/A

Table 10.1
(continued)

Dependent Variables	NEP Study Measurement	WPP Study Measurement
Second-Order Outputs		
Consensus/Agreement	Perceived agreement on six issues: causes of estuary problems, severity of estuary problems, required research, best policy tools, economic consequences of policy, and environmental consequences of policy (Chronbach's alpha 0.86).	Index of level of policy agreement: 0 = no agreement; 1 = agreement on issues to address; 2 = agreement on general goals or principles; 3 = agreement on one or more implementation actions; 4 = agreement on comprehensive watershed management plan.
First-Order Outputs		
New Human and Social Capital	N/A	Scale measuring perceived degree that the partnership has provided (a) "new long-term friendships or professional relationships," (b) "a better understanding of other stakeholders' perspectives," and (c) "a better understanding of the physical or biological processes in the watershed" (Chronbach's alpha 0.75).

Table 10.2
Measurement of Selected Explanatory Variables in NEP and WPP Studies

Independent Variables	NEP Study Measurement	WPP Study Measurement
Structure and Quality of Collaborative Process		
Number of Participants	N/A	Average attendance at meetings
Perceptions of Fairness	Own interests represented; no interest group dominant	Perceived procedural fairness, representation of all critical interests, representation of local community
Intensity of Deliberation	Teamwork among stakeholders	Number of hours per month spent on partnership related activities
Conflict Resolution	Ability to resolve conflict within process	N/A
Neutral Facilitation	N/A	Neutral facilitation (dummy variable)
Enforcement Mechanisms	N/A	Sanction on defectors (dummy variable)
Age of Partnership	N/A	Months since partnership inception
Collaborative Versus Non-Collaborative	National Estuary Program	N/A
Attributes of Stakeholders		
Existing Social Capital	Trust (1-item scale), density of social networks (number of allies mentioned)	Trust in other stakeholders (5-item scale), density of social networks (number of voluntary organizations) and projected stability over 5-year time horizon.
Social Norms	Inclusiveness	Norms of reciprocity and consensus

Table 10.2
(continued)

Independent Variables	NEP Study Measurement	WPP Study Measurement
Conducive Social Values	Environmentalism, property rights, role of government	Anthropocentric conservatism (9-item scale, includes property rights and human relationship to nature)
Value Conflict	N/A	Conflict among stakeholders on policy core values regarding relative seriousness of various problems in watershed (index)
Demographic Controls	N/A	Gender, Participant Versus Observer
Collaborative Context		
Scientific Information	Perceived adequacy of science	Perceived adequacy of information, Perceived access to scientific expertise
Administrative Support	Perceived increased budget commitment, perceived increased political support	Grant funding received ($)
Geographic Scope	Size of estuary (1000 square miles)	Size of watershed (square miles)
Scope of Problems	Perceived scope of behavioral changes required	N/A
Severity of Problems	Perceived problem severity, actual problem severity from EPA	Perceived environmental crisis
Multiple Sovereign Nations	N/A	Tribal land or fishing rights in watershed (dummy variable)
Demographic Controls	Median income, population density	N/A

Table 10.3
Reanalysis of Wave 2 National Estuary Program Data

	Consensus Model (N = 840)	Cooperation Model (N = 840)	Perceived Effectiveness (N = 840)
Outcomes			
Perceived Effectiveness	—	—	—
Third-Order Outputs			
Cooperation	—	—	.07 (.04)*
Second-Order Outputs			
Consensus	—	-.002 (.04)	.22 (.05)**
First-Order Outputs			
Size of Ally Network (Preexisting)	.03 (.04)	.12 (.05)**	.13 (.05)**
Trust (Preexisting)	.13 (.03)**	.03 (.03)	.09 (.04)**
Structure and Quality of Collaborative Process			
NEP Partnership	-.15 (.13)	-.36 (.14)**	1.06 (.17)**
Internal Conflict Resolution	.02 (.02)	-.04 (.02)*	.04(.02)
Intensity of Deliberation	.13 (.04)**	.06 (.03)*	.07 (.04)*
Procedural Fairness	.12 (.04)**	.10 (.04)**	.18 (.05)**
Economic Interests Dominate	-.004 (.02)	.01 (.03)	-.03 (.03)
Environmental Interests Dominate	-.03 (.02)	-.02 (.02)	.08 (.02)*

Table 10.3
(continued)

	Consensus Model (N = 840)	Cooperation Model (N = 840)	Perceived Effectiveness (N = 840)
Attributes of Stakeholders			
Inclusiveness Norm	.005 (.02)	.03 (.02)	.08 (.03)**
Economic Conservatism	−.04 (.03)	−.02 (.03)	.04 (.03)
Environmentalism	.05 (.02)**	−.01 (.02)	.03 (.03)
Context of Collaborative Process			
Perceived Severity of Environmental Problems	.04 (.03)	.06 (.03)*	.04 (.04)
Actual Severity of Environmental Problems	−.014 (.009)*	−.008 (.01)	Insig.
Perceived Scope of Environmental Problems	.005 (.02)	.02 (.02)	−.02 (.03)
Budget Support	.08 (.04)*	.16 (.06)**	.16 (.06)**
Scientific Information	.17 (.02)**	−.05 (.03)*	.09 (.04)**
Political Support	−.08 (.08)	.12 (.08)	.03 (.10)
Median Income (Thousands)	.009 (.01)	.01 (.01)	.009 (.01)
Natural Log Area (Square Miles)	−.09 (.06)	−.02 (.07)	.11 (.08)
Population Density (Thousands per Square Mile)	1.09 (.32)*	−.13 (.39)	−.38 (.43)
Constant	3.30 (.91)**	1.64 (1.05)	−2.41 (1.24)**
Model Fit	$F = 21.48^{**}$ $R^2 = .37$	$F = 3.43^{**}$ $R^2 = .09$	$F = 30.12^{**}$ $R^2 = .43$

Note: All cell entries are unstandardized OLS regression partial slope coefficients, with robust standard errors in parentheses. Null hypothesis tests of parameters = 0; *p < .10; **p < .05

Table 10.4
Reanalysis of Watershed Partnerships Project Data

	Perceived Effect on Human and Social Capital (N = 1286, Individual Level)	Level of Agreement (N = 76, Partnership Level)	Project Implementation (N = 76, Partnership Level)	Perceived Effect on Watershed (N = 1278, Individual Level)
Second-Order Outputs				
Project Implementation	—	—	—	.01 (.004)**
First-Order Outputs				
Level of Agreement Reached	—	—	1.61 (.67)**	—
Structure and Quality of Collaborative Process				
Duration (years[1])	.01 (.01)	.92 (.17)**	.25 (.12)**	.01 (.005)**
Neutral Facilitator/ Coordinator	.03 (.03)	.14 (.07)**	.002 (.01)	.002 (.01)
All Critical Parties Present	.09 (.05)*	-.12 (.10)	.30 (.70)	-.03 (.03)
Sanctions on Defectors	-.05 (.09)	—	3.96 (1.6)**	.05 (.05)
Number of Participants	.004 (.00)*	—	—	-.002 (.00)
Attributes of Stakeholders				
Conflict on Policy-Core Beliefs	-.01 (.01)*	-.04 (.04)	-.22 (.22)	-.01 (.00)**
Social Network Density	-.004 (.01)	.05 (.06)	.81 (.38)**	-.005 (.00)
Trust	.56 (.05)**	-.80 (.42)*	-.41 (1.8)	.39 (.03)**
Interaction: Trust x Duration > 3 yrs	—	1.53 (.52)**	—	—
Norm of Reciprocity	—	.25 (.13)*	—	—
Norm of Consensus	.13 (.02)**	—	—	.06 (.01)**
Stable Policy Networks	.20 (.03)**	—	—	.03 (.02)*
Anthropocentric Conservatism	-.06 (.03)**	—	—	-.10 (.01)**

Table 10.4
(continued)

	Perceived Effect on Human and Social Capital (N = 1286, Individual Level)	Level of Agreement (N = 76, Partnership Level)	Project Implementation (N = 76, Partnership Level)	Perceived Effect on Watershed (N = 1278, Individual Level)
Intensity of Deliberation (Hours/Month)	.01 (.00)**	—	—	.001 (.00)*
Nonparticipant Observer	−.30 (.08)**	—	—	.06 (.04)
Female	.26 (.07)**	—	—	.004 (.04)
Collaborative Context				
Grant Funding ($100,000 s)	−.002 (.02)	—	.07 (.03)*	.003 (.00)**
Geographic Scope (ln 100 sq. miles)	−.02 (.02)	.01 (.04)	−.21 (.26)	.03 (.01)**
Native American Tribes Involved	−.02 (.07)	−.49 (.16)**	.43 (1.1)	−.13 (.04)**
Available Scientific Expertise	.18 (.08)**	.07 (.18)	1.10 (1.2)	.15 (.04)**
Adequate Scientific Information	.18 (.06)**	—	—	−.03 (.03)
Perceived State of Crisis in Watershed	.01 (.01)	—	—	−.01 (.02)
Constant	−.57 (.54)	2.84 (1.4)*	−9.46 (10)	−1.48 (.29)**
Model Fit	F = 32.2** adj. R^2 = .31	F = 6.7** adj. R^2 = .46	F = 5.5** adj. R^2 = .40	F = 36.9** adj. R^2 = .37

Notes: The duration variable is a continuous variable indicating number of years the partnership has existed, with the exception of the "Level of Agreement" model, which uses a dichotomous dummy variable indicating partnerships older than three years. All cell entries are unstandardized OLS regression partial slope coefficients, with robust standard errors in parentheses. Null hypothesis tests of parameters = 0; $*p < .10$; $**p < .05$

data requirements that we do not believe can be met by our data. Thus, we must be satisfied with our simplifications.

Table 10.3 presents the results of the NEP reanalysis. The NEP reanalysis here is different from previous analyses in two ways: (1) all data are from the second wave of the panel study, which has not been analyzed to this point and thus complements earlier analyses; (2) it adds some new variables identified by figure 10.1. Like the previous analyses, this analysis uses individuals from both the NEP and non-NEP watersheds as the unit of analysis, robust standard errors to control for heteroscedasticity and correlated errors across estuaries, and imputed values for missing data due to item nonresponse.

Table 10.4 presents the results of the WPP reanalysis, focusing on four dependent variables: perceived effect on human and social capital, level of policy agreement achieved, project implementation, and perceived effect on watershed conditions. The middle two dependent variables are measured at the partnership level, and the corresponding models are similar to previously published analyses, with a few new variables reported. The first and last dependent variables are measured and modeled at the individual level ($n \geq 1278$). No previously published WPP analysis has modeled these variables at the level of individual respondents—arguably the most appropriate level for modeling stakeholders' perceptions.

New NEP Findings

The NEP reanalysis reiterates some of the broad lessons from previous work. Fairness, social networks, trust, budget support, and scientific analysis (with one exception) remain the strongest predictors of partnership effectiveness at multiple stages. Social values and internal conflict resolution play a secondary role, and estuary characteristics show no effect (probably because of the small number of total estuaries).

As shown by the model fit statistics, the attitudes of consensus and perceived effectiveness are much easier to explain than cooperative behavior. In fact, although NEP stakeholders perceive partnership policies as much more effective (the same is true for consensus when looking at differences in means), levels of cooperation are actually lower in the NEP. This finding highlights the difficulty of changing behaviors, and also the possibility that changes in attitudes could produce only symbolic progress.

The NEP models moderately support our sequential view of partnership outputs and outcomes, with both consensus and cooperation being significant predictors of perceived effectiveness. Interestingly, consensus has a larger substantive influence than cooperation, which again emphasizes that relationships between attitudes are more likely to be significant than relationships between attitudes and behaviors. The fact that behaviors do not always follow attitudes is well known in social psychology. Surprisingly, consensus does not affect cooperation, which may reflect the overall difficulty of predicting behavior, or that both cooperation and consensus are simultaneously necessary for producing successful outcomes.

The NEP reanalysis does have some new findings that were not explored in previous papers. The intensiveness of deliberation, as measured by stakeholder teamwork, has a uniformly positive effect on partnership success. However, in our view the NEP intensiveness variable is probably susceptible to reciprocal causation, so we cannot conclusively determine whether teamwork or success comes first. Like many of the variables, there are probably reinforcing dynamic relationships over time. The cooperation analysis does produce a couple of surprising results. The adequacy of scientific knowledge and internal conflict resolution both appear negatively related to cooperation. These findings are completely contrary to the bulk of previous analyses, and we consider them an aspect of the difficulty of explaining cooperation rather than a serious refutation of previous conclusions.

New WPP Findings

The WPP reanalysis examines two dependent variables at the individual level and two objective measures of partnership outputs. The two individual level measures are perceived increases in human/social capital (which are highly correlated with each other), and perceptions of effectiveness (the closest analogue to the NEP analysis). The two objective variables are derived from analysis of partnership documents and measure the extent of agreement on watershed management plans and breadth of project implementation (see Leach, Pelkey, and Sabatier 2002 for discussion of project implementation scale).

The new analysis reiterates several findings from previous work. First, the results firmly support the sequential view of partnership outputs and outcomes, with trust (one form of social capital) helping to explain policy agreements; agreements in turn predicting project implementation; and project implementation influencing perceived effects on the watershed.

The scope of policy agreements achieved by partnerships is most significantly affected by the duration of the negotiations, neutral facilitation, absence of tribal involvement, and interpersonal trust. The positive effect of trust is concentrated among partnerships three years or older, which suggests that social capital takes some time to emerge and become effective. Project implementation is primarily influenced by time and money (i.e., duration and funding), and augmented by dense social networks and partnerships with mechanisms for imposing sanctions on stakeholders who violate consensus-based policy agreements.

A partnership's perceived effect on watershed conditions is related to three types of partnership resources (time, money, and availability of scientific expertise) plus a key partnership accomplishment (project implementation). However, the most influential variable is the respondent's level of interpersonal trust. A second highly significant predictor is the respondent's general confidence in consensus-based processes. These two measures also influence perceived effectiveness in the NEP analysis. As speculated previously in Leach and Sabatier (2005b), this result suggests that perceptions of effectiveness are subject to a "halo effect" in which stakeholders exhibiting high levels of trust and consensus norms are apt to grade their partnership higher on effectiveness. Reassuringly, however, the significance of the four objective measures of partnership resources and accomplishments suggests that perceptions of success are not totally subjective, as might be suggested by the symbolic policy hypothesis.

Two additional attributes of watershed stakeholders are also significant. First, conservative stakeholders rate their partnerships lower on effectiveness, suggesting that, at least in California and Washington State, conservative stakeholders perceive that partnerships threaten their property rights more so than liberals perceive that partnerships coopt regulatory or land management agencies. Second, perceived effectiveness is lower among stakeholders whose policy-core beliefs vary widely from the average prevailing beliefs in the partnership. This result is consistent with the notion that consensus-based processes generate centrist policy outcomes that are relatively unsatisfying to stakeholders holding more extreme views.

Finally, two contextual variables are also important for explaining perceived effects on the watershed. Perceived effectiveness is higher in larger watersheds, suggesting that the additional complexity of larger watersheds is not a significant obstacle, and that it pays to aim high. This finding contradicts the predictions of both the IAD and ACF frameworks, and also the findings from Lubell (2004b). Perceived effectiveness is lower in watersheds with tribal land or fishing rights (suggesting again that tribal sovereignty and culture prove difficult for nonnative stakeholders to navigate). The significance of the watershed-level contextual variables reiterates the total number of partnerships examined as a major strength of the WPP research design.

The model of perceived effects on new human and social capital yields several results consistent with theory. Respondents who spend more hours working on partnerships and who identify as participants rather than observers are more likely to perceive new human and social capital. These results suggest that the first-order benefits of collaboration are roughly proportional to the amount of time and energy the stakeholders invest, which is one way to measure the intensity of deliberation. Another important variable is the respondent's belief that they will continue to regularly interact with the other partnership participants over the next five years. This result exemplifies Axelrod's (1984) "shadow of the future" hypotheses that individuals are more likely to cooperate in the context of long-term relationships. The model also exhibits large coefficients for trust and consensus norms, as would be expected considering that trust and norms are explicit elements of social capital. Similarly, the influence of scientific expertise and information is expected, as new technical knowledge about the watershed is the primary aspect of human capital captured in the dependent variable.

Watershed Partnerships: Implications for Sustainability

The existing research, previous analyses of the WPP and NEP projects, and the parallel analyses presented in this chapter give some idea of the factors affecting the success of watershed partnerships. Among the most important are perceived fairness, levels of trust, density of social networks, the quality of science, presence of neutral facilitators, intensiveness of deliberation, and availability of financial resources. Interestingly, features of the watershed itself such as size and problem severity have less of an influence on success than the social and structural characteristics of the process. This reinforces the importance of understanding how social and political factors work in the context of uncertain, complex environmental problems.

What are the implications for sustainability? Given the still-growing popularity of watershed partnerships for solving complex environmental problems, understanding what makes them tick is no doubt important. Though the science of watershed partnerships and other forms of collaborative management is still very young, we are beginning to know enough to give some practical recommendations about how to structure partnerships to achieve their goals. And for better or worse, partnerships are well enough established in the environmental policy landscape that their existence must be analyzed.

Perhaps more important for sustainability, the research on watershed partnerships has generated more questions than it has answered. Given the lack of long-term comparative studies, we really have no idea whether or not collaborative partnerships are superior to traditional command-and-control policies for achieving any of the social, environmental, or economic goals of sustainability. At least the environmental goals of watershed partnerships are currently being discussed; the discussion of economic and social goals has barely even started. Also, though we know some of the factors that increase cooperative attitudes and behaviors, we do not know much about how those factors themselves emerge. For example, no existing studies adequately explain why some stakeholders perceive higher levels of fairness, or why some partnerships are seen as being fairer than others. One possible answer from the social psychology literature suggests that fairness is related to stakeholders' ability to have their voices heard and to have some influence on the outcomes of the process (Tyler and McGraw 1986; Lind 1995; Tyler and Blader 2000).

Our research also points to several cautionary tales. For example, we should be wary of potential symbolic policy in partnerships (i.e., consensus without collaboration), which may be one reason for their popularity. Partnerships are not going to work in all situations, such as where existing stocks of social capital or scientific information or funding are very thin, or where decisions must be made expeditiously owing to environmental crises or statutory deadlines. The role of partnerships must also be understood relative to the other existing governance institutions in a particular watershed. Otherwise, partnerships risk transferring cooperative energy away from existing policy venues.

These cautionary tales are echoed by recent troubles in three of the best-known watershed partnerships: the Chesapeake Bay Program, CALFED, and the Comprehensive Everglades Restoration Plan. Despite millions of dollars of expenditures over multiple years, these programs have not solved their main environmental problems. Founded in 1983, the Chesapeake Bay Program is one of the oldest watershed partnerships in the country and has influenced much of the collaborative environmental policy movement. Yet in 2004 the normally collaborative Chesapeake Bay Foundation created a litigation branch that has been involved in several lawsuits, and by 2006 only 29 percent of the water quality goals were achieved (Chesapeake Bay Program 2006), with little possibility of meeting the 2010 nutrient management goals. In 2005, the CALFED program was severely criticized by a government oversight committee and several key officials resigned (Little Hoover Commission 2005), and now in 2008 the California Bay-Delta has record-low levels of key species like the Delta smelt and Chinook salmon, the courts have sharply curtailed water exports. Acting on a recommendation from the Pacific Fisheries Management Council, the National Marine Fisheries Service completely closed the commercial and sport Chinook salmon fisheries in California and severely restricted salmon fishing in Oregon and Washington for the 2008 season. Similar stories are occurring in the Everglades, where phosphorous standards continue to be violated and eight billion dollars of restoration projects are behind schedule. The enormous scale of these partnerships may prove to be a significant barrier to success (Heikkila and Gerlak 2005), and there are some smaller-scale success stories like the Blackfoot Challenge (Weber 2000). But overall, despite the popularity of collaborative approaches, there is no conclusive and systematic evidence that watershed partnerships are more effective than other environmental policy tools.

Given this, we cannot conclude that strong environmental laws and regulations are any less essential today than previously. The three epochs framework articulated in chapter 1 makes clear that each ensuing epoch never fully replaces the policies and programs of the epoch before. However, in the case of watershed management in the United States, perhaps it is more accurate to say that the epoch of sustainability has not supplanted environmental regulation *at all*. State and federal laws governing water quality and endangered species continue to dominate the week-to-week activities of most participants in watershed partnerships, albeit with considerably more flexibility, ingenuity, and collaboration than in days before the partnership movement ascended to dominance in the late 1980s.

Analyses of the WPP and NEP datasets show that relationships between regulatory activity and partnership formation are undeniably complex.

Command-and-control enforcement is associated with both higher and lower incidence of partnership formation depending on the type of enforcement being measured and the type of statistical models used to infer the relationship (Lubell et al. 2002; Leach 2000). It stands to reason, however, that as environmental enforcement is relaxed, regulated parties will at some point lack the incentive to show up at the negotiating table. Unfortunately, debates about whether collaboration and consensus-building are good or bad for sustainability have remained anecdotal at best (Leach 2006b). Until better studies are devised, we should be cautious about implying that command-and-control regulation belongs to a bygone era.

We do not wish to leave the impression that watershed partnerships are useless, because they do indeed address problems that were unresolved in previous epochs and even a troubled watershed partnership may be better than no policies at all. The task for environmental policy research is to further pin down the conditions under which partnerships will work in order to maximize their contribution to sustainability. We believe that resolving the unanswered questions about collaborative environmental management (with respect to both its value relative to alternatives, and to the determinants of successful collaboration) will require ambitious studies employing comparative and longitudinal research designs, large sample sizes, collection of detailed data on partnership structure, participants, and context, and multiple measures of success.

References

Axelrod, Robert. 1984. *The Evolution of Cooperation.* New York: Basic Books.

California Resources Agency. 2002. "Addressing the Need to Protect California's Watersheds: Working with Local Partnerships: Report to the Legislature" (as required by AB 2117, Chapter 735, Statutes of 2000).

CBCRC. 2004. *Evaluation Methods Workshop Summary.* Evaluation Methods Workshop, Community Based Collaboratives Research Consortium, Frisco, Colorado.

Chesapeake Bay Program. 2006. "Bay Health Status." Http://www.chesapeakebay.net/status_waterquality.aspx?menuitem=19646.

Coglianese, Cary. 2003. "Is Satisfaction Success? Evaluating Public Participation in Regulatory Policymaking." In *The Promise and Performance of Environmental Conflict Resolution,* ed. R. O'Leary and L. B. Bingham, 69–89. Washington, D.C.: Resources for the Future.

Colman, James S. 1988. "Social Capital in the Creation of Human Capital." *American Journal of Sociology* 94: S95–S120.

Cronin, Amanda E., and David M. Ostergren. 2007. "Democracy, Participation, and Native American Tribes in Collaborative Watershed Management." *Society and Natural Resources* 20, 6: 527–542.

Heikkila, Tanya, and Andrea K. Gerlak. 2005. "The Formation of Large-Scale Collaborative Resource Management Institutions: Clarifying the Roles of Stakeholders, Science, and Institutions." *Policy Studies Journal* 33, 4: 583–612.

Jostad, Patricia M., Leo H. McAvoy, and Daniel McDonald. 1996. "Native American Land Ethics: Implications for Natural Resource Management." *Society and Natural Resources* 9, 6: 565–581.

Kenney, Douglas S. 2000. *Arguing about Consensus: Examining the Case against Western Watershed Initiatives and Other Collaborative Groups Active in Natural Resources Management.* Boulder, CO: Natural Resources Law Center, University of Colorado School of Law.

Kenney, Douglas S. 2001. "Are Community Watershed Groups Effective? Confronting the Thorny Issue of Measuring Success." In *Across the Great Divide: Explorations in Collaborative Conservation and the American West,* ed. Philip Brick, Donald Snow, and Sarah Van de Wetering, 188–193. Washington, DC: Island Press.

Kenney, Douglas S., Sean T. McAllister, William H. Caile, and Jason S. Peckham. 2000. *The New Watershed Source Book: A Directory and Review of Watershed Initiatives in the Western United States.* Boulder: Natural Resources Law Center, University of Colorado School of Law.

Leach, William D. 2000. "Federal Environmental Law and the Occurrence of Watershed Partnerships." In *Evaluating Watershed Partnerships in California: Theoretical and Methodological Perspectives.* Doctoral dissertation, Graduate Group in Ecology, University of California, Davis.

Leach, William D. 2006a. "Collaborative Public Management and Democracy: Evidence from Western Watershed Partnerships." *Public Administration Review* 66, s1: 100–110.

Leach, William D. 2006b. "Theories about Consensus-Based Conservation." *Conservation Biology* 20, 2: 573–575.

Leach, William D., and Neil W. Pelkey. 2001. "Making Watershed Partnerships Work: A Review of the Empirical Literature." *Journal of Water Resources Planning and Management* 127, 6:378–385.

Leach, William. D., Neil W. Pelkey, and Paul A. Sabatier. 2002. "Stakeholder Partnerships as Collaborative Policymaking: Evaluation Criteria Applied to Watershed Management in California and Washington." *Journal of Policy Analysis and Management* 21, 4: 645–670.

Leach, William D., and Paul A. Sabatier. 2003. "Facilitators, Coordinators, and Outcomes." In *The Promise and Performance of Environmental Conflict Resolu-*

tion, ed. Rosemary O'Leary and Lisa Bingham, 148–171. Washington, D.C.: RFF Press.

Leach, William D., and Paul A. Sabatier. 2005a. "Are Trust and Social Capital the Keys to Success? Watershed Partnerships in California and Washington." In *Swimming Upstream: Collaborative Approaches to Watershed Management*, ed. Paul Sabatier, Will Focht, Mark Lubell, Zev Trachtenberg, Arnold Vedlitz, and Marty Matlock, 233–258. Cambridge, MA: MIT Press.

Leach, William D., and Paul A. Sabatier. 2005b. "To Trust an Adversary: Integrating Rational and Psychological Models of Collaborative Policymaking." *American Political Science Review* 99, 4: 491–503.

Libecap, Gary. 1989. *Contracting for Property Rights*. New York: Cambridge University Press.

Lind, E. A. 1995. *Social Conflict and Social Justice: Some Lessons from the Social Psychology of Justice*. Leiden, the Netherlands: Leiden University Press.

Little Hoover Commission. 2005. *Still Imperiled, Still Important: The Little Hoover Commission's Review of the CALFED Bay-Delta Program*. Report no. 183.

Lubell, Mark. 2003. "Collaborative Institutions, Belief-Systems, and Perceived Policy Effectiveness." *Political Research Quarterly* 56: 309–323.

Lubell, Mark. 2004a. "Collaborative Environmental Institutions: All Talk and No Action?" *Journal of Policy Analysis and Management* 23, 3: 549–573.

Lubell, Mark. 2004b. "Resolving Conflict and Building Cooperation in the National Estuary Program." *Environmental Management* 33, 5: 677–691.

Lubell, Mark, Mark Schneider, John T. Scholz, and Mihriye Mete. 2002. "Watershed Partnerships and the Emergence of Collective Action Institutions." *American Journal of Political Science* 46, 1: 148–163.

Lubell, Mark, and William D. Leach. 2005. "Watershed Partnerships: Evaluating a Collaborative Form of Public Participation." Working paper commissioned by the Panel on Public Participation in Environmental Assessment and Decision Making, National Research Council, Washington, D.C.

Margerum, Richard D. 1995. "Integrated Watershed Management: Comparing Selected Experiences in the U.S. and Australia." *Water Resources Update* 100: 36–47.

Marshall, David. 1998. "Watershed Management in British Columbia: The Fraser Basin Experience." *Environments* 25, 2–3: 64–79.

McCloskey, Michael. 1996. "The Skeptic: Collaboration Has Its Limits." *High Country News* 28 (May 13).

McCloskey, Michael. 2000. "Problems with Using Collaboration to Shape Environmental Public Policy." *Valparaiso University Law Review* 34, 2: 423–434.

Meridian Institute. 2003. *Workshop Summary.* Workshop on Assessing Environmental Outcomes of Community-Based Collaboratives. Snowbird, Utah, September 12–13, 2003.

Olson, Mancur. 1965. *The Logic of Collective Action: Public Goods and the Theory of Groups.* Cambridge, MA: Harvard University Press.

Oregon Watershed Enhancement Board. 2004. *Locally Organized Watershed Councils in Oregon.*

Ostrom, Elinor. 1990. *Governing the Commons: The Evolution of Institutions for Collective Action.* Cambridge: Cambridge University Press.

Pretty, Jules. 2003. "Social Capital and the Collective Management of Resources." *Science* 302, 5652: 1912–1914.

Putnam, Robert D. 1993. *Making Democracy Work: Civic Traditions in Modern Italy.* Princeton, NJ: Princeton University Press.

Putnam, Robert D. 2000. *Bowling Alone: The Collapse and Revival of American Community.* New York: Simon and Schuster.

Sabatier, Paul, Will Focht, Mark Lubell, Zev Trachtenberg, Arnold Vedlitz, and Marty Matlock, eds. 2005. *Swimming Upstream: Collaborative Approaches to Watershed Management.* Cambridge, MA: MIT Press.

Schneider, Mark, John Scholz, Mark Lubell, Denisa Mindruta, and Matthew Edwardsen. 2003. "Building Consensual Institutions: Networks and the National Estuary Program." *American Journal of Political Science* 47, 1: 143–158.

Tyler, Tom R., and Steven Blader. 2000. *Cooperation in Groups: Procedural Justice, Social Identity, and Behavioral Engagement.* Philadelphia: Psychology Press.

Tyler, Tom R., and Kathleen M. McGraw. 1986. "Ideology and the Interpretation of Personal Experience: Procedural Justice and Political Quiescence." *Journal of Social Issues* 42, 2: 115–128.

Washington Department of Ecology. 2003. "Status of Watershed Planning Efforts in Washington State." Publication 03-06-010. Http://www.ecy.wa.gov/pubs/0306010.pdf.

Weber, Edward P. 2000. "A New Vanguard for the Environment: Grass-Roots Ecosystem Management as a New Environmental Movement." *Society and Natural Resources* 13, 3: 237–259.

Wilson, Matt, and Eric Weltman. 2000. "Government's Job." In *Beyond Backyard Environmentalism,* ed. Charles Sabel, Archon Fung, and Bradley Karkkainen, 49–53. Boston: Beacon Press.

11

Sustainability in a Regional Context: The Case of the Great Lakes Basin

Barry G. Rabe and Marc Gaden

The Great Lakes Basin may constitute the ultimate test of a North American region's capacity to adhere to the tenets of sustainable development. Covering a surface area of over 300,000 square miles, the basin holds one-fifth of the world's freshwater supply and is the only glacial feature on the Earth's surface that is visible from the moon (see figure 11.1). One-fourth of the entire population of Canada resides there, and nearly one-half of all Canadian manufacturing occurs within the basin. In turn, one out of every nine Americans lives in the basin, and nearly one-fourth of total American manufacturing takes place in the region. The challenge of forging sustainable strategies for the basin stems not only from its imposing physical scope but also from the concentration of population, intense industrial activity within its boundaries, and political fragmentation that makes the development of coherent environmental policies difficult at best.

The environmental sustainability of the basin first began to be seen as highly jeopardized about four decades ago, at the outset of the modern environmental movement. By the early 1970s, Lake Erie was declared "dead" and the Great Lakes were the butt of national jokes. A series of blazes along waterways such as the Cuyahoga River and mounting evidence that other lakes (particularly Michigan and Ontario) were seriously threatened served to trigger considerable debate over whether ecological health could be regained. Many indeed wondered if the basin was trapped in an irreversible downhill slide. Large surface waters, long residence time for water before it circulates out of the basin, prevailing air currents, and globalization make all five lakes vulnerable. Other pervasive threats to the sustainability of the Great Lakes Basin include haphazard land use, invasive species, groundwater discharge, landfill leaching, pesticide and topsoil runoff from agricultural activity and

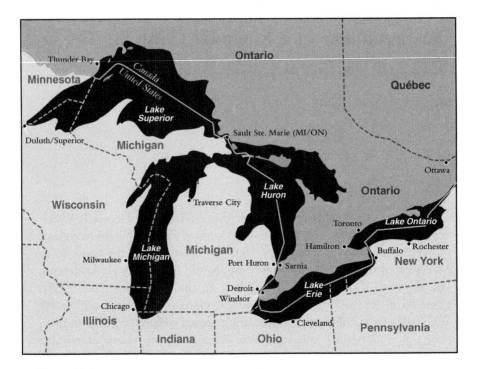

Figure 11.1
Map of Great Lakes Basin area.

residential development, and resuspension of contaminated lake-bottom sediments.

The daunting scope of such problems has served to focus growing interest on ways to view the basin as a unified ecosystem and to assure long-term sustainability. A flurry of collective activity at multiple levels of government has occurred in the basin over the past forty years, much of it linked by the common goal of comprehensive basin protection. Some outright improvements in basin environmental quality involving all media have been registered, most notably in nutrients such as phosphorus, but also in the concentrations of organic compounds and toxic chemicals like polychlorinated biphenyls, pesticides, dioxins, and furans (Environmental Protection Agency and Environment Canada 2007). Stabilization of environmental quality appears to have occurred in other areas, despite continued growth of population and industrial activity. Virtually every unit of government in the basin has played some role in this process. Although they are very loosely coordinated, these numerous strategies and programmatic efforts have contributed to considerable unity and common vision for the basin as a collective whole.

This evolution defies, in many respects, the conventional depictions of how regional ecosystems are most likely to be protected. On the one hand, many analysts contend that only central, hegemonic oversight can be relied on to secure the consent of multiple stakeholders in protection of common resources. Drawing on Garrett Hardin's classic work on the plundering of the commons, Robert Heilbroner, William Ophuls, A. Stephen Boyan, Jr., and others have offered forceful assertions that only strong, top-down authority can foster long-term ecological viability (Ophuls and Boyan 1992). In the Great Lakes, periodic proposals for comprehensive regional "superagencies" with vast powers over development and environmental regulation have followed such lines of analysis (Caldwell 1988, 325–327). Some analysts of the Great Lakes Basin have tended in recent years to attribute most positive developments to the actions of existing central institutions, such as the International Joint Commission (IJC) and its respective Great Lakes Water Quality Agreements (Caldwell 1988; Durnil 1995). Overall, a good deal of published policy analysis on the basin in recent decades is clearly inclined toward more centralized strategies.

This top-down view is countered vigorously by a competing school of thought that perceives bottom-up initiative and partnership as driving forces behind any move toward sustainability. Extremely skeptical of the capacity of central institutions to secure broad stakeholder support for implementable approaches to sustainability, such analysts tend to attribute any positive developments in the basin to arrangements established independently of binational or central government authority. DeWitt John contends that "civic environmentalism" is thriving in American states and localities, unleashing creative approaches to complex environmental issues and filling voids left by prior command-and-control regulatory initiatives from Washington, D.C. (John 1994). Elinor Ostrom and colleagues examining the protection of "common-pool resources," such as river basins, essentially concur with John, and find little if any constructive role for central institutions to play, with creative arrangements for collective choice cultivated through locally based networks (Ostrom 1990; Ostrom, Gardner, and Walker 1994). Applied to the Great Lakes, many observe that the basin's major successes are in part due to enhanced grassroots involvement and a weariness of central government inaction (Francis and Regier 1995; Manno 1994). Such a view would contend that any movement toward sustainability in recent decades can be attributed primarily to local stakeholders working creatively and constructively toward a shared governance system for resource protection.

This analysis of the recent evolution of the Great Lakes Basin acknowledges some merit to the claims of both rival camps, but submits that any shift toward regional sustainability has occurred in a way that defies either a top-down or bottom-up categorization. According to Fikert Berkes, a scholar of institutions and sustainability, "there is a need to design and support management institutions at more than one level, with attention to interactions across scale from the local level up" (Berkes 2002, 293). In the Great Lakes Basin, a multiinstitutional system of regional governance has evolved in that vein, drawing on significant contributions from binational entities, federal, state, provincial, and local governments, and multijurisdictional confederations.

What emerges from this multiinstitutional system is something other than a neat, unified approach to the basin, but one that increasingly appears to embody some core principles of sustainability. It suggests that sustainable development is more than an ethereal construct and can both take institutional form and begin to foster environmental improvement. This appears evident even in a region as physically vast, politically diverse, and institutionally fragmented as the Great Lakes Basin. But it further indicates that conventional depictions, reliant upon either a potent Leviathan or some locally based groundswell of creativity and collaboration, may exaggerate and oversimplify an exceedingly complex, multifaceted phenomenon.

At the same time, this analysis will emphasize that any move toward sustainability within the basin is very much a work in progress. Serious impediments and complex governance structures serve both to limit the impact of current initiatives and to endanger their long-term viability. In particular, the multiinstitutional system that has evolved remains vulnerable to uneven—and ever-changing—levels of commitment from its respective jurisdictions. As certain institutions contemplate a reduced commitment, it remains uncertain whether other institutions have the inclination or capacity to fill the void. Indeed, the links between numerous policy initiatives remain very tenuous, often dependent on policy entrepreneurs who cannot be relied on to serve as permanent champions. These enduring impediments will be the primary focus of the concluding section of this chapter, offering cautionary reminders of both the complexity of the task at hand and the difficulty of sustaining recent progress.

Steps toward Sustainability

Many of the key concepts now associated with sustainability in the Great Lakes Basin evolved over time, starting decades ago. Ideas closely related to pollution prevention and regulatory integration across medium boundaries were clearly evident in the creation of expanded Canadian and American environmental policy systems in the basin during the late 1960s and early 1970s. These ideas tended, however, to be very general in nature, difficult to translate into policy. As a result, they were downplayed in both nations in favor of medium-based, command-and-control systems during these years, consistent with the general North American experience in the first environmental epoch. But if not entirely novel three decades or more later, these ideas were both refined over time and proved persuasive to a growing number of individuals with influence on the shape of environmental policy within the basin. This evolution took increasing institutional form as basin policymaking entered the third environmental epoch.

The growing interest in and legitimacy of alternative, cooperative approaches within the basin proved increasingly appealing to multiple levels of government and multiple institutions within the basin. There was no singular disaster or "focusing event" that triggered public and policymaker attention and directly prompted a shift in policy focus. Episodes such as the Lake Erie collapse in the late 1960s, widely oscillating lake levels starting in the 1980s, and the growing concern over toxics contamination in the late 1980s and into the 2000s all contributed to a sense of serious problems in the lakes and fostered a climate receptive to new policy steps. But these lacked the "big-bang" focus so common in policy formation models, whereby riveting events such as the Three Mile Island, Love Canal, and Exxon Valdez debacles clearly trigger substantial public alarm and foster new policy initiatives (Birkland 1997; Pralle 2006). Instead, a series of problems steadily served notice that the basin warranted serious attention and that extant approaches suffered from demonstrable deficiencies.

This growing recognition of problem intensity and complexity led multiple institutions to make periodic responses, many of which demonstrated a real concern for the basin's sustainability. The policies, however, were often medium-based or not systematically linked such that mutual reinforcement often occurred only by chance. Despite this uncoordinated approach, governments, citizens, and industry moved many of their positions in remarkably similar directions over time. In many of these institutional settings, environmental policy professionals demonstrated growing conversance with the complexity of issues involved, a common recognition of the inherent limitations of prevailing approaches, and a willingness to explore and endorse alternatives. In many of these settings, such professionals demonstrated a capacity to take risks, learn across disciplinary, medium, agency, and intergovernmental lines, and begin to give some semblance of structure to what had once appeared to be little other than a set of slogans. A network of such professionals constituted an informal community of experts with fairly common understandings of the complexity of existing environmental problems, and of policy alternatives with integrative and preventive emphases (Gaden 2007; Montpetit 2003). In concert, different policy professionals sharing views on the future direction of environmental policy in the basin began to influence a policy shift aimed toward sustainable development goals from their respective institutional bases (Rabe 1996).

The Binational Role

None of the regional or binational entities with some responsibility for environmental policy in the Great Lakes Basin are dominant forces in guiding policy in a more sustainable direction. They generally lack the regulatory powers to coerce or the resource bases to entice broad-scale cooperation. Nonetheless, regional policy pronouncements such as a series of Great Lakes Water Quality Agreements (GLWQAs) and recommendations from binational institutions such as the International Joint Commission (IJC) and the Great Lakes Fishery Commission (GLFC) have consistently served to elevate public awareness of the complexity of regional environmental challenges. Moreover, they have provided early and visible endorsement of far-reaching policy reforms consistent with the tenets of the third environmental epoch. Both commissions were formed many decades before the complexities of ecosystem management were understood or appreciated, though over time, the two organizations broadened their foci.

International Joint Commission
The IJC was established by the Boundary Waters Treaty of 1909, an accord between Canada and the United States covering shared waters

along the entire Canadian/American border. Although the treaty is primarily focused on water flow and quantity, a minor provision that prohibited either country from polluting shared waters spawned the first GLWQA, signed by American and Canadian government representatives in 1972. The GLWQA was firmly lodged in the tradition of the first environmental epoch. It focused largely on excessive nutrient loadings and major point sources of water pollution, from industry and municipalities, in parallel with new national initiatives in the United States and, to a lesser extent, Canada. Six years after this agreement, a revised GLWQA reflected a much expanded scope of concern and a philosophy consistent with the third environmental epoch. This new agreement addressed the more complex problem of toxic contamination in the basin and endorsed the proposal that "virtual elimination" of such toxics should be a central goal of future basinwide policy. At the time, this was a particularly bold departure from more conventional pollution control strategies prevalent in the basin and North America more generally. The 1978 Agreement also introduced officially the concept of an "ecosystem approach" for regional policy, emphasizing that Great Lakes policy decisions must "focus on the physical, chemical, and biological relationships among air, water, and land." This emphasis was reiterated in the 1987 Agreement and was linked with an expanded emphasis on the cross-media dimensions of such basin problems as groundwater pollution, contaminated sediments, airborne toxics, and nonpoint source pollution.

These Great Lakes water quality agreements embody the IJC's evolution from narrow responsibilities under a treaty to broader, ecosystemic responses to policy challenges. Although the agreements did not translate into specific legislative proposals imposed uniformly across states and provinces in the basin, they did give unprecedented visibility to these integrative and preventive approaches and indicate significant movement toward sustainability goals in advance of other North American regions, which remained more focused on pollution control and regulatory efficiency into the 1990s. They also served to transform the IJC from its historic status as a near-moribund entity largely responsible for monitoring the levels and flows of boundary waters into a prominent advocate for basin sustainability. Although both American and Canadian governments frequently have ignored IJC recommendations, the IJC has breathed life periodically into the GLWQAs and stimulated a series of other proposals within the basin.

Great Lakes Fishery Commission

The GLFC has also evolved as a binational institution. The GLFC was created in 1955 by the Canadian and U.S. Convention on Great Lakes Fisheries, largely in response to the crisis inflicted on the fishery by the sea lamprey. Sea lampreys are native to the Atlantic Ocean and entered the upper Great Lakes in the 1920s through shipping canals. They latch onto fish with a teeth-filled mouth and feed on the fish, usually until the fish dies. The sea lamprey decimated commercial, sport, and tribal fisheries such that without action, the Great Lakes fishery might well have ceased to exist. Canada and the United States created the GLFC to develop and implement a basinwide sea lamprey control program. The convention granted the GLFC additional responsibilities, which include supporting binational fisheries research, publishing information, and making recommendations to government.

Like the IJC, the GLFC realized that focusing on one primary issue—in this case the sea lamprey—though important, was not sufficient to have a meaningful effect on basinwide sustainability. Consequently, the GLFC formed "lake committees" in 1964 as a way to help the federal, state, and provincial jurisdictions share information about their individual fishery activities. These lake committees were the first permanent institutions to harmonize the disparate fishery policies among the many jurisdictions in the basin after more than a century of failed attempts to do so. The lake committees went through a significant transformation in 1981 with the GLFC-led development of A Joint Strategic Plan for Management of Great Lakes Fisheries, which used the lake committees to help all fishery agencies identify their shared goals and take steps together to achieve them. Thus, the GLFC evolved from mainly a sea lamprey control agency to an agency facilitating multijurisdictional action and making recommendations to government about sustainability. The GLFC has, in recent years, been vocal about invasive species prevention, fish habitat, water quality, research, and a number of other ecosystemic issues.

The Federal Role

The creative steps toward Great Lakes Basin protection promoted by binational action have, in many respects, been complemented by the actions of federal institutions, particularly in the United States. The respective roles of the U.S. and Canadian federal governments in the Great Lakes Basin represent significant contrasts in environmental federalism (Harrison 1996). In the United States, several policy initiatives of the federal government have clearly contributed to environmental improvement in the basin. Launched at various stages during the past three decades, these steps have helped move basin policy in a more preventive, integrative direction. In contrast, the Canadian federal government imprint is much more difficult to discern in the Great Lakes, owing in large part to the continuing Canadian commitment to devolve most environmental policy functions to individual provinces. Ottawa has not made basin efforts comparable to those of Washington, D.C., and, as we will discuss, neither Ontario nor Quebec have fully filled this gap.

These divergent federal cases suggest that federal governments may have extremely important roles to play in fostering regional coordination across jurisdictional lines. Indeed, for all the opprobrium commonly heaped on U.S. federal involvement in environmental policy, its actions in the Great Lakes Basin suggest that it has played a number of constructive roles. This is evident both in early efforts to address pressing basin problems that were not being handled effectively by states or localities and, more recently, in finding new methods to both promote more sustainable policy approaches and find common ground among individual states.

The first significant U.S. federal intervention on behalf of the Great Lakes involved its medium-specific approach to major point sources of water pollution in the 1970s. In many respects, these sorts of pollution sources were not new. Many histories of regional economic development point to huge human health problems stemming from such contamination. In 1885–1886 alone, more than 80,000 Chicagoans died from typhoid, cholera, and dysentery after drinking contaminated water. As late as 1971, only five percent of the basin population living in residences with sewers were served by adequate treatment. The U.S. federal government responded aggressively in the 1970s with new regulatory standards and, in the case of sanitary sewage, major grant programs that led to substantial improvements in related areas of water quality. This action not only had immediate results but also helped clear the way for later initiatives involving the federal and other levels of government. In contrast, the Canadian federal government has never taken comparable steps in this area, consistently deferring to the prerogatives of individual provinces.

The U.S. and Canadian federal governments also have attempted to play a meaningful role in the remediation of some of the region's most degraded sites. Forty-three such sites in Canada and the United States, known as Areas of Concern (AOC), have been identified by the IJC as so impaired by contaminated sediments, sewage discharges, hazardous waste runoff, and habitat degradation that a detailed Remedial Action Plan (RAP) must be developed to guide the cleanup (Hartig 1997). Under the GLWQA, federal, state, provincial, and local authorities and stakeholders work together to formulate and implement RAPs. The IJC monitors progress in remediating AOCs, urges needed actions, and provides progress updates.

Progress on AOCs has been agonizingly slow. Although some AOCs have been improved, remediation of others has been partial, intermittent, or not even begun (Sproule-Jones 2002). In fact, only three AOCs—Collingwood Harbour and Severn Sound, both in Canada, and Oswego in New York—have been removed from the list, and all three constituted relatively straightforward and inexpensive remediation cases. Recognizing the need for more progress, Congress passed the Great Lakes Legacy Act in 2002 (and reauthorized it in 2008) in part to try to reinvigorate AOC cleanup. While millions of dollars have been appropriated through the EPA under the act since 2002, state partners and citizen groups have criticized Congress' unwillingness to appropriate the full $50 million authorized annually despite substantial increases requested from the Bush administration in recent years. In Canada, the Canada-Ontario Agreement outlines how the two levels of government will work to achieve AOC restoration, including pledges of funds and specific government cleanup actions. The agreement, for instance, calls for at least four more AOCs to be delisted by 2010, but given the poor record to date, such success might be elusive. In addition, a Great Lakes Sustainability Fund was established by Environment Canada in 1990 to provide tens of millions of dollars in support of AOC remediation, particularly in the application of cleanup technologies, but has had little demonstrable impact.

Interstate/Interprovincial Institutions

Neither the U.S. nor Canadian constitutions were drafted with serious consideration of mechanisms to facilitate problem solving among neighboring states or provinces. Water basins pose a particularly complex question of interjurisdictional governance, as they tend to render political boundaries meaningless. Artificial political boundaries have precipitated many environmental squabbles and to avoid conflict, the subnational governments must often come up with creative ways to share and protect multijurisdictional natural resources.

U.S. states have for decades responded to jurisdictional problems through the use of interstate agreements, establishing on at least thirty-five occasions formal compacts for joint oversight of common water management. Each member state's legislature must approve compacts, making them statute in each signatory state and, therefore, binding (Zimmerman 2004). There is no comparable formal process yet to emerge among provinces in Canada, though it is generally settled that provinces can freely enter into agreements with each other and with foreign governments, so long as the agreement pertains to provincial authority. In fact, there is a growing number of agreements that involve two or more provinces over a particular environmental or natural resource concern, and provinces have on occasion signed onto U.S. state agreements.

Nowhere in the basin is the application of a formal interstate or interprovincial compact more salient than with water use and diversion. Water quantity in the basin and the concern over the fluctuating lake levels have continually triggered interstate interest in devising new institutions to promote research and facilitate consensus building. As early as the 1950s, these concerns led to the development of the Great Lakes Commission (GLC) as a formal advisory and advocacy body. In turn, the Council of Great Lakes Governors (CGLG) was created in the early 1980s to provide a regular forum for basin governors to explore cooperative approaches to economic development and environmental protection. Although the GLC and the CGLG lack the authority of federal, state, and provincial governments, they have played prominent roles in managing the use and diversion of Great Lakes water.

By the mid-1990s, concern over the diversion of Great Lakes water, fueled by historic lows in the water levels, triggered an intensified effort to create a contractual agreement among the jurisdictions. This agreement—first outlined in 2001 and formalized as the Great Lakes–St. Lawrence River Basin Water Resources Compact in 2005—was spearheaded by the region's governors and premiers, working together through the CGLG. All ten governors and premiers signed the compact in December 2005, and by July 2008, with Michigan's passage of the compact, all Great Lakes states had approved the agreement, thus sending the compact to Washington for its consideration. With remarkable speed, Congress agreed to the compact and, in September 2008, sent it to the president, who promptly signed it. (In contrast, the Great Lakes Basin Compact, another major agreement in the Basin, took thirteen years for approval.) The Water Resources Compact is momentous in establishing a clear and legally binding process—driven by the states and the provinces—to protect Great Lakes water from diversion. The compact also addresses withdrawals within the Great Lakes Basin and mitigation of water degradation caused by withdrawals. Because the compact was approved by state legislatures and Congress, the agreement is binding. Ontario and Quebec, though not legally bound, adhere to an "International Agreement" that resembles the compact and allows them to continue to work with the states (Annin 2006).

Overall, multijurisdictional action in the Great Lakes region, particularly in the absence of compelling federal leadership, has blossomed in the previous decades and illustrates the movement of environmental policy into the third epoch. The state and provincial jurisdictions appear to understand that by identifying shared goals and objectives and by leveraging resources, they can implement coherent policies that promote sustainability.

Single-State Institutions

Reflecting their differing political cultures and levels of support for environmental protection, states and provinces vary enormously in both their degree of commitment and demonstrated capacity to pursue goals consistent with sustainability and ecosystem management principles. Nonetheless, every state or province in the basin has experimented with a wide range of initiatives that attempt to translate sustainability principles into institutional forms.

Minnesota emerges as a clear leader among basin states and provinces in addressing contamination, having devised a host of pollution prevention and regulatory integration programs during the past two decades. The Minnesota approach reflects a blend of incentives and regulatory measures, all linked by the common goal of minimizing environmental contamination and explicitly directed at a statewide commitment to sustainability. Building on earlier efforts to provide technical assistance to industry for pollution prevention, Minnesota enacted a far-reaching Toxics Pollution Prevention Act in 1990, which emphasized preventing pollution "at the source." One cornerstone of the act was mandatory pollution prevention planning, which requires Minnesota firms to incorporate national Toxics Release Inventory (TRI) data into their planning processes. In turn, the state sets fees based on volume and type of toxic substances released, with resulting revenues providing both a disincentive to releases and a substantial source of funding for expanded technical assistance efforts. Facility plans are to be revised through annual progress reports, contributing to a systematic evaluation of progress in pollution prevention that remains novel among states and provinces in the basin.

Minnesota has supplemented its pollution prevention initiatives by revisiting virtually every step of the conventional regulatory process. Permitting, for example, has been modified to offer participating firms substantial flexibility in determining how to reduce emissions in exchange for firm commitment to dramatic emission reductions and installation of sophisticated systems of continuous emissions monitoring. State officials have also attempted to work creatively with federal counterparts in these initiatives, seeking ways to modify existing regulatory programs to promote approaches more consistent with the 1990 act (Marcus, Geffen, and Sexton 2002). Minnesota has also been the most active state in the basin in taking steps to combat climate change through a series of programs to promote renewable energy and energy efficiency and played a central role in a 2007 initiative designed to foster formal collaboration on climate policy among states in the basin. In 2006, the state established an Emerging Issues Team to anticipate future environmental health threats, such as those posed by nanotechnology, and weigh early policy responses.

Michigan has exerted singular leadership in another major policy area: stopping the introduction of alien invasive species through the discharge of ballast water. Foreign ships enter the Great Lakes through the St. Lawrence Seaway and when they discharge their stabilizing ballast water to take on cargo exotic hitchhikers are often mixed with the water. Invasive species are particularly insidious in that they reproduce, spread, and inflict damage on the ecosystem. Some of the notorious nonnative species that entered the Great Lakes through ballast water include zebra mussels, round goby, and spiny water fleas.

Despite knowing the extreme, irreversible damage caused by ballast water invaders, neither the federal government of Canada nor that of the United States has taken meaningful action to prevent new introductions. While the states (and the shippers) would prefer a single ballast water regime for the Great Lakes Basin, the lack of federal action has been frustrating, prompting some states to consider taking matters into their own hands. Michigan passed a law in 2005 requiring a permit for ocean-going vessels that wish to discharge ballast into Michigan waters. The law, spearheaded by State Senator Patty Birkholz and State Representative David Palsrok, both Republicans, and signed by Democratic Governor Jennifer Granholm, was met by strong resistance from shippers, who argued they should not be subjected to a hodgepodge of state regulations. Shippers threatened to sue Michigan over its ballast water regulations and avoid Michigan ports if subjected to ballast discharge permits. Though they followed through (unsuccessfully) on their first threat, Senator Birkholz has observed that vessel operators have applied for ballast discharge permits, indicating that the law has not deterred ship visits to Michigan.

Cities and Sustainability

No level of government is closer to the Great Lakes than the city, town, or village. The region's mayors are responsible, as such, for an astonishing suite of duties that impact sustainability. Municipalities oversee the water supply, maintain sewers and wastewater infrastructure, zone for development and greenspace, manage trash and recyclables, operate transportation systems, and provide access to the resource through ports, harbors, and beaches. Increasingly, mayors in the Great Lakes are also more fully appreciating their role in traditionally regional, national, and international matters including climate change and water quantity. Mayors have much to gain from a healthy Great Lakes Basin and much to lose when practices are unsustainable. Their interest in sustainability stems from their fundamental responsibility to maintain a high quality of life for local residents and to promote economic strength. As the region's mayors noted in a 2007 joint statement, "The local, action-oriented nature of cities and municipalities make them the ideal order of government for sustainability-related improvements and piloting projects. Citizens are more directly engaged with their city or municipality than their state or nation" (Great Lakes and St. Lawrence Cities Initiative 2007).

In 2003, sensing the need for municipalities to play a greater role in regional policy, Chicago's mayor Richard M. Daley founded, and Toronto's mayor David Miller joined shortly thereafter, the Great Lakes

Cities Initiative (later renamed the Great Lakes and St. Lawrence Cities Initiative, or GLSLCI). The two mayors, already progressive in instituting sustainable policies in their own cities, sought to increase municipal clout, basinwide, in the two countries. Nearly fifty municipalities are now members of the GLSLCI including large cities like Duluth, Rochester, and Montreal and small towns like Parry Sound, Goderich, and Waukegan.

The emergence of the GLSLCI is further evidence of the Great Lakes Basin's movement into the third epoch of sustainability. Through the GLSLCI, mayors focus on traditional municipal concerns like trash collection and zoning, but they do so in ways that explicitly link their local actions to basinwide sustainability. Mayors seek to educate each other about what works and what does not work at the city level and to secure greater attention and resources from the federal, state, and provincial governments for environmental initiatives. The mayors have, for instance, together pressed the U.S. Congress to implement comprehensive Great Lakes restoration plans, pass invasive species legislation, improve their commitment to protecting water quality, and invest in water protection infrastructure. The mayors have also developed a Water Conservation Framework through the GLSLCI to help them share best practices for reducing water use by at least 15 percent by 2015 (Great Lakes and St. Lawrence Cities Initiative 2006).

Because of the GLSLCI, mayors view themselves as partners in sustainability, not simply elected officials seeking more state, provincial, or federal funding. The emergence of the GLSLCI, and the active participation by scores of mayors in local and basinwide governance, is an emerging, novel, and potent force in the region. More than just a bottom-up, grassroots approach, the mayors are working with each other and with other levels of government to move forward as a group toward sustainability.

The Great Lakes Regional Collaboration: A New Paradigm?

As the 1990s came to a close, discontent had mounted about the limited ability of governments at all levels in the Great Lakes Basin to mount a cohesive approach to sustainability. The absence of a common plan to restore the region's resources was further evidence that regional governance needed a fresh look. Observers both inside and outside of government were worried that the resolve to protect and improve the Great

Lakes was weakening and the momentum from earlier environmental laws was slowing. Areas of concern were not being de-listed, invasive species were coming at an all-too-regular pace, the Great Lakes Water Quality Agreement was in need of review, Congress was confused about how federal dollars were spent in the basin, and Canada seemed plagued by inertia at federal and provincial levels. Innovative structures for collaboration among governments and stakeholders would be needed to move Great Lakes sustainability to the next level.

New discourse in the common pool resource literature acknowledges that "vertical integration" (communications across levels of government) is essential for managing large-scale resources (Berkes 2002; Stern et al. 2002) and that a "coordinating unit," some entity that can bring together government and nongovernment actors, can move policy forward effectively (McCay 2002). The U.S. Environmental Protection Agency estimates that no fewer than 140 federal programs operate in the region to manage and protect natural resources, and scores of additional state, tribal, and municipal efforts play a role in regional governance. Vertical collaboration among these government units, to the extent it even occurs, is relatively happenstance.

A recent drive to expand basinwide collaboration in the Great Lakes region began in the early 2000s and came from an unlikely place: the Florida Everglades. After years of discussion and wrangling, Congress in 2000 approved a multi-billion-dollar restoration package to "replumb" the heavily altered Everglades. Restoration would be based on a detailed plan and would depend on collaboration among federal, state, and local agencies; industry; and citizen groups. When governors and constituents in the Great Lakes region subsequently approached Congress for restoration legislation and dollars, they were advised that there would be little chance of an Everglades-like program without a regional plan for sustainability. Developing a plan in a region with diverse interests and complex governance structures would require a change in relationships, and basin stakeholders sought a model that might trigger federal restoration efforts comparable to the one that Congress had launched for the Everglades. The process that helped to change relationships began in May 2004, when President Bush issued executive order 13340 that recognized the Great Lakes as a "national treasure" and formed the Great Lakes Interagency Task Force, a committee of federal cabinet secretaries whose agencies administer programs for the Great Lakes. The president's order envisioned the federal agencies better coordinating their programs and activities, with the goal of developing a more targeted and cost-effective response to sustainability. The order also put into motion an unprecedented collaborative process that, while still in its infancy, has changed the way business is done in the region and moved all participants squarely into the third epoch.

To implement the order, the president directed EPA's Great Lakes National Program Office in Chicago to lead the so-called Great Lakes Regional Collaboration (GLRC), a process through which thousands of federal, state, tribal, and local officials and outside stakeholders work together systematically to identify specific restoration needs and develop action plans for implementation. Although the executive order would be led by the federal EPA, the GLRC was intended to help all Great Lakes participants cooperate to develop a restoration plan. Could the federal government be the coordinating unit that would spur true collaboration?

In December 2004, with an escort of bagpipers and a color guard, EPA administrator Michael Leavitt welcomed his fellow cabinet secretaries, governors, mayors, tribal leaders, members of Congress, IJC and GLFC commissioners, and NGO officials to a GLRC kickoff meeting in Chicago. Using a list of priority issue areas developed by the CGLG as the framework for the collaboration, the EPA created eight strategy teams to investigate and create action plans for aquatic invasive species, habitat, coastal health, areas of concern, nonpoint source pollution, toxic pollutants, indicators and information, and sustainable development. The strategy teams comprised a wide variety of government and non-government officials and operated by consensus. The executive order also called for enhanced cooperation with Canada, and Canadians were thus invited to participate as observers in the GLRC process.

After about a year of intense discussions, face-to-face meetings, conference calls, and emails, the eight strategy teams submitted their action plans in December 2005. The plans and their appendices contain detailed recommendations for sustainability and identify responsible implementing parties. Overall, the combined price tag of all eight action plans amounts to approximately $20 billion, shared among the levels of government, with the lion's share of those dollars recommended for combined sewer overflow infrastructure to protect public health (Environmental Protection Agency 2005). The plans reflect a remarkable level of consensus in the region about how sustainability should be achieved.

Less clear is the long-term future and the overall impact of the GLRC, as implementation of the GLRC blueprint is off to a slow start. Immediately after the GLRC action plan was finalized in 2005, members of Congress introduced the Great Lakes Collaboration Implementation Act, a large bill that reaffirmed several existing programs and authorized many of the collaboration's recommendations. The act was introduced and died in both the 109th and 110th Congresses. The GLRC recommendations have fared equally poorly on the funding front. To date, federal budgets have contained neither influxes of federal dollars for the Great Lakes nor proposals for major refocusing of agency efforts. Moreover, no initiative similar to the GLRC has been launched in Canada.

On the other hand, the GLRC was not exclusively intended to be the primary catalyst for new federal restoration dollars; rather, it was intended to create a new way for government officials and citizens to work together for sustainability. As such, the process itself may prove valuable, as it institutionalizes relationships among government officials at all levels and calls for ongoing interactions with industry and nongovernmental organizations. Such a process not only helps government officials leverage resources, but it provides a way for nongovernmental officials to work continually with government officials toward a common vision for restoration. The GLRC has only been in existence for a few years but already it has produced an action plan that guides restoration and rhetoric throughout the region and in Washington. Although many, including a bipartisan group of nearly forty House and Senate members (Great Lakes Task Force 2007), have complained that the process has fizzled owing to a lack of leadership from the EPA, the GLRC does represent a major new cooperative approach that is dependent on both top-down and bottom-up participation. If the process continues, networks that build trust, coalitions, and capacity among the participants will likely be solidified, though funding will prove crucial to implementation of key initiatives.

Enduring Impediments

Developments at binational, national, multistate, state, and municipal levels all indicate progress toward Great Lakes Basin sustainability. Institutions at each level have demonstrated some capacity to not only articulate a vision of a more comprehensive commitment to the region but also begin to work together to translate those statements into specific policy initiatives.

Basin policy remains, however, in a period of transition and uncertainty. Numerous conditions continue to impede the further development of cross-jurisdictional cooperation toward common environmental goals and, in fact, may serve to retard recent gains. Just as each institutional level has played some role in moving policy in the directions already noted, each also retains limitations that brake further progress. Recent developments in regional approaches may serve to overstate the ease with which common commitment to resource protection can occur. Indeed, the basin constitutes a massive "community," involving enough people to exceed the populations of all but eleven nations, diverse jurisdictional and institutional actors, and externality problems galore. Its environmental protection remains a daunting collective-action challenge, even for governing institutions with substantial resources and creative energies. Its recent strides toward sustainability, given those realities, represent a remarkable success story. However, substantial impediments endure. The following points illustrate significant stumbling blocks to further realization of shared sustainability goals.

Limits to Central Guidance

Binational institutions have undergone a remarkable evolution in recent decades, becoming outspoken advocates for basinwide policy shifts compatible with sustainability goals. But there are limits to their influence on broad, basinwide policy. The IJC's role remains largely symbolic; it generally acts only in response to specific requests from U.S. or Canadian federal governments, and often sees its recommendations go ignored or only superficially implemented. Even policy innovations under IJC auspices, such as Remedial Action Plans (RAPs) and lakewide management plans, are almost completely dependent on the resources and cooperative goodwill of federal, state, provincial, and local governments. As a result, for every Oswego- and Collingwood Harbour-type breakthrough, dozens of other RAPs remain mired in the very early stages of evaluation. The Great Lakes Fishery Commission is perhaps more successful in the direct delivery of a program (sea lamprey control) and in coordinating fishery management through the Joint Strategic Plan, though its mandate is narrower than the IJC, thus limiting the scope of its influence. Moreover, success of the GLFC's coordination role often depends on the cooperation of the participating agencies—goodwill that becomes fleeting during times of budgetary shortfalls.

Federal Government Shirking

Federal leaders in both Ottawa and Washington, D.C., have habituated the practice of offering immediate and energetic embraces of IJC or GLWQA policy pronouncements. However, these endorsements do not necessarily translate into shifts in federal policy. This lag is particularly evident in Canada, where the federal government not only maintains a minimalist presence in environmental policy but also remains overwhelmingly committed to medium-based, pollution control strategies. Canadian federal environmental policy continues to be remarkably dependent on prior U.S. federal experience. Consequently, Canada is just beginning to consider a number of promising alternatives.

In instances in which Canada has begun to embrace more preventive and integrative approaches, these often prove very superficial. The launching of the so-called Green Plan and related initiatives in the 1990s was heralded as a major breakthrough whereby diverse grant programs would be unified behind the common cause of sustainability. Subsequent analyses of the plans reveal a thinly disguised strategy more closely resembling conventional developmental policy initiatives, with little evidence of any significant shift in funding from traditional priorities. In turn, periodic efforts to modify major pieces of Canadian federal legislation, such as the Canadian Environmental Protection Act (CEPA), represent little other than cosmetic efforts to move beyond traditional approaches. Instead, Canada has continued to devolve many key policy decisions to its provinces. Ottawa has generally eschewed the command-and-control model common in U.S. federal environmental law and has also been less receptive to market-based tools such as emissions trading (Rabe 2007). In virtually every area where U.S. federal and state governments have begun to devise policy alternatives more compatible with sustainability goals, Ottawa clearly lags behind (Boyd 2003).

The federal government contribution is somewhat more heartening on the U.S. side of the basin. Earlier and more aggressive water and air pollution control efforts enacted by the U.S. federal government led to significant environmental improvements and also paved the way for more preventive, integrative initiatives in recent years. However, many key components of federal environmental policy in the United States continue to adhere to conventional, medium-based emphases. Enabling legislation, the organizational design of the EPA, and an agency culture that continues to foster turf protection all augur against more far-reaching evolution of federal policy. In turn, respective Congresses and presidents have had great difficulty updating and revising many core pieces of environmental legislation for the past decade or so (Kraft 2006). Moreover, both Canadian and U.S. federal environmental agencies face uncertain fiscal futures, and the lack of a budget initiative to implement the recommendations of the Great Lakes Regional Collaboration draws into question the U.S. federal commitment to any restoration plan. Any future commitment of federal governments to areas with direct bearing on sustainability thus remains highly uncertain.

State and Provincial Government Shirking
In the absence of clear marching orders from binational or federal authorities, states and provinces bear the brunt of responsibility for securing collaborative approaches that best represent the region. Even the GLRC envisioned substantial subnational investment in Great Lakes restoration. As we have seen, most units in the basin have made some effort to move toward more preventive and integrative policies in recent years. Some, such as Minnesota, have unilaterally pursued a host of promising new policy departures. On the whole, however, individual states and provinces continue to face considerable budget constraints and incentives to shirk responsibility for basinwide well-being. Subnational units working to reduce emissions and waste volumes may largely be serving neighboring states and provinces, given prevailing currents of pollutant transfer and patterns of waste export. They may, in short, have limited incentive to act on their own, especially when their own environmental problems may endure as a result of contamination transferred from other jurisdictions. Given the economic and political costs associated with imposing new requirements on regulated parties, it may be enticing for individual states or provinces to stick with traditional routines. State and provincial caution in these matters may also be reflected by periodic efforts to cut environmental staff and total expenditures significantly and propose "customer-friendly" regulatory alternatives that may constitute an emphasis on a new form of efficiency so central to the second epoch. Such a shift has been most visible in Ontario and Michigan, each of which has experienced significant reduction in environmental agency staff since the mid-1990s (McKenzie

2002; Dempsey 2001) and has focused heavily on easing regulatory burdens.

Interstate variation is reflected in the enduring problem of cross-boundary transfer of pollutants and wastes. In the United States, federal policy has periodically attempted to address serious pollution "balance of trade" problems after states failed to resolve such difficulties on their own. States like Illinois, Ohio, and Pennsylvania have continued to contribute substantial quantities of air pollution, much of which becomes land or water pollution problems elsewhere in the basin or in other regions. For example, nearly half of the sulfate levels found in New York's Adirondack Mountains emanates from Midwestern air pollution sources. As political scientist William Lowry has noted, the current federal structure "creates incentives for states to export pollution" (Lowry 1992, 44). Moreover, relatively limited sharing of information and ideas occurs among officials across state and provincial boundaries, one of a series of continuing challenges for decentralized approaches to basin well-being.

Conclusions

To paraphrase Mark Twain, reports anticipating the death of the Great Lakes issued more than thirty-five years ago have proven inaccurate. Several important indicators of lake water quality and basin ecosystem health have stabilized or improved, despite increases in population, industrial activity, and automobile usage. Many of these salutary developments can be traced directly to interventions from various levels of government. These developments should not serve, of course, to obscure enduring challenges facing the basin. Even with the GLSLCI and the GLRC, coordination of efforts across governmental levels remains difficult and translating a common vision into action has been elusive. Moreover, individual states and provinces have mixed records in addressing regionwide concerns. Many of the most promising new innovations, such as the GLRC, remain in early stages of implementation, with their long-term performance or capacity for replication in other basin jurisdictions unclear. Moreover, the recent history of the basin reveals an ever-expanding set of challenges to ecosystem health. At the same time that external contaminants and exotic species continue to confound basin policymakers, there is a growing indication that the next round of internal policy development must focus on ubiquitous sources of contamination from within the basin. Far beyond the traditional emphasis on large point sources of pollution, such as major industry and municipalities, nonpoint water pollution may be the next—and most substantial—challenge yet faced. Nonpoint sources include virtually all residents in the basin, including farmers and home owners, whose penchant for land development and pesticides invariably compound water quality problems.

Viewing environmental sustainability in the basin from this perspective, and attempting to shift the focus of its citizenry toward sustainability goals, remains a formidable challenge. Nonetheless, the past four decades of experience within the basin reflects an evolution largely consistent with the epochs outlined in chapter 1. After earlier emphasis on command-and-control strategies and experimentation with regulatory efficiency measures, many areas of basin policy are making a clear shift into the third epoch and reflect its emphasis on sustainable development. Most notably, one can discern a movement from pollution control strategies toward more preventive and integrative efforts in recent years. Such contributions toward this transformation are evident at binational, federal, state, provincial, and municipal levels of governance within the basin. In some instances, new systems are now being tested that appear to hold considerable promise for placing environmental policy efforts into a more comprehensive context and for confronting some of the most serious challenges to basin sustainability. This transition is not seamless, and could indeed be undermined by a variety of factors, such as possible reluctance or inability of individual states, provinces, and municipalities to participate fully in this collective effort and a reversion to regulatory efficiency goals so central to the second epoch. Nonetheless, the Great Lakes Basin, despite its physical breadth, population density, and industrial intensity, demonstrates the potential on a regional basis for supplanting conventional approaches to environmental protection with an emphasis on collaboration and pursuing sustainability.

Acknowledgments

The authors thank David Ullrich, Daniel Mazmanian, and Michael Kraft, whose comments greatly improved this chapter. We are also very grateful to Judy Stopke for technical assistance in producing our map.

References

Annin, Peter. 2006. *The Great Lakes Water Wars.* Washington: Island Press.

Berkes, Fikert. 2002. "Cross-scale Institutional Linkages: Perspectives From the Bottom Up." In *The Drama of the Commons*, ed. Elinor Ostrom, Thomas Dietz, Nives Dolsak, Paul C. Stern, Susan Stonich, and Elke W. Weber, 293–322. Washington, D.C.: National Academy Press.

Birkland, Thomas. 1997. *After Disaster.* Washington, D.C.: Georgetown University Press.

Boyd, David R. 2003. *Unnatural Law: Rethinking Canadian Environmental Law and Policy.* Vancouver: UBC Press.

Caldwell, Lynton K., ed. 1988. *Perspectives in Ecosystem Management in the Great Lakes.* Albany: State University of New York Press.

Dempsey, David. 2001. *Ruin and Recovery: Michigan's Rise as a Conservation Leader.* Ann Arbor: University of Michigan Press.

Durnil, Gordon K. 1995. *The Making of a Conservative Environmentalist.* Bloomington: Indiana University Press.

Environmental Protection Agency. 2005. "Great Lakes Regional Collaboration Strategy to Restore and Protect the Great Lakes." Chicago: EPA, Great Lakes National Program Office. Online at www.glrc.us. Accessed 8 August 2007.

Environmental Protection Agency and Environment Canada. 2007. "State of the Great Lakes 2007: Highlights." Ottawa and Washington: Environment Canada and EPA.

Francis, George, and Henry A. Regier. 1995. "Barriers and Bridges to the Restoration of the Great Lakes Basin Ecosystem." In *Barriers and Bridges to the Renewal of Ecosystem and Institutions*, ed. Lance Holling, C. S. Holling, and Stephan S. Light, 239–291. New York: Columbia University Press.

Gaden, Marc. 2007. "Bridging Jurisdictional Divides: Collective Action through a Joint Strategic Plan for Management of Great Lakes Fisheries." Unpublished Ph.D. Dissertation. Ann Arbor: University of Michigan.

Great Lakes and St. Lawrence Cities Initiative. 2006. "Water Conservation Framework." Chicago: Great Lakes and St. Lawrence Cities Initiative. Online at www.glslcities.org/watercons.htm. Accessed 10 July 2007.

Great Lakes and St. Lawrence Cities Initiative. 2007. "Resolution 7-2007M: Sustainable Cities and Municipalities." Chicago: Great Lakes and St. Lawrence Cities Initiative. Online at www.glslcities.org/documents/Resolutionpackage072307.pdf. Accessed 10 July 2007.

Great Lakes Task Force. 2007. Letter from Members of Congress to President George Bush. July 31, 2007. Washington, D.C.: Northeast-Midwest Coalition Great Lakes Task Force.

Harrison, Kathryn. 1996. *Passing the Buck: Federalism and Canadian Environmental Policy.* Vancouver: University of British Columbia Press.

Hartig, John H. 1997. "Great Lakes Remedial Action Plans: Fostering Adaptive Ecosystem-based Management Processes." *American Review of Canadian Studies* 27, 3: 437–458.

John, DeWitt. 1994. *Civic Environmentalism*. Washington, D.C.: Congressional Quarterly.

Kraft, Michael E. 2006. "Environmental Policy in Congress." In *Environmental Policy: New Directions for the Twenty-first Century*, 6th ed., ed. Michael E. Kraft and Norman J. Vig, 124–147. Washington, D.C.: CQ Press.

Lowry, William. 1992. *The Dimensions of Federalism*. Durham: Duke University Press.

Manno, Jack. 1994. "Advocacy and Diplomacy: NGOs and the Great Lakes Water Quality Agreement." In *Environmental NGOs in World Politics*, ed. Thomas Princen and Mathias Finger, 69–120. London and New York: Routledge.

Marcus, Alfred A., Donald A. Geffen, and Ken Sexton. 2002. *Reinventing Environmental Regulation*. Washington, D.C.: Resources for the Future.

McCay, Bonnie J. 2002. "Emergence of Institutions for the Commons: Contexts, Situations, and Events." In *The Drama of the Commons*, ed. Elinor Ostrom, Thomas Dietz, Nives Dolsak, Paul C. Stern, Susan Stonich, and Elke W. Weber, 361–402. Washington: National Academy Press.

McKenzie, Judith I. 2002. *Environmental Politics in Canada*. Don Mills, ON: Oxford University Press.

Montpetit, Éric. 2003. *Misplaced Distrust: Policy Networks and the Environment in France, the United States, and Canada*. Vancouver: University of British Columbia Press.

Ophuls, William, and A. Stephen Boyan, Jr. 1992. *Ecology and the Politics of Scarcity Revisited: The Unraveling of the American Dream*. New York: W. H. Freeman.

Ostrom, Elinor. 1990. *Governing the Commons*. Cambridge: Cambridge University Press.

Ostrom, Elinor, Roy Gardner, and James Walker. 1994. *Rules, Games, and Common-Pool Resources*. Ann Arbor: University of Michigan Press.

Pralle, Sarah B. 2006. *Branching Out, Digging In: Environmental Advocacy and Agenda Setting*. Washington, D.C.: Georgetown University Press.

Rabe, Barry G. 1996. "An Empirical Examination of Innovations in Integrated Environmental Management: The Case of the Great Lakes Basin." *Public Administration Review* 56 (July/August): 372–381.

Rabe, Barry G. 2007. "Beyond Kyoto: Climate Change Policy in Multi-level Governance Systems." *Governance* 20, 3: 423–444.

Sproule-Jones, Mark. 2002. *Restoration of the Great Lakes: Promises, Practices, Performances*. Vancouver: University of British Columbia Press.

Stern, P. C., T. Dietz, N. Dolsak, E. Ostrom, and S. Stonich. 2002. "Knowledge and Questions After 15 years of Research." In *The Drama of the Commons*, ed. Elinor Ostrom, Thomas Dietz, Nives Dolsak, Paul C. Stern, Susan Stonich, and Elke W. Weber, 445–490. Washington, D.C.: National Academy Press.

Zimmerman, Joseph. 2004. *Interstate Economic Relations*. Albany: SUNY Press.

IV

Overview and Implications for a Sustainable Future

12

Conclusions: Toward Sustainable Communities

Michael E. Kraft and Daniel A. Mazmanian

Nearly a decade into the twenty-first century, environmental policy in the United States is experiencing the early stage of what we hope will be a profound transition toward a new epoch of sustainability. It is too early to speak confidently of how far or how fast this transition will go, or how successful it will be in addressing the myriad of environmental and ecological challenges facing the nation and the world. Yet there is no question that shifts in the way we understand the problems, the tone of policy dialogues, the number and array of policy actors, and the steps being taken have dramatically changed. The nation is moving from the era of problem denial, adversarial relations among key actors, and top-down environmental regulation that dominated the second half of the twentieth century to one of more sophisticated and complex understanding of the challenges, comprehensive thinking and planning, and public and private sector initiatives directed at the long-term goal of sustainability.

The conversation has been joined from all corners of society. At the current stage, the choices that loom before us concern the design of public policies to facilitate and encourage the transition and how to govern toward a green future while working within the broad framework of checks and balances of our constitutional democracy. The case studies provided in this book clearly suggest that one of the major avenues of change working from within the constitutional system, and perhaps the most important one, will come from the subnational, regional, city, and community level. These provide the pilot efforts at policy innovation and the often remarkable illustrations of what can be accomplished when policymakers are freed from the chains of national political gridlock (Klyza and Sousa 2008; Portney 2003; Rabe 2004, 2006; Rabe and Mundo 2007). The levels of government serve, in short, as the policy and idea incubators for the nation. We hope this book contributes to understanding how and why this transition has unfolded to date and that it stimulates others to inquire about additional cases and circumstances that can fill the gaps in our knowledge about this increasingly visible and important movement toward a more sustainable society.

In this concluding chapter, we consider the implications of the preceding discussions and case studies for both theory and practice and suggest lines of further inquiry to help clarify our conceptual thinking and expand on the findings in the cases presented. We revisit our thesis about the nature of the transition toward sustainable communities and offer some observations about lessons learned, particularly the factors that seem most to affect the character and pace of the transition to environmental sustainability.

Findings and Implications

The previous chapters have examined a variety of environmental policy developments within different regions, states, and communities around the nation. The case studies consider the pertinent issues within their own policy arenas while also addressing the broader conceptual issues raised by the book. We first turn to considering these findings in relation to one another and with respect to the framework presented in chapter 1.

As introduced in chapter 1 and examined in depth in chapter 2, sustainability has many meanings, from an ecologically determined set of goals to smart growth and quality of life principles by which community and industry activities may be assessed for their long-term impacts on society. It is not essential to agree on a single or narrow definition of environmental sustainability, sustainable development, or sustainable communities to study the important transitions now taking place in American society. It is important, however, to understand the broad thrust of the concept of sustainability—utilizing resources more efficiently; moving to closed-loop systems of production, consumption, and reuse; reducing dependence on fossil fuels; improving the quality of life for all through reducing pollution and repairing damaged ecosystems—the social movements it is inspiring, and the analytical challenges of measuring progress toward identified goals.

In turning to the issue of governance, each of the many community sustainability initiatives has incorporated in one form or another a commitment to greater civic engagement and cooperation among the public, private, and nonprofit sectors in pursuit of long-term community goals. As Robert Putnam (1993) has so persuasively argued, however, such ambitious collective action depends on the existence of sufficient "social capital," or the "norms and networks of civic engagement." To the extent that some communities and regions succeed in identifying shared social, economic, and environmental goals, and in fostering the development of a new generation of public policies grounded in sustainability, they merit close attention and analysis. The implications extend well beyond environmental policy. In fact, hundreds of communities across the nation have initiated sustainable community projects that include working together to develop indicators and benchmarks for the core components of community sustainability: social well-being and justice, economic vitality, and ecological integrity (Portney 2003; Smart Communities Network 2007; Sustainable Measures 2007).

Although it is beyond the scope of this book, political scientists should be well equipped to ask how these profound changes have come about and what is likely to sustain them over time. Indeed, what will it take for the core ideas of sustainability to spread around the country (and the world) and fundamentally to shift policy in this direction, that is, to speed up the transition to which we refer? A fairly well-developed literature on policy change (e.g., Baumgartner and Jones 1993; Sabatier and Jenkins-Smith 1993) hints at the likely variables that make a difference, from local political and economic leadership to supportive public values and attitudes. At least some empirical work that seeks to explain successes and failures in sustainability initiatives contributes to this line of inquiry (Portney 2003), but much more could be done. We hope that the case studies and analyses in this volume inspire others to take on these tasks, and we elaborate below on what we think are some of the key research needs.

The most striking consequence across all of the case studies where we see movement toward sustainability is that the understanding of "the problem" and the "policy objectives" in environmental protection has undergone dramatic change, even in the most traditional policy arenas such as in air (chapter 4) and water pollution control (chapters 5, 10, and 11) where the guiding policy directives reach back to the beginning of the first epoch of the environmental movement. The problems of environmental pollution are now understood as inextricably tied to the way in which we produce and consume, and envision life's quality, from the individual up through the societal level. Moreover, the problems faced will not be solved or even largely mitigated by a dedicated but ultimately small number of individuals making different, more sustainable life choices, or add-on emission control devices on cars, smokestacks, and wastewater outlets, or even efforts to insist on proper behavior and impose regulation on all of business and industry. Solutions are going to require rethinking and changing fundamentally how we produce, consume, and live.

Recognition of this reality is evident in Daniel Fiorino's discussion (chapter 3) of why the regulatory approach of the first epoch is no longer suited to the realities of the twenty-first century's fast-moving, diverse, global economic order, especially when juxtaposed with the requisites of sustainability spelled out by Lamont Hempel (chapter 2). Governing on behalf of the environment will require bringing economic development into balance with environmental protection around the five design principles laid out by Fiorino that are nothing less than an implementation philosophy for guiding the government–business relationship in the third epoch:

• use legally enforceable, stringent performance standards
• differentiate among firms based on past and likely future performance
• promote continuous improvements in environmental performance
• measure environmental performance
• create mechanisms and relationships that build trust

The transformation in problem identification and policy objectives is equally evident in the communities that have adopted sustainable strategies, as difficult as they are proving to achieve, as Kent Portney points out (chapter 9) and as does Michael Kraft with respect to watershed cleanup (in chapter 5). This more comprehensive and profound understanding of the depth of the problems and the fundamental changes that will be required to remedy them means that the point of intervention cannot be simple or limited, but must permeate the social, political, and economic institutions and activities of society. In this process the subnational cities and regions examined here are proving to be useful starting points in that they already operate as planning and governing arenas. They are large enough to act at the systems level yet small enough where entrepreneurial leaders can move to work quickly, not having to wait for national or even statewide consensus, formal authorization, and only or even mainly public resources. It is at the subnational levels that leaders from the public, private, and nonprofit sectors who are more accustomed to working together to solve their community's problems have been able to step in as first movers; in this way they have become exemplars in the transition to sustainability.

The case studies also reveal the generally tepid embrace of second epoch implementation approaches that were the focus of the debates in Congress and the White House during the 1980s and 1990s (Eisner 2007; Klyza and Sousa 2008; Vig and Kraft 2006). Although much lip service was paid during those years to the importance of cost-effectiveness, managing pollution through market-based mechanisms, and the need to introduce pollution prevention, little appears to have trickled down to the subnational "on-the-ground" level of the cases studied. What did occur was a shift in responsibility and expectation of funding from the federal government to the states, but this appears to have been more a reflection of the diminution of the federal effort than the adoption of second epoch thinking, strategies, and tools at the subnational levels. There are exceptions, however, and an important one was the initiation of the RECLAIM program by the South Coast Air Quality Management Program in Los Angles (chapter 4), which continues to stand out as one of the nation's leading market-based emissions reductions programs at either the local or regional level.

Given the backlash against the federally dominant regulatory approach of the first epoch and political pressures to reach accords if not outright consensus on both remedial actions and new development projects in the second epoch, significant *process* changes were introduced. They came in several forms, from consensus-building exercises, community and stakeholder dialogues, collaborative processes, and citizen participation to transparent decision making. Rather than facing off in confrontations at regulatory agency hearings or in the courts as in epoch one, all the stakeholders—private, nonprofit, and public—were asked to work together in search of common ground (Durant, Fiorino, and O'Leary 2004; Fiorino 2006; Layzer 2008; Weber 2003). This approach characterized many of the policy arenas examined herein, as evidenced by Daniel Press and Nicole Nakagawa's assessment of open space policy-making and strategies (chapter 6) and the city sustainability programs described by Portney (chapter 9). Blueprint planning, as an extension of the dialogue process, elevated the discussion of priorities and trade-offs from the local to the regional level in California, according to Elisa

Barbour and Michael Teitz (chapter 7); this brought to the table not only regional interests but a greater array of stakeholders. Similar process changes were adopted in the struggle over the Fox-Wolf Basin cleanup in Wisconsin, according to Kraft (chapter 5), and as part of the even larger Great Lakes Basin program described by Barry Rabe and Marc Gaden (chapter 11).

In one of the more systematic assessment of these consensus process efforts, Mark Lubell, William Leach, and Paul Sabatier reveal that a good deal has been learned about the dimensions of a successful consensus process. Though their study is based on watershed management efforts, the most important qualities of a successful effort would seem to be generalizable—perceived fairness, levels of trust, density of social networks, the quality of science, presence of neutral facilitators, intensiveness of deliberation, and availability of financial resources (chapter 10).

It is evident from a number of the cases that introducing an open and sincere dialogue process does not ensure that a consensus about how to proceed will emerge, thus removing the necessity of ultimately invoking the legal process and the regulatory approach to bringing an issue to resolution. The case that best illustrates this point and serves as a cautionary tale on the limits of dialogue and consensus building is the outcome in the Fox-Wolf Basin watershed remediation effort (chapter 5). A cautionary note is also sounded in the blueprint planning discussion of Barbour and Teitz on the possible limitations on the outcome of the recent round of comprehensive regional planning in California, that without the authority to implement, even the most consensus-based regional plan may lead to naught. These conclusions echo the findings of other recent studies of ecosystem-based management, where collaboration has not lived up to all of the expectations of its proponents in either processes or outcomes (Press 2007; Layzer 2008).

In a manner not foreseen when this book project was launched and the cases commissioned, the case studies have underscored why the second epoch is, in fact, aptly characterized as transitional. The second epoch represents a backlash against both the top-down command-and-control strategy of the first epoch and the acrimony and political and economic turmoil it precipitated. Yet the problems of environmental pollution and the public's strong support for remedying them could not be ignored, so it was not possible to revert to the policy frameworks that existed prior to the 1970s. Instead, a compromise strategy was sought between the warring business, environmental, and governmental forces.

Less emphasis would be placed on federal top-down policymaking and enforcement, and attention would be given instead to judging actions to the extent possible by the standards of economic efficiency, and consensus building and political accommodation on the ground. This worked, to an extent, but to no one's complete satisfaction.

With the rise of sustainability as the preeminent policy objective of the new millennium, not simply pollution reduction and remediation, and acceptance of the argument that this would require a paradigm shift in thinking and action, the third environmental epoch has been shepherded in. Attention is rapidly moving beyond the compromise strategies and focus on process of the second epoch, and even beyond the substantial environmental pollution goals of the first epoch. Although the goal of reducing pollution and the regulatory regime that it created have faded into the background in the public and political dialogue, the fact of the matter is that most environmental policy is still conducted through the regulatory apparatus established in the first epoch, albeit now pushed in large part from the federal down to the state and even local levels of government (Eisner 2007; Klyza and Sousa 2008; Rabe 2006; Scheberle 2004). Also, seeking the most efficient approach, working across the public-private divide, and using consensus-building processes remain important dimensions of the sustainability movement. What is critically different is the new vision for a sustainable future, the fundamental transformation it will take to be achieved, and the recognition by business and industry that it is in their best interest to apply their entrepreneurial and technical skill to leading the transformation.

We think the case studies we have assembled here provide ample illustration of the potential for subnational entrepreneurial activities in the public and nonprofit sectors as well. State and local government officials, often in cooperation with environmental organizations, citizen groups, and area scientists and other technical experts, bring considerable knowledge and experience to the task of identifying and addressing local and regional environmental problems. Federal and state officials can assist substantially in strengthening these capacities, as they have over the past decade, through well-targeted grant programs, education and training initiatives, sharing of information, and similar actions. Recognizing and fostering the best practices in smart growth planning, pollution prevention, waste minimization, energy and water conservation, and the like demonstrates how the federal government can work cooperatively and creatively with state and local officials even while the environmental protection policies and programs of the first epoch remain firmly in place.

Implications for Further Research

As is seemingly the case with all research undertakings that set out to develop a framework for understanding an evolving phenomenon and then to answer an initial set of questions, we have uncovered a host of new issues that call for further exploration. In this final section we turn to a number of questions that the case studies suggest are prime candidates for additional inquiry. These include research that looks into the empirical cases in greater depth and that extends the conceptual dimensions of the epochs framework—for example, the evolution of policy objectives, implementation philosophy, and political and institutional contexts. We also think research that broadens the scope of inquiry by expanding it beyond the subnational and communities level would be valuable.

The following is a list of ten research questions and areas of needed inquiry that emerged out of each of the chapters. Although the list is by no means comprehensive of the questions that were identified in the chapters or that can be imagined given the enormity of the topic, drawing them together in one place helps to underscore the range of possibilities and richness of research waiting to be explored.

1. What are the most effective mechanisms of partnering in the protection of threatened ecosystems? In the words of Lubell, Leach, and Sabatier (chapter 10), we need to "further pin down the conditions under which partnerships will work in order to maximize their contribution to sustainability." Moreover, "we believe that resolving the unanswered questions will require ambitious studies employing comparative and longitudinal research designs, large sample sizes, collection of detailed data on partnership structure, participants, and context, and multiple measures of success." Even research that falls short of these demanding stipulations could help to inform both scholars and policymakers of what realistically can be expected from partnerships and collaborative decision making in different areas of environmental policy (Layzer 2008).

2. Can there be effective sustainability planning without enforcement mechanisms and a framework for resolving the multiplicity of land use and cross-jurisdictional controversies? Barbour and Teitz conclude with

the observation that lacking prioritization and state planning guidelines, this is unlikely. This raises the question of the extent to which blueprints can "help set a frame for integrated planning to help achieve state, regional, and local sustainability goals." In the California case, in particular, to what extent might the greenhouse gas emissions goals about to be set by the California Air Resources Board become the guiding targets for blueprints? And, if this comes about, might this prove to be a "historic compromise to shift environment-development conflicts from the piecemeal, project-by-project level to a more proactive, regional frame"?

3. Many cities across the nation have stepped up to the climate change challenge, but how viable are they as major actors in the needed paradigm shift to sustainability? Portney concludes (chapter 9) that the potpourri of different city initiatives "have ushered in an era replete with opportunities for extensive research to determine which of these policies and programs seems most effective in achieving sustainability goals." He identifies a substantial array of interesting questions in need of further research including, "What is the long-term environmental effect of the policies pursued in Seattle, Portland, and elsewhere? What kinds of programs seem better able to contribute to balancing long-term societal and natural system needs? How do these policies influence the kinds of economic development in the city, and the patterns of economic development outside of the city? What kinds of urban political and governance structures seem best able to embrace the pursuit of sustainability?"

4. To what extent should we understand the transition to sustainability as invariably two steps forward, one step back? Illustration one. In tracing the history of the Fox-Wolf Basin cleanup project over the course of all three epochs, Kraft concludes that process matters and that an effective dialogue can bring successful resolution; "the outcomes in this case suggest that collaboration among community stakeholders works best when diverse parties are seeking agreement on general cleanup goals—particularly as they deal with the inherent uncertainty of environmental and health risks and the anticipated costs of cleanup." He suggests, however, that "this approach to decision making may be less suitable when consensus cannot be easily achieved on specific cleanup schedules, the means to be used, and the allocation of costs—and where participants believe they will benefit from deferring decisions." As the Fox-Wolf experience revealed, "under these conditions, the continuing

presence of stringent federal environmental laws and standards" of the first epoch may be necessary.

5. Two steps forward, one step back? Illustration two. Barry Rabe and Marc Gaden examine the spatially largest subnational regional environmental case in the volume in their Great Lakes Basin study. While they see clearly the "movement from pollution control strategies toward more preventive and integrative efforts in recent years," they wonder to what extent comprehensive sustainability can endure when implementation must be coordinated and carried out in a multiplicity of binational, federal, state, provincial, and municipal political jurisdictions. They tell us that "in some instances, new systems are being tested that appear to hold considerable promise for placing environmental policy efforts into a more comprehensive context and for confronting some of the most serious challenges to basin sustainability." Yet, "this transition is not seamless, and could indeed be undermined by a variety of factors, such as possible reluctance or inability of individual states, provinces, and municipalities to participate fully in this collective effort and a reversion to regulatory efficiency goals so central to the second epoch." Which of the forces wins out would be fascinating to explore.

6. To what extent can the lessons learned at the subnational level be scaled up to state, national, and international levels, what Michele Betsill and Barry Rabe characterize as the verticality problem? Illustration one. The growing specter of climate change and the challenge it presents to think globally while acting locally is playing a significant role in ushering in the third epoch. This leads Betsill and Rabe to discuss the importance of linking local, regional, state, national, and international efforts at greenhouse gas emissions reductions, in thought and action—that is, thinking vertically not just horizontally, which up until now has been the dominant activity in the myriad of emerging subnational climate change action plans. The need to better understand the interrelation between arenas of action—local to global—and the learning between them is a topic of enormous importance and future research. The issue can be approached from the bottom up, asking to what extent the kinds of collaborative and consensus processes that have evolved at the subnational level can be scaled up to national and international levels. Conversely, to what extent can policies at the global and national level be designed so as to accomplish their performance objectives, such as reduction of greenhouse gases, while remaining sufficiently flexible and incentive-driven to be embraced at the subnational level without resorting to top-down command-and-control regulatory approaches?

7. Scaling up, illustration two. When it comes to verticality and the ability to think globally while acting locally, Hempel (chapter 2) believes the likely success in doing so, at least in the context of the United States, is far from clear, thus opening an interesting avenue of research. He posits that "it remains to be seen if the U.S. political system will adjust to this kind of thinking. The goals of sustainable community may be too Jeffersonian to suit a society shaped predominantly by Hamiltonian precepts. Then again, they may provide an important stimulus for rethinking what quality of life requires in the new millennium." After all, he goes on to muse, "In *Democracy in America* (1835), de Tocqueville observes that among the key enabling features of American politics are 'those township institutions which limit the despotism of the majority and at the same time impart to the people a taste for freedom and the art of being free.'"

8. Scaling up, illustration three. One of the more intriguing extensions of the RECLAIM market mechanism, discussed by Mazmanian (chapter 4), is the use of a cap-and-trade program widely under consideration today at the state, multistate, national, and international levels. Although the experience of RECLAIM would seem to have a great deal to offer in informing these considerations, relatively little effort has been made to utilize the knowledge gleaned on the ground in Los Angeles in contemplating scaling the program up to a much wider and more complex societal setting. Yet a close inspection of the experience in Los Angeles suggests this will be far more difficult than imagined.

9. Are the public and policymakers prepared to make more than highly visible and symbolic investments in a sustainable future? Daniel Press and Nicole Nakagawa raise this issue in the context of open space preservation, but it would seem to extend much further than that. They join the issue by asking rhetorically, "How can it be that Americans willingly pay billions of dollars to acquire valuable open space, but turn miserly and short-sighted when it comes to stewardship?" And their answer would seem to have implications for many such situations.

Stewardship suffers partly because a wicked combination of short political attention spans along with extremely tight annual budgets conspire to favor acquisition [i.e., a major policy action] over stewardship [i.e., ensuring implementation over long periods of time]. The drama in preservation is in the acquisition deal, not in the day-to-day management. Donors far prefer to have their name on a high-profile project (a building, a new open space preserve) than to pay for seemingly prosaic maintenance. For their part, community leaders and politicians need to demonstrate their achievements within short time spans (usually measured by electoral cycles); a long-term restoration project or invasive species eradication won't fit the bill as well as a well-publicized acquisition.

The authors go on to observe that "It's also a lot easier to raise money for one-time, unique expenditures than committing an institution to making payments for many years, as anyone managing an overstretched annual budget can attest."

10. If it is true that transformational changes occur only when a society is on the brink of crisis, is climate change the crisis that precipitates the transformation into the sustainability epoch? Daniel Fiorino suggests so.

What may at some point break the gridlock are the demands of pressing issues. The prospect of global climate change and its consequences has generated controversy, but it also has stimulated creative dialogue about policy options and approaches. We are seeing efforts to draw varied interests into a search for solutions; to integrate energy, transportation, and other policy sectors with environmental strategies; to use emissions trading, a carbon tax, and other policy tools in fashioning solutions; to improve the capacity for measuring and benchmarking performance; and to combine voluntary with what almost surely will be regulatory solutions at some point. The need to respond to climate change may stimulate relationships among government, industry, and others that build trust and thus create more opportunities for dialogue that promotes innovation.

These kinds of institutional and policy developments are intriguing to consider and will be grist for research for many years to come.

Transitions and Transformations Revisited

It is important as we conclude to acknowledge once again the impressive gains the United States has made, especially in the past three decades, in controlling air, water, and land pollution and protecting the nation's precious natural resources. Dozens of major environmental laws have been enacted and implemented at the federal level, and at all levels of government a vast array of significant changes has been instituted in the way we make decisions that affect the environment. Environmentalists and government officials can justifiably claim credit for having moved the nation toward a greener future.

Several of the chapter authors also remind us that these processes of social, institutional, and policy change need to be carefully assessed. We ought to be asking about the real impact that policies adopted over the past thirty-five to forty years have had on the environment and resource use. Equally important is asking about the likely effects of the new policy approaches that have been proposed over the past twenty-five years to correct perceived deficiencies in first epoch policies. Scholars and policy analysts should be open to exploring both short-term and long-term impacts, whether positive or negative, as they affect both the processes of policy implementation and actual effects on the environment and other sustainability goals (Davies and Mazurek 1998; Fiorino 2006; Kraft 2007; Morgenstern and Pizer 2007; Press and Mazmanian 2006). As several of the case studies suggest, before abandoning regulatory policies that have been moderately effective, if not always efficient, we ought to have some degree of confidence that improvements in environmental quality will follow.

As we noted above, where new approaches such as the use of market incentives, provision of information, and collaborative decision making are indeed producing improved results, it would be useful to know why. What helped to bring about the desired behavioral and institutional changes? Such knowledge obviously is of central importance for further efforts at policy design, adoption, and implementation (Coglianese and Nash 2006; Dietz and Stern 2003; Durant, Fiorino, and O'Leary 2004; Eisner 2007; Layzer 2008; Sabatier et al. 2005; Prakash and Potoski 2006; Wondolleck and Yaffee 2000).

Final Observations

We hope the analyses and conclusions we have summarized here stimulate others to revise and extend the work represented in this volume. However insightful it may be, research based on case studies and analytic narratives is inherently limited in terms of generalization to other cases, with their varying timetables and with features unique to time, place, and focus. The eight case studies in the book are illustrative, we think, of the problems faced in hundreds of other communities and regions across the country, and of the challenges facing citizens and policymakers as they seek to reform environmental policy and reconcile it with economic development and other social needs. We believe the cases are sufficiently suggestive of the existence of the transformations underway that they facilitate understanding and further inquiry and involvement in these remarkable experiments in democracy.

For the environmental policy arenas developed most fully during the first epoch—that is, air, water, noise, and toxic wastes that focused on specific media—the transformation from epoch one to epoch two has been taking place across the board of policy domains. In these major areas of explicit environmental protection policy, the framework of the three epochs finds the strongest application.

In some instances, such as with water pollution in the Great Lakes, the evolution across the epochs has been more evolutionary—underway, in concept at least, from the outset and linking relatively easily to the ideas being put forth today—and guided by some of the key principles of sustainability. Realization of these principles, of course, has not been easy in the Great Lakes, and practice does not always following theory.

In the area of land-use policy, management and planning go back much further than the 1970s and are related to many more consider-ations than environmental protection. If anything, modern-day land-use practices are being affected by the sustainability movement, but it is not clear that practices are keeping apace. Quite simply, managing the land in the United States is more difficult than managing clear air and clean water.

In terms of information and management needs, there is no question that the demand for sound and credible scientific data is growing by leaps and bounds, as is the quantity of data being produced both in and outside government. The most difficult challenge for today is not simply to acquire more data, but how to link the data that scientists and monitoring systems can provide with prudent resource management decisions. This requires creative solutions for bringing together scientists, agency managers, citizens, and other stakeholders in a way that facili-tates assessment of the data, however limited at any given time, and fosters a public discourse over implications for public policy and com-munity well-being. We have a long way to go to find the best way to achieve these goals.

One of the important messages to come out of the collection of spe-cific, real-world case studies is the extent to which the processes and trends key to the transformations underway in environmental policy in the 2000s have a parallel in other fields of inquiry. Our epochs model is very much akin to the idea of punctuated equilibrium models of agenda setting and policy change (Baumgartner and Jones 1993, 2002). The long-standing debate between the efficacy of top-down and bottom-up policy implementation, discussed by Rabe and Gaden, has been tested empirically over time in the environmental arena, and it appears that some version of bottom-up, or at least bottom-level involvement and collaboration, is more efficacious.

The cases included here illustrate, on the one hand, that no simple analytical framework can do full justice to the realities of environmental policy as it is designed, adopted, and implemented. On the other hand, understanding the broader contours of the many changes now occurring in environmental policy and practice, in terms of more encompassing epochs, is a genuine aid in helping to see basic dimensions and directions of change.

The analytical framework we offer in this volume provides a useful way of thinking about these changes in the evolution of environmental policy and politics. It can be applied in broad, sweeping terms—moving from the first through the third epoch as a way of providing an historical sweep and narrative. It identifies the full range of particular dimensions of epoch-level change, from ideas through implementation strategy. As presented here, the framework emerged out of the transformations underway in the air pollution arena—so dominant in the United States beginning in the early 1970s. It appeared to fit that arena well in both general and specific terms.

Whereas the general transformations are equally applicable in each of the other arenas examined, the timing and close fit of detailed changes are less applicable as we move from air to watershed, open-space, and public lands policies. The closeness of fit in particular aspects of change is even less apt in viewing the more multimedia arenas that are brought into consideration in energy use and climate change, urban sustainability initiatives, watershed protection, and supraregional, transnational arenas, such as the Great Lakes. The effects of epoch one are evident in each of these arenas, as well as the emergence of epoch three. However, epoch two is far less clearly demarcated in these cases.

Inquiry into other cases and other venues will surely help refine the framework and broaden our understanding of the dynamics of environmental policy as the twenty-first century further unfolds. We believe that such research can also provide much needed strategic advice to planners, analysts, policymakers, and citizens who will have to choose and live with the policies that govern environmental quality over the next several decades, when the nation and the world must come to terms with the challenge of environmental sustainability.

References

Baumgartner, Frank R., and Bryan D. Jones. 1993. *Agendas and Instability in American Politics*. Chicago: University of Chicago Press.

Baumgartner, Frank R., and Bryan D. Jones, eds. 2002. *Policy Dynamics*. Chicago: University of Chicago Press.

Coglianese, Cary, and Jennifer Nash, eds. 2006. *Leveraging the Private Sector: Management-Based Strategies for Improving Environmental Performance*. Washington, D.C.: RFF Press.

Davies, J. Clarence, and Jan Mazurek. 1998. *Pollution Control in the United States: Evaluating the System*. Washington, D.C.: Resources for the Future.

Dietz, Thomas, and Paul C. Stern, eds. 2003. *New Tools for Environmental Protection: Education, Information, and Voluntary Measures*. Washington, D.C.: National Academy Press.

Durant, Robert F., Daniel J. Fiorino, and Rosemary O'Leary, eds. 2004. *Environmental Governance Reconsidered: Challenges, Choices, and Opportunities*. Cambridge, MA: MIT Press.

Eisner, Marc Allen. 2007. *Governing the Environment: The Transformation of Environmental Regulation*. Boulder, CO: Lynne Rienner.

Fiorino, Daniel J. 2006. *The New Environmental Regulation*. Cambridge, MA: MIT Press.

Kraft, Michael, E. 2007. *Environmental Policy and Politics*, 4th ed. New York: Pearson Longman.

Klyza, Christopher McGrory, and David Sousa. 2008. *American Environmental Policy, 1990–2006: Beyond Gridlock*. Cambridge, MA: MIT Press.

Layzer, Judith. 2008. *Natural Experiments: Ecosystem Management and the Environment*. Cambridge, MA: MIT Press.

Morgenstern, Richard D., and William A. Pizer, eds. 2007. *Reality Check: The Nature and Performance of Voluntary Environmental Programs in the United States, Europe, and Japan*. Washington, D.C.: RFF Press.

Portney, Kent E. 2003. *Taking Sustainable Cities Seriously: Economic Development, the Environment, and Quality of Life in American Cities*. Cambridge, MA: MIT Press.

Prakash, Aseem, and Matthew Potoski, 2006. *The Voluntary Environmentalists: Green Clubs, ISO 14001, and Voluntary Environmental Regulations*. New York: Cambridge University Press.

Press, Daniel. 2007. "Industry, Environmental Policy, and Environmental Outcomes." *Annual Review of Environment and Resources* 32: 1.1–1.28.

Press, Daniel, and Daniel A. Mazmanian. 2006. "The Greening of Industry: Combining Government Regulation and Voluntary Strategies." In *Environmental Policy*, 6th ed., ed. Norman J. Vig and Michael E. Kraft, 264–287. Washington, D.C.: CQ Press.

Putnam, Robert. 1993. *Making Democracy Work: Civic Traditions in Modern Italy*. Princeton: Princeton University Press.

Rabe, Barry G. 2004. *Statehouse and Greenhouse: The Emerging Politics of American Climate Change Policy*. Washington, D.C.: Brookings Institution Press.

Rabe, Barry. 2006. "Power to the States: The Promise and Pitfalls of Decentralization." In *Environmental Policy*, 6th ed., ed. Norman J. Vig and Michael E. Kraft, 34–56. Washington, D.C.: CQ Press.

Rabe, Barry G., and Philip A. Mundo. 2007. "Business Influence in State-Level Environmental Policy." In *Business and Environmental Policy: Corporate Interests in the American Political System*, ed. Michael E. Kraft and Sheldon Kamieniecki, 265–297. Cambridge, MA: MIT Press.

Ringquist, Evan J. 1995. "Evaluating Environmental Policy Outcomes." In *Environmental Politics and Policy*, 2nd ed., ed. James P. Lester, 303–327. Durham: Duke University Press.

Sabatier, Paul A., and Hank C. Jenkins-Smith. 1993. *Policy Change and Learning: An Advocacy Coalition Approach*. Boulder, CO: Westview Press.

Sabatier, Paul, Will Focht, Mark Lubell, Zev Trachtenberg, Arnold Vedlitz, and Mary Matlock, eds. 2005. *Swimming Upstream: Collaborative Approaches to Watershed Management*. Cambridge, MA: MIT Press.

Scheberle, Denise. 2004. *Federalism and Environmental Policy: Trust and the Politics of Implementation*, 2nd ed. Washington, D.C.: Georgetown University Press.

Smart Communities Network. 2007. Http://www.smartcommunities.ncat.org/. Accessed 27 November 2007.

Sustainable Measures. 2007. Http://www.sustainablemeasures.com. Accessed 27 November 2007.

Vig, Norman, and Michael Kraft, eds. 2006. *Environmental Policy*, 6th ed. Washington, D.C.: CQ Press.

Weber, Edward P. 2003. *Bringing Society Back In: Grassroots Ecosystem Management, Accountability, and Sustainable Communities*. Cambridge, MA: MIT Press.

Wondolleck, Julia M., and Steven L. Yaffee. 2000. *Making Collaboration Work: Lessons from Innovation in Natural Resource Management*. Washington, D.C.: Island Press.

Index

American and Comparative Environmental Policy
Sheldon Kamieniecki and Michael E. Kraft, series editors

Russell J. Dalton, Paula Garb, Nicholas P. Lovrich, John C. Pierce, and John M. Whiteley, *Critical Masses: Citizens, Nuclear Weapons Production, and Environmental Destruction in the United States and Russia*

Daniel A. Mazmanian and Michael E. Kraft, editors, *Toward Sustainable Communities: Transition and Transformations in Environmental Policy*

Elizabeth R. DeSombre, *Domestic Sources of International Environmental Policy: Industry, Environmentalists, and U.S. Power*

Kate O'Neill, *Waste Trading among Rich Nations: Building a New Theory of Environmental Regulation*

Joachim Blatter and Helen Ingram, editors, *Reflections on Water: New Approaches to Transboundary Conflicts and Cooperation*

Paul F. Steinberg, *Environmental Leadership in Developing Countries: Transnational Relations and Biodiversity Policy in Costa Rica and Bolivia*

Uday Desai, editor, *Environmental Politics and Policy in Industrialized Countries*

Kent Portney, *Taking Sustainable Cities Seriously: Economic Development, the Environment, and Quality of Life in American Cities*

Edward P. Weber, *Bringing Society Back In: Grassroots Ecosystem Management, Accountability, and Sustainable Communities*

Norman J. Vig and Michael G. Faure, eds., *Green Giants? Environmental Policies of the United States and the European Union*

Robert F. Durant, Daniel J. Fiorino, and Rosemary O'Leary, eds., *Environmental Governance Reconsidered: Challenges, Choices, and Opportunities*

Paul A. Sabatier, Will Focht, Mark Lubell, Zev Trachtenberg, Arnold Vedlitz, and Marty Matlock, eds., *Swimming Upstream: Collaborative Approaches to Watershed Management*

Sally K. Fairfax, Lauren Gwin, Mary Ann King, Leigh S. Raymond, and Laura Watt, *Buying Nature: The Limits of Land Acquisition as a Conservation Strategy, 1780–2004*

Steven Cohen, Sheldon Kamieniecki, and Matthew A. Cahn, *Strategic Planning in Environmental Regulation: A Policy Approach That Works*

Michael E. Kraft and Sheldon Kamieniecki, eds., *Business and Environmental Policy: Corporate Interests in the American Political System*

Joseph F. C. DiMento and Pamela Doughman, eds., Climate Change: *What It Means for You, Your Children, and Your Grandchildren*

Christopher McGrory Klyza and David J. Sousa, *American Environmental Policy, 1990–2006: Beyond Gridlock*

John M. Whiteley, Helen Ingram, and Richard Perry, eds., *Water, Place, and Equity*

Judith Layzer, *Natural Experiments: Ecosystem Management and the Environment*

Daniel A. Mazmanian and Michael E. Kraft, editors, *Toward Sustainable Communities: Transition and Transformations in Environmental Policy*, 2nd edition

CPSIA information can be obtained at www.ICGtesting.com
Printed in the USA
LVOW04s0859140815

450095LV00002B/2/P